Praise for

MARGARET FULLER

"Megan Marshall's *Margaret Fuller: A New American Life* is the best single volume ever written on Fuller. Carefully researched and beautifully written, the book brings Fuller back to life in all her intellectual vivacity and emotional intensity. Marshall's Fuller overwhelms the reader just as Fuller herself overwhelmed everyone she met. This book is a masterpiece of empathetic biography. You will not be able to put it down."
—Robert D. Richardson, author of *William James: In the Maelstrom of American Modernism* and *Emerson: The Mind on Fire*

"[Marshall] brings her powers of research and her eye for story to the life of Margaret Fuller." —*Minneapolis Star Tribune*

"Fascinating, and well-researched . . . should help to remedy Fuller's obscurity . . . It is Marshall's prescient reading of Fuller's life that makes this book worthy of its subject." —*Daily Beast*

"Megan Marshall gives new meaning to close reading—from words on a page she conjures a fantastically rich inner life, a meld of body, mind, and soul. Drawing on the letters and diaries of Margaret Fuller and her circle, she has brought us a brave, visionary, sensual, tough-minded intellectual, a 'first woman' who was unique yet stood for all women. A masterful achievement by a great American writer and scholar."
—Evan Thomas, author of *Ike's Bluff: President Eisenhower's Secret Battle to Save the World*

"[Marshall] inhabits Fuller's dramatic, oft-told story with unique intimacy by virtue of her fluency in and judicious quoting of Fuller's extraordinarily vivid letters . . . A magnificent biography of a revolutionary thinker, witness, and writer." —*Booklist*, starred review

Also by Megan Marshall

The Peabody Sisters: Three Women Who
Ignited American Romanticism

MARGARET FULLER

· A NEW AMERICAN LIFE ·

Megan Marshall

MARINER BOOKS
HOUGHTON MIFFLIN HARCOURT
BOSTON   NEW YORK

In memory of —
E.S.
E.S.M.
&
E.W.M.M.

First Mariner Books edition 2014
Copyright © 2013 by Megan Marshall

www.hmhco.com

Library of Congress Cataloging-in-Publication Data
Marshall, Megan.
Margaret Fuller : a new American life / Megan Marshall.
pages cm
ISBN 978-0-547-19560-5 (hardback)   ISBN 978-0-544-24561-7 (pbk.)
1. Fuller, Margaret, 1810–1850. 2. Authors, American — 19th century — Biography.
3. Feminists — United States — Biography. I. Title.
PS2506.M37 2013
818'.309 — dc23
[B]   2012042179

Book design by Melissa Lotfy

Printed in the United States of America
DOC 10 9 8 7 6 5 4 3 2 1

PAGES VI–VII: Houghton Library, Harvard University,
MS Am 1086 box 4, Rome Diaries.

Where I make an impression it must be by being most myself.

—Margaret Fuller to her editor John Wiley, 1846

Mr O Clarke justly pleads
that it is nonsense for the
Pope to threaten excommunication
for encroachment on his temporal
power & (such things are thought
& spoken in Rome now) advises the
priests to beware lest the remains
of authority be lost in ridicule.

Eveg of 17th Meeting at Teatro
Metastasio called by the Tuscan
deputies for the costituente Cannoniere
spoke, De Boni. things were said
such as never before, surely, echoed
from the walls of modern Rome.
A man named Cola answered from
the pit with considerable spirit.

18th A public meeting at the
Consistorew to nominate members
for the Constituente I was not
present. but understand it was
a great meeting and unanimous
in laughing to scorn the excommunication and pushing forward
liberal measures.

17ᵗ Just before I went to the public meeting at the Tordinona stopped the funeral procession of a princess Barberini, last relic of their papal splendors.

(&c.) was proclaimed at the Tordinona that the ministry had now taken measures for a Constituente not only Romovea but Italiana. Now, indeed, Italy has taken a great step onward.

Saw today the address of Mickiewicz to Louis Napoleon on presenting the Polish emigration.

19ᵗ Treachery! The troops of the line have fired on the dragoons crying viva Pio. All will be dark indeed, if there be disunion within as well as foes without.

20ᵗ 21ˢᵗ The suffrages for C. A. have been given & all passed off peaceably The first day they came in slowly each waiting to see what the other

CONTENTS

LIST OF ILLUSTRATIONS

Margaret Fuller, engraving by Henry Bryan Hall Jr.

PROLOGUE

THE ARCHIVIST PLACED THE SLIM VOLUME, AN ORDINARY composition book with mottled green covers, in a protective foam cradle on the library desk in front of me. When I opened it, I knew I would find pages filled with a familiar looping script, a forward-slanting hand that often seemed to rush from one line to the next as if racing to catch up with the writer's coursing thoughts.

But this notebook was different from any other I'd seen: it had survived the wreck of the *Elizabeth* off Fire Island in July 1850, packed safely in a trunk that floated to shore, where grieving friends retrieved the soggy diary and dried it by the fire. The green pasteboard cover had pulled away from its backing; the pages were warped at the edges in even ripples. This was Margaret Fuller's last known journal. Its contents were all that remained to hint at what she might have written in her famous lost manuscript on the rise and fall of the 1849 Roman Republic, the revolution she had barely survived. The manuscript itself—"what is most valuable to me if I live of any thing"—had been swept away more than a century and a half ago in a storm of near hurricane force, along with Margaret, her young Italian husband, and their two-year-old son, all of them passengers on the ill-fated *Elizabeth*.

I opened the cover and read what appeared to be a message directed to me, or to anyone else who might choose to study this singular document. The words, written on a white index card, had not been penned in Margaret Fuller's flowing longhand, but rather penciled in a primly vertical script formed in a decade closer to mine—by a descendant? an earlier biographer? a library cataloguer? Two brief lines carried a judgment on the volume, and on Margaret herself: "Nothing *personal*, public events merely." The nameless reader, like so many before and since, had been searching Margaret Fuller's private papers for clues to the mysteries in her personal life—Had she really married the Italian marchese she called her husband? Was their child conceived out of wedlock? — and found the evidence lacking.

I turned the pages, reading at random. In the early passages, Margaret recalled her arrival at Naples in the spring of 1847 at age thirty-six, her "first acquaintance with the fig and olive," and sightseeing in Capri and Pompeii before traveling overland to Rome. Having grown up a prodigy of classical learning in Cambridge, Massachusetts, Margaret had long wished to make this journey. Yet perhaps it was for the best that a reversal in family fortune kept her in New England through her early thirties. She had made a name for herself among the Transcendentalists, becoming Emerson's friend and Thoreau's editor before moving to New York City for an eighteen-month stint as front-page columnist for Horace Greeley's *New-York Tribune,* which led to this belated European tour in a triumphal role as foreign correspondent, witness to the revolutions that spread across the Continent beginning in 1848.

Flipping ahead to January 1849, I read of the exiled soldier-politicians Garibaldi and Mazzini greeted in Rome as returning heroes and of a circular posted by the deposed Pope Pius IX, excommunicating any citizen who had aided in the assassination of his highest deputy the previous November: "The people received it with jeers, tore it at once from the walls." Then — "Monstrous are the treacheries of our time"! — French troops, dispatched to restore the pope to power, had landed just fifty miles away on the Mediterranean coast, at Civitavecchia. Finally, on April 28: "Rome is barricaded, the foe daily hourly expected." These vivid entries, brief as they were, would anchor my narrative of Margaret's Roman years. Public events "merely"?

How extraordinary it was to find a woman's private journal filled with such accounts. Yet the inscriber of the index card had found the contents disappointing. Would any reader fault a man — especially an internationally known writer and activist, as Margaret Fuller was — for keeping a journal confined to public events through a springtime of revolution? Margaret well understood this limited view of women and the consequences for those who overstepped its bounds. She herself had scorned those who censured her personal heroines, Mary Wollstonecraft and George Sand, for flouting the institution of marriage; Margaret had been appalled that critics "will not take off the brand" once it had been "set upon" these unconventional women, even after they found "their way to purer air"—in death. Margaret's own legacy had been clouded by the same prurient attention, often leading to condemnation, always distracting attention from her achievements.

For a time I believed I must write a biography of Margaret Fuller that turned away from the intrigues in her private life, that spoke of public events solely, and that would affirm her eminence as America's originating and most consequential theorist of woman's role in history, culture, and society. Margaret Fuller was, to borrow a phrase coined by one of her friends, a "fore-sayer." No other writer, until Simone de Beauvoir took up similar themes in the 1940s, had so skillfully critiqued what Margaret Fuller termed in 1843 "the great radical dualism" of gender. "There is no wholly masculine man, no purely feminine woman," she had written, anticipating Virginia Woolf's explorations of male and female character in fiction. Margaret Fuller's haunting allegories personifying flowers presaged Georgia O'Keeffe's sensual flower paintings; her untimely midcareer death set off a persistent public longing to refuse the facts and grant her a different fate, similar to the reaction following the midflight disappearance of Amelia Earhart nearly one hundred years later. Although she had titled her most influential book *Woman in the Nineteenth Century*, heralding an era in which she expected great advances for women, Margaret Fuller fit more readily among these heroines of the twentieth century. She deserved a place in this international sisterhood whose achievements her own pioneering writings helped to make possible.

But while I never gave up the aim of representing Margaret Fuller's many accomplishments, as I read more of her letters, journals, and works in print, I began to recognize the personal in the political. Margaret Fuller's critique of marriage was formulated during a period of tussling with the unhappily married Ralph Waldo Emerson over the nature of their emotional involvement; her pronouncements on the emerging power of single women evolved from her own struggle with the role; even her brave stand for the Roman Republic could not be separated from her love affair with one particular Roman republican. It was not true, as she had written of Mary Wollstonecraft, that Margaret Fuller was "a woman whose existence better proved the need of some new interpretation of woman's rights, than anything she wrote." Her writing was eloquent, assured, and uncannily prescient. But her writing also confirmed my hunch. Margaret Fuller's published books were hybrids of personal observation, extracts from letters and diaries, confessional poetry; her private journals were filled with cultural commentary and reportage on public events. Margaret did not experience her life as divided into public and private; rather, she sought "fulness of being." She maintained important correspondences with many of the significant thinkers and politicians of her day — from Emerson to Harriet Martineau to the Polish poet and revolutionary Adam Mickiewicz — but she valued the letters she received above all for the "history of feeling" they contained. She, like so many of her comrades, both male and female, valued feeling as an inspiration to action in both the private and public spheres. I would write the full story — operatic in its emotional pitch, global in its dimensions.

Margaret Fuller's mind and life were so exceptional that it can be easy to miss the ways in which she was emblematic of her time, an embodiment of her era's "go-ahead" spirit. Her parents grew up in country towns in Massachusetts, their families eking out a tenuous subsistence in the early years of the republic; both were drawn to city life, and they met by chance, crossing in opposite directions on the new West Bridge, the first to connect Cambridge and Boston. Their life together through Margaret's childhood was urban, following a national trend: the population of the United States tripled during Margaret's lifetime, transforming American cities. The advent of railroads and a massive influx of immigrants from overseas stimulated urban growth.

By the late 1830s and '40s, when Margaret was a young single woman living in Providence, Boston, and Cambridge, New England had become the first region in the country with a shortage of men. The overcrowded job market and economic volatility that drove her lawyer father back to farming and her younger brothers to seek employment in the South and West created this imbalance, leaving one third of Boston's female population unmarried. Little wonder that Margaret toyed for a while with the notion that only an unmarried woman could "represent the female world." Her argument was theoretical: American wives belonged by law to their husbands and could not act independently. Yet she also spoke for a surging population of women, many of them single, who sought usefulness outside the home and who readily joined the political life of the nation by advocating causes from temperance to abolition long before they gained the right to vote.

Despite her allegiance to women's rights and her important alliances with reform-minded women, Margaret Fuller was never a joiner. She took to heart the example of the French novelist George Sand, whom she met in Paris, a woman who effectively articulated her ideas through both conversation and published writing and who chose an independent path in life. She was impressed by the way Sand "takes rank in society like a man, for the weight of her thoughts." In a time when "self-reliance" was the watchword—one she helped to coin and circulate—Margaret had, by her own account, a "mind that insisted on utterance." She too insisted that her ideas be valued as highly as those of the brilliant men who were her comrades. She refused to be pigeonholed as a woman writer or trivialized as sentimental, and her interests were as far-ranging as the country itself, where, as she wrote in a farewell column for the *Tribune* when she sailed for Europe, "life rushes wide and free." In England, France, and Italy, Margaret found, as the stay-at-home Ralph Waldo Emerson predicted, even more members of her "expansive fellowship": radical thinkers, revolutionaries, and artists of the new age. Yet even in this journey to the Old World she was marking out a new American life—a route traced in the future by the likes of Henry James, Edith Wharton, Mary Cassatt, John Reed, Ernest Hemingway, and countless other seekers of inspiration and new theaters of action abroad.

Nathaniel Hawthorne, a friend of Margaret Fuller's in Concord who followed her path to the Continent several years after her death, undertook an experiment in fictional form when he put aside writing stories in favor of longer narratives. He preferred to call his books "Romances," not novels. "When a writer calls his work a Romance," Hawthorne explained in his preface to *The House of the Seven Gables,* "he wishes to claim a certain latitude, both as to its fashion and material, which he would not have felt himself entitled to assume had he professed to be writing a Novel." The novelist, in Hawthorne's terms, aims to achieve "a very minute fidelity" to experience, whereas the author of a romance may "bring out or mellow the lights and deepen and enrich the shadows of the picture" while still maintaining strict allegiance to "the truth of the human heart."

My book is not a work of fiction, but I have kept in mind Hawthorne's notion of the "Romance" as a guiding principle in my factual narrative. Or, to borrow from Margaret Fuller herself, "we propose some liberating measures." I have brought out lights and deepened shadows, intensifying focus, for example, on Margaret's friendships in a circle of young "lovers" who were drawn to the flame of her intelligence during the years of her closest friendship with Emerson, and on her experience as a mother separated from her infant son during wartime. My account lingers on such points to render the complexity of her lived experience and to make full use of the rich documentation of these key episodes. At other times the narrative takes a more rapid pace to chart the swift trajectory of this "ardent and onward-looking spirit" whose life spanned only forty years.

Margaret Fuller maintained that all human beings are capable of great accomplishment, that "genius" would be "common as light, if men trusted their higher selves." Still, she was always mindful of her own extraordinary capabilities. "From a very early age I have felt that I was not born to the common womanly lot," Margaret wrote to a friend as her thirtieth birthday approached. This awareness was a source of frequent inner turmoil as she strove to realize her talents in an era unfriendly to openly ambitious women. Yet she achieved almost inconceivable success, with remarkable poise. After talking her way into the library at Harvard to complete research on her first book, Margaret did not allow the gawking undergraduates, who had never before seen a woman at work in their midst, to break her concentration. A few years later she occupied a desk in another all-male setting, the newsroom at Horace Greeley's *New-York Tribune*, where she turned out editorials and cultural commentary aimed at shaping the opinions of her fifty thousand readers on subjects from literature and music to Negro voting rights and prison reform. In Rome, offering her views in a *Tribune* column on the U.S. government's need to appoint an ambassador to the new Roman Republic, Margaret conjectured, "Another century, and I might ask to be made Ambassador myself." But in this case, she was forced to admit, "woman's day has not come yet."

In the twenty-first century, woman's day may almost have arrived. American women vote and hold high office as elected representatives, judges, diplomats, even secretaries of state, if not as president. Yet Margaret Fuller's journalistic descendants still risk their lives, not just because they work in dangerous places, but because they are female, objects of scorn and worse, in many parts of the world, for daring to serve in the public arena. What was it like to be such a woman—the only such woman, the first female war correspondent—a half-century after America's own revolution?

I have written Margaret Fuller's story from the inside, using the most direct evidence—her words, and those of her family and friends, recorded in the moment, preserved in archives, and in many cases carefully annotated and published by scholars of the period. A close reading of this now well-established manuscript record yielded many perceptions that I hope will strike readers familiar with Margaret Fuller's life as fresh and true. I have also relied on a number of previously unknown documents that emerged during my years of research on the Peabody sisters and later as I tracked my current subject in archives across the country: two newly discovered letters by Margaret Fuller, a record in Mary Peabody's hand of Margaret Fuller's first series of Conversations for women held in Boston in 1839, the Peabody sisters' correspondence during the months following the wreck of the *Elizabeth,* and a letter written by Ralph Waldo Emerson to the Collector of the Port of New York, itemizing the trunks and valuables lost in the fatal storm.

"The scrolls of the past burn my fingers," Margaret Fuller wrote to her great friend Ralph Waldo Emerson concerning some particularly painful letters the two had exchanged; "they have not yet passed into literature." So impassioned are her words, they burn our fingers yet, two centuries later. *Margaret Fuller: A New American Life* is my attempt to transport those letters into literature, to give her magnificent life "a little space," as she asked from Emerson, so that "the sympathetic hues would show again before the fire, renovated and lively." As for Margaret herself—if she reached a heaven, we may hope it is like the one she once imagined, "empowering me to incessant acts of vigorous beauty."

· I ·

YOUTH

Timothy Fuller,
portrait by Rufus Porter

Margarett Crane Fuller,
daguerreotype, c. 1840s

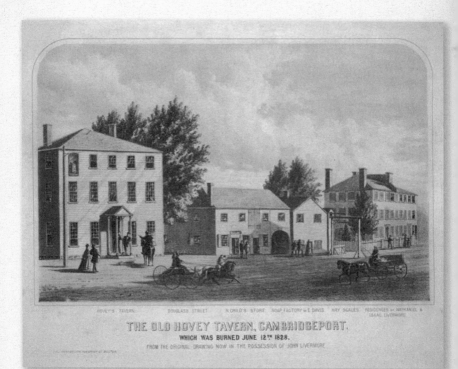

Street scene in Cambridgeport, early 1820s,
with soap factory at center

Three Letters

"DEAR FATHER IT IS A HEAVY STORM I HOPE YOU WILL NOT have to come home in it." So begins the record of a life that will end on a homeward journey in another heavy storm, a life unusually full of words, both spoken and written.

Sarah Margaret Fuller is six years old when she writes this brief letter on a half-sheet of paper saved by the devoted and exacting father who receives it, next by his widow, then by their descendants. Which one of them thinks to label it "*First* letter"? All of her survivors understand that there are, or will be, biographers, historians, students of literature who care to know.

But first it is the father who treasures his daughter's message of concern, this lurching unpunctuated parade of runes, from the moment he unfolds the page—a father nearing forty and eager to set his young daughter, already an apt pupil, to a "severe though kind" education. And the mother, just twenty-one at her daughter's birth, only twenty-seven now: she is known to find any words her firstborn child scribbles on bits of paper "*original*," worthy of preservation.

At seven, the little girl—a tall little girl with plain looks and auburn hair, whose height and imperious manner set her apart from her age mates—writes again to her father, Timothy Fuller, a brash and for the moment successful lawyer in Cambridge, Massachusetts, a U.S. congressman whose career in politics takes him away to Washington half the year, in winter and spring. It is January of 1818. In the new year, the girl's concern for her father has transmuted into the desire to earn his good opinion—and so into more words, into the wish to show off her inquiring mind.

"I have learned all the rules of Musick but one," she writes now in a fine spidery script, and "I have been reviewing Valpy's Chronology" (a verse narrative of ancient and English history). And: "I should have liked to have been with you to have seen the pictures gallery at NYork."

Sarah Margaret's claims of accomplishment, her carefully worded wish to join Timothy in New York, are meant to forestall what she has already come to expect from her overbearing father: the torrent of criticism—of her penmanship, of her rate of progress through his curriculum, of her "*stile*" of expression, as he prefers to spell the word—all intended to bring his precocious daughter "as near perfection as possible." Timothy, proud to have been a "high scholar" at Harvard, has been her only teacher, starting her on Latin at age six, requiring that she recite her lessons only to *him* during his months at home, insisting she be kept awake until his return from work to stand before him on his study carpet late at night, her nerves "on the stretch" until she has finished repeating to him what she had learned that day. Already she has experienced more severity than kindness in her father's pedagogy.

And so the anxious, eager-to-please seven-year-old Sarah Margaret Fuller apologizes to her father, a man with "absolutely no patience" for mistakes, as she will to no one else in the voluminous correspondence that follows after this second letter: "I do not write well at all," and "I have written every day a little but have made but little improvement." And: "I hope to make greater proficiency in my Studies."

But the verbs tell all—she has *learned* and *reviewed*, she would like to *see* and to *make improvement*. These verbs are hers. The nouns also: *music, art, chronology* (the unfolding of world events, the progress of society). These are her concerns, her aims, her occupations at age seven. And they will remain so for the girl who, to her father's and her own dismay, struggles through years of singing lessons, unable to shine at this one accomplishment. "To excel in all things should be your constant aim; mediocrity is obscurity," Timothy will prod when he offers to buy her a piano. But she continues to *write every day* that she has paper and pen to hand, except in times of sickness, until she becomes a woman. And then too, when she will write of music, art, literature, politics, and travel for a nation of readers. She takes her father's cue, embraces the discipline: she refuses to be mediocre, to be obscure.

The seven-year-old girl must stop writing this second letter, however, a letter that announces her intellect to her father even by way of apology, because her mother—Margarett Crane Fuller—has asked her to "hold the baby," a new little brother, William Henry, the second after brother Eugene. Three-year-old Eugene "speaks of you sometimes," the girl tells her father, but he is not old enough to write—or to hold the baby, which he would not have been asked to do anyway, as a boy. Sarah Margaret must hold the baby while her mother, Margarett—a head taller than her bluff, domineering husband, with a slender, elfin beauty; sweet-tempered, but not a woman *of letters*—writes her own letter to Timothy.

Baby, little brother, elder sister, mother, all crowd around a writing desk with the absent Timothy foremost in their minds—his demanding presence felt across the miles. Missing from this tableau is Julia Adelaide, the "soft, graceful and lively" much-adored second-born daughter who died four years ago, just past her first birthday, when Sarah Margaret was three years old. The abrupt loss, the never-forgotten moment when the baby's nurse, tears streaming, pulled Sarah Margaret into the nursery to view her sister's tiny corpse in all its "severe sweetness," shocked the older girl into consciousness. "My first experience of life was one of death," she will write years later—so that even now, as she takes her infant brother in her arms and cedes the pen to her mother, she feels alone.

"She who would have been the companion of my life" was "severed from me": Julia Adelaide might have been Sarah Margaret's ally in their father's more "severe" than "kind" school. Julia Adelaide's death too was far more "severe" than "sweet," for in the following months Margarett was also severed—or withdrew—from Sarah Margaret, growing "delicate" in health as her grief turned to depression. The sorrowing mother spent hours in her garden, working the flower beds or simply sitting among the fragrant roses, fruit trees, and clematis vines, turned away from her living daughter. And then the brothers came, first Eugene and then William Henry. In dreams, Sarah Margaret sees herself joining a procession of mourners "in their black clothes and dreary faces," following her mother to her grave as she already has her sister. She has been told, but does not remember, that she begged "with loud cries" that Julia Adelaide not be put into the ground. She wakes to find her pillow wet with tears.

Two years later, Sarah Margaret starts again: "My dear father." By now, January 16, 1820, she has written many more letters to Timothy, signed them "Your affectionate daughter, Sarah M Fuller" or "S M Fuller" or "Sarah-Margaret Fuller." She has sent him compositions in which "I assure you I . . . made *almost* as many corrections as your critical self would were you at home." Obedient to Timothy alone (her mother finds her difficult, "opinionative"), she has let him know she is translating Oliver Goldsmith's long poem of rural decline, *The Deserted Village*, into Latin, as he has asked; she is pushing herself through the *Aeneid* in answer to his challenge—wasn't she yet "*profoundly* into" the work? Within six months she will have puzzled out the entire savage-heroic tale in the original Latin.

It is a greater pleasure, almost easy, for the girl to accomplish such intellectual feats during the half-year her father is away. Even though she quarrels with Margarett, is unable to feel her love, she will at times, whether to imitate her mother or to seek her mother's distilled essence or simply to please herself, sit alone in the garden, at ease among the violets, lilies, and roses: "my mother's hand had planted them, and they bloomed for me." Like Persephone, she is free above ground during the two seasons her father is away, when her mother's "flower-like nature" prevails, when she need answer only to Timothy's exhorting letters.

In this third letter she begins to test Timothy's strictures. Twice before she has written asking his permission to read an Italian thriller, *Zeluco*, and twice she has recommended for his own reading a novel—"Do not let the name novel make you think it is either trifling or silly," she urges—called *Hesitation: or, To Marry, or Not to Marry?* In the pages of *Hesitation* she has encountered, along with the novel's pair of indecisive lovers, the extraordinary comtesse de Pologne, a witty conversationalist, happily single, with the "power to disengage herself from the shackles of custom, without losing one attribute of modesty": a woman whose personal magnetism draws both men and women to her circle. Does she hope Timothy will find the comtesse too and approve?

Sarah Margaret is writing fiction herself, "a new tale called The young satirist," she tells her father, in the loose rolling hand she has acquired only recently, which will be recognizably hers from now on. Despite Timothy's criticisms, she is beginning to feel how bright she is, even brilliant, a commanding presence in her mind's eye, if not in daily life — the tall girl will soon reach five feet two inches and stop growing, becoming short, plump, and awkward as an adolescent. She too can play the critic, the provocateur, the "young satirist," when she wishes. She is nine years old. Her mother, Margarett, just thirty, is newly pregnant with a fifth child. She closes her letter:

P S I do not like Sarah, call me Margaret alone, pray do!

2

Ellen Kilshaw

THE FIRST LETTER SHE WROTE AND SIGNED "MARGARET," even before she asked her father to "call me Margaret alone" (which he refused to do), was sent to Ellen Kilshaw, "first friend." Ellen was older, a grown woman in her early twenties, "an English lady, who, by a singular chance, was cast upon this region for a few months," Margaret would write years later, unconsciously adopting the language of the romantic novels she loved as a girl. And why not? She had fallen in love with Ellen Kilshaw: "Elegant and captivating, her every look and gesture tuned to a different pitch from anything I had ever known."

This "region" upon which Ellen Kilshaw was cast, where Margaret Fuller lived, was not the Cambridge of Harvard College, of elegant mansions on Brattle Street's "Tory Row" or gently sloping Mount Auburn. It could have been a world away. Margaret's "region" was the upstart community at Cambridgeport, two miles east of Old Cambridge through marshes and pastureland, where squat frame houses like her own "comfortable" yet "very ugly" three-story house on Cherry Street clustered near the new West Bridge. Spanning the Charles River where it emptied into Boston Harbor, and leading directly to fashionable Beacon Hill, the West Bridge, when it was completed in 1793, had inspired Cambridgeport's founders to drain riverside swamps, dredge canals, and construct wharves in hopes of luring trade ships away from Boston's waterfront. But the financial failure, early in the new century, of the Middlesex Turnpike, an inland toll road intended to bring farm goods to market in Cambridgeport, followed by Jefferson's devastating foreign trade embargo, then the War of 1812, turned the bustling district into a virtual ghost town of vacant house lots and unused warehouses during the years of Margaret's childhood.

Ambitious Timothy Fuller, thirty-one, the fourth of ten children and the oldest of five brothers, bought the house at 71 Cherry Street for $6,000 in the summer of 1809, a few months after marrying twenty-year-old Margarett Crane. The price was high for a man who had paid his way through college and legal studies as a schoolteacher, but affordable now that he'd opened a law office in Boston and begun to make a name for himself in Republican party politics. Timothy expected to raise a large family (his father was also one of ten children), and he could walk to work in under an hour. He could not have managed so ample a house in Boston, and he chose to ignore the signs of Cambridgeport's imminent decline. The birth of Sarah Margaret—named for his mother and his wife—on May 23, 1810, scarcely a year after his wedding, confirmed the rightness of his decision.

The Fullers' Cherry Street block was primarily residential, but across the road stood an "unsavory" soap factory, which, by the time Margaret was making her way through the *Aeneid*, seemed an ironic commentary on the commercial bubble that had so swiftly burst. There were other families hanging on to residential and commercial investments in Cambridgeport during the second decade of the new century whose daughters might have played more often with Margaret if she'd gone to school with them. Or perhaps not. A "child of masculine energy," she preferred "violent bodily exercise"—boys' games of chase and tag—to girls' tamer pastimes on the few occasions when she pulled herself away from reading, now "a habit and a passion."

The neighborhood girls didn't dislike her, Margaret recalled. They recognized her "hauteur," she thought, as justified: "the girls supposed me really superior to themselves." True or not, and likely it *was* true, Margaret's reputation as an intellectual prodigy had spread quickly through Cambridgeport and beyond—before she could feel the sting of their rejection, she'd "given up" any wish for the girls' friendship, "for they seemed rude, tiresome, and childish, as I did to them dull and strange." Perhaps it was the neighbor girls she had in mind when, years later, she dismissed Cambridgeport as presenting a *"mesquin"* — mean, paltry — and "huddled look."

Within easy walking distance of Cherry Street stood a freshly built parish church, where Margaret caught her first glimpse of the visiting Ellen Kilshaw — "a new apparition foreign to that scene" — and a newly opened college preparatory school for boys, where girls were invited to study Latin and English composition as well, although Timothy had not yet permitted Margaret to leave his home school. Until Ellen Kilshaw was "cast upon" Cambridgeport, nearly all that Margaret Fuller liked about her neighborhood was the view as she walked away from it across the West Bridge over the gently winding Charles and into Boston — "the river, and the city glittering in sunset, and the undulating line all round, and the light smokes, seen in some weathers."

A glittering city shrouded in "light smokes": a setting reminiscent of London in the popular novels Margaret was beginning to read and her father to discourage. But Ellen Kilshaw's England was not London any more than Margaret's "region" was Old Cambridge or Boston. Ellen had come from Liverpool, and she returned there after an eighteen-month American sojourn, with her last months spent in Cambridgeport — her project, as Margaret was fully aware, the search for a husband. Yet to Margaret's way of thinking, Ellen brought with her the "atmosphere of European life," the very stuff of her bookish fantasies: "I saw in her the storied castles, the fair stately parks and the wind laden with tones from the past, which I desired to know." Ellen Kilshaw, with her "face most fair" and long hair of "graceful pliancy," was a merging of heroines — a clever yet vulnerable ingénue whose father's business reversals threatened her chances in the marriage market, and a refined English-style comtesse de Pologne. For Ellen enchanted not just Margaret, but also her parents. Three years after Ellen returned to England, in 1820, Timothy and Margarett would name their fifth child, their second surviving daughter, Ellen Kilshaw Fuller.

With Julia Adelaide lost to her, the neighbor girls tiresome, and her mother preoccupied, Ellen Kilshaw was "my first real interest in my kind." My kind? Ellen painted in oils, and she allowed eight-year-old Margaret to watch the pictures "growing beneath her hand." She played the harp, and Margaret listened as if the sweet arpeggios were "heralds of the promised land I saw before me." Ellen was a spellbinder—this was Margaret's kind.

Ellen Kilshaw beckoned Margaret toward that hazily imagined adulthood promising more than mediocrity, obscurity. Margaret's days of reading and study now seemed drab to her; she lived for invitations to join Ellen and the other adults on country walks, when she could draw the older woman to her side and stroll hand in hand. Or for Ellen's visits to the Cherry Street parlor, where Margaret studied Ellen "from a distance" and memorized "all her looks and motions." She recognized that Ellen had "in its perfection the woman's delicate sense for sympathies and attractions." In company, she offered to all a "sweet courtesy" that "hung about her like a mantle," even as "her thoughts were free": she could "live two lives at the same moment."

Although her recollections of Ellen were written decades after the brief girlhood friendship, the child Margaret had sensed in Ellen the complexities of a lone woman's life. A man would not need or wish to "live two lives" at the same moment—nor hope to cultivate that "delicate sense" of social alliances forming and re-forming. A man would not have to maintain a "reserve" like Ellen's, which seemed, significantly to Margaret, the result of "self-possession" rather than "timidity." Ellen's virtues were feminine, as were her "accomplishments" in music and art: shown off to admiring friends in parlor and salon, not to strangers in a concert hall or gallery.

Margaret's parents observed their daughter's fascination with Ellen Kilshaw and encouraged her attachment to a woman they also saw as embodying a feminine ideal—the perfection "in all things" that Timothy envisioned for his daughter, who, to his distress, was developing a slouch as her growth spurt worsened a congenital spinal curve, and whose intensive studies had given her a nearsighted squint. "*All* accomplishments, & the whole circle of the virtues & graces should be your constant aim, my dear child," he pressed her, and recommended she follow a program of marching through the house banging a drum harnessed to her shoulders, in hopes of improving her posture.

Although Timothy was educating his oldest daughter to be "the heir of all he knew," as Margaret would later recall, he was a man of conventional, if not retrograde, views of women. The two impulses warred within him: to cultivate his prodigy-daughter's mind through the curriculum that had won him entry to Harvard, and to foster conventional, even ultra-feminine behavior, the sort that had drawn him to marry Margarett Crane.

The same ambivalence caused him, one day in Washington, to pick up Mary Wollstonecraft's *Vindication of the Rights of Woman*—a book that, thirty years ago in England when it was published to great acclaim, had opened the question of equality of the sexes. It was a volume, Timothy wrote to his wife, that now "no woman dares to read, but she should be charged with libertinism," because the author had been "discountenanced" as a result of her affair with a man "she loved so ardently & would not marry, but had a child by him." Indeed Wollstonecraft, who'd taken her first lover while living in Paris, drawn there by the spirit of revolution, had conceived two children out of wedlock before dying in childbirth with the second. After reading *Vindication*, however, Timothy declared he was "so well pleased" he might send home a copy—only to waver yet again as he considered the matter, suddenly worrying that his course of instruction for Margaret had left her lacking "knowledge of household affairs, sewing etc."

Timothy Fuller was something of a libertine himself. Fresh out of college and teaching at a young ladies' academy in rural Leicester, Massachusetts, he'd had no qualms about romancing his students, recording in his diary "*delicious* hour[s]" spent with one or another of the girls, enjoying "repeated contact of souls *through our lips!*" He prided himself on being "capable of *plurality* of loves" and took his time selecting a wife—ultimately settling on a novice schoolteacher, the daughter of a gunsmith in Canton, a country town south of Boston. Just nineteen when they met after crossing paths on the new bridge, Margarett Crane must have reminded Timothy of the "delicious" yet demure young ladies, "well informed, delicate, & amiable," whom he'd dallied with at Leicester Academy, to the occasional tittering of their less "judicious" classmates. This young bride from a few rungs down the social ladder would certainly acquiesce to his wishes, even if her enchanting looks and greater height set the stocky redheaded Timothy at a physical disadvantage. Little wonder that their oldest child would form the impression that, in most marriages, "the man looks upon his wife as an adopted child."

The Crane family, with four daughters to marry off, viewed Timothy's marriage proposal as a "piece of good fortune," and Margarett herself thrilled to her husband's "throbs of ambition," rarely questioning where they might lead him. If she wasn't precisely a politician's wife — did not often entertain his Republican cronies in Cambridgeport, follow him to Washington as hostess-companion, or attempt to influence his legislative agenda — she willingly tended to house and children while he was away and applauded, by letter, whenever he reported having entered into congressional debate.

Margarett Crane Fuller also found relief in her husband's regular absences, long months during which she sometimes took the children to stay at her girlhood home in Canton or brought her mother and sisters to Cambridgeport. Timothy, who admitted to a "hasty temper" and could be, as his daughter later wrote, "a tyrant in his home," was no less hotheaded and tyrannical in the letters he sent to his wife from Washington. Several weeks into their initial separation, after his wife had written that the receipt of his first letters had caused "such an overflowing of joy" that she had rushed upstairs to hide her tears, Timothy wrote back that he loved her "*more romantically* now than when we were married." But in other letters he ordered her to write every day, whether or not he reciprocated, charged her with extravagance, and refused her access to funds managed by his brother Abraham, reminding her that "your absent *Lord*" will be "hold[ing] the purse strings" as long as he wasn't near enough "to *enforce* respect for my just command." More bewildering, Timothy chastised his "disobedient spouse" for imagined "wayward" behavior with "light and frivolous *chaps*" simply because he'd had a dream in which she'd been riding with another man in a carriage as Timothy walked alongside. "Are our little ones neglected because you are listening to the flatteries & fooleries of fine fellows?" he pestered her. He demanded that she "tell the whole": "If any thing is suppressed, I shall certainly know it."

Timothy worried that his younger wife would find men of her own age more attractive in his absence and regretted being too far off to have "you in my eye constantly," as he had walking carriage-side in his dream. Yet he compulsively engaged in the very behavior he was forbidding his wife. He wrote home to her, boasting of a plurality of flirtations in Washington households, often stressing the superior beauty of women of "*low* stature" — women shorter than she — when compared to those of "Herculean size." He prattled on about his dinner party infatuations despite her requests that he stop. Even her barbed comment that perhaps he was "*envious* at the superiority I have over you in size" had no effect. If he had any thoughts of his wife joining him in Washington, she warned, only half teasing, she now had "no inclination" to "exhibit myself" where Timothy would find himself at a "disadvantage." She was reluctant to appear in society where he had shown himself to be an incorrigible flirt.

Little wonder that Timothy was powerfully attracted to the "highly cultivated" Ellen Kilshaw and that Margarett Crane was just as powerfully determined to have an equal part in the friendship, her own means of keeping her husband "in my eye constantly." Both may have felt relief when Ellen's focus turned out to be their daughter, "so surprising for her years, and [who] expresses herself in such appropriate language upon subjects that most of twice her age do not comprehend." Ellen had been charmed instantly when Margaret's passion revealed itself on her first visit to the Fuller home. When Margaret opened the door to Ellen, the girl's cheeks had "flushed" red, then she scampered to hide behind her parents' chairs before emerging again to engage the visitor in that "so surprising" conversation.

Ellen was the first adult besides her parents to take a serious interest in Margaret. It is hard to find a distinct Ellen Kilshaw in Margaret's over-wrought depictions of this woman she claimed to love "better than my life," but more important, Margaret felt Ellen had found a distinct—the *true*—Margaret. Ellen saw past the girl's flushed cheeks to "the lonely child whose heaven she was, whose eye she met, whose possibilities she predicted." With Ellen, Margaret experienced and never forgot the affirmation that comes when "the voice finds a listener" and is inspired to "more and more clearness."

Timothy's ambitions for Margaret were his own: Margaret must attain the perfect shining image he held in his mind's eye. Ellen, an emissary from the wider world—"a region of elegant culture and intercourse"—saw and "predicted" Margaret's own "possibilities": qualities of mind and spirit that, ironically, would carry her on a quite different route out of obscurity. After several years of tribulations—a broken engagement, a term as a governess—Ellen's many accomplishments took her to the altar with a socially acceptable Englishman, the Fullers would learn, as they followed their friend's progress by overseas mail.

By then, Margaret had recognized something "shallow and delicate" in Ellen's voice, in Ellen herself. But that was long after Ellen was severed from Margaret on her return to England and the days of "melancholy" and "profound depression" that followed Ellen's departure. Margaret's books, her mother's garden, no longer delighted or consoled. The girl was plagued by headaches, welcomed them because they kept her from studies that now seemed meaningless. She had learned that she needed real companions, "would not be pacified by shadows"—the characters in books and in her imagination. But where would she find true companions in dull, "*mesquin*" Cambridgeport? "All joy seemed to have departed with my friend, and the emptiness of our house stood revealed."

But the Cherry Street house, with a brood of Fuller children, wasn't empty; it was the tangle of parental disappointments and demands that left Margaret feeling empty. Both lonely and overmanaged, Margaret understood that her father's plurality of loves in fact was focused on just two females: "In the more delicate and individual relations, he never approached but two mortals, my mother and myself." She was one of "my *pair* of Ms," along with her mother, her father's possession, his prize. In Timothy's letters home, read by both wife and daughter, Margaret learned that as the Washington dinner party invitations thinned out, her father spent idle, "effeminate" evenings toying with a lock of her mother's hair in his rooms. He even admitted that "sometimes I try the memory & judgment of my daughter by questions in chronology, history, Latin &c." Although he'd taken a stand in Congress against the Missouri Compromise, an early fugitive slave law, and the Seminole War, he was not making a mark in Washington, and the fault was his own. He confided to his wife, "I am rather too indolent or unenterprising for the slight skirmishes . . . & the great questions require too much trouble and thought." At night, instead of troubling himself over the "great questions," he dreamed of Margaret practicing the piano—that lesson "she could never play in true time." Timothy's attention to his star pupil was intense, even disturbing, in a man who had once so blithely ignored the boundary between romance and pedagogy. Timothy was fanning a rivalry, as he had done in his letters to his wife detailing the charms of Washington's women. His complex involvement with Margaret elevated her sense of importance in the family, made her want to be "Margaret alone," surpassing even her mother in her father's estimation.

Did Margaret enjoy it when Timothy used a common Latin phrase—

O tempora, O mores!—in a letter to his wife, and followed it with a jab—"Sarah Margarett must interpret for you"—that also accorded his daughter the maternal spelling of their shared name? It was from her father that Margaret learned the art of cruel disparagement, and she practiced it first on her mother. When Margarett Crane finally agreed to accompany Timothy to Washington for a term, her daughter advised her to give up thoughts of acting as his secretary. It was not "a very feasible plan," wrote eleven-year-old Margaret: "I fancy you will be too much engaged besides you do not write half so fast as he can, and are not sufficiently fond of letter writing; do tell my father that I expect some letters from him." Timothy had his wife's company for scarcely a month before she returned to Massachusetts—to nurse her two little boys through a case of the measles, to retreat to the quiet fragrance of her garden.

With her mother, Margaret was "impertinent," begging to be allowed to put aside her household chores—minding the baby, tutoring her brothers—to take that favorite walk across the West Bridge into Boston. Margaret read her father's letters home, but she did not read her mother's to Timothy, wherein she would have found reports of her misbehavior, along with unexpected insights. Margarett Crane Fuller's philosophy of child rearing could not have been more different from her husband's, at least when it came to their older daughter. "I see in Sarah M. much to be proud of and much to correct, but I wish above all things to preserve her confidence & affection & not appear to be a severe judge," she wrote, in an effort to rein in her husband's criticisms.

Margarett Crane was questioning Timothy's authority too. "I have long thought that constant care of children narrowed the mind," she wrote her husband, impatient after a decade of marriage, concerning her household duties when he was away. The plan to join him in Washington had been the result of her challenge: "I intend sometime to leave you in the same situation I am placed in just to see how much real patience and philosophy you possess." Had he sent her Wollstonecraft's *Vindication*? Margarett Crane Fuller was more willful than Timothy had suspected when he had fallen in love with her as a nineteen-year-old he imagined he could shape and control—as he then tried to shape and control their daughter, "to make" of her "a good scholar & a good girl."

Margarett Crane may have been even more perceptive about the "very uncommon *child*," as she described her older daughter, the girl she struggled with, who felt unloved, than Timothy was. Had Margaret known that her mother had written this about her to Timothy—"Whenever I find any little scraps of her writing, I find something *original* & worth preserving in them"—would she have felt such emptiness, or sought throughout her life so desperately for validation of her originality, her worth, from other Ellen Kilshaws, and from other Timothys? Her father's proprietary vigilance felt like a loss to Margaret: "how deep the anguish, how deeper still the want, with which I walked alone in hours of childish passion, and called for a Father often saying the Word a hundred times till it was stifled by sobs."

After Ellen Kilshaw's departure, Margaret would seek other guides to realms beyond Cambridgeport. Yet her memory lingered. Ellen left Margaret a keepsake, "a bunch of golden amaranths or everlasting flowers." Overpoweringly fragrant, the flowers came from Madeira, Ellen said. Margaret saved them long after she'd grown disenchanted with Ellen Kilshaw, long into adulthood—"'Madeira' seemed to me the fortunate isle, apart in the blue ocean from all of ill or dread. Whenever I saw a sail passing in the distance,—if it bore itself with fulness of beautiful certainty,—I felt that it was going to Madeira."

3

Theme:
"Possunt quia posse videntur"

"THEY CAN CONQUER WHO BELIEVE THEY CAN." THE WELL-known line from Virgil's *Aeneid* describes a team of rowers who will themselves to win a race. Chosen by Margaret, or by her father, the inspiring words became the starting point for an essay she wrote as a girl. This time Margaret herself saved the manuscript, noting on its final page decades later, "Theme corrected by father; the only one I have kept; it shows very plainly what our mental relation was."

Yet strangely, few corrections appear from Timothy—that "man of business, even in literature," as Margaret later wrote, who "demanded accuracy and clearness in everything: you must not speak, unless you can make your meaning perfectly intelligible to the person addressed; must not express a thought, unless you can give a reason for it, if required; must not make a statement, unless sure of all particulars." Timothy's marks on the handwritten composition—six pages long—are minimal, just a phrase or two deleted, several ambiguous antecedents queried. By now, Margaret had absorbed so many of her father's views that he found little else to criticize.

This was what she preserved in the manuscript: the implicit presence of her father, both resented and loved, in her thought as a girl. "As nothing more widely distinguishes man from man than energy of will," Margaret begins, "so can nothing be more interesting than an inquiry into the nature of that enthusiastic confidence in the future which is a chief element of this will." Surely the forthright statement, an endorsement of democratic striving and Yankee zeal, pleased her father. Timothy suggests that she substitute "energy" for the final word, "will," for the sake of clarity; and he questions the phrase "in the future." Timothy's query teaches Margaret this about her father: he too is anxious. Can the "high scholar," the striving lawyer and politician, maintain his position by force of will? There is no choice but to summon the "energy" to try.

"Imagination is necessary to this confidence," Margaret continues; imagination enables us to apprehend beauty and to "enliven our hearts" once we have attained our goals. But imagination "cannot nerve the will to perseverance," she admonishes her reader (and herself, perhaps), cannot support the "unwearied climbing and scrambling" necessary to accomplishment. Years later, Margaret came to understand that her father "had no conception of the subtle and indirect motions of imagination and feeling," had "no belief in minds that listen, wait, and receive." The girl Margaret's mistrust of the imagination, of *her* imagination, was her father's.

And "so I must put on the fetters," she recalled of her unwearying scramble up the hill of knowledge as defined by Timothy: "I had no natural childhood." At a younger age than Ellen Kilshaw, Margaret learned to live two lives, safeguarding her imagination, her listening, feeling self: "My own world sank deep within." And that "true life was only the dearer" for being "secluded . . . veiled over by a thick curtain"—not a mantle of courtesy, like Ellen's, but a mantle of "intellect."

Most telling of all, "man" is the subject of Margaret's essay—not generic "mankind," but *man, not woman*. Napoleon, Michelangelo, Demosthenes, Brutus are her examples of energetic will. "I thought with rapture of the all-accomplished man, him of the many talents, wide resources, clear sight, and omnipotent will," she recalled of the years spent in her father's home school. At age nine she had written a page called "Beauties of Nature," enumerating the delights of garden, hill, cavern, and sea, concluding, "What employment [is] so noble as that of a naturalist. How must his mind be exalted and ennobled."

Negative examples, those who falter, are men too: "The *coward* never enters the lists,—the *weakling* failing once never enters them *again*." "Possunt quia posse videntur" is an essay about the power of the will, confidence in the future, written by an ambitious little girl who has learned that men are heroes, who must imagine herself, though her imagination is suspect, into the forward-looking conclusion she herself has written, a sentence that shows "very plainly" what she has to say on her own, although that sentence excludes her: "It is not in the power of circumstance to prevent the earnest will from shaping round itself the character of a great, a wise, or a good man."

One sentence allows for an ambiguous subject, neither male nor female, a sentence that speaks of learning from defeat, of redoubled effort: "The truly strong of will returns invigorated by the contest, calmed, not saddened by failure and wiser from its nature." Margaret has learned to rebound from her father's criticism; she has, she believes, "too much strength to be crushed." Those heroes were not who she could become, but she "loved to conquer obstacles, and fed my youth and strength for their sake," she would later recall. It will be many years before that girl envisions womanly valor, attains a "fulness of beautiful certainty"—before she makes her voyage to "Madeira," bearing her mantle of intellect not as a cloak but as a shield. Always she will strive, manfully, though she is a girl, and later a woman.

Now Margaret's hidden self spoke, beyond her control. By night she was "a victim of spectral illusions, nightmare, and somnambulism." She dreamed of walking in her mother's funeral procession, dreams inspired by her reading of the *Aeneid:* "of horses trampling over her," of "trees that dripped with blood, where she walked and walked and could not get out" as the bloody tide rose over her feet, then higher, finally reaching her lips, threatening her ability to speak, to cry for help, to live. She walked in her sleep, moaning, till her father found her, shook her awake, and, when she confessed her nightmare visions, ordered her "sharply" to "leave off thinking of such nonsense." The man who leveled jealous accusations at his wife on the basis of one dream brushed aside his daughter's recurring nightmares as nonsense—"never knowing that he was himself the cause of all these horrors of the night" by keeping her up long past any normal child's bedtime for late-night recitations, by forcing her through Virgil's lurid battle scenes, by inciting a rivalry between his *"pair* of Ms." Finally, to everyone's relief, Timothy sent Margaret to school.

At nine and ten Margaret walked down Cherry Street and around the corner each day to the newly opened Cambridge Port Private Grammar School with her brother Eugene, now six. There, in an arrangement unusual for the time, boys preparing for Harvard and girls with progressive-minded parents studied together, although seated in separate "classes," facing each other from benches on opposite sides of the room. Margaret, the girl with "no natural childhood," who "came with the reputation of being 'smart,'" as one classmate remembered, nevertheless made friends with Harriet Fay, one of the few girls on Cherry Street whose parents also favored a classical education for their daughter, and with several other girls who walked the mile and a half from high-minded Old Cambridge or across the river from Brookline and Boston.

Boys noticed her, not always favorably. Young Oliver Wendell Holmes, who found the fair-haired Harriet Fay "a revelation" of feminine charms, remembered Margaret, by contrast, as exhibiting an "air to her schoolmates [that] was marked by a certain stateliness and distance, as if she had other thoughts than theirs and was not of them." But again, Margaret was justified in holding this view of herself. She had come to school adept in translating Caesar, Cicero, and Virgil, the Latin texts her classmates were studying, and her compositions in English were closely reasoned and distinctive—original, as her mother had noted. The eleven-year-old Holmes chanced on a copy of one of Margaret's essays and began to read "with a certain emulous interest," hoping to find that his own written work was better—after all, he was a full year older. Margaret's essay began, "'It is a trite remark' . . . I stopped. Alas! I did not know what *trite* meant." For the future physician and poet, the evidence of Margaret's "superiority" was a "crushing discovery." That Margaret so quickly "got ahead of me" was likely the reason young Holmes derided her "long, flexile neck"—that slouch—and the "aqua-marine lustre" in her squinting eyes. What the boy didn't know was that Margaret also kept watch on competitors, usually older ones. When Margaret learned that "Miss Mary Elliot went through Virgil in thirty days," she determined to study "with renewed vigor."

But Margaret did not stay long at the Port School, as it was nicknamed by its pupils. Timothy had begun to hear of her "deficiencies" in "female *propriety*, & disposition," and he wanted a girls' school for his daughter. Margaret herself was uncomfortable with her body as it grew more womanly, lacing herself into too small dresses in hopes of containing the feminine flesh, making her seem "very corpulent," one boy judged harshly.

Once while visiting the house of a school friend, a maid had to be summoned to tighten the corset strings when her dress came undone. Now it wasn't just her intellect that made her seem much older than she was; it was her body. Entering her teens, Margaret was a "robust" girl who "passed for eighteen or twenty."

Although her mother argued for a boarding school in suburban Jamaica Plain that emphasized "polite forms of etiquette in social life," Timothy instead chose, at Margaret's urging, the most academically rigorous girls' academy in Boston, Dr. Park's Lyceum for Young Ladies, a day school across the river on Beacon Hill's Mount Vernon Street. There Margaret could continue her Latin and English composition, and add Italian, French, history, geography, geometry and trigonometry, and the natural sciences. As for the social graces, she began lessons at a nearby dancing school, which brought regular invitations to cotillions. Now her love of strenuous exercise had an outlet, and the physically mature girl soon found herself dancing with "grown up gentlemen"—to her parents' distress. Might she "display" her "attainments" too soon? But Margaret felt more comfortable conversing with college men, and even the handful of college professors who sometimes appeared, than with schoolboys.

In the classroom, Margaret gravitated to older girls as well, although less as friends than as objects of the competitive zeal fostered by Dr. Park's teaching methods: here was an opportunity to "conquer obstacles." At the end of each week, the student with the highest marks in a particular subject was awarded a medal and became the "head" of that class. A girl who collected twenty-one medals would earn the coveted "eye of Intelligence," the Lyceum's highest honor. Fourteen-year-old Susan Channing, niece of the eminent Reverend William Ellery Channing, had earned an impressive seventeen medals during her three months in the school previous to Margaret's arrival. But this didn't stop eleven-year-old Margaret from vowing to take the head in English away from Susan and rack up her own twenty-one in as short a time—and she did.

Once again, a reputation for genius, if somewhat distorted, had preceded her and grew with her accomplishments. Margaret was that "prodigy of talent and accomplishment" and that "wonderful child at Dr. Park's school, talking pure mathematics with her father, at 12 years." Her forthright manner and awkward appearance may have contributed to another impression circulating: the girl "had not religion." Margaret certainly made no effort to exhibit conventional piety in conversation or demeanor; anyone who heard her talk knew that Greek and Roman heroes, not Christian saints, were her lodestars. Her precocious reading of adult novels put her beyond the experience, at least imaginatively, of her peers and even many grown women.

Before coming to Dr. Park's school, she had seized on another novel from her father's bookshelves, an English translation of the German author Christoph Wieland's *Oberon*. At nine she wrote to Timothy that she had "never read anything that delighted me so much as that book." Cleverly, she had not asked his permission to read it the first time, but she begged his approval for a second reading, once "I get the card that has *Best* upon it" at the Port School; there was no point in denying her. A medieval fantasy of Charlemagne's court, with the fairy king and queen hovering in the background, *Oberon* is the tale of two fervid lovers, the pagan Princess Rezia and her devoted knight Huon, who struggle to obey Oberon's order that they remain chaste while they travel by ship to Rome to ask permission for a Christian wedding. Even if the nine-year-old did not precisely understand the rapturous island scene in which Huon "defies the god," Rezia "yields," and "their secret union" is achieved, she could have perceived the couple's transgression when they gave in to love's "sweet control," along with the passionate feelings that left them, afterward, "embath'd in bliss." And she would have felt the tragedy when Oberon sends a storm their way as punishment, ordering Huon to give up his life to save his lover and the ship. Instead, both lovers leap overboard to drown together.

The girl who thrilled to this tale, in which pagan sensuality and Christian law collide to tragic effect, could not pretend to "have religion" in the conventional sense. She could not settle down to the business of becoming one of "the dashing misses of the city," dancing with schoolboys and giving herself over to "fashion and frivolity" with her new classmates. As Susan Channing's younger brother William Henry, Margaret's age mate, later recalled, "a sad feeling prevailed" that Margaret "was paying the penalty . . . in nearsightedness, awkward manners, extravagant tendencies of thought, and a pedantic style of talk" for having been "overtasked by her father, who wished to train her like a boy." Little wonder that Margaret was "exposed to petty persecutions" and became "a butt for the ridicule" of the more "frivolous" girls at Dr. Park's Lyceum. She was a girl who found inspiration in male heroism, male transgression, hubris. She responded to the taunting "with indiscriminate sarcasms," the weapon she had taken from her father's arsenal along with his erudition, and "made herself formidable by her wit, and, of course, unpopular." Perhaps even Dr. Park, for whom she had quickly become a prized pupil, would not have understood her, had she revealed to him her hidden "true life." German literature, which he considered polluted with "rhapsodical intimations," was not taught in his school.

Although Margaret never spoke of the unpleasantness at Dr. Park's Lyceum to her parents, Timothy withdrew her after eighteen months, sending her back to the Port School where she could supervise her two younger brothers in Latin. She was thirteen years old, and he kept her under his rule again while he searched for a boarding school to provide the "finish" for his oldest daughter's education. No American college had yet opened its doors to women, and few parents, not even Timothy, thought it an opportunity lost. Although he was ambitious for his daughter, his plans for her future could have been no more definite than her own, and certainly featured a brilliant marriage as its centerpiece. As she entered her teens, Margaret became, to her parents, "this hopeful of ours." Timothy began to fret more over his oldest child's "manners and disposition" than her facility with Latin declensions and to insist she attend to "her musick & her sewing as well as to her Greek."

Dr. Park was sorry to let his prize pupil go. He drew Margaret aside to deliver a parting "address," saying "that he never *flattered*," yet stating outright, Margarett Crane reported to Timothy, that "he had never had a pupil with half her attainments at her age." Her classmates were less sorry. Hoping, at the last, to gain in their affection, Margaret planned a farewell dancing party at Cherry Street. Timothy was in Washington, but her Fuller uncles Elisha and Henry hired the musicians, and her mother paid out another fifty dollars for refreshments—after gaining Timothy's permission and extracting the sum from tight-fisted Uncle Abraham. Margaret told her father it would be a party for forty friends, but she sent out ninety invitations to girls in Boston and her old Port School friends. Two days before the dance, only nine had responded.

Margaret was chagrined, not hurt. Or she pretended not to be. When, deterred by the snowy evening or their young hostess's "formidable" wit, scarcely more than the nine appeared for the dance, Margaret made matters worse by fawning over the few Boston girls and ignoring her old Cambridge friends. She never gave her father the full account of the proceedings he pressed for. The dance had been "exceedingly agreeable," she lied. The event was "*well over*," her mother summarized. If, as a result of the fiasco, Margaret was forced to realize she had become "notoriously unpopular with the ladies of her circle," as Henry Hedge, the equally precocious son of the Harvard professor Levi Hedge, put it, she maintained a proud silence. Margaret had her "true" life to rely on, as she always had. In a letter she had written at age nine but never sent to Ellen Kilshaw, Margaret had spun out a fantasy of her family's "nobility of blood," with her brother William Henry as king, Eugene the "prince of Savoy," and Margaret herself both "queen [and] the duchess of Marlborough." It was a notion that would sustain her in later years as well, that "my natural position . . . is regal. — Without throne, sceptre, or guards, still a queen!" She would not let "circumstance" — her residence in dreary Cambridgeport, her difficulties with girls her own age, her alternately bullying and neglectful parents — erode her "enthusiastic confidence in the future."

· 4 ·

Mariana

A DISFIGURING RED "FLUSH" ROSE TO HER CHEEKS AND forehead, and would not go away. Timothy believed the "eruption" on Margaret's face was caused by her high spirits, the force of will she had extolled in her essay and that he had once approved in her; Margaret sensed he was "mortified to see the fineness of my complexion destroyed." Timothy harped on her need for "instruction" in "feminine discipline . . . female *propriety*, & disposition." She began to think of herself as "an odd and unpleasing girl." It didn't help to have a flawlessly beautiful and accommodating mother, "much taller than I," and an apple-cheeked baby sister who seemingly could do no wrong. Ellen's arrival in the family aroused Timothy's sense of correctness: his sons could be energetic, *boyish*, but his daughters must display "the virtues & graces." And a third son, Arthur, was born two years after Ellen, in 1822, while Margaret was accumulating medals at Dr. Park's school. Margaret was already "too independent," a poor example for three-year-old Ellen. But it was too late to change the habits of mind that Timothy himself had fostered in his oldest child. When no remedy cured the skin condition (probably acne), Margaret put aside her own "wounded" vanity and "made up my mind to be bright and ugly."

It was a vow more easily stated than adhered to, especially when she once again found herself surrounded by girls each day, and all night as well. Margaret had begged to attend the new girls' academy in Boston opened by the former principal at Boston's English Classical School, George B. Emerson; there she'd be able to learn Greek, a language she had not yet studied systematically. But her pleas to expand her classical education no longer affected Timothy. He objected, instead, to the daily commute into Boston, whether she rode or walked — "for I should grieve to have your complexion ruined past remedy by exposure to the heat & violent exercise."

Both parents were eager to send Margaret away from the city, where, despite having been "disappointed" by her farewell party, as she finally admitted to her mother, Margaret continued to attend cotillions, dancing with Harvard men — George Ripley and Edward Emerson, Ralph Waldo's younger brother and cousin to George B. What if his daughter were to "cheapen her value by too frequent appearance in company," Timothy worried. "She certainly begins to think herself a Lady among the Beaux," her mother had written to Timothy, disturbed by a parlor scene in which thirteen-year-old Margaret had refused the polite request of an attentive young schoolmaster, Mr. Frost, to see some of her writing. "He looked surprised & I was amazed at the girl's daring. What do you think of such a beginning?" Margarett Crane asked.

Margaret had no choice but to agree to a summer at Miss Susan Prescott's school in rural Groton, Massachusetts, the same small town where Timothy had been born. His father, a stubborn-minded minister turned politician, had refused to vote in favor of the U.S. Constitution because the document had not banned slavery. Being "too independent" was a Fuller family trait. "I hope you will not keep me there very long," Margaret wrote plaintively to Timothy, reminding him that if she stayed at school through the fall, she would "not see you the whole year round" because of his term in Washington. Once Margaret had acquiesced, Timothy sent her a hymn to the virtues of Susan Prescott, daughter of a prominent judge: the "judicious country lady, who will be *free & faithful* in watching & correcting your faults, & in imparting a relish for *rural scenes,* & rural *habits,* & rural *society,*" which would "contribute immensely to your immediate *worth,* & to your permanent happiness." After he had made his firstborn "the heir of all he knew," he now was determined to turn her into a demure country miss, as her mother had been when he met her. In the end, Margaret stayed in Groton a full twelve months.

As Timothy's political aspirations reached a plateau, his concern for Margaret's future—the match she might make—deepened. Yet her *immediate* happiness troubled him too. Familiar with the stinging slights of judgmental schoolgirls, Timothy hoped Miss Prescott's academy would offer Margaret "a fair opportunity to *begin the world anew,* to avoid the mistakes & faults, which have deprived you of *some esteem,* among your present acquaintances." Margaret must have shared the same hope as she boarded the stage, chaperoned in her father's absence by her uncle Elisha, for the six-hour journey over thirty miles of rutted roads leading north and west of Boston in May of 1824, two weeks before her fourteenth birthday.

Nestled in a verdant landscape that Margaret never mentioned in her letters to Timothy, Miss Prescott's academy at Groton was not a school for scholars, despite its extensive offerings: "Orthography, Reading, Poetry and Prose, Writing, English grammar; Geography, ancient and modern, Arithmetic, Projection of Maps, History, Composition, Rhetoric, Logic, Natural and Intellectual Philosophy, Geometry, Astronomy, Chemistry, Botany, French Language," as advertised in a Boston newspaper the month before Margaret arrived. "I feel myself rather degraded from Cicero's Oratory to One and two are how many," Margaret wrote her father after just a few days, reporting that the texts assigned to her were standard volumes in rhetoric and logic, plus Warren Colburn's "Arithmetick." She wished he would write to Miss Prescott, "for I do not know myself exactly what were your wishes with regard to the course of my studies," she tweaked her once vigilant father. The strongest indication of Timothy's turnabout in guiding Margaret's development was his apparent lack of interest in her academic program at this last stop in her formal schooling.

But Miss Prescott, whom "I did not intend to like," Margaret admitted, turned out to be a woman "I really love and admire." The lessons she would learn at boarding school—in matters "those who had sent her forth to learn little dreamed of"—had nothing to do with the intellect. The most profound of them came from that "judicious country lady" whose nurture of her wayward pupil would have surprised the exacting Timothy, had he learned of it. Many years later, Margaret turned the episode into a fictional piece, representing herself as Mariana, a girl who had "been unfortunately committed for some time to the mercies of a boarding-school." The story has the flavor of a Charlotte Brontë novel, although both Margaret's experience at the school and her telling of it anticipate *Shirley* and *Jane Eyre* by decades.

Mariana is different from the other girls—she is "on the father's side, of Spanish Creole blood." Mariana's unusual paternal inheritance makes her a "strange bird" at the school, "a lonely swallow that could not make for itself a summer," just as Margaret's uncommon education by her father set her apart as a scholar when she arrived at Miss Prescott's. One can assume that with Margaret, as with Mariana, the other girls immediately recognized her "touch of genius and power." The story makes no mention of Mariana's mother; Margaret's own mother was likely preoccupied when she left for school: within days of her daughter's departure Margarett Crane gave birth to a fourth son, Richard.

At first Mariana is an enchanting figure to her schoolmates—"always new, always surprising, and, for a time, charming." The other girls are "captivated" by her trick of spinning in circles till her onlookers are "giddy" with watching, then pausing to tell stories woven from "the scenes of her earlier childhood, her companions, and the dignitaries she sometimes saw, with fantasies unknown to life, unknown to heaven or earth"—which bring her schoolgirl audience to laughter or tears. With her gift for theater, Mariana is chosen for the lead in school plays, where she shines "triumphant." But there is "a vein of haughty caprice in her character," along with a "love of solitude," which annoy and perplex the other girls. She refuses to join in their gossip and flouts the "restraints and narrow routine" of the school. She soon gains a reputation as a "provoking non-conformist" who is "always devising means to break" rules: feigning headaches in order to skip tedious mealtimes or simply dallying on an upstairs balcony, "gazing on the beautiful prospect," when the dinner bell rings.

Mariana takes to wearing her stage makeup on schooldays, dipping into "her carmine saucer on the dressing table" each morning to paint her cheeks, and the other girls, once tolerant of her eccentric dress—"some sash twisted about her, some drapery, something odd in the arrangement of her hair"—finally begin to tease her for it. Mariana persists in the habit, at first saying she likes to "look prettier" and then responding with silence. The detail has the ring of painful truth, as if Margaret, not nearly so reconciled to being "bright and ugly" as she'd vowed, had adopted the same routine herself at Miss Prescott's, wishing to cover her acne. One day at dinner, Mariana looks up from her plate to see that the other girls have all painted large circles of rouge on their cheeks; they laugh at her down the table as teachers and servants look on with barely suppressed giggles.

Mariana maintains her composure through the meal, relying on her "Roman" spirit to carry her through the ordeal. But she collapses in hysterics afterward in her room, only to rise up transformed. She cannot forget that not one of her former companions took her side by refusing to take part in the prank. Her outward "wildness, her invention" are gone, replaced with somber studiousness and a sudden interest in the other girls' gossip, which she cleverly manipulates until those who have wronged her are consumed with jealousy and spite. She has become a "genius of discord" rather than a genius of the imagination. And then she is found out, accused—rightly, she admits—by the older girls of "calumny and falsehood." The "passionate, but nobly-tempered" Mariana throws herself on the floor, dashes her head against the iron hearth in shame. She knows that by seeking vengeance she has committed a greater wrong than those who injured her first.

It is left to the headmistress to calm and console Mariana—and she does so as Ellen Kilshaw might have: by expressing complete sympathy and confiding errors from her own youth. "Do not think that one great fault can mar a whole life," she exhorts Mariana. The girl is changed again, "tamed in that hour of penitence": "The heart of stone was quite broken in her. The fiery life fallen from flame to coal." Mariana asks her schoolmates' forgiveness, and they accept her as a "returning prodigal." She emerges from this "terrible crisis" as one who "could not resent, could not play false."

Although Margaret's account of Mariana is fictional, it derives from genuine suffering Margaret endured but never revealed to anyone outside the school. Five years after she left Miss Prescott's academy, she was still writing to her teacher of "those sad experiences," which continue to "agitate me deeply." And still grateful to Miss Prescott, "my beloved supporter in those sorrowful hours." Her memory of "that evening subdues every proud, passionate impulse," Margaret wrote: "Can I ever forget that to your treatment in that crisis of youth I owe the true life,—the love of Truth and Honor?"

Margaret's tale of Mariana has many elements of popular morality tales of the time: a high-spirited, nonconforming girl is "tamed," inducted into womanhood and its gentler ways. Yet Margaret's story has a twist. Mariana's "fiery life" may have "fallen from flame," but it is not extinguished: the embers remain, banked coals that burn steadily or may be reignited. The lesson she learns is not submission but perseverance when faced with ill will, and authenticity: she "could not resent, could not play false." These are the qualities Margaret thanks Miss Prescott for in her letter: "the love of Truth and Honor."

Whatever transpired at Groton, and between Susan Prescott and Margaret Fuller, left the girl stronger and steadier of purpose when she returned home for her fifteenth birthday. Margaret's first letter to Susan Prescott from Cambridgeport told of following a rigorous course of language studies — reading French and Italian on her own for several hours each day, morning classes in Greek — along with metaphysics, piano practice, regular walks, and evening journal writing. "I feel the power of industry growing every day," she wrote, driven by the "all-powerful motive of ambition." If Timothy had hoped that a year at boarding school would help focus Margaret's sights on the domestic sphere, he was wrong. "I am determined on distinction," she confided in Miss Prescott, "which formerly I thought to win at an easy rate; but now I see that long years of labor must be given." But she would not be one of those "persons of genius, utterly deficient in grace and the power of pleasurable excitement." Rather, "I wish to combine both." She was still the Margaret who yearned for power and influence, and for someone to share it with — who, as she wrote Miss Prescott again three years later, was capable of feeling "a gladiatorial disposition" along with "an aching wish for some person with whom I might talk fully and openly."

· II ·

CAMBRIDGE

Margaret Fuller,
sketch by James Freeman Clarke

James Freeman Clarke, sketch by his
sister, Sarah Freeman Clarke

The Dana mansion, Cambridge

· 5 ·

The Young Lady's Friends

I T WAS BACK IN CAMBRIDGE THAT MARGARET ENCOUNTERED the "dignitaries" she later wove into her story of Mariana. She had been away at Groton in August of 1824 when the marquis de Lafayette arrived in Boston at the start of a triumphal American tour, which drew grateful crowds to roadsides everywhere he passed. Now, in June of 1825, the aged hero of the American Revolution was back in the city again, preparing for his return to France, and Margaret was allowed to tag along with her parents to an opulent reception hosted by Boston's mayor, Josiah Quincy. The fifteen-year-old girl insisted on making her own introduction, by way of a letter composed earlier that same day.

"I expect the pleasure of seeing you tonight," Margaret began. Though she admitted to being only "one of the most insignificant of that vast population whose hearts echo your name," she could not "resist the desire of placing my idea before your mind if it be but for a moment." The idea of Margaret Fuller: already she sensed herself to be a significant personage, as much idea in the minds of others as reality to herself. She wished to tell him, "La Fayette I love I admire you"; and she wanted him to know how much his example inspired in her "a noble ambition." This was a fan letter, and an "ardent" one (the word peppered her letters now), but self-deprecation had vanished by the closing line: "Should we both live, and it is possible to a female, to whom the avenues of glory are seldom accessible, I will recal my name to your recollection."

Whether her letter reached Lafayette in time, or whether Margaret managed the personal encounter she hoped for, is not known and does not finally matter. What matters is this: even at fifteen Margaret could not contemplate glory without placing herself in its presence. Yet she had also begun to confront the inevitable difference between her future prospects and those of a similarly talented, nobly ambitious boy. Was it "possible to a female" to wield power? And if so, how?

Contemplating the heroic example of the Greeks in an essay written for her father was one thing: *They can conquer who believe they can.* She could imagine herself into that earlier world as, perhaps, an Amazonian warrior, or even as a member of Aeneas's crew. Margaret's mind could take her anywhere; she delighted, she wrote to her teacher Susan Prescott, in being "translate[d]" through her reading or in daydreams to "another scene," where she became absorbed, "to tears and shuddering," by the "spirit of adventure." Most recently she had become immersed in the novel *Anastasius,* which "hurls you," alongside its protagonist, "into the midst of the burning passions of the East." But at a formal social occasion for a living hero of her own day, the ritualized behavior and dress—the stark differences between dark-suited men and puffy-sleeved, corseted women as they sat at table, gathered after dinner in separate rooms—must have seemed incontrovertible evidence of feminine constraint. Was there "pleasure" to be had in Lafayette's company that night for a girl like Margaret, who wished herself—willed herself—onto the avenues of glory with the likes of her hero?

The following year, in support of Timothy's ambitions for himself and for Margaret—could they be separated?—the Fullers moved into the former home of Chief Justice Francis Dana, giving up their drab Cambridgeport house for a grand Georgian residence perched on a terraced hillside in Old Cambridge, a quarter of a mile east of the Harvard campus. With a private drive leading up from the road to Boston across spacious lawns dotted with specimen fruit trees, the Dana mansion offered an expansive view over the Charles River, "so slow and mild," Margaret wrote. From her second-story window she could see all the way to the "gentle" Blue Hills of Dedham in the south and to Mount Auburn in the west, which glowed in the late-afternoon sun beyond the slate rooftops of Harvard's handful of classroom and dormitory buildings. The prospect was far superior to the Cambridgeport soap works, which her four-year-old brother Arthur, lording it over the two younger Fuller boys, Richard and the new baby, Lloyd, in the nursery at Dana Hill, mischievously claimed to miss.

But the greater luxury only highlighted Margaret's increasingly ambiguous position in the family as she neared adulthood. What was she to do with her prodigious learning and restless ambition? At sixteen, she was now the eldest of seven Fuller siblings, with the cherubic six-year-old Ellen her only sister. Had she been a boy, Margaret would have begun classes at Harvard. Instead she was required to start the little ones on their first lessons and hear daily recitations from Eugene and William Henry, ages eleven and nine, while pursuing an ambitious self-imposed curriculum of her own devising. Most days she made time for Greek and Italian language study, French philosophy and literature, and piano practice — all preparation for an only dimly foreseeable future in which marriage was the sole achievement expected of her, but the last thing on her mind. No wonder she allowed the rosy sunset over Mount Auburn to draw her attention away from Harvard's imposing brick and stone campus: she could never walk those avenues of glory as a scholar or, as might one day have been appropriate to her talents, professor.

Timothy Fuller had quit representing the Middlesex district of Massachusetts in the U.S. Congress, where he'd never gained influence, and turned to state politics, swiftly becoming speaker of the Massachusetts House of Representatives. His law practice, which thrived now that he was in residence year-round, paid the bills for the Dana estate. But Timothy wanted more: a diplomatic posting to Europe under the new administration of John Quincy Adams. And he encouraged Margaret to expect a Continental finish to her education.

Scarcely a month after the move from Cambridgeport, Timothy used the Dana house to press his case, hosting a lavish dinner dance in the president's honor. The event promised to be the first Fuller social success, erasing the memory of Margaret's failed midwinter ball several years earlier, and even afterward it was said to have been "one of the most elaborate affairs of the kind" since pre-Revolutionary days. But Timothy too was forced to count his extravaganza a failure. Adams, still mourning the death of his father, the first President Adams, two months earlier, left before the dancing began and never did offer Timothy Fuller a place in his diplomatic corps. The gala came to seem another case of ill-advised merriment; there would be no more balls in the capacious Fuller home.

If Timothy had hoped his older daughter would display herself as an appealing commodity on the marriage market that night, he was disappointed in this also. At least one young woman present found Margaret unchanged from the days of her catastrophic dancing party, describing her at the Adams ball as "a young girl of sixteen with a very plain face, half-shut eyes, and hair curled all over her head." Margaret had laced herself too tightly, "by reason of stoutness," and she wore "a badly cut, low-necked pink silk, with white muslin over it." Her dancing was awkward too, the result of being "so near-sighted that she could hardly see her partner."

Margaret was still a precocious half-child half-adult, and anyone who chose to evaluate her in these days solely on the basis of manners and appearance was sure to find her lacking. She had not bothered to notice that the fashion for a full head of curls had given way to a mere fringe of ringlets around the face; her heavy honey-colored hair was difficult to manage anyway, even if it was her one point of pride. She had done her best job of corseting to show off her waist, but hers wasn't thin. Daring others to overlook her ungainly posture and ill-fitting clothes if they wished to know her, Margaret wasn't yet ready to admit that her appearance *should* matter. She longed not for Boston's elegant ballrooms but, as she wrote to Susan Prescott, for the ancient "feudal hall" where an assembled company might fall under "the romance of the minstrel" rather than the sway of a politician, and would venerate "nature, not as high-dressed and pampered, but as just risen from the bath." Words, not looks, were her stock in trade, but it remained to be seen what reward they would bring.

Fortunately there were many now who were drawn to Margaret's way of speaking and to her bookish, passionate nature. Despite Harvard's inaccessibility to women, the intellectual atmosphere of Old Cambridge was congenial to members of both sexes. "There is a constant stimulus to improvement," one female contemporary wrote of Cambridge in the 1820s, and "even if you know today more than some others they may sit up all night and put you down tomorrow." A "born leader" who was capable of directing parlor games with a wave of a handkerchief, and always ahead of the rest in her studies, Margaret could hold her listeners in thrall. "How did she glorify life to all!" one friend recalled, inspired like many to superlatives when it came to describing Margaret's talk: "all that was tame and common vanish[ed] away in the picturesque light thrown over the most familiar things by her rapid fancy, her brilliant wit, her sharp insight, her creative imagination, by the inexhaustible resources of her knowledge."

While Margaret's "sarcastic, supercilious" teasing, her "inclination to quiz," and her obvious disdain for "mediocrity" still made enemies of those who felt the heat of her scorn (her critic at the Adams ball may have been one of these), she began to have admirers who plotted to gain her favor. Some girls tried imitating Margaret's half-shut eyes and habitual slouch, in the apparent belief that mimicking her mannerisms would enable them to "know as much Greek as she did." When others observed her trick of converting her long hooded cloak for use as a satchel to carry home the armloads of books she borrowed at the local subscription library, hoisting them over her shoulder for the trek back to Dana Hill, they begged their mothers to buy them hooded cloaks so they might do the same.

From her gang of adorers, Margaret chose particular favorites: Amelia Greenwood and Almira Penniman, Ellen Sturgis and Elizabeth Randall. "Each was to her a study," wrote a close male friend of the time. He saw Margaret's girl friends as a young man would: "There was A — a dark-haired, black-eyed beauty," who was "bright" but "cold as a gem"; then "there was B — , the reverse of all this, — tender, susceptible, with soft blue eyes, and mouth of trembling sensibility." C — was "all animated and radiant with joyful interest in life"; D — "half-voluptuous"; and E — "beautiful too, but in a calmer, purer style." And then there was M — Margaret. She was their ringleader, too formidable and too physically awkward for a teenage boy to see with a would-be lover's eyes.

But Margaret too enjoyed the sensuality of girls her own age. The hours spent lounging on drawing room sofas after tea, on shady porches, or under parasols at summer visits to the seashore provided a respite from her schoolroom duties at home. The girls huddled in conversation, always conversation, for Margaret "never rested till she had found the bottom of every mind, — till she had satisfied herself of its capacity and currents, — measuring it with her sure line." Margaret expected her friends to "be capable of seeking something." She cared little what that something was, only that her friends "should not be satisfied with the common routine of life,—that they should aspire to something higher, better, holier, than they had now attained."

In many ways, Margaret wasn't a girl at all anymore. In letters she addressed her teacher Susan Prescott as an intellectual equal and wrote to her of her childhood days as if they were many years in the past. When visiting friends, she often drifted away to speak with their mothers; two of her closest friends were accomplished adult women.

Margaret most likely met the novelist Lydia Maria Francis in 1825 when Maria, who also preferred to use her middle name, was at the height of her early fame; at the reception for Lafayette, *she* had won a personal introduction and a kiss on the hand, which she vowed never to wash off, from the celebrated French general. Not long before that giddy moment, Maria Francis had published her first novel, *Hobomok*, the story of a romance between a Pequod Indian and a white woman, set in colonial New England, which "marked the very dawn of American imaginative literature," in one critic's estimation, and made Francis a celebrity overnight.

Eight years older than Margaret, Maria Francis had been raised by an older sister in backwoods Maine after their mother's early death. Self-taught, self-made, and self-reliant, she was unlike any woman Margaret had known before, yet they had a great deal in common. Maria too was filled with "restless insatiable ambition," as she once wrote, which burned in her heart "like a fiery charm," promising deliverance from obscurity. As with Margaret, the "harmless arrow" of Maria's "playful wit" was often mistaken "for the poisoned darts of sarcasm," and despite her celebrity status Maria soon earned "enemies as well as friends" in Boston society. The publication of her second novel, *The Rebels*, a thinly fictionalized account of a prominent Loyalist family in Revolutionary Boston, shocked and ultimately turned her public against her, once they decoded its source.

Prophetically, Maria Francis had created in *The Rebels* a heroine who, like herself, "possessed a large share of that freedom of thought, that boldness of investigation, which renders exalted talents a peculiarly dangerous gift." Shunned by those who once feted her, Maria Francis put aside novel-writing and retreated from Boston to Watertown, just beyond Cambridge, to teach school, preferring that "honest independence" to mingling with "those who possess merely the accidental advantages of rank and fortune." It was during this period of exile that Margaret and Maria became close friends.

Margaret recognized Maria Francis as honest and forthright, "a natural person,—a most rare thing in this age of cant and pretension," she wrote to Susan Prescott. Maria looked beyond Margaret's "accidental advantages"—the imposing Dana mansion with its servants—to praise her young friend as "full of thought, raciness, originality." As the two women contemplated their uncertain futures, feeling the dangerous inner heat of ambition, they undertook a comparative study of two European philosophers: the English empiricist John Locke and the French Romantic Germaine de Staël.

Inevitably they favored the "brilliant" de Staël, who in Margaret's words operated "on the grand scale, on liberalizing, regenerating principles." They were captivated as much by the author's role as intellectual diva in Revolutionary France as they were by her writing. De Staël—whose *De l'Allemagne* brought the fervid idealism of German Romantic philosophy to the rest of Europe, and whose Paris salon attracted political refugees and international luminaries alike—was the model both young women needed, even as her example must have seemed impossible to match in parochial New England of the 1820s.

Looking back on her own brief burst of fame, Maria confessed that she had felt at times "like a butterfly under a gilded glass tumbler; I can do nothing but pant despairingly, or beat all the feathers off my wings, thumping against the glittering walls of limitations." And at twenty-four, in retreat at Watertown, Maria had begun to worry that she'd end up as "a poor isolated spinster"—a more distant prospect for Margaret, but perhaps a troubling one after her several resounding failures in formal social settings. De Staël, who had inherited a fortune, had also managed to secure her social standing by marrying, though she lived apart from her husband and carried on love affairs without bothering to hide them.

As their year of study drew to a close, Margaret watched Maria's growing attachment to David Child, an idealistic Boston lawyer and newspaperman who would prove to be as improvident as he was in love with Maria Francis. When the couple married in October 1828, Child was out of work, so it was Maria who purchased the thirty-five pounds of cake they served at their wedding, drawing on her own new income as editor of the *Juvenile Miscellany*. Such "was the beginning of the married life of a woman of genius," observed one of the guests. Lydia Maria Child would always be the financial mainstay of her marriage, and in less than a decade she had once again achieved fame, though this time not as a novelist. An outspoken abolitionist, she wrote *An Appeal in Favor of That Class of People Called Africans*, the most influential anti-slavery work before *Uncle Tom's Cabin*, and, in a different vein, published *The Frugal Housewife*, one of the era's most popular domestic advice manuals.

Although Margaret and Maria remained friends, after her marriage the older woman became too busy for shared study, and her place in Margaret's life was quickly filled by Eliza Farrar, who had married in 1828 as well, at age thirty-seven. Eliza's husband was the Harvard mathematics and natural philosophy professor John Farrar, a fifty-two-year-old widower who installed his European-born bride in a Cambridge house not nearly as grand as the Fullers' Dana mansion, but comfortably large and conveniently located near the college on the newly established Professors' Row (now Kirkland Street).

Born to American parents but raised in France and England, Eliza Farrar had, like Margaret's beloved Ellen Kilshaw, come to America as an adult after her father lost his fortune. She lived with family in New Bedford and looked for a husband—not to secure a "*mariage de convenance,*" as she referred to unions arranged for the sake of money, but to find the love of a suitable man who would overlook her lack of a dowry. Eliza would later write in her memoirs—which told of her acquaintance, in palmier days, with London's literati—of the closed society she had known in England, where "love matches" were encouraged, but only among members of the same social set, and young people met and fell in love at weekend house parties, closely supervised by parents eager to preserve and augment the family fortune. Had she stayed in England, an unlucky young woman like Eliza, with no dowry to bring into a marriage, might well have been pressured to accept a husband below her in social status or a wealthy suitor for whom she felt nothing. Better to go to America, where her European refinement would show to good effect, where men were less "careful" in the financial matters bearing on marriage, and where social class was more fluid.

Eliza Farrar, like Maria Francis, was already a published author when Margaret met her, but her first book, a children's tale with a subtle anti-slavery message, had not won her fame—nor did Eliza seek it. Her chief interest was feminine propriety, although, in tune with the liberal social order of her adopted country, she espoused "an American freedom from purely conventional standards," according to one of her neighbors on Professors' Row, Charles Eliot Norton. Still, when she published a popular advice manual on dress and deportment, *The Young Lady's Friend*, nearly a decade after meeting Margaret, she did so anonymously, as "A Lady," in order to obtain not public recognition, but needed income, because her husband's health had suddenly declined. If Eliza Farrar provided a less adventurous model of womanly achievement than Maria Francis—or their shared ideal, Germaine de Staël—Margaret learned more from her.

Margaret was eighteen now and suddenly eager to acquire the poise and worldly sophistication—key sources of female power, as Margaret was coming to understand—that Eliza Farrar so obviously possessed. She was also attracted to the companionable marriage of the lady cosmopolite and the learned professor. Both were adept in what Eliza Farrar termed the "art" of conversation—with Eliza the superior talker. Despite the age difference, in this marriage husband and wife, unlike Timothy and Margarett Crane Fuller, were intellectual equals; in fact, the wife's personality dominated. For several years, Margaret spent so much time in the Farrar household, where the childless couple held open house for Harvard students, some of whom were boarders, that she came to think of Eliza Farrar as her "elected" mother.

Eliza, who was new to Cambridge and still reconciling herself to a permanent American residence, saw Margaret's "extraordinary promise" as clearly as Ellen Kilshaw had, and made a project of her young neighbor. Her plan was to "mould her externally," as a mutual acquaintance observed, "to make her less abrupt, less self-asserting, more *comme il faut* in ideas, manners, and even costume." If Margarett Crane was stung by her daughter's defection to another household, Timothy could not have minded the results. Eliza gave new orders to Margaret's dressmaker and hairdresser and took Margaret on social calls to refine her manners. Shedding pounds along with her adolescence, Margaret would never again be faulted for ill-fitting clothes or frowsy hair. Her slouching posture, the result of kyphosis, an S-like curvature of the spine, now began to seem swanlike, not slumping. By the end of this education, Margaret looked back on her younger self as "the most intolerable girl that ever took a seat in a drawing room." Crucially, however, she was not being schooled in deference; Eliza Farrar's ideal woman was no demure drawing room fixture, as Margarett Crane so easily became in social settings. Margaret was learning to play the lady bountiful, to become a "gentlewoman," as Eliza recommended in *The Young Lady's Friend*, who could actively demonstrate her ability to "behave courteously and delicately to all." From Eliza Farrar she was discovering, above all, that a strong-willed woman could give lessons to other women on what to think and how to behave.

Although its publication was some years in the future, Eliza Farrar's *Young Lady's Friend*, which adroitly linked Yankee frugality and high-mindedness with Old World cultivation and noblesse oblige, speaks with the force of moral authority that Eliza must have exerted over Margaret. Eliza's code of etiquette was based on a notion of class privilege within a democracy, and she gave her female readers instruction on upward mobility through displays of refinement—the means through which she had won her marriage to a distinguished Harvard professor. Her message must have registered with Margaret, who as a child had fancied herself a queen even as she thrilled to tales of the Roman Republic. "In no country is it more important to cultivate good manners, than in our own," Eliza Farrar wrote, "where we acknowledge no distinctions but what are founded on character and manners." America's aristocracy of merit, still taking shape in the first decades of the nineteenth century, was open to all but the "person who is bold, coarse, vociferous, and inattentive to the rights and feelings of others," for she "is a vulgar woman, let her possessions be ever so great, and her way of living ever so genteel. Thus we may see a lady sewing for her livelihood, and a vulgar woman presiding over a most expensive establishment."

Eliza Farrar admonished her readers to master and perform daily household chores—making their beds, tidying their rooms, even if they had servants on hand to discharge these tasks—as a means of showing respect to their social inferiors and earning their good favor. In fashion, Farrar declared, the way a woman carried her shawl—whether "dragged round the shoulders" or "worn in graceful folds"—mattered more than the quality of the fabric, because "true taste will generally be found on the side of economy." A "love of finery" was to be discouraged; mothers were advised to give their daughters plainly dressed dolls so as to ward off an infatuation with "tawdry ornament." To American women struggling to make ends meet in the financially turbulent decade of the 1830s, when many fortunes made in the early years of the republic were lost in what came to be known as the Panic of 1837, this was welcome news.

She filled a chapter with recommendations on proper behavior at lectures, one of the few popular entertainments of the day that women could attend unescorted. Lectures provided opportunities for women to gather material for conversation and to practice their manners in mixed society. Those "who attend lectures together," Eliza wrote, "meet on terms of perfect equality." The lecture hall was a place where a ladylike seamstress might well attract a gentleman's notice, so it was best to remember that a "gentlewoman" would not arrive late, or wear a large hat that might obstruct the view of those behind her, or "run, jump, scream, scramble, and push, in order to get a good seat." Neither would a gentlewoman stand at the podium to address the crowd; so well understood was this prohibition that there had been no need to state it.

Eliza Farrar's program culminated in her chapter on conversation, "one of the highest attainments of civilized society," yet rarely cultivated in the United States, she lamented. Americans excelled in verbal "fluency," she conceded, but few had trained themselves to become "correct and methodical thinkers," and many were given to "careless and thoughtless volubility." She counseled young ladies to avoid superlatives, slang, and repetition; to listen as well as to speak; and never to gossip or tease. For those who became adept in the conversational "art," social discourse was the "way in which gifted minds exert their influence."

At eighteen, Margaret had already made herself a prime example of a gifted mind exerting influence through conversation. A natural speaker, trained in "correct and methodical" thinking by her father, she had also learned to restrain her tendency to tease and quiz, making herself less "intolerable" in the drawing room. She could now hold in reserve her barbed wit, a faculty she had too often resorted to as an offensive tactic when sparring verbally with young America's sometimes less-than-well-mannered gentlemen and as a defensive one when she felt hurt.

Margaret needed her "elected" mother's guidance far more in matters of dress and comportment than in conversation; where she already sensed her own expertise, she would not take all of Eliza Farrar's advice to heart.

But Margaret accepted wholeheartedly another of Eliza Farrar's gifts—
the friendship of Eliza's cousin Anna Barker, a New York society girl
with family ties to the freethinking Quaker merchants of New Bedford.
Three years younger than Margaret, Anna often stopped in Cambridge
on her way to Newport, Rhode Island, for summer holidays. Attracted as
Margaret was to older women as mentors, she was still, as Eliza phrased it
in her book, at "the precious morning of life." And so was Anna, a lithe,
dark-haired beauty as naturally alluring as Margaret was forceful. Both
were entering that "season full of danger and temptation," Eliza warned,
when school is over and young ladies must guard against the feeling that
their education is finished.

· 6 ·

Elective Affinities

M ARGARET FOLLOWED POLITICS — READ THE PAPERS FAITH-fully or listened to her father read the news aloud after dinner. In this way she learned, in early 1826, that the Russian throne had passed to Nicholas rather than to the "brutal" Constantine, his brother. "We may now hope more strongly for the liberties of unchained Europe," Margaret rejoiced in a letter to Susan Prescott. She had come to care passionately for the cause of Greek independence after Lord Byron joined the fight and died there in 1824. (The poet-revolutionary would become an obsession; two years later Margaret wrote to a friend, "My whole being is Byronized . . . my whole mind is possessed with one desire — to comprehend Byron once for all.") Now she waited in "anxious suspense" for the results of negotiations between Russia and England that would determine the country's fate.

But when her father urged her to pay attention to his friend Albert Tracy, an unmarried congressman from upstate New York whom Timothy invited for a long visit during Margaret's first summer back from school at Groton, she wasn't interested. Later she would recall that despite Tracy's obvious charms — his "powerful eye" and "imposing maniere d'être" — she had not been "inclined to idealize lawyers and members of Congress" or, most especially, "*father's friends*." Instead she was smitten by her distant cousin George Davis, who had moved to Cambridge from his home on Cape Cod to join Harvard's class of 1829. Ironically, he would go on to become a lawyer and politician—a liberal Whig congressman and editor—but now, as he joined the Fuller household for evening meals and after-dinner talk and frequented the Farrars' open house, he seemed simply the only one of a bright crowd of Harvard men who could match wits with Margaret and keep pace with her dynamic thoughts, a man with whom she could be "truly myself."

Others in their set included her once sharply critical Cambridgeport schoolmate Oliver Wendell Holmes; the sometimes pedantic Henry Hedge, whose years of study in Germany before entering Harvard earned him the nickname "Germanicus" from the envious Margaret; the mathematician Benjamin Peirce; and the future Unitarian ministers James Freeman Clarke, William Henry Channing, and William Green-leaf Eliot, who later founded Washington University in St. Louis. Eliot complained, as many of the others might have, that Margaret treated him "like a plaything." Years later she wrote of a fictional "friend": "Her mind was often the leading one, always effective." This was Margaret, even among the stars of Harvard's brilliant class of '29, the class that might have been hers, had she been a man. George Davis—bright-eyed, with regular features and a soft complexion—was her nearest equal in a roomful of fervent talkers. Like Margaret, he was capable of "intellectual abandon," had the "habit of *letting himself go* in conversation," drawing on his vast store of literary references—and he shared her inclination to analyze their friends, sometimes mercilessly. George Davis and Margaret liked to "pull people to pieces to see what they were made of, and then divert themselves with the fragments," one less-than-willing participant in their "college frolics" recalled.

But the attraction, on Margaret's side at least, was more than a matter of verbal jousting and elevated gossip. While George Davis may have inspired the "gladiatorial disposition" she reported to Susan Prescott, Margaret was also losing interest in "light conversation." She was drawn to George Davis's "contempt for shows and pretenses." For a time she believed he would answer that "aching wish for some person with whom I might talk fully and openly." Long after their initial intimacy, Margaret would remember that the two of them could "communicate more closely with one another than either could with the herd." The connection was "so open" and the "intimacy," through several seasons of Cambridge evenings, "so long, so constant," that she felt their mingling of souls to be "conjugal."

Then why didn't he return her love? They exchanged letters, both flirtatious and sincere. Margaret told George Davis he had the "brilliant vivacity and airy self-possession" of the rogue Robert Lovelace in Samuel Richardson's novel of seduction, *Clarissa:* she admired his "character . . . based on the love of power and the spirit of enterprize." George Davis wrote asking for a statement of Margaret's religious beliefs, a common query from a young man considering a marriage proposal. Margaret could easily have taken his question as a preamble to courtship—a step beyond the sort of intellectual challenge she encouraged in her male companions. Best of all, he may have wished to pay suit *and* to contend.

Margaret answered frankly, almost imperiously, with a bold admission of religious doubt, accompanied by a highhanded dismissal of anyone who didn't share her skepticism: "I have determined not to form settled opinions at present. Loving or feeble natures need a positive religion, a visible refuge, a protection . . . But mine is not such." As a child, Margaret had thrilled to tales of Greek and Roman conquests; the *Aeneid* was her text, not the Bible. Church was a place to let her mind wander on Sunday mornings, to find Ellen Kilshaw, that avatar of aesthetic culture and feminine refinement, far more inspiring than any sermon. If she had faith at all it was in "Eternal Progression" and in "a God" (not *the* God, or even *God*) that was synonymous with "Beauty and Perfection," she wrote to George Davis.

In words she might later come to regret but would never renounce, Margaret went further: "When disappointed, I do not ask or wish consolation,—I wish to know and feel my pain, to investigate its nature and its source." She acknowledged herself "singularly barren of illusions" for a nineteen-year-old and unwilling to have "my feelings soothed" by religious dogma. But Margaret did harbor the illusion that George Davis would receive her confidences sympathetically. Whether she saw his question as a romantic overture or as a comradely inquiry into her first principles, Margaret had revealed more to him of her private beliefs than she had ever admitted to anyone, and she counted on him to "read understandingly!"

Could he? Was George Davis the man Margaret willed him to be: a powerful, scintillating Lovelace who wouldn't mind—might even treasure—a woman as powerful and scintillating as himself, a woman whose "pride," as she confessed to him, "is superior to any feelings I have yet experienced"? Margaret readily answered a second letter from George Davis on the topic of religion. He had declared himself "satisfied" with her initial response, yet something in this dry remark prompted her to clarify her position: no, she had not yet experienced "Christian Revelation," the conversion experience widely recognized as a badge of Christian piety, and "do not feel it suited to me at present." Reading this blunt reply, George Davis—dazzling conversationalist, yet no daring Lovelace after all—must have wondered what sort of woman he had nearly fallen for. Perhaps he was one of those "feeble natures" who required a positive religion—along with most Americans of the time.

George Davis finished his college courses and left Cambridge for western Massachusetts to prepare for a career in law. He'd already tapered off his visits to the Fuller house, and after the exchange on religion, his letters trailed off too. "Ah weakness of the strong," Margaret wrote in her autobiographical story of Mariana, who returned from boarding school to fall in love, instantly, with Sylvain, a man she believed to be her equal "in the paths of passion and action": "everything about him was rich and soft" and "of a noble character." But—"it is a curse to woman to love first, or most." Margaret had loved George Davis both first *and* most. Had Davis loved her at all?

Silence is the cruelest means of rejection, even if it only masks confusion or regret. The spurned lover is left to guess, to hope, to search her soul and her memory of past events for an explanation. All this Margaret did as she suffered George Davis's silence. It wasn't until years later, writing the story of Mariana, that she was able to interpret what she decided was his "insincerity and heartlessness": "Thoughts he had none, and little delicacy of sentiment." Mariana, Margaret's double, loved Sylvain, George Davis's stand-in, so much that she failed to recognize his shallowness; she had "imagined all the rest"—his attentiveness and understanding. In the story of Mariana, the couple marries and Mariana dies young, suffering from "the desolation of solitude" and the "repression of her finer powers" by her careless, uncomprehending husband, who never recognized the "secret riches within" his bride. In remembered bitterness, Margaret made George-as-Sylvain a beautiful, vain villain. Marriage to George Davis would have been a disaster. If "separation" was possible, she would ultimately conclude, "real intimacy had never been."

But at nineteen-turning-twenty, the pain was intense, made all the worse by the sudden death of her youngest brother, Edward, the ninth Fuller child, born the year before on Margaret's eighteenth birthday. The boy had been assigned to her special care, "given" to her then as "my child." Her mother had too many others to care for, and Margaret was nearly as old as her mother had been when she agreed to marry Timothy Fuller. In the fall of 1829, as the infant Edward grew weak from an unknown illness, Margaret shared the night watches, carried the boy in her arms to soothe him "while night listened around," did her best to answer the "pleading softness of his large blue eyes" with reassurance in her own. This wordless communion at life's precipice yielded "some of the sweetest hours of existence." Although the trial was not enough to cause Margaret to reconsider her brave renunciation of the comforts of faith, she envied Edward his freedom from suffering when "at last . . . death came." Margaret's first awareness of life had been the death of her sister Julia Adelaide; she left childhood behind when George Davis failed to answer her "aching wish" and her brother Edward died in her arms.

George Davis's friend and Harvard classmate James Freeman Clarke became Margaret's friend. She found it difficult at first to "talk fully and openly" with another man and resisted James Clarke's initial advances — even though his were those of a would-be comrade, not a lover. But James persisted. He told Margaret they too were cousins, although the relation, as the two construed it, was at a "thirty-seven degrees" remove; in fact, they were descended from entirely different Fuller lines.

When James Clarke wrote asking Margaret to open her "answering store" of emotional honesty to him, she responded by telling him of her "stifled heart" and of the "sad process of feeling" she had recently endured. She didn't need to mention George Davis by name; James knew. "Now there are many voices of the soul which I imperiously silence," she wrote of her bitter discovery that, in regard to Davis, "the sympathy, the interest [were] . . . all on my side." She consented to tell James Clarke "the truth of my thoughts on any subject we may have in common" but promised no "limitless confidence." She closed by asking him to show her letter to "no other cousin or friend of any style."

Still, she may have hoped that James would tell George Davis of her suffering, let him know, if he didn't already, how he had hurt her and how much she longed for him. Could his sympathy and interest still be kindled? Or could he be made to suffer some regret? Even if James heeded her prohibition and none of this came to pass, Margaret could now look to *him* for the male companionship—the "pleasure . . . of finding oneself in an alien nature"—that the close childhood bond with her father had established in her as a persistent need. And James Clarke was a much better match.

Born the same year as Margaret, James Freeman Clarke had experienced a hothouse childhood similar to Margaret's in its intense focus on cultivation of the intellect, though the method had been different. The third child of an improvident doctor-druggist, James had been sent to live until age ten with his step-grandfather James Freeman, the minister at Boston's King's Chapel and a founder of the liberal Unitarian sect. Every day was a free-ranging tutorial in the classics and liberal religious texts, the course of inquiry dictated by the boy's own curiosity. When James returned to his parents' house, crowded with siblings, to attend Boston Latin School and then Harvard, where rote learning and competition for class rank prevailed, he chafed at the regimen as Margaret had at Miss Prescott's logic and rhetoric texts. When Margaret and James established a friendship during James's first year of divinity school at Harvard, they were perfectly matched study partners: Margaret with her self-imposed discipline and voracious appetite for knowledge, eager to keep pace with a divinity school curriculum closed to her by virtue of her sex; James with his questing spirit, open heart, and surprising acceptance of a woman as his intellectual superior, impatient to satisfy an innate desire for an education beyond the narrow offerings within the brick walls of Divinity Hall. There would be no rivalry, no confused love between them.

The two new friends embarked on a joint venture: they would master the German language well enough to read the foundational texts of Romanticism that they knew so far only secondhand from commentary in Germaine de Staël's *De l'Allemagne,* Coleridge's *Aids to Reflection,* and the rare English translation. The movement that had arisen among artists and intellectuals toward the end of the eighteenth century in a semifeudal Germany, still a disorderly collection of principalities and independent city-states under the waning control of the Hapsburg dynasty, held enormous appeal for young freethinking Americans. The German intelligentsia sought an ideology to stimulate a movement for national unification; American intellectuals hungered for a philosophy to support a nation newly born, a democracy in the process of inventing itself. The argument for the "rights of man" that had inspired the American Revolution needed only a little pressure to depart from its Enlightenment roots and bind itself to the Romantic cult of the individual, with its emphasis on inward inspiration, free self-expression, and freely expressed emotion—impulses that had already begun to stir a new century of democratic revolution in Europe.

Margaret was a quick study, as always, becoming a fluent reader and accurate translator in just three months, to James's astonishment. No longer Byronized, Margaret read Schiller, Novalis, Jean Paul Richter, and above all Goethe. "It seems to me as if the mind of Goethe had embraced the universe," she wrote to James. "He comprehends every feeling I have ever had so perfectly, expresses it so beautifully." She read with such absorption that "when I shut the book, it seems as if I had lost my personal identity." The two "cousins," as they addressed each other, related by blood or not, took as their common credo Goethe's phrase "extraordinary, generous seeking" and used it to spur their studies and their personal ambitions. James dreamed of an influential role in the Unitarian ministry; Margaret yearned—for what, she still did not know.

Margaret's unfocused striving and rankling frustration over family obligations found answering chords in Goethe's Romanticism. She began, and hoped to publish, a translation of his play *Torquato Tasso*, based on the life of an Italian Renaissance poet whose close confidante, an unmarried, intellectually gifted princess, complains of feeling stifled in her gilded cage. Margaret was captivated as well by his novel *Elective Affinities*, which put into fictional play Goethe's view, borrowed from new science, that romantic attractions resulted from unalterable chemical "affinities" and should be obeyed regardless of marital ties. Shocking to many readers in its day, the book provided a refreshing glimmer of hope to Margaret, who was beginning to doubt she'd ever make a conventional marriage. One after another, her female friends had found husbands—even her teacher Susan Prescott had closed her school to marry

John Wright of Lowell—and, rumor had it, George Davis was courting Harriet Russell, a younger woman still in school in Greenfield, Massachusetts, where Davis worked now as a law clerk.

The closest Margaret had come to a romantic involvement in recent months had been her compulsive meddling in James Clarke's courtship of Elizabeth Randall, Margaret's friend since their days together in Dr. Park's Boston school. Margaret granted that the sweet-tempered and strikingly attractive "E." should "suffice" for James as "a present type of the Beautiful to kindle Fancy," but she did not believe the two were suited for marriage, nor James ready for it. Perhaps she was disturbed when James confided that the woman he desired for a wife would have to be a "loved and loving one, twining her arms about me and gazing in my face with eyes full of passion and dependence." This was not the way Margaret envisioned marriage; possibly she knew her friend Elizabeth Randall didn't either. She may have been troubled too that James, who understood Margaret so well and prized her friendship, would wish to be loved by someone so unlike herself and with a submissive devotion she would never wish to tender.

In response to James's sufferings over what they came to call "the Elizabeth affair," so similar to her own misdirected passion for George Davis, Margaret wrote with the wisdom—and arrogance—of the freshly wounded: "What you have felt has answered every purpose in aiding to form your character," but "I do not think you are now capable of feeling or inspiring a constant and ardent attachment." Acting impulsively to stall the courtship before it advanced any further, and with an imperiousness learned from her commanding father, Margaret pocketed a letter of apology James had written after a disagreement with his "fair Elschen," as the two cousins referred to Elizabeth in their letters, and never delivered it. Even if Margaret wasn't competing for James's heart, she could ensure they both remained single as they pursued their Germanic studies, their "extraordinary, generous seeking" together.

When James discovered Margaret's deception, he accused her of deliberately preventing the reconciliation he had hoped to achieve, but then meekly accepted her explanation. "I looked upon you at that time as a man infatuated," Margaret told James, "and thought your fever must work itself off and that your pains would not be lessened by such sympathy as [Elizabeth] could offer." She might as well have been writing about herself and George Davis. And James's surprising deference only confirmed Margaret's opinion that he wasn't ready for marriage.

Nevertheless, their parallel romantic failures, their obvious intimacy, and their frequent appearances together at social gatherings stirred speculation on the nature of James and Margaret's friendship. James's doting grandfather Freeman, disturbed by a visit the two friends paid him in which he had been surprised by Margaret's "cross mouth," worried that his grandson would "go and marry that woman and be miserable all the days of his life." Yet their common romantic yearnings for lovers who had spurned them made their friendship safe and fueled their mutual passion for the great Romantic texts — Goethe's *Sorrows of Young Werther* and Novalis's *Hymns to the Night* — which featured protagonists suffering in equal measure from lost loves and undirected ambition.

The spring of 1831 brought Margaret's twenty-first birthday, and soon after, the startling news that Timothy, discouraged with politics and the law, planned to move the family out of Cambridge and set himself up as a gentleman farmer. Timothy would spend his new leisure writing a history of the United States; if he couldn't make history, he would write it. In the "bitter months" that followed, Margaret suffered the first onslaught of the fierce headaches that would plague her recurrently through much of her adult life, often accompanied with fatigue and depression.

Timothy called in a doctor. Margaret was bled, and plied with medications, and allowed to sleep away her days until "my nerves became calmed." Still, her father put the spacious Dana mansion up for sale in late summer and made arrangements for the family to share quarters with his brother Abraham while he looked for a country property to buy. The youngest and the only one of the Fuller brothers not to attend college, Margaret's rich uncle Abraham had made a point of displaying his greater prosperity, achieved through crafty real-estate investments during the lean years of the Jefferson embargo, by acquiring a Cambridge showplace, the Brattle House on old Tory Row, a stone's throw from Harvard Yard and situated on elaborately cultivated grounds that stretched down to the Charles River. Even more imperious than Timothy, Abraham Fuller had never married but fancied himself a ladies' man; more likely he'd had trouble finding a woman willing to live with him in the Brattle House, which he ran like a small fiefdom. Margaret had already experienced Abraham's dictatorial manner. During the months her father had been away in Washington, Abraham managed the family accounts, doling out only on request the modest sums her mother required and faulting her for any expenditures he considered frivolous.

The immediate prospect of living once again under her exacting uncle's supervision felt to Margaret like entering "prison." Long-range prospects appeared even worse: to be removed from the friends, libraries, cultural events, and social gatherings she depended on to spark her thoughts was an intellectual death sentence. She later posed her alter ego Mariana gazing dreamily at the green landscape from a boarding school modeled on Miss Prescott's rustic academy, but Margaret preferred nature within easy reach of an urban perch—the blooms in her mother's garden in Cambridgeport, the view of the Blue Hills from the upstairs windows of the Dana mansion, the gentle slopes of Mount Auburn reached after a brisk walk from Harvard Yard. And country life meant little relief from her role as spinster older sister, consigned to tutoring a large brood of younger siblings as well as carrying out a long list of daily household chores. The loss of "my child" Edward, who might have been a consolation, accentuated what already seemed "a great burden of family cares." Was this all that her precocity would amount to? Timothy Fuller, once eager to see his daughter make a propitious match, seemed to think so, now promising Margaret a trip to Europe only as a distant reward for seeing all of her brothers enrolled at Harvard. Little Lloyd was just learning his alphabet.

Margaret's longing for George Davis flared in the crisis. He became "a walking memento mori—haunting [my] day-dreams," she would write to James. In her depression, she thought once again how George Davis had seemed her ideal mate, "the only person who can appreciate my true self." In her journal she confided that "there is no person whose companionship would be endurable to me—except one—and reason forbids me even to wish for that person's society—reason alas! pride too—In a profound but not a cold reserve I must shroud my heart, if I would escape the most deadly wounds." She had taken the language of Goethe's *Sorrows* as her own.

The passions Margaret allowed herself to feel and respond to now were for women. During the past year she had enjoyed climbing the rocks above the harbor at Lynn, ten miles north of Boston, with Elizabeth Randall—"more sweet and lovely than ever and I in highest glee"—nearly as much as James might have, and she regaled him with the story. The younger Anna Barker, when in town, held Margaret fascinated. Anna was her "divinest love," Margaret would write; theirs was "the same love we shall feel when we are angels."

Just as Margaret had divined the truth about James's attraction to Elizabeth Randall, James intuited the source of Margaret's passion for Anna: "how she idolizes you, how happy it must make you to be loved by her so much." But even if Anna's adoration served to soothe Margaret's wounded heart, "the sympathy, the interest" were not, by any means, all on Anna's side. "I loved Anna for a time," Margaret wrote in a later reminiscence, "with as much passion as I was then strong enough to feel—Her face was always gleaming before me, her voice was echoing in my ear, all poetic thoughts clustered round the dear image." While Margaret's idealizing passion for Anna resembled her exalted feelings for George Davis, and the two young women sometimes shared a bed at night while visiting each other, the love between them, as James's reaction shows, would not have provoked gossip or carried the same label— homosexual—as it would a century later. Such same-sex "loves" might be exclusive and rhapsodic, but they did not brand the lovers as outside the norm, as lesbians. The key to Margaret's ability to feel such a love just now, however, may not have been Anna's safely tantalizing femininity, but her lengthy absences; as long as Anna remained more "image" than reality, she was no threat to Margaret's disciplined study.

For it was the friendship with James Clarke, their shared enterprise, that supplied Margaret with all she had missed from George Davis, and without the distracting romantic heat or tussle for dominance. James recognized, as George-Sylvain had not, Margaret's "secret riches within"— her extensive resources of mind, heart, and soul. He catalogued them in his journal as an extraordinary mix of "sympathies most wide, with reasoning powers most active and unshackled," and "an understanding that revels in the widest prospects." James understood too, as few men ever would, the bind Margaret was in. To have, as he saw it, so clear a "consciousness" of her abilities that she must suffer acute frustration from their lack of outlet was the chief "evil" of life for Margaret: "her powers immeasurably transcend her sphere." In his journal James could not help but wonder "what is the effect of these powers. She is not happy—it all ends in nothing . . . she has no sphere of action. Why was she a woman?" A despairing Margaret asked herself the same question, noting bitterly, with the same astute consciousness Clarke identified, that "men never, in any extreme of despair, wished to be women."

Perhaps it was because he too was suffering more than heartache that James could summon such empathy for Margaret. At the start of their year of intense German study, he'd been forced to take a year off from divinity school to teach at the Port School in order to raise tuition money; then, partway through his year of teaching, his father died suddenly of a cerebral hemorrhage, with James standing by. His mourning for the impecunious yet goodhearted Samuel Clarke was deepened with the death that same year of the intellectual father he shared with Margaret: Goethe died in Weimar at eighty-two. Unwilling to turn to his grandfather Freeman, who had refused to pay for the second year of his divinity school training, James relied on Margaret as his chief emotional support; she was the one person he could go to "full of self dissatisfaction" and come away "excited & ready to exert myself."

Margaret was fortunate that the impulses of Romanticism had brought her together with James Clarke; the literature they explored was suffused with emotionality, suffering, and struggle. By their own example, Goethe, Schiller, and the others gave their male readers permission to be more expressive of their feelings and so to understand and accept a woman's emotions more readily. Although they were not lovers, Margaret and James could still offer each other small gestures of physical comfort. On one occasion, "her kind pressure of my hand when I was in as miserable a mood" had "rejoiced" James, and he offered her the same one day when she had come to him "with tears glistening in her eyes . . . [and] expressed feelings of infinite capacities unsatisfied, powers unemployed & wasting, wants & burning desires unmet." Whether Margaret had intended to or not, she had established with James a "limitless confidence" that served them both well.

Yet even James could make a misstep. When he suggested to Margaret, in the fall of 1832, that she solve her problems by becoming a writer — "you are destined to be an author," he had written; "I shall yet see you wholly against your will and drawn by circumstances, become the founder of an American literature!" — she was affronted that James "should think me fit for nothing but to write books." If she were to "fulfil your prediction," Margaret snapped, "it will be indeed 'against my will' and I am sure I shall never be happy." Her "bias" was not toward writing, as he should have known, but "towards the living and practical." Although she was always on the lookout for the work of those she considered serious women writers, Margaret had developed an abhorrence for the sentimental novels that seemed a woman's best route to literary fame; she wrote James that she had little in common with "women authors' mental history."

And she was right. What man with similar powers of reasoning and speech would have been advised to confine his ambitions to the printed page? Timothy Fuller had given Margaret a lawyer's training in rational argument; he'd coached and prodded until she could think on her feet just as well as he could. On her own, she had given herself an education equal to that of the young men around her studying for law or the ministry; in their company she could argue or sermonize on almost any subject as well as or better than all of them. Indeed, James had already sent her a draft of a sermon he was preparing and asked her opinion. Some years later Margaret would write to James, after hearing an elite roster of Massachusetts statesmen deliver eulogies on the death of Lafayette to an enthusiastic crowd, "I felt as I have so often done before if I were a man decidedly the gift I would choose should be that of eloquence — That power of forcing the vital currents of thousands of human hearts into *one* current." The power of captivating an audience, however fleeting, attracted her above "a more extensive fame, a more permanent influence" in literature. The sad truth was, she already had that power, but no way of exercising it.

Rebuffed, but still concerned for his friend, James wrote about Margaret in his journal, "She has nothing to do — no place in the world & fears she never shall have." Privately he wished she might fall in love with someone more responsive than George Davis and "have someone to reverence." Such a love might give her a "sphere of duty," if not of "action," and a man into whom she could transfer her ambitions and see them realized. As much as he loved his friend, he could not imagine for her any other means to happiness than the kind of marriage he looked for — with wife as helpmeet.

If she had known of these thoughts, Margaret would surely have been even more angry than she'd been at James's suggestion that she become a writer. Guessing that, he withheld them. Yet part of Margaret's struggle during these months was with this very question. She had an instinct, she would later write, "from a very early age . . . that I was not born to the common womanly lot. I knew I should never find a being who could keep the key of my character; that there would be none on whom I could always lean, from whom I could always learn." In time she would become convinced that she was not meant to experience "more extended personal relations" and that "self-dependence," as she called it, would have to suffice, making her a lone "pilgrim and sojourner on earth." Her questing would never end, and she must learn to "be my own priest, pupil, parent, child, husband, and wife." But for now, she felt only anxiety about the future.

Margaret's greatest frustration was to undergo all this while still living as a dependent in her father's household—subject to his whims about where the family would live, even what she must do each day. Timothy, who she recognized had given her the gift of treating her, when a child, "not as a plaything, but as a living mind," had nonetheless failed to help her find an outlet for the capabilities he once fostered so avidly. She began to see that he had made the mistake of so many well-meaning parents who try to make children "conform to an object and standard of their own" rather than help them to "live a new life." Now their frustrations mirrored each other's—neither had yet found a way to be effective in the world, to have their talents appreciated. Timothy had molded Margaret in his own image of frustrated ambition, and that had left her with nothing to do and no place to go, except his home.

Margaret had Timothy's bullheadedness too, so when he ordered her to go to church on Thanksgiving the year she turned twenty-one, this young woman who had six volumes of the godless Goethe's complete works in her room, who "always suffered much in church from a feeling of disunion with the hearers and dissent from the preacher," went only grudgingly, and sat in the family pew feeling a "strange anguish, this dread uncertainty." She thought of her "unrecognized" powers, of how "the past was worthless, the future hopeless," yet "my aspiration seemed very high." She waited impatiently for the sermon to end so she could escape the confining space, the predictable worship service—"that I might get into the free air." Church was no place for Margaret, nor for any woman who wished to lead, to be eloquent, to be heard.

She left the church and walked fast, almost running, over the barren fields stretching between Old Cambridge and the Port, her old neighborhood. She found a stream she'd observed in springtime as a rushing torrent, now "voiceless, choked with withered leaves," yet, she marveled, "it did not quite lose itself in the earth." She pressed on to a grove of trees surrounding a "pool, dark and silent," a place that would serve for reflection, for resolution, as the late-afternoon sun shone out "like the last smile of a dying lover." She stood still, yet her thoughts continued to race, casting her back to childhood, to her earliest awareness of her questing self. She recalled a day, just an ordinary day when "I had stopped myself . . . on the stairs, and asked, how came I here? How is it that I seem to be this Margaret Fuller? What does it mean? What shall I do about it?"

She began to remember "all the times and ways in which the same thought had returned," how she had struggled "under these limitations of time and space, and human nature" to find the meaning of Margaret Fuller, and was struggling still. The torment, the uncertainty, the "earthly pain at not being recognized" had at last become intolerable. Could Margaret really hold to her vow not to seek "a positive religion, a refuge, a protection"? Not on this day. She looked around at the barren landscape, the reflecting pool, which may have yielded up the very picture of her misery — loose hair, disheveled dress, anxious face, neither pretty nor plain. She was tired of seeking and not finding, asking and not knowing. She wanted to leave her noisy questing "self" behind in that pool — not by tumbling in, like Narcissus, but by rising up. The answer came to her: "I saw there was no self; that selfishness was all folly . . . that I had only to live in the idea of the ALL, and all was mine."

Margaret rushed home in the moonlight, stopping to offer a prayer in the churchyard she had fled just hours before, grateful for this epiphany — this "communion with the soul of things" — grateful to be "taken up into God," to find her place in "the grand harmony." She would bid farewell to the "epoch of pride," move beyond her "haughty, passionate, ambitious" youth, and follow her father to whatever country village he chose, educate her brothers, inspire her sister, help her mother — and never again allow herself to be "completely engaged in self." But it was a hedged bet, and deep down she knew it. Give up the self, so that "all" could be *mine*.

· III ·

GROTON AND PROVIDENCE

The Fuller farmhouse in Groton as it appeared in 1902,
with wings added in the 1890s

The Greene Street School, Providence

"My heart has no proper home"

THE SQUARE WHITE FARMHOUSE TIMOTHY FULLER PUR-
chased in Groton, from another scion of the prosperous Dana family, was set on a hill at the edge of town, with ample fields for tillage and
commanding views of Mount Monadnock and Mount Wachusett from
the topmost of its ten spacious rooms. It seemed an ideal retreat to the
would-be historian, but not to his daughter. This was the "too tamely
smiling and sleepy" New England village with pretensions to nobility
where Margaret had suffered through a year at Miss Prescott's boarding school as a teenager, learning unwanted lessons in humility from her
small-minded classmates. The sense of being a social and intellectual
misfit recurred as soon as Margaret began to meet her new neighbors,
who, in contrast to her city friends, seemed to her "neither beautiful nor
heroick," their "characters" so unformed as to hardly be "amusing." In
the months before the move, Margaret had steeled herself to "live alone,
to all intents and purposes,—separate entirely my acting from my thinking world, take care of my ideas without aid." Now she had arrived, as
she'd written to James Clarke, "where there is never a spirit to come, if I
call ever so loudly"—or, as she put it less dramatically to her Cambridge
school friend Almira Penniman Barlow, "This is the first time in my life
that I have known what it is to have nobody to speak to."

Groton's main street was dotted with the elegant homes of Massachusetts men wealthy enough to retire to the country without the necessity of

working a farm. The Fullers were different. Once Timothy abandoned his political career and the daily practice of law, his family was left with scant resources, a fact he'd managed to keep from his wife and children as long as they'd boarded with his rich brother Abraham in Cambridge. After the family settled in Groton in the spring of 1833, there could be no more illusions. Timothy Fuller's income was reduced to the meager rents he could not always manage to collect on the Cherry Street house in Cambridgeport and a few other tumbledown properties—he was no Dana when it came to real estate—along with the occasional legal matter that still took him into Boston, a six-hour trip by stage. Timothy and his sons would have to work the Groton farm by themselves in hopes of turning a profit. Once capable of serving up a lavish feast for Boston's finest in honor of the president, Timothy now expected his family to subsist on corn, potatoes, pumpkins, and beans from the fields, milk from three dairy cows, and the occasional chicken butchered from the flock. Timothy himself dined almost exclusively on bread and milk, a diet he insisted was as healthful as it was economical, and he urged his family to follow suit.

To avoid the expense of private school tuition, Timothy required Margaret to run a family school for all her siblings, not just the youngest ones. Eugene was in his third year at Harvard, disappointing Timothy and Margaret with his mediocre performance and lack of ambition, despite being, Margaret thought, "a sweet youth"; sixteen-year-old William Henry, prone to rages— "collisions," Margaret called them—against his father, left home to look for office work in Boston almost as soon as he learned of Timothy's plans to make a farmer of him. That still left thirteen-year-old Ellen, who, with their mother's winsome looks, missed city life almost as much as Margaret did, and the three boys, Arthur, Richard, and Lloyd, ages eleven, nine, and seven. Always resistant to discipline and beginning to show signs of the erratic behavior that would later blossom into mental illness, Lloyd was nearly hopeless in the classroom. Richard was steadier, but Arthur, the Fuller child who, after Margaret, showed the most intellectual promise, had suffered a serious injury shortly after the move, when a farmhand, soon released from service, clumsily tossed a piece of stove wood in the boy's direction and hit him in the face. Margaret became her brother's nurse, spending her first weeks in the country "in a dark room" where Arthur lay in bed "burning with fever"; the boy recovered from infection, but lost the sight in one eye.

The shock of her favorite brother's injury may not have been the only reason "I greeted my new home with a flood of bitter tears," as Margaret wrote to Eliza Farrar in Cambridge. The *"only* grown-up daughter" in the family, Margaret shared her mother's burden of household chores, often taking full charge when Margarett Crane, still given to bouts of depression and illness, could not manage. The Fullers occasionally hired a servant to assist with cooking and cleaning, but the family needlework fell to Margaret alone: the "sitting-still occupations," she called them, of cutting out and sewing new clothes, mending and darning old ones, which all too often left "my spirit faint from inanition." When Margaret sat to read or write, she never felt confined, but sewing prevented the mental activity she craved even more than physical freedom. "My fingers have been busy, my eyes wide open but my mind has been so still," she fretted that first summer in Groton; "my feelings seemed sunk down so deep—I almost believed I should never hope nor fear perhaps never *think* again."

Margaret's submerged feelings included alarm at her father's escalating despotism on the isolated Groton homestead, where there was little to distract or curb his repressive nature. Grandiose plans for the history he had not yet begun to write clashed with his nagging sense of failure in public life, turning Timothy Fuller into a figure Margaret would one day term the "domestic tyrant," unpredictably liberal or restrictive with his family members, always controlling. When her brothers Richard and Arthur, initially enchanted by farm life, appealed to their father to let them skip their studies and devote their first Groton summer to field work, Timothy agreed to the bargain—then refused to release them from it once they'd gotten a taste of the "hardening" labor he demanded. He woke the boys at dawn, berating them if they weren't out of bed at first call, and saw to it that plowing, planting, and the work of building a new barn on the property continued with little respite through the long hot days. In fact, had the boys not proposed the arrangement, Timothy would likely have forced it on them out of necessity. Yet he never asked more of his sons than of himself, and the sight of their fifty-five-year-old father, whose work had previously been conducted exclusively at a desk or on the floor of a legislative chamber, prostrate for hours after loading grain in the midsummer heat, made as deep an impression on his children as the nature walks he led on the occasional holiday, offering up bits of wisdom to mingle with the birdsong.

Margaret bristled at Timothy's mixed signals. Not quite ready to see his oldest daughter, the intellectual prodigy he'd nurtured with late-night drills, become a household drudge, Timothy built Margaret a shaded seat at the entrance to a pinewood down the hill, which he dubbed "Margaret's Grove." But she refused to go there on her own and never made the time to visit the spot with her father; Timothy could control her workday, but not her few leisure hours. She preferred a stand of trees farther off, on the banks of the Nashua River. She named the spot "Hazel-grove," and in her few private moments took what solace she could from the nearby mountains. "I used to look at them," she later wrote, "towering to the sky, and feel that I, too, from birth, had longed to rise, and, though for the moment crushed, was not subdued."

Margaret would always question her father's "ill-judged exchange" of city living for hard country labor, in which mother and children were "violently rent from all their former life and cast on toils for which they were unprepared." But certain habits of mind remained, even intensified, for both Timothy and Margaret in rustic isolation. She could not have acknowledged it directly, but Margaret suffered from the same smoldering intellectual drive and frustrated social ambition that consumed her father. Although she was twenty-three and had the skills to earn her independence as a governess or schoolteacher, Margaret did not, like the older Fuller boys, see her future in terms of escape from the family. After years of aiming higher, she knew full well that "some might sneer at the notion of my becoming a teacher." She was also reluctant to advertise her family's — and her own — fall from fortune by taking a job away from home. A profound sense of identification with and a grudging loyalty to the man who had once taken such pride in her genius bound Margaret to her father and fostered a need to serve as her mother's support and protector. She would not leave.

Groton nights were for study and writing — at first primarily letters. Margaret could dash off more than a dozen at one sitting as she worked to secure her connections with friends who all too often disappointed her when they came to visit. Her life was now so different from theirs. During her first year at Groton, her friend Amelia Greenwood's engagement "seems to have changed our relation to one another," Margaret wrote bluntly. Once married, Amelia was "entirely absorbed": "All her thoughts now revolve around one centre"—her new husband. As a nine-year-old, Margaret had refused to employ the title "Miss" when addressing a letter to her friend Ellen Kilshaw, objecting to it as not "half so friendly." Amelia's newly acquired "Mrs.," along with her change of surname to Bartlett, signified a nearly unbridgeable gap.

For visits from Elizabeth Randall, the Boston school friend she had once shielded from James Clarke's romantic overtures, Margaret put aside her needlework to spend lazy afternoons or moonlit nights drifting in a rowboat on the river. The Randalls owned a summer house nearby, but Elizabeth, with no family school to keep and a new beau she was testing as a marriage prospect, had a habit of prattling on in a way that could "oercloud my courage of soul," Margaret groused. Worse, Elizabeth's connections in Groton "brought me into a closeness of contact with the townspeople" that felt "profaning or at least un*nun*like." Despite her complaints about the isolation, Margaret stubbornly wished to maintain a hermit's seclusion if she had to be in the country. At times she even boasted of feeling "wild and free" and claimed to "mourn [th]at I was not brought up in this solitude." But those moments were rare and passed all too quickly. "I am not a nun," Margaret wrote emphatically to James Clarke, whose first visit to Groton in June stirred a nearly amorous declaration from him. "How free" their conversation had been, he wrote after he'd gotten home to Cambridge, "yet what unity!" James reveled in the memory: "I felt as if our minds were embracing."

Yet uncertainty about *what* she was—or was to be—clouded this friendship as well, creating new tensions between the two "cousins" as they left their years of companionable study behind. James had completed his training for the ministry at Harvard, relying on Margaret's advice in crafting several of his first sermons. On one of her last days in Cambridge, she heard him deliver a homily on a biblical text they both treasured, knowing it as Goethe's favorite: "Whatsoever thy hand findeth to do, do it with thy might." Unlike Margaret, James *had* found something to do. He'd accepted a post as minister to a small congregation in Louisville, Kentucky, aiming to spread a liberal gospel to the evangelical West. "The wor[ld] receives you as a man," Margaret acknowledged when she had absorbed the news that James would soon embark on his vocation, while she was left to sew for and school a quartet of younger siblings. When James appeared in Groton a second time to say good-bye, Margaret's loneliness and longing for her own "engrossing object of pursuit" overwhelmed her as she attempted to "compress all I had ever thought and felt towards you in the retrospect of a few hours."

What were those thoughts and feelings? James had upset a delicate balance by conjuring that cerebral embrace; a month later, in a first letter from Kentucky, he would recall "thrilling at the heart" with "the slight sympathetic touch" of Margaret's fingers "one night when I parted from you at Elizabeth [Randall]'s door in an hour of gloom." Neither was in love with the other in the conventional sense. James, who'd once asked, in sympathy with Margaret's plight, "Why was she a woman?" could never imagine Margaret as his wife; and Margaret, bruised by George Davis's rejection, depended on the refuge from courting rituals that her friendship with James offered, a safe haven of open, fraternal communion. Their connection was deep, defying categorization, borrowing freely from the language and gestures of romance, friendship, familial affection, and a mentorship that ran in both directions. "Fair, pure, noble lady moon," James saluted Margaret by letter, or "my sweet confidant" and "best, truest one." Yet on the day he traveled to Groton to say good-bye, he clammed up rather than resume singing his hymn to their unity of mind. Margaret was hurt. "Your manner repressed me," she scolded afterward, and she passed up the opportunity to reprise her feelings, "to give you my *blessing*."

Margaret's ambivalence silenced her. She knew James had made a difficult choice. He too would have preferred to stay near Boston, but there were few ministerial openings in New England. Most of the brilliant young Harvard men Margaret had known had been "disappointed and tortured" as they surveyed a diminished job market before deciding to leave for the West; Henry Hedge would land the closest, in backwoods Bangor, Maine. Margaret had been "prepared" to see James "never estimated as you deserved, to see the results of all your efforts imperfect." Some part of her wished to continue seeking and *not finding* with James. At the moment of parting, which she feared might signal "the breaking up of our intimacy," she willed herself to assert the intellectual superiority they had both acknowledged long ago by positioning herself as one who could *bless* the newly minted minister. But she could not get the words out.

She wrote them instead, a crisp farewell augury, in her first letter to James at Louisville—"you are gone and you will prosper"—and then worked to regain an equal footing. "We must I think be both of us quite grown up now," she proposed. But if James had become a man, what was she? No nun, but still living at home as a disgruntled "grown-up daughter," still playing "Margaret Good child," her own self-mocking appellation. She struggled to find words to measure being "grown up" in a woman like herself, a woman of genius but, as James had recognized, with "no sphere of action." The measure would have to be internal; her metaphors became tangled as she sought a meaningful way to chart her inward progress. "I feel as if my characte[r] had taken its tone," she claimed, "and as if there might be ornaments added and wealth accumulated there or the reverse but as if the fabrick was now shaped into proportion and its altar dedicated." Was she singer or seamstress, banker or bride—or vestal virgin?

From nine hundred miles away in Louisville, where he had been confronted instantly with fire-and-brimstone resistance to his Romantic theology when a half-dozen church women walked out on one of his first sermons, James could say it outright. "You envy me my situation without which your powers are useless," he wrote to Margaret. "I envy you your abilities without which I cannot fulfill the demands of my situation. You are the Bengal tiger confined in a cage to leap over a broomstick for the amusement of staring clowns. I am a broken-winged hawk, seeking to fly at the sun, but fluttering in the dust."

James urged Margaret to keep a journal of daily life and send it to him; he would do the same in return. She refused, then wished she'd done it, telling him, "Now that I have lost you I think of you constantly." She took her reading down to Hazel-grove and held "imaginary conversations" with James about poetry and novels, and wrote it all in "foolishly frank uninterpreted letters," proposing, "Let us be free in friendship." Long-distance, through the mail, she would be free with James as she could be nowhere and with no one else, now that "there is no escaping from the dust and weariness and burden of this state of seclusion— 'Free?'—Vain thought!" As for friendship in her state of exile, she had concluded that "my heart has no proper home only can prefer some of its visiting-places to others."

And visit she did, taking the stage to Cambridge to stay with the Farrars when Timothy granted her liberty to "lay on the shelf books needles and children." She made a first trip to New York City with James's widowed mother and his sister, Sarah, an aspiring landscape painter. They toured art galleries, and Margaret deepened her acquaintance with the enchanting Anna Barker, meeting her for the first time on her home turf. Best of all, in the young metropolis Margaret "collected quantities of those most desirable articles new ideas."

Back home, as winter came on, her father's despotism crested in the "*icy* seclusion of Groton"; he insisted the younger children adopt his routine of morning ice-water baths and made the boys run barefoot with him in the snow for exercise. In the evenings, though, he revived some of the Old Cambridge gentility, asking Margaret to read Jefferson's letters along with him in preparation for his historical work. "I rejoice," Margaret wrote of the shared project; "all my other pursuits have led me away from him." The collaboration brought a respite from Timothy's exacting command; the best she'd been able to say of her dealings with him in recent months was that "my Father has not once seemed dissatisfied with me."

But what Margaret really wanted to do was study and write her own work—to "try my hand at composition," she admitted to Amelia Greenwood. Once the idea of becoming a writer had rankled, but now she understood—as James Clarke had foreseen—that publication was her best and possibly only means to deliver her opinions and exert her will beyond her circle of intimate friends. She may also have taken her father's sudden decision to turn into a man of letters as a gauntlet thrown down. Why should Timothy entertain any greater expectation of literary success than she? Here was a chance to compete with—and perhaps exceed—the man whose pedagogical tyranny she had both thrived on and suffered under, who had made her "the heir to all he knew," instilling in her a child's restless will to surpass the father.

To James she confided plans to read "ten-thousand, thousand things this winter": history, geography, the principles of architecture, more Goethe and Schiller. She was drawn to philosophy, which, she wrote, quoting Novalis, "is peculiarly home-sickness; an overmastering desire to be at home," and religion, where she hoped to find "a system" of belief "which shall suffice to my character." The epiphany she reached after fleeing the Thanksgiving church service the year before had not sustained her: "I wish to arrive at that point where I can trust myself, and leave off saying, 'It seems to me,' and boldly feel, It *is* so to me."

She began drafting sermons. Maybe if she tried setting down her views, she could persuade herself of them. And she told James about them: could she have hoped he'd deliver her sermons in Louisville? Writing from a biblical text he'd also used, she teased James that she could do as well as or better than he. But in the end she was dissatisfied. Instead of unfolding spiritual lessons, she "could only write reveries," Margaret explained to James, and threw out the drafts. Writing sermons with no particular audience in mind, with no prospect of delivering them herself, was bound to lead to frustration. The experience of being shut out from the ministry fed her religious doubt; confronting exclusion so directly was painful.

She tried essays next, submitting them to the *Christian Examiner*, the prestigious Unitarian journal that had solicited James's speech at graduation from Harvard Divinity School the summer before—only to see them turned down. She finished her translation of Goethe's *Tasso* and sent it to James, who was enthusiastic. But the prospect of publication, offered initially through a connection of Eliza Farrar's, vanished. She'd let herself hope she might put her facility with languages to use in translating for an income, but the scheme now seemed untenable, especially as she so far lacked the brazenness to "walk into the Boston establishments and ask them to buy my work." Here, "I have no friend at once efficient and sympathizing," she wrote in a letter asking James to try publishers in the West on her behalf. Women writers frequently leaned on a male relative or friend to handle such negotiations, and then, in order to show a properly feminine lack of ambition, claimed in a preface to have had publication pressed on them. But James could perform no such magic in a territory where most residents didn't even know the German Romantic writers well enough to despise them, he explained.

The question nagged—what was she to become? Margaret liked encouraging James in his vocation—he'd written to thank her for the inspiration of her "onward spirit"—so long as she didn't think too hard about the disparity, her sense that "your progress is vast compared to mine." Perhaps she should accept that she was meant simply "to feed" James's "intellectual burner with pine chips," as she proposed in a letter. There might even be some distinction in an indirect path to power. "Was I not born to fill the ear of some Frederick or Czar Peter with information and suggestions on which he might reflect and act"?

After more than a year at Groton, her situation had changed little, except that seventeen-year-old William Henry returned for a brief stint in her classroom before departing to the West Indies to seek his fortune. When he left, she added three village children to her home school, receiving a small income of her own. "Earning *money*—think of that," she wrote to James. "I shall be a professional character yet." Perhaps she could save enough eventually to support a trip to Italy. But the excitement of "beginning to serve my apprenticeship to the world," as she half-jokingly described her experiment in wage earning, faded as a second Groton winter approached: "Life grows scantier, employments accumulate," and "I feel less and less confidence in my powers," she wrote to James.

The sense of being unmoored, of not belonging wherever she went, persisted. "I am more and more dissatisfied with this world, and *cannot* find a home in it," Margaret confided to Almira Barlow, recently married to a minister in Brooklyn. "Heaven knows I have striven enough to make my mind its own place. I have resolution for the contest, and will not shrink or faint, but I know not, just at this moment, where to turn." And then, a chance conversation with her father landed her in print.

The two had read an essay by George Bancroft in the *North American Review* in which the young historian, hoping to stir up controversy, dissected the character of Brutus, a cherished idol to many in the fledgling American republic. Bancroft charged Brutus with being impulsive and lacking "coolness of judgement," and he faulted Roman historians for making him a hero simply for assassinating Julius Caesar. Timothy and Margaret were incensed—particularly Margaret, whose passion for the ancients was the great legacy of her early studies with her father. Although she had mixed feelings about her father's teaching methods, "Roman virtue" was, for Margaret, an ideal never to be disputed. "ROME! it stands by itself, a clear Word. The power of will, the dignity of a fixed purpose is what it utters," she had come to believe through her childhood reading. Brutus, "mild in his temper" and with "a greatness of mind, that was superior to anger, avarice and the love of pleasure," was one of the chief exemplars of Roman virtue, she would soon argue in the pages of the *Boston Daily Advertiser*, refuting Bancroft's charge.

As Margaret told Henry Hedge afterward, "My father requested me to write a little piece in answer" to Bancroft's attack, which Timothy then sent to the *Advertiser*, a newspaper that circulated widely in Massachusetts. Margaret's essay ran unsigned under the title "Brutus" on November 27, 1834. Her argument was a more sophisticated version of the "Possunt quia posse videntur" theme she'd written for her father in adolescence; she defined the elements of a noble character, then illustrated their presence in Brutus. If her defense of the Roman politician as mild of temper and superior to anger seemed to tweak Timothy, it was also an oblique articulation of her domestic struggle: she was reluctant "to lose this object of reverence from among the heart's household gods," she confided at the start of the essay.

Why did Timothy turn over this writing task to Margaret? He'd moved the family to Groton intending to make a name for himself with a historical work. Perhaps a mere letter to the editor was beneath his dignity. Or was he stepping aside? Timothy may have sensed Margaret's more powerful ambition, her will to succeed. If the publication of "Brutus" was the result of Timothy's "request"—a final assignment—it was a gift, unlike the shaded arbor in Margaret's Grove, that his oldest child and best pupil truly needed and was happy to accept. Timothy had acted as the "friend at once efficient and sympathizing" that Margaret claimed to lack.

Yet Margaret's letter to Henry Hedge is her only account of the venture. Could she have contrived this explanation, or played up her father's role, to disguise her ambitious foray as the design of a man, her father? However the publication came about, Margaret had an important taste of victory—she had reached an audience at last. Her "little piece" even provoked a rebuttal from a reader in Salem, who nonetheless praised her "ability" as a writer. He "seemed to *consider me* as an elderly gentleman," Margaret wrote to Henry Hedge. Never one to shy away from disputes, she took this as a compliment.

The step into print proved energizing. Margaret may have needed Timothy's assignment and his connections to gain a foothold, but this would be the last time her father figured in her plans for publication. In the spring, James Clarke wrote announcing the start of a literary journal to be published in Cincinnati, for which he would serve as one of the editors, and asked Margaret's help in filling the first issues. He welcomed essays on "topics of religion, morals, literature, art, or anything *you* feel to be worth writing about." In a second prodding letter he urged: "Don't be afraid, there is no public opinion here. You are throwing your ideas to help form one." She could even "be as transcendental" as she wished.

By August of 1835, Margaret had published two lengthy book reviews in successive issues of Clarke's *Western Messenger* and proposed a third. The first appeared in the June debut issue, a review of memoirs by two English writers of the infamous Blue Stocking Club, George Crabbe and Hannah More, in which Margaret traced their paths into London's "most brilliant circle," a circle centered on women writers and intellectuals, and beyond. For the August issue she reviewed Edward Bulwer-Lytton's historical novel *The Last Days of Pompeii*, taking the opportunity to analyze the author's complete body of work, observing a progression from the satirical toward "the ideal." Margaret's first literary essays—both of which revealed her interest in the formation of important literary careers—appeared unsigned in a fledgling journal published for an audience its founder considered barely educated. But the *Western Messenger* was widely read in New England, where most of its writers were born and educated, though many had migrated west along with James Clarke. Margaret was the only female writer whose work appeared in these pages; James had not left her behind.

Margaret's first reviews may have been the pieces rejected by the *Christian Examiner* the previous year; both were ambitious in intent but were haphazardly structured. Even Clarke, who published them gratefully, was aware of their flaws. When Margaret pressed him for criticism, "no matter how severe," he responded that the essays were too digressive: "We feel like an explorer in a Kentucky cavern; there are so many side-passages, opening to the right and left, leading upward and downward." Further, her language was "too elevated," and her wide literary reference escaped her readers: "They know nothing of books." Margaret wrote the way she spoke, Clarke told her, and her sparkling conversation could at times be "too lofty." The digressions and allusions that entertained and impressed in Cambridge parlors were off-putting in print.

Yet Margaret was true to her word, accepting James's "severe" criticism and eager to correct the missteps of "one [who] has talked so much and written so little." Margaret understood that she had not yet learned to craft her thoughts in formal prose, and her isolation—her desperate need to converse—fed the problem. "This going into mental solitude is desperately trying," she'd written to Henry Hedge; "to me the expression of thought and feeling is to the mind what respiration is to the lungs." These awkward early attempts convinced Margaret, whose innate verbal facility had never failed her, that "the art of writing, like all other arts, requires an apprenticeship," and she was now willing to serve it. "My grand object is improvement," she assured James, to whom she had once admitted her fear that she might "die and leave no trace." Now she wished to leave more than a trace: an indelible mark of distinction.

Where once she had resisted mixing with the "common-place people" of Groton, Margaret now made up her mind to "engage" with them. At times she would "talk incessantly" with her neighbors, "full of intense curiosity" to understand "that strange whole the American publick" she hoped to address. The real possibility of reaching a public through her writing began to ease the sense of deprivation and envy she felt at being barred from the ministry. A year before she had written with regret to Henry Hedge that "I am not yet *intimate* with any of the lower class. I have not the advantages of a clergy man." Her break into the writing profession gave a purpose and legitimacy to seeking out both the "common" and the "low," as she initially perceived Groton's gentry and its working class.

By August too, Margaret had spent several weeks with the Farrars on a tour of upstate New York's natural wonders. She'd begged her father for his "consent" to the time off and for the funds to support the trip: "Oh do sympathize with me—do feel about it as I do—." She even proposed that Timothy reduce the sum of her eventual inheritance, her "portion" of the family estate, by two hundred dollars, if advancing her the fifty-seven dollars necessary to cover the cost of the excursion created anxiety for him now. Timothy agreed to the plan without making the deduction, and soon Margaret was on her way by steamboat up the Hudson River to West Point and Trenton Falls in a traveling party that included one of the Farrars' student boarders, Sam Ward. Seven years younger than Margaret and captivatingly handsome, the son of a Boston financier, Sam Ward was wealthy and talented enough to toy with the idea of a career as an artist after graduation from Harvard. The two became fast friends on the journey, and Sam readily agreed to serve as Margaret's escort to Newport on her way back to Boston, where she planned to introduce him to Anna Barker, his female counterpart in youth, good looks, and, for Margaret, magnetic power.

The "romantic rocks" at Trenton Falls and the "gorgeous prospect" from the summit of Kaatskill Mountain, its "immense hotel" seemingly "dropped there by magic," contrasted with the social whirl of "dressed dolls" (excluding Anna, of course) and moneyed men at Newport, gave spice to Margaret's letters home. Here was an opportunity to try out her skills as a travel writer. When, in late summer, the Farrars proposed that Margaret join them, along with Sam Ward and Anna Barker, on a yearlong tour of Europe, departing from Boston in the summer of 1836, Margaret began working to persuade her father of the necessity—and practicality—of this longer and far more costly journey. She needed the schooling of a European tour to fulfill her promise as a writer; the investment now would yield rewards later. Despite her family's straitened finances, Margaret began to believe it would happen.

Her determination to make the journey intensified after her meeting at summer's end with Harriet Martineau, England's best-known woman writer, who was traveling in the United States to gather material for a book on contemporary life in Britain's former colonies. Martineau, who had made her name with a series of popular books explaining the principles of political economy to general readers—the audience Margaret hoped to win with her own writing—was staying with the Farrars in Cambridge. Margaret expected to "see her," she wrote to James Clarke, "but it is not probable I shall become acquainted." She knew that "many will be seeking" out Martineau, "and as I have no name nor fame I shall not have much chance." Earlier that summer she had failed, despite her proficiency in the German language, to attract the interest of Dr. Francis Lieber, a German reformer passing through Boston. Though a friend of James, Lieber evidently did not possess his capacity to appreciate intellectual distinction in women: "I was to him only Miss Fuller, an unmarried female of no mark or likelihood," Margaret sighed.

But Martineau, like Eliza Farrar and Ellen Kilshaw before her, instantly saw Margaret's promise—indeed, recognized her as a kindred spirit. The two attended Harvard commencement together. Seated beside her new friend—a true international celebrity—as a succession of talented seniors took the podium to exhibit their public speaking abilities, Margaret inwardly prayed that "I should not be haunted with recollections of 'aims unreached occasions lost,'" she wrote afterward in her journal. She prayed, as well, that Harriet Martineau might become the "intellectual guide" she still sought, the friend who "would do—what none has ever done yet, comprehend me wholly, mentally and morally, and enable me better to comprehend myself." More than either Eliza Farrar or Maria Child, Margaret recognized, Harriet Martineau "has what I want": "vigorous reasoning powers, invention, clear views of her objects, and she has trained to the best means of execution." When Martineau learned of Margaret's projected European trip, she shifted her own return voyage so that she could sail with the Farrars, and she offered to serve as Margaret's entrée into society—Martineau's own "brilliant circle"—once the party arrived in England.

Margaret was also edging into influential circles close to home. Ralph Waldo Emerson had settled halfway between Boston and Groton in the county seat at Concord, Massachusetts, on returning from his own year-long European tour. The third in a line of influential ministers stretching back to colonial times, Emerson had shocked Boston by resigning a prestigious pulpit when his congregation refused to support him in abandoning the ritual of communion—a practice he considered primitive and idolatrous. His firm defiance had gained him followers in the younger generation of Unitarian ministers—Clarke, Hedge, and others who were Margaret's friends; Emerson's proud self-exile conferred dignity on their own errands into the wilderness. Whenever possible, they attended Emerson's increasingly popular Boston lectures espousing a nonsectarian inquiry into human nature, which, as one early listener, the gifted teacher and Transcendentalist writer Elizabeth Peabody, wrote, gathered together "all the most important ideas—which we value—as this age's *spirit*."

Now that they were almost neighbors, Margaret angled for a meeting with "that only clergyman of all possible clergymen who eludes my acquaintance." She considered his the most powerful "of any American mind," and she wished to "know him in private." But Emerson, who continued preaching in country pulpits on a "supply" basis, always seemed to appear in Groton when Margaret was away. Henry Hedge aided the cause by sending Emerson the manuscript of Margaret's translation of

Tasso. Now Waldo, as he was known to close friends, the name passed down from an ancestral Puritan family, was asking to meet Margaret. In the summer of 1835, she wrote James that a correspondence had commenced and "the reverend, and I are tottering on the verge of an acquaintance"—even as she learned that the widower was engaged to marry for a second time.

Margaret had heard that Lydia Jackson, or "Lidian," as Waldo insisted on renaming his fiancée, evoking the Greek "Lydian" musical scale and preventing the awkward elision of vowel sounds in "Lydia Emerson," was a woman "of character and manners entirely unlike" Ellen Tucker Emerson, the child bride Waldo had married six years before, when she was eighteen and he twenty-six, and who had died of tuberculosis after only seventeen months of marriage. Lidian was a year older than Waldo, at thirty-three a woman of settled personality, unlikely to remind him of the pretty young poetess he still actively mourned. Despite his status as an engaged man, Waldo's position as "reverend" allowed him a freedom in forming relationships with other women as counselor, confessor, or spiritual guide—even with an "unmarried woman of no mark or likelihood," but with a fierce appetite for distinction, like Margaret. But could Margaret make a place for herself in the threesome of Waldo, Lidian, and the shade of Ellen?

Even as she was publishing her first essays, circulating her translation of *Tasso,* and expanding her range of acquaintance, Margaret confessed to Henry Hedge a "restless desire to write stories . . . which have nothing to do with my present purpose." Although she felt most secure in her critical powers, she did not yet value criticism as highly as fiction or poetry; perhaps she could adapt to fiction her talent for social observation and witty insights about the personalities in her circle. James Clarke's sister, Sarah, had suggested she "write a novel and make myself a heroine." Margaret thought Anna Barker would make a better protagonist. Probably a novel inspired by both characters—"the most gentle Anna and the most ungentle Margaret," as she'd described their contrasting temperaments in a recent letter to James—would have been best.

But Margaret told none of her friends when she sent out a story—"Lost and Won"—to the *New England Galaxy,* where it appeared in print on August 8, 1835, her fourth publication in less than a year. She intended this one to go unnoticed: she'd taken as her subject the court-ship of George Davis and Harriet Russell, spinning her story out of re-ports that, after the engagement, Harriet had "coquetted" with the rakish Cambridge bachelor Joseph Angier. The minor scandal fascinated Mar-garet, perhaps because it drew on the Goethean concept of elective affini-ties (the notion that sexual attractions sometimes defied convention yet must be obeyed) or because Margaret was secretly pleased to see the man she believed had jilted her pained by his fiancée's public vacillation — or both. Yet before writing, she satisfied herself that Harriet had returned to proper form, and wrote up the incident as a morality tale illustrating the errant heroine's restoration to virtue. Margaret portrayed her hero, modeled on George Davis, as having lost, and then regained, his fiancée in this ironically subtitled "tale of modern days and good society."

All might have been well, had James Clarke not traveled home to New England in late summer, picked up a copy of the magazine, and recog-nized the thinly disguised lovers as George and Harriet — and himself as model for one of the more admirable male characters. As ever in sym-pathy with Margaret's aims, he considered she had spun gold from the straw of his friends' premarital spat. The story delivered its moral su-perbly, and he sent a copy to the newlyweds. He seemed to believe that the couple should be proud to serve as inspiration for Margaret's tale. In-stead George and Harriet were outraged, and Margaret turned on James for betraying her secret.

James's sister, Sarah, attempted to intercede, but by then, in an epi-sode that seemed to enlarge the frame of the story, Margaret had fallen sick with a severe headache and fever — typhoid fever, she said after-ward. Her family called it brain fever and feared for Margaret's life as she grew weaker, shaking with chills and suffering nightmare visions day after day. The fever did not break. Timothy offered a benediction: "My dear," Margaret recalled him telling her one morning at her bedside, "I have been thinking of you in the night, and I cannot remember that you have any *faults*. You have defects, of course, as all mortals have, but I do not know that you have a single fault." From Timothy, who consid-ered compliments "hurtful to his children" and "who had scarce ever in my presence praised me," the words of blessing sounded "strange," but also moving. So accustomed was Margaret to her father's criticism that she did not register the stinginess of his message: she had no faults. She heard, instead, a pronouncement of her perfection, which "affected me to tears."

On the ninth day, her fever broke. Weak and chastened, Margaret survived the autumn. Timothy did not. In late September, almost as soon as his daughter was well, he collapsed one evening after a day spent in the fields, flushed with fever and retching uncontrollably. Eugene was in Virginia teaching, but when Timothy, directing even his last hours, announced he would surely die, the rest of the family, including William Henry, who had returned from the West Indies to a clerkship in Boston, gathered to say their farewells. After suffering two days of intensifying fever and chills accompanied by painful spasms, Timothy Fuller was dead of Asiatic cholera, contracted while working the lowland acres of his Groton farm. He was fifty-seven. At his bedside, Margaret reached out to close her father's eyes.

· 8 ·

"Returned into life"

Timothy's death brought back feelings Margaret had experienced with the loss of her sister Julia Adelaide in childhood. Again her mother receded into grief, "worn to a shadow" with cares she could not face. Margaret felt like an "orphan" now. Summoning an "awful calm," she gathered her siblings together around "the lifeless form of her father," their mother later recalled, and "kneeling, pledged herself to God that if she had ever been ungrateful or unfilial to her father, she would atone for it by fidelity" to his children.

This was not simple mourning, and little wonder when Margaret was grieving a father whose scant blessing just days before his death had left her at once tearfully grateful and empty-handed. Margaret had been restored to health—"returned into life," as she wrote to Almira Barlow—only to "bear a sorrow" the consequences of which she could scarcely fathom. She was consumed, for a time, with self-reproach. "My father's image follows me constantly," Margaret wrote in her journal of the weeks following his death. "Whenever I am in my room, he seems to open the door," yet when Margaret looked up in hopes of receiving his "complacent, tender smile," the empty room mocked her, reminding her of all the ways she had "fallen short of love and duty": her ill-concealed resentment of the move to Groton, her refusal to visit the shaded seat Timothy had constructed for her in Margaret's Grove.

Neither Eugene nor William Henry would return to oversee the farm.

Surprising for a lawyer, Timothy had left no will, and stern Uncle Abraham, who had always handled family business in Timothy's absence, stepped into the breach, informing Margaret and her mother that the estate was worth even less than expected. There was little cash on hand to support daily existence. Timothy's investments had been in properties, primarily the Groton farm, which, for lack of a will, could not be sold until the estate was settled in court. Accustomed to deference and ill prepared to handle the family finances, Margarett Crane ceded her widow's right to manage the estate to Abraham, who doled out funds, advanced against the eventual sale of Timothy's properties, in the stingy manner Margaret and her mother had always chaffed under, insisting on accountings for everything from food and clothes to schoolbooks and fees for fifteen-year-old Ellen, who, Margaret argued, now needed the polish of a private school in Boston or Cambridge. It was time to let Ellen make the most of her good looks — an advantage that Margaret, despite her personal magnetism, did not possess.

"I have often had reason to regret being of the softer sex," Margaret wrote to a friend, "and never more than now." Where once she had "hated the din" of business affairs and "hoped to find a life-long refuge from them in the serene world of literature and the arts," she found herself "full of desire" to learn "the management and value of property . . . that I may be able to advise and act." Yet the fact remained: Margaret could never be "an eldest son," a role that would have permitted her to serve as "guardian to my brothers and sister, administer the estate, and really become the head of my family." Instead she was left to play mediator between her mother and Uncle Abraham, pleading with him to continue delivery of one newspaper, searching the attic of the Groton house for receipts to document Timothy's holdings, apologizing for not having lent "a more heedful ear" to her father when he spoke of his financial concerns, and urging her uncle to "make things as easy to Mother as you can." Margaret's awareness that the childless Abraham Fuller was leading a life of plenty in his Cambridge mansion made this supplication all the more bitter. Still, he might one day make Timothy's children his heirs, so she did her best to restrain her indignation.

James Clarke and George Davis both visited Groton to offer condolences. The ruckus over "Lost and Won" belonged to a distant past now, and Margaret was glad to receive the sympathy of the two most significant men in her life after Timothy — and then see them depart. The loss of her father and her sharp feelings of regret brought Margaret a deeper sense of isolation, but also of mission. She had long referred to the younger brothers she educated from childhood as "my boys." Her father's family was *her* family now. Resolved to honor this commitment, and in some ways freed by it from the restless uncertainty of recent years, Margaret found it possible finally to admit, in a letter to James after he'd left again for Kentucky, that she expected never to "become more tenderly attached to any other man," even as she urged him to find another woman to love and marry.

James could not be her husband, but he had given her a vocation — first the nudge toward a writing career that she deflected but later embraced, then the means of publishing her first literary essays. Despite the anguish of the early autumn, she'd finished the review of Henry Taylor's *Philip van Artevelde*, a historical drama in verse, that she'd promised to the *Western Messenger* over the summer. Experiencing a greater sense of mission in her writing too, she moved beyond biographical insight to articulate her own critical aesthetic. "Art is Nature, but nature, new modelled, condensed, and harmonized," she wrote of Taylor's play about a medieval governor's call to power in place of his dead father — a plot that must have reverberated with her present circumstances, and she had always thrilled to tales from the feudal hall. "We are not merely like mirrors to reflect our own times to those more distant," she explained. "The mind has a light of its own, and by it illumines what it recreates." This statement of purpose, achieved at age twenty-five, would guide her writing hereafter; there would be no more fictional portrayals of her friends' drawing room intrigues.

When the review appeared in December 1835, Margaret was already immersed in a more ambitious project, also bequeathed her by James but originating from her own mind's light. The previous spring she had suggested to James that he "write a *Life* of Goethe in 2 vols . . . accompanied by criticisms of his works." She confessed, "This vision swims often before mine own eyes," but a biography was an enormous undertaking, and her imagination was already "swimming" with plenty of smaller, more manageable ideas; she would happily see this one "realized" by James. Yet her friend quickly divined that Margaret expected his prompting to make this project her own. "If *I* do it," she had added, "there shall be less eloquence perhaps but more insight than a De Stael." James delivered the needed stimulus: "I should like to see your '*View of Goethe*, 2 vols . . . Philadelphia, Carey Lea & Co.—' Send me a copy of it, will you?" When Margaret mentioned the idea to Harriet Martineau in late summer, she received further encouragement. "She thinks the time is ripe, she thinks I can do it," Margaret reported to James, asking him to lend her his set of Goethe's works, forty volumes in German. She could not "at present, afford to buy them" herself.

Although she was attending to her father's estate, negotiating on her mother's behalf with Uncle Abraham, forming plans for her Goethe biography, continuing her family schoolroom duties, and taking on several adult pupils for foreign language study, Margaret would also remember the season following Timothy's death as "the first winter of my suffering health." She had not yet fully recovered from her own fever—sometimes she would say she never did—and though she had inherited Timothy's tenacity, her mother's example of retreating from overwhelming responsibility into illness was not lost on her. Migraine and back pain, the result of the spinal curvature that caused her slouching posture, plagued her when her spirits flagged.

Despite the dismal news about family finances, she had been reluctant to give up plans for the trip to Europe with the Farrars. How could she write Goethe's biography without traveling to Germany and speaking to people who knew him? Staying home would mean having "to tear my heart, by a violent effort, from its present objects and natural desires." Those objects and desires also included her passion for Anna Barker, with whom she'd begun to count on sharing this transformational journey.

During the fall, she wrote a series of six poems dedicated to Anna, whom she'd last seen in August at the height of her summertime confidence. After the shock of her father's death, Margaret began to idealize Anna as her rescuer from despair, imagining the time they might spend together as if on "some isle far apart from the haunts of men." In her journal she explained her attraction to women, in part, as the result of having "masculine traits," and so "I am naturally often relieved by . . . women in my imaginary distresses." But with Anna it was more than relief from anxiety Margaret dreamed of. As she wrote in another of the poems—"When with soft eyes, beaming the tenderest love, / I see thy

dear face, Anna! Far above,— / By magnet drawn up to thee I seem."
Margaret was in love with Anna—perhaps a no more realistic love than
her anguished passion for the standoffish George Davis—and her longing to have a share in Anna's carefree existence, maybe the greatest share,
was acute.

She worked out calculations. A two-thousand-dollar advance from her
father's estate—about the sum of her eventual portion—could finance
the trip, she proposed, despite Uncle Abraham's warning that the court
might soon act to deprive her mother of household furnishings and live-
stock. At this critical time of need, could Margaret bring herself to leave
the family she'd vowed to support in her miserly uncle's care while she
traveled to enhance her professional skills and ease her own distress—
even if investing in her happiness and future success as a writer might
help them all? The internal debate wore her down.

Sometimes she simply needed the cover of illness or exhaustion to regain her bearings. During the winter of her complicated grief and her
indecision about Europe, she continued her investigations of Groton's
townsfolk, and volunteered one night to watch over a young woman dying of consumption—or so Margaret was told. Once she arrived at the
house "full of poverty . . . and fragments of destiny," Margaret learned
from the young unmarried woman, perhaps Margaret's own age, that she
was pregnant and had attempted to abort the fetus: this act, not tuberculosis, brought on her lethal affliction. Margaret had entered a scene not
just of poverty and illness, as she'd expected, but of a particular female
desperation that was almost too horrifying to register. As at her father's
deathbed a few months earlier, Margaret experienced "a sadness of deepest calm." She gathered into her arms this lonely woman, who had committed and was suffering for a "crime for the sake of sensual pleasure,"
as Margaret saw it then; she sank back in Margaret's embrace and died.
How different this was from the death of Margaret's small brother Edward in her arms several years before, or the death of Timothy: both son
and father had been attended by loving if weary family members through
their final hours.

Margaret reached home just before sunrise and, rather than seek out
her mother, went straight to "the silent room" where "but late before my
human father dwelt." She lay down on her father's bed—his deathbed—
and watched "the cold rosy winter dawn and then the sun" cross the sky

through the tall windows, refusing to eat, making this day "unintention-ally a fast." Lying there, Margaret began to take in the meaning of her future life, to assemble the fragments of her own destiny in the space left empty by her father and in reaction to that night's scene of solitary female ruin.

Hers would have to be "an ascetic life." She would renounce sensual-ity—the sort that had claimed a nameless single woman and her unborn child—and embrace winter's "bareness, her pure shroud, her judgment-announcing wind." She would summon from within herself the "strength to wait as a smooth bare tree forever." It was time to give up the Eu-ropean journey, "to forget myself, and act for others' sakes." And she would "ask no more" of "my friends for leaves and flowers or a bird haunted bower"—she would get along without feminine care and affec-tion, the metaphoric fruits of her mother's garden, the sequestered isle she selfishly dreamed of inhabiting with Anna Barker.

At the day's end she rose from Timothy's bed and opened the door into her family's home to take his place. "I *was* called back to this state of things," she wrote afterward to her old school friend Almira Barlow, "to perform some piece of work which another could not." No one else could care for her family now as Margaret would; she became "a tower of strength in this emergency," her brother Richard would recall. And perhaps her biography of Goethe, her own great work that, like her fa-ther's projected history of the United States, honored a personal found-ing father, would one day be another "piece of work" that she could per-form as no one else. She would practice patience—"wait as a smooth bare tree," dedicated in spirit to her task, preparing as best she could on limited means—and hope the wait would not last "forever."

But could she support her family while staying with them on the Gro-ton farm? A second dark epiphany occurred in the spring. Again Mar-garet had gone on an errand of mercy—and of curiosity—to the house of impoverished neighbors, setting out by moonlight with a "happy sort of feeling" when "nature's song of promise was chanting in my heart." She'd visited this place before, a one-room farmhouse where a ninety-year-old widow, whose "husband, sons, strength, health, house and lands, all are gone," lived on donations from townspeople, cared for by her unmarried daughter, an elderly woman herself. This time when Mar-garet entered the hut, where "everything is old and faded, but at the same time as clean and carefully mended as possible," she found the two figures huddled before a low fire, despite the warm night air. In the dim light of the glowing embers, she saw the pair—"mother and daughter!"—as phantoms in a Platonic shadow play enacting a nightmarish destiny: they were "all frost" and had "long ceased to know what spring is."

Margaret's attention was drawn to the daughter, who, starved for company, chattered on about "the price of pounds of sugar, and ounces of tea, and yards of flannel." She had nothing else to talk about; her "only intellectual resource," Margaret guessed, was "hearing five or six verses of the Bible read every day" by her nearly "imbecile" mother, who suffered from senility. "Can we think of spring, or summer, or anything joyous or really life-like, when we look at the daughter?" Margaret wondered.

Still the woman clung to "this sordid existence" with a "self-sacrificing constancy," as women were expected to do; she had "ever been good," in stark contrast to the young unwed mother who died as the result of her "crime" of sensuality. Yet this aged daughter's fate was just as horrifying to Margaret, who could not imagine herself ever equaling such self-sacrifice. How could this daughter not wish for extinction, her mother's and her own? This life was already a kind of death. The two women rose each morning "without a hope" and reached the end of each day "vacant or apathetic": "all they know of pleasure is to get strength to sweep those few boards, and mend those old spreads and curtains." After so many years of this routine, the poor daughter "would not know what to do with life," even if freed from her "narrow and crushing duties" to her mother. It was a frightening prospect: could Margaret's own suddenly reduced circumstances, her resolution to serve her mother and younger siblings, lead to a life—a death-in-life—like this?

Leaving the house, escaping "into the open air," Margaret renewed her vow to follow the "Ought"—her commitment to duty, the care of her mother and siblings. But she could not abide the idea of dedicating herself to a course of action—or inaction—that might result in such "grub-like lives" for her mother and herself, "undignified even by passion,—these life-long quenchings of the spark divine."

Out of these twin encounters with female destitution and despair, Margaret forged twin resolves: to support her family *and* to follow a personal destiny. She would leave Groton to seek her fortune in the city— play the wage-earning eldest son or father, even though she was of the "softer sex." On her twenty-sixth birthday, May 23, Margaret took stock of her present situation, in light of her choice to forgo the "intellectual re-sources" and restorative companionship she might have acquired in travel-ing to Europe: "What I can do with my pen, I know not. At present, I feel no confidence or hope. The expectations so many have been led to cherish by my conversational powers, I am disposed to deem ill-founded. I do not think I can produce a valuable work. I do not feel in my bosom that confidence necessary to sustain me in such undertakings, — the con-fidence of genius. But I am now but just recovered from bodily illness, and still heart-broken by sorrow and disappointment. I may be renewed again." In the meantime, "I will make up my mind to teach."

Afterward Margaret would understand she had come late to the party at Bronson Alcott's Temple School. But at the time she accepted the job in Boston as Alcott's teaching assistant in the fall of 1836, she believed she was joining a crusade in full swing that would also supply the employ-ment she needed to "get money, which I will use for the benefit of my dear, gentle, suffering mother, — my brothers and sister." She didn't yet know that her predecessors, the self-educated historian and innovative schoolteacher Elizabeth Peabody and her younger sisters, Mary and So-phia, had not been paid a cent for their work over the past two years since the school's founding in September 1834, when Elizabeth had gathered pupils from the progressive-minded families of Beacon Hill and the still fashionable residential districts near the waterfront and offered them up to the dreamy idealist Alcott for his educational experiment.

The sisters, in particular Elizabeth, had made certain the Temple School was both an academic and a popular success by conducting the school's regular lessons in Latin, math, and geography, leaving Bron-son Alcott free to lead his young pupils in the daily Socratic dialogues on "spiritual philosophy" that formed the centerpiece of his progressive pedagogy, which the sisters faithfully recorded. Elizabeth had turned these transcripts into a book, *Record of a School*, which, appearing in the spring of 1835, commenced a flood of Transcendentalist publications — including James Freeman Clarke's *Western Messenger* with Margaret's reviews, as well as Emerson's first book, his rhapsodic *Nature* — that put the reformers' ideas before the public. Alcott believed, along with Eliza-beth Peabody, that children already possessed the seeds of knowledge —

all that was needed was an able facilitator, such as Alcott, to "cultivate the heart, and to bring out from the child's own mind the principles which are to govern his character." The conversations reported in *Record of a School* showed children as young as five uttering naive wisdom on surprisingly weighty matters, from "the advantage of having an imagination" to the immortality of the human soul. It was a system bound to appeal to Margaret, who so far had little practical experience in a classroom, even more powerfully than it had to Elizabeth Peabody, who had been running her own schools for more than a decade before joining forces with Alcott.

Elizabeth Peabody, who liked to act as an intellectual impresario among Boston's freethinkers, should have been the one to introduce Margaret to Bronson Alcott. Since Timothy Fuller's death had left Margaret responsible for her family—a situation Elizabeth Peabody understood, with her own ne'er-do-well younger brothers and an impecunious dentist for a father—she had done all she could for Margaret, whom she remembered from her years as a wunderkind in Dr. Park's Boston school. A free-ranging conversation with the eighteen-year-old Margaret while she still lived in the Dana mansion in Cambridge had left Elizabeth feeling "I had seen the Universe," she later recalled.

In the spring of 1836, when Margaret still held out the hope of earning a living by her pen, Elizabeth had paved the way for Margaret's publication that year of three ambitious essays on British and German literature in the *American Monthly Magazine*, edited by Elizabeth's friend Park Benjamin. In the last of these, Margaret made a case for the Romantic poets Coleridge and Wordsworth as "the pilot-minds of the age," whose work allowed readers to glimpse "that which lies beyond" while simultaneously being "roused to do and dare for ourselves." These prophets of the new era had found a way to express what Margaret termed the "mind-emotions"—the feelings that fueled her thoughts and aspirations with a passion more intense than the "heart-emotions," the province of poets from earlier times. It was important writing, but before accepting Elizabeth's aid she had imperiously sniped at the older woman, "I would gladly sell some part of my mind for lucre . . . but I will not sell my soul . . . I am *not* willing to have what I write mutilated, or what I ought to say dictated to suit the public taste." Never mind that she had spent the greater part of the past year, as she later wrote to Sam Ward, pursuing a

"liberal communion with the woful struggling crowd of fellow men"—
and women—with the precise aim of discerning the needs and interests
of the reading public.

Elizabeth had also wangled an invitation for Margaret to stay with the
Emersons in Concord in January. Postponed until the summer, this first
visit nonetheless turned out to be a success. Waldo, at first put off by
Margaret's forthright manner and obvious efforts to charm him, was ultimately won over. "I believe we all here shared your respect for Miss
Fuller's gifts & character," Waldo wrote to Elizabeth, grateful she had
pressed for the visit. Perhaps Margaret read to Waldo and Lidian a poem
she had composed and published that spring in a Boston newspaper, expressing sympathy after Waldo's favorite brother, Charles, died of tuberculosis in early May, a loss that was felt deeply by all who knew the family; writing of efforts to "assuage grief's dread excess," Margaret may
also have recalled her own periods of mourning for infant brother and
father. In return, Waldo read aloud to Margaret his "little book called
'Nature,'" then still in manuscript. But it was Margaret's ready wit that
Waldo remarked on to Elizabeth Peabody: "She has the quickest apprehension & immediately learned all we knew & had us at her mercy when
she pleased to make us laugh." His wife, Lidian, wrote more plainly: "We
like her—she likes us." In a letter to his brother William, the ruggedly
handsome six-foot-tall Concord sage said more: talking to Margaret
Fuller was "like being set in a large place. You stretch your limbs & dilate
to your utmost size." Margaret's stay in the large white frame house on
the main road from Cambridge, where she occupied a guest room on the
ground floor across the hall from Waldo's study, was extended to a week
and more.

But that summer, Elizabeth Peabody had a long-overdue falling-out
with Bronson Alcott when she withdrew her support from the new volume of conversations he planned to publish. His insistence on including
passages in which children discussed the processes of human conception
and birth, taboo in polite society, threatened the future of the school,
she'd warned him. Already, concerned parents were withdrawing their
children. Elizabeth received a letter from her younger sister Mary advising her to resign before her reputation was ruined. Mary had come to
believe that, aside from the scandalous content, Alcott's conversations
with the children were not so innocent in method: he was planting his

own ideas in his young pupils' minds, leading them to conclusions he favored, even "question[ing]" them "out of their opinions." Not particularly known for tact, Elizabeth had nevertheless attempted to conceal the depth of her reservations about Alcott's system as a whole in order to keep the peace. But when she moved into the Alcott household that summer, accepting room and board in partial payment of the back salary she was owed, Bronson's wife, Abigail, had opened a packet of Mary's letters to Elizabeth and found out their true opinions. Elizabeth, outraged at the violation of her privacy and frightened by Abigail Alcott's spiteful accusations of disloyalty, packed and left the house—with its brood of three small daughters, Anna, Louisa May, and the baby Elizabeth, named for Peabody as another form of payment in kind—and the city of Boston to live with her family twenty miles north in the old port town of Salem.

So it was that during Margaret's summertime visit with the Emersons, she met Bronson Alcott, the flaxen-haired aging faun of the Transcendentalist inner circle, who arrived in Concord the same day Elizabeth Peabody fled Boston, casually speaking of his need for a substitute. A self-taught country-bred improviser—some would say charlatan—Alcott really did need a second teacher in his school: he simply didn't know enough to teach the basic academic subjects. Elizabeth's wayward youngest sister, Sophia, had taken her place for the time being, moving into the Alcott house and siding with Abigail, but he understood that Sophia's rebellion from Elizabeth's authority couldn't last long.

Alcott may also have hinted that Margaret (whom he would ultimately deem "more liberal than almost any mind among us" and certain to "add enduring glory to female literature") could do better than Elizabeth, which would have appealed to Margaret's vanity. Elizabeth Peabody was so far the most active female Transcendentalist, succeeding where Margaret had failed. Her published translations from the French philosopher de Gérando's *Self-Education* and *Visitor of the Poor* influenced Emerson's thought and the younger rebellious Unitarian ministers' actions, and her three-part series of essays on the historical sources and contemporary relevance of the Old Testament appeared in the *Christian Examiner* the same year Margaret's reviews had been rejected. A fourth essay had been slated for publication, but the conservative editor Andrews Norton, known as the Unitarian "Pope," had balked at Elizabeth's introduction of the concept of "transcendentalism"—a term, until then, not seen in print in the United States—and put an end to the series. So she had suffered the sanctifying martyrdom of censorship by the Unitarian establishment as well. If Elizabeth had been, like Harriet Martineau, a visitor from Europe, only temporarily on the scene, Margaret might have put herself under her sway. Instead, only six years older than Margaret and with a reputation for sloppy hair and clothes, and a style of assertiveness that almost always managed to "offend," as Waldo Emerson ultimately concluded, Elizabeth Peabody was another disturbing model of femininity that Margaret preferred to look away from during the pivotal year after her father's death—despite Elizabeth's persistent offers of help, which Margaret nearly always accepted.

In September of 1837, Margaret settled into a room in her uncle Henry's house on Avon Place in Boston and, with Elizabeth Peabody out of the way in Salem, took on some of the many roles the older woman had played for over a decade in the more populous, forward-looking city. She accepted Bronson Alcott's offer of employment but delayed starting until December, gathering a brood of older teenage and young-adult women for classes in French, German, and Italian literature, many of them former pupils of Elizabeth Peabody in her advanced world history classes. But Margaret won them over in an entirely different way. Margaret was, by disposition, more galvanizer than teacher. She was proud of her "magnetic power over young women," as she described her ability to draw pupils "into my sphere." She saw to it that within three months the beginning German class was translating twenty pages per lesson, the advanced language students reading whole volumes of Goethe and Dante. But the "sympathy and time" she offered in sometimes taxing amounts to a handful of the girls, particularly Caroline Sturgis, the high-spirited daughter of the China-trade baron Captain William Sturgis and youngest sister of Margaret's girlhood friend Ellen, pointed her teacher-student relationships in the direction of deeper friendship. In truth, Margaret never liked the formal relationship of teacher and pupil, which reminded her too much of her straitened circumstances. It was best to be paid for what she might have done anyway: befriend and inspire.

Margaret also began making weekly evening visits to the Boston household of the Reverend William Ellery Channing, the charismatic minister who had introduced the concepts of Unitarianism, at first deemed blatantly heretical, to America. In a series of stirring sermons beginning in 1815 and widely circulated in print, Channing outlined his precepts of man's "likeness to God," arguing that every human soul is fed by its unique spark of the divine and the essential humanity—not divinity—of Jesus. Taken together, these radical notions dismantled the Holy Trinity, leaving Unitarians to believe in the one God residing in the human heart. But by the time Margaret began spending evenings with Channing, his liberal religion had, within two short decades, been codified into an establishment credo that emphasized intellection over intuition, and the new generation was now straying from it, toward Transcendentalism's more secular, nature-oriented humanism. As Emerson would confide to Elizabeth Peabody when he decided to further distance himself from the institution of the church by putting an end to his supply preaching two years later, "Whoever would preach Christ in these times must say nothing about him!"

Margaret offered Reverend Channing her services in translating aloud for him the works of her favorite German writers, although Channing professed a disdain of Goethe on moral grounds. It was the old *Elective Affinities* taint, amplified by some real-life gossip: Goethe was rumored to have lived unmarried with his lover, Christiane Vulpius, for many years, marrying her only after the birth of their son. Margaret herself had been "greatly pained and troubled" when she'd learned of the story earlier in the year, writing to James Clarke, "I had no idea . . . [he] went so far with his experimentalizing in *real life*. I had not supposed he '*was*' all he '*writ*.'"

Channing reciprocated by reading Coleridge and Wordsworth aloud and offering his gloss on the poems, as he had done with Elizabeth Peabody some years earlier. For Margaret, these sessions comfortably recalled the nights spent reading with her father and became a means of indirectly mourning Timothy: in devoting her evenings to the older man, she was refusing, unlike so many of her friends in Transcendentalism, to "forget what he has done." But she may also have had the pragmatic aim of seeking the blessing of this Boston celebrity—the Unitarian Evangelist—whose views were far more liberal than her father's. When Margaret returned to Boston on her own in 1836, it was to make a place for herself in a sphere different from her father's Republican political arena. Reverend Channing was the elder statesman of the movement she hoped to join. When the men and women of Transcendentalism began to speak of her as simply "Margaret," dropping her surname, she was pleased;

for better or worse, she had truly become "Margaret alone," as she had insisted her father address her so many years ago.

The Reverend George Ripley was one of those who tended to forget Channing—one of the young men Emerson wrote about admiringly as having been "born with knives in their brain," ready to "dissect" the status quo, maybe even act to undo it. A few years older than James Clarke and Henry Hedge, Ripley, also a Harvard-trained Unitarian, had taken one of the few available ministerial openings in Boston, at the Purchase Street Church, but felt restless there. He shared Emerson's view that spiritual reform could not take place within established religious institutions, which were, as Ripley came to believe, "vicious in [their] foundations." He didn't want to go it alone, however; he'd become interested in the writings of European "Associationists" and, with his wife, Sophia Dana Ripley, granddaughter of a Harvard president, dreamed of gathering together like-minded seekers to form an ideal community where they could implement their principles in daily life. In 1836, Ripley was taking a first step by making arrangements to publish a series of books in translation he called Specimens of Foreign Standard Literature; he deliberately planned to include works by Goethe, whose personal peccadilloes seemed to him beside the point. When Ripley learned of Margaret's plan for a biography, he signed her on, with a three-year deadline, and invited her also to translate for the series Johann Peter Eckermann's biographical *Conversations with Goethe in the Last Years of His Life*, which she planned to study closely as part of her research.

But the prospect of payment for these works was far in the future, and her income from the foreign language classes was not enough to support her, let alone send money home. In December, the same month that the first volume of Bronson Alcott's new *Conversations with Children on the Gospels* appeared in print, Margaret began spending her days at the Temple School, the one-time showplace of Transcendental pedagogy. More than a year earlier, Waldo Emerson had taken a seat on the classroom's green velvet visitors' couch, bringing Lidian too, shortly before their wedding in September 1835. Impressed with what he'd seen, Emerson went on to declare Elizabeth Peabody's *Record of a School* "the only book of facts I ever read" that was as "engaging" as a novel. Harriet Martineau had listened in on Alcott's morning dialogues as well and planned to include an account of the school in her book. But by December 1836, the numbers in the school had dwindled from the robust thirty of the year before. The spacious classroom on the second floor of Boston's towering new Masonic temple, with busts of Plato, Socrates, Shakespeare, and Walter Scott arrayed in its four corners, was beginning to look empty in the weak winter sunlight that filtered through its single enormous Palladian window.

The disaster that Elizabeth Peabody predicted hit fast. After volume two of *Conversations* appeared in February, "Pope" Andrews Norton blasted it as "one third absurd, one third blasphemous, and one third obscene," and assailed its author as "an ignorant and presuming charlatan," either "insane or half-witted." The book was "more indecent and obscene," a second reviewer charged, "than any other we ever saw exposed for sale on a bookseller's counter." By then, Margaret had given up keeping a record of Bronson's further conversations; he had so far omitted to pay her salary, and while she would make good on her commitment to teach through the end of term in April, she began making plans to leave, as most of the pupils would. For the remainder of the school's brief existence, Bronson was forced to move into the Masonic temple's basement, where only a handful of children, including his oldest daughter, Anna, and an African American child whose presence brought even more defections, continued through the following year, after which the Temple School closed and Alcott, who had once dreamed of reforming the American system of education, left the teaching profession for good.

Privately, Margaret had no dispute with Alcott's philosophy or methods, although she considered him "one-sided" and "impatient of the complex." Alcott was a "star of purest ray serene," she argued to Henry Hedge, whose "elevated aim" had been undercut by his "practical defects": he was inclined to become "lost in abstractions, and could not illustrate [his] principles," she told her former employer outright a few years later. But Margaret shared Bronson Alcott's inclination to form collegial relations with his students and had instinctively developed a teaching style that featured the give-and-take of conversation rather than the conventional memorize-and-recite method. Even if she didn't fully agree with Alcott that her students already possessed profound knowledge, she preferred to cultivate in them—particularly the girls—the ability to express what they learned from her, to ask questions and find the answers.

If Margaret learned anything from working with Alcott, it was to drive a harder bargain when negotiating her terms of employment. When another idealist in the field of education from Providence, Rhode Island, Hiram Fuller (no relation), learned that Margaret was free of her Temple School obligations and offered her work at his new Greene Street School, she insisted on a salary of $1,000 per year, the equal of a Harvard professor's yearly income, and the freedom to teach as she pleased. A few years younger than Margaret and as charismatic with investors as Alcott had been with his young pupils, Hiram Fuller had successfully raised funds to build a schoolhouse, modeled after a Greek temple, on one of the city's main streets. When Hiram Fuller agreed to Margaret's conditions, she had reason to believe he could deliver. Despite misgivings about leaving Boston's more stimulating intellectual atmosphere, when the Greene Street School opened in its new quarters in June 1837, Margaret was there for the start of the new term — along with Ralph Waldo Emerson.

· 9 ·

"Bringing my opinions to the test"

I F BOSTON WAS OLD MONEY AND NEW IDEAS, PROVIDENCE was simply money. Or so it seemed to Margaret after her first weeks in the city fifty miles to the south, with one quarter the population. "Here is the hostile element of money getting but with little counterpoise" of cultural or spiritual aspiration, she wrote to Bronson Alcott. Providence seemed "low" on intellectual stimulation compared with even some of the "villages" surrounding Boston—Concord or Cambridge, she must have been thinking. Margaret missed the "liveliness of mind" in the Temple School children, which she attributed not so much to their innate genius, as Alcott had, as to their enlightened parents. Yet the solid prosperity of the Greene Street School families increased her confidence in the school's success—and in receiving her pay—and their relative lack of intellectual sophistication promised relief from the scrutiny of a cannier Boston elite: "there is an affectionate, if not an intelligent sympathy in this community with Mr. Fuller and his undertaking," she reported to Alcott.

Margaret had ended her teaching days in Boston pleased with all she had accomplished in her first "public position"—and suffering a raging headache. Yet that too was something to boast about: "all my pursuits and propensities have a tendency to make my head worse," she wrote to James Clarke, still in Kentucky. "It is but a bad head; as bad as if I were a great man." Although she still hadn't accomplished anything worthy of greatness, an ambition evident in all her letters to James, "I flatter myself it is very interesting of me to suffer so much." Margaret had retreated to Groton to be coddled by her mother, whose habitual submissiveness was receding along with her grief. Margarett Crane had married at twenty, "too young," in her older daughter's view, stunting her own development while "growing to earthly womanhood with your children." The forty-eight-year-old widow would soon launch a successful appeal to Uncle Abraham for the funds to keep Ellen in school, and while it still fell to Margaret to lecture her sister on the need to accustom herself to wearing "faded frocks" in company—"Now that every one knows our circumstances it is no disgrace to us not to wear fine clothes, but a credit" —Margaret could "vegetate" this spring, for perhaps the first time in her life, in her mother's "sunny kindness." Margarett Crane saw to it that her overtired daughter "had a grand reading time at home," broken only by a week's visit to Waldo and Lidian Emerson and their new infant son in late April.

Margaret had last seen the Emersons on a brief stopover in October, a few weeks before the birth of the couple's first child. In advance of that visit, Waldo had urged her to come "as soon as you can," writing that Margaret's company was sure to be more healthful to the ailing Lidian than "poppy & oatmeal," referring to the opium that both women sometimes took to ease headaches. But the visit itself proved to be a disappointment for Margaret. Her aim was friendship with Waldo, whom she saw as her intellectual counterpart and potential soul mate, not with Lidian, much as she esteemed her "holiness." Once she arrived, Waldo maintained a surprising reserve after the past summer's volubility, retreating to his study to keep to a regular work schedule and responding coolly to Margaret's verbal sallies. "We lead a life of glimpses & glances," he had written to Margaret afterward, in oblique apology—and warning. He might have been referring to himself rather than to his fleeting thoughts: "We see nothing good steadily or long, and though love-sick with Ideas they hide their faces alway."

Leading up to this third stay in Concord, Margaret had turned the tables, playing Waldo's game. "I am sure you will purify and strengthen me to enter the Paradise of thought once more," she wrote effusively in advance, while privately "schooling" herself—her "heart," she specified—"not to expect too much." Lowering her expectations helped. This time in Concord, evening conversation proved so stimulating that "the excitement . . . prevents my sleeping," she wrote to one of her Boston language students. The resulting headaches brought good cover too: if Waldo withdrew to his study during the day, Margaret, when feeling unwell, could seal herself up in the first-floor guest room across the hall. Alternatively she could earn her host's gratitude by playing with the six-month-old "beautiful" baby boy, who "looks like his father, and smiles so sweetly on all hearty, good people." She was rewarded at the end of the week with a Sunday-morning drive, alone "with the Author of '*Nature*'" on his way to Watertown, several villages away, to deliver a guest sermon. All "care and routine" were forgotten as the pair wound through the woods, the tall pines sighing "with their soul-like sounds for June." It was to be one of the last sermons the renegade minister preached from a pulpit.

Margaret was eager for June as well. Waldo had agreed to deliver the inaugural address at the opening of the Greene Street School's new building at the start of the month, filling in for Hiram Fuller's mentor, the recently disgraced Bronson Alcott. Stopping again in Concord for a night at the end of May on her way to Rhode Island, Margaret left armed with a stack of books loaned by Waldo—Coleridge, Milton, Jonson, Plutarch, Goethe—and the draft of a poem, Waldo's "Compensation," which reverberated with Margaret's own sense of solitary mission:

> *Why should I keep holiday*
> *When other men have none?*
> *Why but because when these are gay*
> *I sit and mourn alone.*
>
> *And why, when Mirth unseals all tongues*
> *Must mine alone be dumb?*
> *Ah late I spoke to the silent throngs*
> *And now their turn has come.*

Many had predicted it, but few saw just how it would happen: a crash of the fragile new American economy. On May 4, the first bank suspension took place in Natchez, Mississippi, followed within the week by sharp reductions in lending at banks in Alabama, New York, Connecticut, and finally Boston and Providence. By the end of the month, nearly all American banks were conducting business only in specie—gold or silver. Enormous paper fortunes, all based on speculation, were lost. The Panic of 1837, which brought the worst recession in the history of the young nation, not to be matched for another forty years, was under way.

When Waldo Emerson spoke on June 10 at Providence's Westminster Unitarian Church in honor of the opening of the Greene Street School, he told the overflow crowd that attempting to make sense of such unprecedented calamity felt to him like "learning geology the morning after an earthquake." The world had split apart, and he would read the "ghastly diagrams" of "cloven mountain and upheaved plain." Margaret, who had been thinking of little but "Concord, dear Concord" since arriving in Providence the week before, was in the audience, buoyed already by a letter from Waldo. "These black times," he had written, as news of the bank suspensions reached him in the village, "discover by very contrast a light in the mind we had not looked for." He would shine that light to good purpose in Providence.

The "peculiar aspects of the times," Waldo Emerson informed his listeners, "advertise us of radical errors somewhere" that can be corrected only by "reform of our culture": a new system of education. A moment like this one, of "calamity and alarm," when "a commercial or political revolution has shattered" the calm of daily life, was no time to be "afraid of change, afraid of thought." It was time, instead, to throw off the "desperate conservatism" that "clings with both hands to every dead form in the schools, in the state, in the church."

"The disease of which the world lies sick," he argued, is "the inaction of the higher faculties of man." He called on educators to provide the nation's deliverance, but they must do more than teach numbers, words, and facts, and instead make use of the "capital secret of their profession, namely, to convert life into truth, or to show the meaning of events." They must "teach self-trust," allow the student to explore "the resources of his mind" and there discover "all his strength." "Amid the swarming population how few men!" he scolded, a charge that would serve as impetus for the revelatory speech he delivered two months later to Harvard's Phi Beta Kappa Society at commencement. In "The American Scholar" he would define the ideal citizen as *Man Thinking.*"

And then he was gone, leaving a bewildered audience—few, as Marga-

ret might have predicted, could follow or approve his train of thought—
and a deeply inspired twenty-seven-year-old schoolmistress. Margaret
now had to make sense of her new assignment, to somehow "convert life
into truth" and "show the meaning of events" to the girls in her charge:
sixty of them, ages ten to eighteen, seated in long rows filling one half of
the Greene Street School's enormous interior room and facing her expectantly. On the opposite side of the white-walled, orange-carpeted Great
Hall, sixty boys worked their lessons under Hiram Fuller's guidance.

The well-appointed schoolroom, with a grand piano against one wall
and visitors' couches ranged against another, with classical statuary and
a portrait of Hiram Fuller for decoration, gave an air of theater to the
experiment. Divide and hope to conquer was all Margaret could manage at first, however, organizing her pupils into Latin sections according
to ability, and composition, elocution, ethics, world history, and natural
history classes by age. Two other women taught mathematics, French,
drawing, and dancing to the girls, so these need not be her concern. Margaret arranged for regular sessions with each group in the antechambers
designed for recitations, insisting on conversation instead. The rule was
simple: in order to remain in the class, each girl must be "willing to communicate what was in her mind." Soon she was writing to Elizabeth Peabody, "I believe I do very well."

"There is room here," she wrote to Waldo Emerson, as if in answer
to his call for reform, "for a great move in the cause of education." Many
of the girls "begin already to attempt to walk in the ways I point . . .
Activity of mind, accuracy of processes, constant looking for principles,
and search after the good and beautiful." As she pushed the girls to express their thoughts vocally and in their journals each day—girls whose
"hearts are right" but whose minds had previously been "absolutely torpid," she wrote to Elizabeth Peabody—she discovered that "this experience here will be useful to me, if not to Providence, for I am bringing my
opinions to the test."

Hiram Fuller liked nothing better than to show off his Greene Street
School pupils to town dignitaries or visiting celebrities, and he held public exhibitions every two weeks. But only boys participated, a convention
he would not break. Margaret chafed at having her girls sit silently in the
audience as the boys spoke their pieces or answered questions. She began
calling attention to the girls' superior performance in beginning Latin,

her one coeducational class, and she formulated a curriculum in her other classes designed to persuade the girls of their intellectual strengths. In natural history, she coaxed them out of their "antipathy" to worms and caterpillars and told them the myth of Arachne—"an ambitious young lady who wanted to weave as fine as the goddess of Minerva," one young student recorded in her journal—when they studied spiders.

Margaret "spoke upon what woman could do," another student recorded, and "said she should like to see a woman everything she might be, in intellect and character." Whenever possible, she dwelled on examples of powerful women from classical history and myth: Atalanta, who "wished to live in the enjoyment of 'single blessedness,'" Daphne, Aspasia, Sappho, and Diotima. She required reading by women authors, from the Connecticut poet Lydia Sigourney to the British essayist Anna Jameson, who wrote on literary and historical heroines, and of course de Staël. When teaching Wordsworth, she singled out his poems about women: "Lament of Mary Queen of Scots" received a full lesson and a written analysis as homework. Even Hiram Fuller seemed to catch on, calling the entire school—boys *and* girls—to attention at midsummer with the news of the eighteen-year-old Princess Victoria's ascension to the British throne.

Margaret herself provided the best model of all. When she felt her students weren't striving for original thought in their journals, she started one herself and read passages aloud. "How and when did she ever learn about everybody that existed?" one of her older students asked in her own journal. "I wonder if I shall know an eighth part of what she does." Another student wrote to her brother, who was studying law at Harvard, "I wish you could hear her talk a few moments. I almost stand in awe of her, she is such a literary being."

But again Margaret was wearing herself out. At least once a month, with a regularity that suggests an underlying hormonal cause of her migraines, she missed school for a half-day or more because of illness. Through her first summer at Greene Street, she held herself to a punishing daily schedule. She had been receiving books selected and shipped from Europe by the Farrars, Anna Barker, and Sam Ward, to help with her research on Goethe, and she woke herself at 4:30 or 5:00 each morning to dress quickly, then read and take notes until breakfast at 7:30. By 8:30, when she arrived at the handsome school building and passed between its enormous white columns to enter the Great Hall and take up her teaching duties, she was often exhausted and resentful at having to "serve two masters": her own inner drive for literary achievement and the requirement to support herself and her family.

Sometimes her frustration showed in impatience with her students, whose "barbarous ignorance" at times seemed to Margaret almost a personal affront: teaching sixty "miserably prepared" young girls was not the professional life she had imagined for herself. The girls' journals registered fear of the sometimes "satirical" or *very severe* Miss Fuller—who "is very critical and sometimes cuts us up into bits"—along with admiration for "the infinite capacity of her mind" and a craving for her attention. When one older student burst into tears after being singled out for failing to prepare for class, Margaret later extended a written apology—"I often regret that you have not a teacher who has more heart, more health, more energy to spend upon you than I have." Although she admitted she may have been "too rough" with the girl, Margaret still hoped to "teach her more confidence and self-possession." She would rather her students learn to stand up to pressure than be indulged for shortcomings well within their power to correct: "I dare not be *generous* lest I should thus be unable to be *just*." In the end, all her students learned that "we must *think* as well as *study*, and *talk* as well as *recite*."

When school closed for a summer recess in late August, Margaret left Providence for Cambridge, an invited guest in the audience for Waldo Emerson's Phi Beta Kappa address and in his Concord home for the week following. The summer months had proven New England steadier in the financial crisis than other parts of the country; at Harvard, Waldo's message of "self-trust" turned less despairing and more visionary. For those who were ready for it, his "American Scholar" speech would mark a new era: "Our day of dependence, our long apprenticeship to the learning of other lands, draws to a close," they heard. He challenged his listeners to become intellectually "free and brave," to cultivate "heroic" minds, and more: the scholar must rise from his desk—"Life is our dictionary"—and become a man of action. "The one thing in the world, of value, is the active soul," he exhorted. "The soul active sees absolute truth; and utters truth, or creates. In this action, it is genius; not the privilege of here and there a favorite, but the sound estate of every man." In answer to his earlier complaint at Providence ("how few men!"), he looked to the time when all men's minds would become active, and offered this prediction: "A nation of men will for the first time exist."

Some years later Margaret would write of Waldo Emerson's "sermons" that "several of these stand apart in memory, like landmarks of my spiritual history," and this may have been one of them. She was accustomed to finding inspiration in literature and lectures aimed at men. Why shouldn't Waldo direct his words on this day to the male Harvard graduates, faculty, and president? But Margaret soon adapted Waldo's theme to her own use, drawing him into conversation a few days later in Concord on the subject of women. "Who would be a goody," she asserted, employing the old-fashioned term for housewife, "that could be a genius?" Women too, as Margaret had been entreating her pupils all summer, must cultivate "the active soul." And they would prefer to, if given the chance. Her question and its ramifications stayed with Waldo, possibly as a key to Margaret's character rather than women as a group, but he recorded her comment in his journal, his personal storehouse of overheard wisdom.

All summer the two had traded views by letter on the possibilities of friendship in general and, by implication, theirs in particular. In June, after they parted in Providence, Waldo had offered a tantalizing premise: "what is any friend but a holiday good for nothing if it lasts all the time, and intensating its good always as the interval." At least Margaret could hope their connection was "intensating" through her long summer absence. Then Waldo had written again, injecting Aristotle's bleak formulation "O my friends, there is no friend" with even darker meaning: "*O my friends, there are no friends.*" The statement struck Margaret with "a paralyzing conviction," she wrote back: she was overcome by a "misanthropic" skepticism of "the existence of any real communication between human beings"—or with Waldo. But when he welcomed her visit to Concord at summer's end, she delivered a teasing acceptance to "my dear *no friends,* Mr and Mrs Emerson."

The subject of women had come up in the wake of Margaret's incursion into another all-male bastion, again at Waldo's instigation. For the past year a group of rebel ministers had been meeting at one another's houses to discuss ideas for reform, calling themselves variously "Mr. Hedge's Club," the club of the "Like-Minded" ("because no two of us thought alike"), or simply the Transcendental Club. Margaret's friend Henry Hedge's frequent trips to Boston from Bangor set the timing of the meetings. Waldo, as elder statesman, had already persuaded the group to relax its qualifications to admit one lay member, Bronson Alcott. The other regulars included James Clarke when he was in town, George Ripley, Theodore Parker (who'd read his way through the Harvard curriculum on his own to win entrance to Harvard Divinity School), and John Sullivan Dwight, another newly minted preacher with a yen for German Romantic music and poetry. Margaret already knew Dwight because he had solicited her translations from Goethe for a volume of German verse he was collecting for George Ripley's series Specimens of Foreign Standard Literature.

The club was set to meet the day after Waldo's Phi Beta Kappa speech for an "all-day party" in Concord, with discussion of "the progress of Society" as the order of the day. Awkwardly, Waldo hinted to Margaret in advance that he would invite her as well, along with two women of his extended Concord family, Elizabeth Hoar and Sarah Ripley: "who knows but the wise men in an hour more timid or more gracious may crave the aid of wise & blessed women at their session." The three women swelled the ranks of the "like-minded" that day to eighteen, primarily listening as the men talked and Lidian Emerson hovered in the background as *genius domi*, plying the "Spiritualists" with a "noble great piece" of beef, a leg of mutton, cucumbers, tomatoes, lettuce, applesauce, and rice pudding with currants. A week later, Margaret attended a second session, at James Clarke's mother's house in the Boston suburb of Newton, on her way back to Providence; there Sarah Clarke and Elizabeth Peabody joined in, confirming the group's openness to female participation, although the numbers would remain few.

Margaret left no record of these historic meetings in her letters or journals at the time, but they made their mark. When she returned to Providence, where autumn brought out the city's intelligentsia, she found herself welcomed into the Coliseum Club, a group of men and women writers, politicians, and other professionals who were themselves debating the question of "the progress of Society": had civilization advanced over the centuries? It was a lightning-rod topic; some members defended the status quo, while others—fewer—saw signs of trouble lurking in the country's financial crisis and a need for change. Every two weeks, one member presented a paper, and Margaret became the fourth to give her ideas on the subject.

Margaret was a skeptic on the topic of progress and a proponent of reform. She found "incompleteness" in the reasoning of her more optimistic Coliseum Club colleagues, as well as in the arguments presented at the Transcendental Club session devoted to the same subject — "a meeting of gentlemen" she had attended "a few months since." She allowed that society as a whole may have improved, but what of the individual? The very signs of progress others pointed to — innovations such as the railroad and the steamship — created or exacerbated "immense wants" in the individual: "the diffusion of *information* is not necessarily the diffusion of knowledge," she explained, and "the triumph over matter does not always or often lead to the triumph of Soul." And "when it is made over easy for men to communicate with one another, they learn less from one another." It was time to "reassert the claims of the individual man." The signs were plain, in the increasing numbers of "men tired of materialism, rushing back into mysticism, weary of the useful, sighing for the beautiful."

And what of women? Margaret could write a book on the subject, she told the Coliseum Club. She rejected the argument that women's status in contemporary society — respected as wives and mothers, or simply as creatures of a "softer sex" — was an indicator of progress. Yes, education for women had improved, and more girls attended better schools. But "a woman may learn all the ologies" and still hold "no real power," as long as physical beauty was considered her only significant attribute, as long as she could choose among only three professions: "marriage, mantua-making" (needlework), "and school-keeping," as Margaret had once enumerated them. Even Margaret's beloved Wordsworth fell short on the issue; for him, she quoted ruefully, the ideal woman should not be "Too bright and good / For Human nature's daily food."

Margaret drew on examples from ancient myth, wherein "the idea of female perfection is as fully presented as that of male," to show that women had been accorded greater respect in earlier times. In Egyptian mythology, "Isis is even more powerful than Osiris," and "the Hindoo goddesses reign on the highest peaks of sanctification." In Greek myth, "not only Beauty, Health and the Soul are represented under feminine attributes, but the Muses, the inspirers of all genius," and "Wisdom itself

. . . are feminine." Margaret's dream was to bring the dispirited "individual man" together with the disempowered woman—unite the two sides of the Great Hall's classroom—and create, by merging the best attributes of each, "fully" perfected souls. Then, a nation of *men and women* will for the first time exist, she might have said, amending Waldo Emerson's visionary claim.

Although Providence wasn't Boston, and Margaret felt the difference every day, living and working there bolstered her sense of effectiveness. "I feel increasing trust in mine own good mind," she wrote to her mother. "We will take good care of the children and, one another," adding, "things do not trouble me as they did for I feel within myself the power to aid—to serve." To her Boston student Caroline Sturgis, with whom a friendship was still "intensating" from afar, she wrote even more emphatically: "I grow impatient and domineering—my liberty here will spoil my tact for the primmer timider sphere." Margaret had even read "the most daring passages in [Goethe's] Faust" to a "coterie of Hanna Mores," a group of women devoted to the works of the British moralist and writer on women's education Hannah More, a progressive but hardly open-minded thinker of a previous generation.

At Greene Street that winter, Margaret was finally able to launch a "school for more advanced culture," with the addition of a half-dozen older girls "from eighteen to twenty, intelligent and earnest, attracted by our renown," to the group she had already established. Margaret had sympathized with Bronson Alcott's notion that "those who would reform the world should begin with the beginning of life"—by teaching young children—but she preferred to engage with minds on the cusp of adulthood. "This was just what I wanted," Margaret wrote to Cary, as she had begun to call Caroline Sturgis, at the start of the new year in 1838. The young women were proud to be part of Margaret Fuller's "row"—her favored class. Margaret felt "a happy glow, that many minds are wakened to know the beauty of the life of thought. My own thoughts have been flowing clear and bright as amber." Teaching had brought "the unfolding of powers which lay comparatively dormant in me," as well as in her students.

But she still suffered periods of illness, sometimes feeling for weeks at a time as if "there were no great stock of oil to feed my wick." She was bled by a physician, and when that didn't help she consulted a mesmerist—a blind girl who only afterward confessed to Margaret that she believed she was losing her powers of clairvoyance. The girl had told Margaret to stop reading or she would never recover her health; Margaret had come to a similar conclusion on her own. "It is no longer in my power to write or study much," she wrote to her mother. "I cannot bear it and do not attempt it." The stress of "serving two masters" had become too much. She read and worked for her own purposes only "a little" each day now and attempted to reconcile herself to the possibility that "Heaven, I believe, had no will that I should accomplish any-thing great or beautiful." Instead she took on a class of ten adults in German, six of them men. She needed the income.

Margaret had thought of quitting her job as early as her first weeks at Greene Street, when she wrote to Waldo Emerson, "I *must* leave Providence at the end of another term"; it was not a suitable place for the "citizen of the world" she felt she had become. There was so much she was missing: Transcendental Club meetings, and each season another series of Waldo's Boston lectures. She implored him to schedule a few of them for her school breaks or, failing that, to send her the manuscripts of his lectures "Holiness" and "Heroism." But most of all, she missed all she could have been learning in conversation with trusted—or coveted— friends. "There are noble books but one wants the breath of life sometimes," she wrote to Waldo, "you, unsympathizing, unhelpful, wise good man."

She had written separately to James Clarke and Henry Hedge, asking for accurate information—"all the scandal"—about Goethe's marriage. But propriety kept both men from answering a woman's questions on sexual *im*propriety by letter, whereas they might have spoken to her more freely in person. At moments like this she considered herself "a poor, lonely, '*female*,'" as she signed herself in one letter to Henry Hedge— and she hated that feeling. When she discovered, too late to arrange a visit, that the British celebrity author Anna Jameson, whose books on female sovereigns and Shakespearean heroines Margaret taught in school, had passed through Boston, she was almost inconsolable. Jameson had been an intimate friend of Goethe's daughter-in-law, Margaret learned, making her "the very person in the world who could best aid me."

Margaret wrote Jameson a despairing letter, offering to come to New

York City to meet her before she returned to England. Margaret's schedule would permit travel only on the weekend, however. "You must not get an ugly picture of me because I am a schoolmistress," she fretted. "I am only teaching for a little while." It was a darker, more operatic version of Margaret's early letter of self-introduction to the marquis de Lafayette. "How I wish that I was famous or could paint beautiful pictures and then you would not be willing to go without seeing me," she lamented. "But now—I know not how to interest you . . . Yet I am worthy to know you, and be known by you, and if you could see me you would soon believe it." Her distress over the Goethe biography she had scarcely begun welled up at the thought of this lost opportunity. Margaret was reluctant to describe the full dimensions of the book she planned to write, and she asked Jameson to keep the project a secret, for "precarious health, the pressure of many ties make me fearful of promising what I will do.—I may die soon—you may never more hear my name." Margaret heard nothing in response.

She devised a plan to combat her loneliness: Cary Sturgis would come live with her for a few months of intensive language study. The scheme would save money, since Cary's father would cover half the cost of the rooms they would rent together. But Cary's initial enthusiasm quickly waned, and after weeks of strained correspondence Margaret learned that Cary's father had forbidden his eighteen-year-old daughter to share quarters with her. Margaret's public alliance with the members of the Transcendental Club tarnished her in the eyes of the wealthy China trader, whose daughter's rebellious nature—she'd been expelled from the prim Dorothea Dix's Boston day school several years earlier—was worrisome enough as it was. Waldo Emerson's "American Scholar" address opened a rift in Boston's cultured elite that would only grow wider when he delivered a still more incendiary speech to the graduating class at Harvard Divinity School the following summer, daring to suggest that the young men follow his lead in refusing to preach from the pulpit, that true religion could be found almost anywhere but in church.

When Margaret found out that Captain Sturgis had put a stop to her plan, she was indignant but no longer hurt by what she'd taken to be Cary's indifference. She responded directly to her friend: "As to transcendentalism and the nonsense which is talked by so many about it—I do not know what is meant. For myself I should say that if it is meant that I have an active mind frequently busy with large topics I hope it is so—If it is meant that I am honored by the friendship of such men as Mr Emerson, Mr Ripley, or Mr Alcott, I hope it is so—*But* if it is meant that I cherish any opinions which interfere with domestic duties, cheerful courage and judgement in the practical affairs of life, I challenge any or all in the little world which knows me to prove such deficiency from any acts of mine since I came to woman's estate." Margaret would miss Cary's company, although the younger woman's insistence that their rooms be decorated with "nothing striped diamonded or (above all things) *square*" had both amused and put her off. Captain Sturgis's prohibition only spurred Margaret's efforts to draw Cary further into her circle. She wrote to Waldo Emerson about Cary's talent for poetry, her ardent spirit—she has "the heroic element in her," Margaret believed—and promised to bring her to Concord on a future visit. By letter, the friendship with her former pupil deepened as Margaret began signing herself first with the shorthand "S.M.F.," then "M. F.," and finally, "M."

Despite her brave declaration of faithfulness to "domestic duties" in her letter to Cary, Margaret had had enough. To Waldo she wrote, "I keep on 'fulfilling all my duties' as the technical phrase is except to myself." As her letter to Anna Jameson revealed, having to work as a "schoolmistress" rankled, despite any "unfolding" of dormant powers the job may have brought. To her brothers Arthur and Richard she now wrote frankly of having given up "three precious years at the best period of life" to their education while living at Groton—years that "would have enabled me to make great attainments which now I never may"—followed by "two years incessant teaching" to raise money for their support. She goaded them on to accomplishment—"that I may not remember that time with sadness," that "you may . . . do what I may never be permitted to do."

"There is a beauty in martyrdom," Margaret wrote to Cary, "if one cannot succeed." But she was not ready to sacrifice everything yet. She willed herself to find a way to "devote to writing all the time that I am well and bright," without appearing to desert her responsibilities. Although she had put aside her work on Goethe, she had managed two reviews for the *Western Messenger*, which brought gratifying compliments from Waldo. "Its superior tone its discrimination & its thought," he wrote of her analysis of the Unitarian minister William Ware's historical novel *Letters from Palmyra,* "indicate a golden pen apt for a higher service hereafter." Waldo asked her to bring "a portfolio full of journals letters & poems"—hers and Cary Sturgis's—when she next visited. She did not want to disappoint.

In the same letter to Cary in which she wrote about the attractions of martyrdom, Margaret asserted that her "natural position" was far from that of a saint: instead "it is regal.—Without throne, sceptre, or guards, still a queen!" She made light of the conceit, one she had entertained since girlhood, in a "May-day" ode she composed for the Greene Street children to sing on their outing to the seashore at the end of the spring term in 1838:

> *We are the children of the Spring*
> *Our home is always green*
> *Green be the garland of our King*
> *The livery of our Queen!*

But in Providence she felt like an exiled ruler, forced to employ "those means of suppression and accommodation which I at present hate to my hearts core" in order to converse with even the best minds of the lesser city. She had "gabbled and simpered . . . till there seems no good left in me." If springtime brought any "May-gales" to "blow warm & glad / And charm the heart from pain," as the Greene Street children sang, it was the stiff wind that would drive her to Concord again at the close of school.

By letter, Waldo had turned increasingly confiding—if only about his daily chores. She heard about his pig, his forty-four newly planted pines, his tomatoes and rhubarb, the bugs that "eat up my vines," and Little Waldo, "as handsome as Walden pond at sunrise" at a year and a half. Sequestered in Providence, she missed him most of all her friends, even as the grounds of their friendship remained uncertain. She had resorted to advertising herself: "I am better than most persons *I* see and, I dare say, better than most persons *you* see," she wrote to him while still in her queenly mood. "But perhaps you do not need to see anybody," she teased, tweaking Waldo for his perennial pessimism on the subject of friendship.

He wrote back consolingly—up to a point. "It seems to me that almost all people *descend* somewhat into society," Waldo commiserated. "All association must be a compromise." But "what is worst," he continued distressingly, "the very flower & aroma of the flower of each of the beautiful natures disappears as they approach each other. What a perpetual disappointment is actual society even of the virtuous & gifted." Did Waldo prefer tending his garden to cultivating friendship? He had already written that he favored communing with his own thoughts in private over communicating with others: "persons except they be of commanding excellence will not work on heads as old as mine like thoughts." Waldo Emerson was hardly old—only thirty-five. Still, experience had aged him, with the death of his young first wife seven years before and the sad loss of two beloved brothers to tuberculosis since then. "Persons provoke you to efforts at acquaintance at sympathy which now hit, now miss, but lucky or unlucky exhaust you at last," he temporized. "Thoughts bring their own proper motion with them & communicate it to you not borrow yours."

Still, Waldo's sporadic expansiveness—and Margaret's need—brought a new intensity to the relationship. Once she left for Providence, he began addressing her as "My dear friend" rather than "My dear Miss Fuller" in letters; through the wearying spring of 1838, Margaret progressed from signing herself "Devoutly, if not worthily yours, S. M. Fuller" to the fervent "Always yours, S.M.F." When Cary Sturgis, now nineteen and ready to defy her father, made a visit to Concord that summer, Waldo was grateful to Margaret for bringing them together: "For a hermit I begin to think I know several very fine people." Margaret was one of them, and when the opportunity presented itself, he wanted her close by. At the end of summer, when Margaret confided her hope to leave teaching before winter, Waldo insisted she spend the following year in Concord. "Will you commission me to find you a boudoir," he offered, "or, much better, will you defy my awkwardness & come & sit down in our castle, summon the village before you & find an abode at your leisure? I really hope you mean to come & study here. And to come now." Waldo needed Margaret too, reluctant as he was to partake of her language of passionate friendship.

Finally illness rescued Margaret. By the fall of 1838 she felt exhausted nearly all the time and missed more days of teaching. She sent for her sister, Ellen, to stay with her and then to serve as her substitute for several weeks. Traveling to Boston, Margaret consulted Dr. Walter Channing, Reverend Channing's brother and the most respected doctor to women in Boston. In early November, "I heard with unspeakable pain Dr. Channing's opinion that I must go away." She would not go away to Concord, but to Groton — "to the quiet of home, and the care of my mother." She felt sure of a cure there — "I am by nature energetick and fearless; if I should recover my natural tone of health and spirits, I shall not dread labor nor shrink from meeting a circle of strangers as I do now." Her mother had at last sold the property, and the family needed to vacate the premises by April. "I do not know what we shall do," Margaret had to admit. "But I do not look beyond." It was enough to count on "these three months of peace and seclusion after three years of toil, restraint and perpetual excitement."

At the eleventh hour Margaret found a reason to regret her departure: Charles King Newcomb, the eighteen-year-old son of one of the "coterie of Hanna Mores," "a new young man, very interesting, a character of monastic beauty, a religious love for what is best in Nature and books." Charles had just returned from a year at the Protestant Episcopal Theological Seminary in Virginia; he was one of those men "rushing back into mysticism" — possibly even Catholicism — whom she had envisioned in her Coliseum Club talk. His spiritual quest intrigued her, as did the opportunity to influence his development — attractions that would draw her to other younger men in coming years. They walked in the evening moonlight in the woods above the city; he wrote her letters "full of affection and faith," which she had little time to answer, "for all the little imps of care are round me." Still she urged him, "Write to me, if you will; it gives pleasure."

But "a new young man" was not enough to lure Margaret from the close proximity of enigmatic, "unhelpful, wise" Waldo Emerson. In December, after a tearful parting with her "row" of pupils, who presented her with an "elegantly bound" set of Shakespeare, Margaret was off to the "vestal solitudes" of Groton. "I do not wish to teach again at all," she declared. She knew she might not have her wish, but she expected to devote at least a year to "my own inventions" before attempting once more to effect "my dreams and hopes as to the education of women," if necessary. And: "What hostile or friendly star may not take the ascendant before that time?" For now, making her escape from Providence mattered most of all. She had felt there "always in a false position," teaching when she would rather be writing, gabbling when she wished to converse. Margaret had advised her students that a woman must strive to discover and attain "everything she might be." "Who would be a goody that could be a genius?" she had demanded of Waldo Emerson. It was time for Margaret to answer her own question.

· IV ·

CONCORD, BOSTON,
JAMAICA PLAIN

Caroline Sturgis

Samuel Gray Ward

Anna Barker Ward

Margaret Fuller

Ralph Waldo Emerson

Ellery Channing

Ellen Kilshaw Fuller

"What were we born to do?"

M ARGARET RARELY THOUGHT THE POETRY SHE WROTE —
to express private longings or, at times, rhapsodic joy — was pub-
lishable. The elegy to Waldo Emerson's brother Charles, published in
a Boston newspaper in 1836, had a specific occasion and also a purpose:
to communicate her sympathy to the grieving older writer in the weeks
before their first meeting. But when James Clarke printed several verses
that she'd sent him by letter in his *Western Messenger*, without asking
her permission, she was outraged: "all the value of this utterance is destroyed by a hasty or indiscriminate publicity," she complained. She felt
"profaned" to have these "overflowings of a personal experience" — they
were lines she'd written to comfort herself in the months of crisis after
Timothy Fuller's death — offered up to strangers' eyes. There was nothing "universal" in them that might "appeal to the common heart of man,"
as the works of a true poetic genius like Byron or Goethe would. Fortunately, only her mother had recognized the lines as her work; James at
least had the sense not to print Margaret's name.

Yet when John Sullivan Dwight asked if she'd like to attach her name
to the two verse translations he'd chosen for his anthology *Select Minor
Poems of Goethe and Schiller*, Margaret was happy to be identified, even
though she considered her renderings of Goethe's lyrics into English
"pitiful" and "clumsy" compared to Dwight's. But what name would she
choose? Three years before, her "Lines" on the death of Charles Chauncy

Emerson had appeared with an ambiguous "F" as signature. Now, at Margaret's request, "Eagles and Doves" and "To a Golden Heart, Worn Round His Neck" were listed on the contents page of *Select Minor Poems* as the work of "S. M. Fuller" — concealing, for those who didn't know her, the fact that she was the only female among the contributors to the volume, and signaling to those who *did* that she was one of the boys. Margaret had not graduated from Harvard with them, but here at last she joined the triumvirate of young, disaffected Unitarian ministers, James Clarke, Henry Hedge, and her old friend William Henry Channing, their names printed in full alongside a handful of New England literary men: G. W. (George Wallis) Haven, N. L. (Nathaniel Langdon) Frothingham, and C. P. (Christopher Pearse) Cranch. Here too appeared George Bancroft, who'd earned his doctorate at Göttingen and whose screed against Brutus had prompted Margaret's first anonymous publication five years earlier, before her father's death. Now she was Bancroft's equal in the pages of a landmark volume, the first translation from German in George Ripley's ambitious series Specimens of Foreign Standard Literature.

Perhaps some of the verses she'd submitted to Dwight were clumsy, but these two were not. And even if they weren't her own private "overflowings," the Goethe lyrics expressed poignantly Margaret's twin preoccupations with frustrated ambition and failed love. In the first, a fledgling eagle, wounded in the wing by a "huntsman's dart," loses the "power to soar"; as the young eagle stares longingly into the heavens, "a tear glistens in his haughty eye." A pair of doves befriend the "inly-mourning" bird and remind him that although he cannot fly or hunt, he can still feed on the "superfluous wealth of the wood-bushes," drink from the brook, take pleasure in flowers, trees, and sunset: "the spirit of content / Gives all that we can know of bliss." It was a lesson Margaret would never fully master, but rehearsing the lines surely eased her hungry soul.

"To a Golden Heart" sings a darker tune, but one that must have provided Margaret the solace of fellow feeling as she worked out her translation, still lacking a love to replace her infatuation with George Davis. A spurned lover wears a heart-shaped medallion around his neck, a "Remembrancer of joys long passed away," a gift from his beloved Lili. The poet laments, "Stronger thy chain than that which bound the heart," yet he cannot bring himself to put aside "the prisoner's badge." His lost love binds him, defines him.

Both poems speak a man's feelings; Margaret was, after all, translating Goethe. Was it the masculine voice of these griefs that made her consider them "universal," appealing to the "common heart of *man*," unlike her own "overflowings"? It would take several years for Margaret to move beyond the relative safety of critical writing, to feel certain that her private thoughts *as a woman* had universal appeal, and longer still to bring "Margaret" into her byline. For now, she was gratified to have a place in the anthology and to find her biography of Goethe announced in Dwight's preface: "there is reason to expect, before long, a life of Goethe, from one qualified, in an eminent degree, for such an arduous task."

Home in Groton for the first months of 1839, the last months she would have a home there, Margaret turned her attention to completing her translation of Johann Peter Eckermann's *Conversations with Goethe in the Last Years of His Life*, also advertised by Dwight as "in course of preparation." She had not lived at home since the last years of Timothy Fuller's life, and the stern family patriarch loomed large in her imagination as she walked the grounds each morning, then returned to her papers, "lying in heaps" about her, to work over the words of her adopted father figure. The book amounted to a "monologue" by Goethe, not a true conversation, she observed in her translator's preface. There had been no chance to listen to Timothy reminisce about his life and work in the manner of Goethe's young disciple Eckermann, nor had Margaret been inclined to draw him out, to her regret. Yet she remembered how, even when he was alive, she had always missed her father, a man so full of his own plans for his oldest daughter that he failed to see her clearly. Goethe's words and life example, summarized in her preface, answered her need now: "He knew both what he sought and how to seek it."

Margaret felt relieved to have escaped Providence and the grueling round of classes, and she hardly missed Boston, where "it was all tea and dinner parties, and long conversations and pictures" on her stolen visits over the past two years, she recalled in a letter to James Clarke. But as the April deadline to vacate the Groton homestead neared, reserving time for the translation became increasingly difficult. She spent hours sorting through her father's papers — a "hackneyed moral" might be drawn from them, Margaret decided, as she catalogued the remnants of an ultimately frustrated career. Timothy's bitter withdrawal from public life had been his undoing. Certainly it had brought the family nothing but hardship, compounded now with "the disorders of a house which has lost its head." Her guilty grief for Timothy was beginning to include more rancor than reverence.

Packing, arranging for the rental of a farmhouse in Jamaica Plain that she would share with her mother and brother Richard (five miles from Boston, with land enough to pasture the family cow), playing a few final melodies on the piano her father had bought her—all this brought on headaches and back pain. The piano, which would be sold at auction along with many of Timothy's books and other family belongings, was a relic of that distant time when Margaret had idealized Ellen Kilshaw and imagined for herself a life of feminine accomplishment rewarded by an advantageous marriage. Marriage, she would one day write, "is the natural means of forming a sphere, of taking root on the earth"—how much "more strength" was required "to do this" alone!

Now Margaret refused to give up the task near to hand—her translation—even if it meant dictating to her brother Richard and correcting his pages, a process nearly as laborious as writing them out herself. The work, and the knowledge that it was expected, kept her driving toward completion—"as if an intellectual person ever had a night's rest," she sputtered to Waldo Emerson. On her twenty-ninth birthday, May 23, 1839, she signed her translator's preface at her desk in the new house, Willow Brook, in Jamaica Plain, and sent the manuscript to press, a full volume from the pen of "S. M. Fuller."

Waldo was delighted with her *Conversations*, and with Margaret's preface in particular—"a brilliant statement." The translation was "a beneficent action for which America will long thank you." Most of all, the book gave him confidence that "you can write on Goethe" with "decision and intelligence," and in "good English"; already she had managed, in *Conversations*, to "scatter all the popular nonsense about him."

Margaret had confided in Waldo her worry that she might not be capable of the larger biographical project, and he'd commiserated as he worked to finish his own first book of essays, a more ambitious undertaking than the slim volume *Nature* and one that, like a full biography, so easily "daunts & chills" a writer. Trusting in her powers would help conquer the fear that she might not write a book worthy of her subject:

"self possession is all," he counseled, and "our hero" — Goethe — "shall follow as he may." The knowledge that Waldo Emerson accepted her as a comrade in authorship may have boosted Margaret's confidence as much as his backhanded compliment: "I know that not possibly can you write a bad book a dull page, if only you indulge yourself and take up your work proudly." She had grown up with praise phrased mostly in negatives.

Yet how much could Margaret afford to "indulge" herself? Could she "ransom more time for writing," as she once expressed her ever-present need, than the few months she'd set aside while still in Groton and the stolen moments since the move to Willow Brook? Writing a book was far different from translating one, albeit one with a "brilliant" preface. She promised Waldo she would write a trial chapter of her Goethe biography that summer — "speed the pen," he'd urged — and then threw herself "unremittingly" into several months of "thought and study," knowing she would have to reckon with finances come fall. She'd already begun negotiations with the parents of three former Greene Street School pupils for the girls to board with the Fullers in Jamaica Plain, sharing the rent and paying Margaret to complete their education. Ever since Bronson Alcott had shorted her on wages, Margaret had been careful to set terms precisely and well in advance; in Providence she had instituted the practice of billing by the quarter-hour for private language lessons, so as not to let her instinctive generosity erode her profits.

Taking a ten-day vacation in Bristol, Rhode Island, in August, at the home of an old friend from Miss Prescott's school, Mary Soley DeWolfe, who had married a wealthy descendant of the triangle-trade baron James DeWolfe ("the richest and the worst" of those slave traders, as was commonly known), Margaret was able to revive some of the carefree feelings she enjoyed when her own family's fortunes were more stable. She put aside her foreign language texts and read a biography of Sir Walter Scott that she found in the "ill stocked" library of the mansion house, rode in an open carriage up gently sloping Mount Hope (part of her host's extensive properties) for a view of Narragansett Bay, stretched out to rest on boulders at the seashore, and, with Mary, narrowly escaped a trampling by a charging stallion pastured on the estate — they drew their parasols in self-defense. It was all delightful, but Margaret was fully aware that her friend must see her as "destitute of all she thinks valuable": "beauty, money, fixed station in society." Occupied with matters of dress and household decoration, the teasing yet gracious Mary DeWolfe was "ignorant of my mental compensations"—the satisfaction that Margaret, the only "live wire" in the DeWolfe household that week, took in study and conversation with intellectual companions. Mary, even more than Margaret, was distressed that her guest was "unsustained" and "uncertain as to the future."

Visiting the "fine houses" of the rich "makes my annoyances seem light" compared to the tiresome burdens of wealth, Margaret would eventually conclude. She had come far enough not to wish herself back again; experience had taught her "how much characters require the discipline of difficult circumstances" to develop their full powers. Would she have achieved the little so far to her credit without the spur of necessity? "I am safer," she believed, for "I do not sleep on roses," and a vacation among the rich "will not last long enough to spoil me." She would continue to savor weeks of recuperation from overwork at the homes of her more prosperous friends without compunction, never minding that she could not reciprocate. What troubled her far more than her lack of funds and the uncertainty of her position were the real limits imposed upon her sex, both by external prohibitions on schooling and employment and by the self-restraint that women learned and internalized: "A man's ambition with a woman's heart.—'Tis an accursed lot," she wrote in her journal at summer's end.

In the final weeks of August, Margaret devised a plan to unite the two—her professional ambitions and her concerns on behalf of women. She borrowed the idea from Bronson Alcott, who since losing his Temple School had taken up an itinerant "Ministry of Talking," as he called it, leading conversations for adults on the spiritual topics that had gotten him into trouble in the classroom—and getting paid for it. Margaret determined to try the same with a class of adult women in Boston. Her aim was more practical than spiritual, however: to "ascertain what pursuits are best suited to us in our time and state of society, and how we may make best use of our means for building up the life of thought upon the life of action," as she wrote in a letter to Sophia Ripley, proposing a series of weekly "Conversations" to begin in the fall of 1839 and continue through the spring, if interest remained strong. She asked both Sophia Ripley and Elizabeth Peabody to help her gather a "circle" of women "desirous to answer the great questions. What were we born to do? How shall we do it?" Too often, Margaret observed, thinking perhaps of her mother or the aged women in the Groton cabin, it is only when "their best years are gone by" that women begin to ask these questions—too late to profit from the answers.

Margaret had been asking the "great" questions of *herself* since childhood—"How is it that I seem to be this Margaret Fuller? What does it mean? What shall I do about it?"—struggling "under these limitations of time and space and human nature" to find answers. But in adulthood the scope of her questions had widened to take in all women, as she recognized how much even *her* answers had to do with her sex. In the years since Timothy's death, as she was thrown upon her own devices in a "time and space" inhospitable to a woman of ambition, she could no longer see herself as a proxy oldest son, no longer imagine herself an oarsman in the *Aeneid*, pulling toward victory—nor did she want to. She longed to experience life with her "woman's heart."

Still, her plan was to make the classics—in particular classical myth—the focus of discussion. She wanted other women to feel the impulse to action she'd received from these tales as a child drawn to stories of Greek and Roman vitality rather than to parables of Christian piety and submission. Her passion for Greco-Roman myth had only been heightened through her German studies when she discovered that Goethe and Schiller, whose adulatory poem "The Gods of Greece" she knew well, also viewed Apollo, Jupiter, Venus, and Minerva as exemplars of human virtues, or, as Margaret herself phrased it, "great instincts—or ideas—or facts of the internal constitution separated & personified." As she wrote to Cary Sturgis, "These Greeks no more merged the human in the divine than the divine in the human." In them, the real and the ideal were united, thought and deed fused in the "active soul" Margaret wished to become. "I cannot live without mine own particular star; but my foot is on the earth and I wish to walk over it until my wings be grown." Despite painful seasons of self-doubt or retreat from the workaday world into illness, Margaret reveled in the "majesty of earth": "its roaring sea that dashes against the crag—I love its sounding cataract, its lava rush, its whirlwind, its rivers" as much as the distant, serene "blue sky" of the ideal. "I will use my microscope as well as my telescope."

The radicalism of Margaret's plan would be evident to anyone at the time. Boys read Ovid's *Metamorphoses*, his exuberant accounts in Latin of the lusty Greek gods and goddesses (the best source of these tales before Thomas Bulfinch's English translations, *The Age of Fable,* appeared in 1855). Girls did not. Margaret, with her boy's education and full immersion in German Romantic "mythomania," had stories to tell and lessons to draw from them that few of her adult female contemporaries knew or could access.

More radical still was her intention to promote an open discussion in which all participants could freely "state their doubts and difficulties with hope of gaining aid from the experience or aspirations of others." As with her advanced class at the Greene Street School, Margaret would insist that each woman be "willing to communicate what was in her mind." This was, she wrote elsewhere, "an age of consciousness"—an "era of experiment," of "illumination"—and she was determined that the women of her circle experience the gains that the men of the Transcendental Club fraternity derived from focused group discussion, whether or not their essential subject was woman. She would bring them together "undefended by rouge or candlelight," dispense with the pointless, artificial conventions of feminine parlor chat—"digressing into personalities or commonplaces," in a word, gossip—and require instead a "simple & clear effort for expression."

Some might at first "learn by blundering," but Margaret hoped all the women would eventually discover in themselves the capacity "to question, to define, to state and examine their opinions," to "systemize" their thought and achieve "a precision in which our sex are so deficient." This was the verbal exactitude that Margaret had learned from her lawyer father, which caused many who heard her speak extemporaneously to identify her mind as "masculine"; without it, she knew, most women felt "*inferior*" when it came to entering "the business of life." Even the most rigorous young ladies' academies provided "few inducements to test and classify" information taken in. After receiving a superficial education in a girls' school, many women now lacked even "that practical good sense & mother wisdom & wit which grew up with our grandmothers at the spinning wheel." Margaret's Conversations would provide those needed inducements, and Margaret herself would serve as the model for "application of knowledge" in speech, the all-important first step toward action.

Margaret relied on that "magic about me which draws other spirits," as well as on the practical aid of Sophia Ripley and Elizabeth Peabody, whose historical classes for adult women through the 1830s had set a precedent, to gather her class. Soon twenty-five women had bought ten-dollar tickets for an initial thirteen-week series, a rate of pay about two thirds of Waldo Emerson's take for a similar course of lectures. The high sum signaled both the value Margaret placed on the enterprise and her own refusal to assume an "inferior" position when it came to conducting the "business of life." The class included three Sturgis sisters—Anna, Ellen, and Cary, the older two married to the Hooper brothers Sam and Robert, heirs to a Boston mercantile fortune; Elizabeth Bancroft, the wife of the historian George Bancroft; Mary Jane Quincy, the wife of future Boston mayor Josiah Quincy Jr. and daughter-in-law of Harvard president Josiah Quincy; Margaret's longtime friend Lydia Maria Child; and an assortment of Elizabeth Peabody's friends and former students.

Elizabeth offered her sister Mary's rented room at 1 Chauncy Place, a few blocks east of the Common, for the Wednesday midday sessions. Mary was out during the day, teaching school, although she could join the class after morning lessons. Participants who traveled to Boston from other towns—as Elizabeth did from Salem—could combine Margaret's Conversation with Waldo Emerson's Wednesday-evening lecture. His 1839–40 series on the "Present Age," a paean to the era of experiment that Margaret's Conversations were helping to usher in, began several weeks after Margaret's opening session on November 6, 1839.

Of course many women signed on just to hear Margaret Fuller talk. Waldo Emerson, who'd been treated to her sallies over dinner, in his parlor, and on walks in the Concord woods, considered Margaret's "the most entertaining conversation in America." James Clarke also thought Margaret's verbal powers unequaled: her speech was "finished and true as the most deliberate rhetoric of the pen," but always had "an air of spontaneity which made it seem the grace of the moment,—the result of some organic provision that made finished sentences as natural to her as blundering and hesitation are to most of us."

If she'd been a man, Margaret might have become a popular lecturer, perhaps even more successful than Waldo, who persisted in reading his essays from manuscript pages, using the lecture hall as a workroom for his books rather than a performance space. But, bold as she was as a thinker and writer, Margaret never considered mounting the podium, despite her extraordinary capacity for extemporaneous speech. In 1839, only a few fervent abolitionist women dared to cross that barrier, stirring up outrage wherever they held forth, as much for speaking in public as for their reformist views. Margaret still clung to the few vestiges of Boston prestige that remained to her, and she continued to emulate an Old World gentility, the elegance she had admired in Ellen Kilshaw and refined under Eliza Farrar's direction. Situating her Conversations in a private household—even a Boston schoolteacher's boarding house—and offering them to a handpicked audience underscored her belief that conversation was an art as well as an impetus to action, and implied that hers was an elite company, such as Madame de Staël's salon or London's Blue Stocking Club. Nevertheless, her sessions soon gained the reputation of "a kind of infidel association," an appraisal that was at least half accurate: the Conversations were more of a club than a class.

For Margaret did not want to be listened to; she "dreaded" the feeling of being on "display," like "a paid Corinne," the heroine of a novel by de Staël who entertained parlor audiences as an *improvisatrice*, holding forth on the splendors of Italian art. She wanted to serve as the "nucleus of conversation," only "*one* to give her own best thoughts on any subject that was named, as a means of calling out the thoughts of others." If the group was a circle, she would be "its moving spring." She laid out her plan to the assembled women on that first Wednesday in November and waited for the second meeting, she wrote to Waldo Emerson, for "the real trial of whether they will talk themselves."

She needn't have worried. As Margaret launched into a description of Greek mythology as "playful as well as deep" and remarked on the "joyous life" of the Greeks themselves—"we sometimes could not but envy them submerged as we are in analysis & sentiment"—Mary Jane Quincy grew alarmed. Mrs. Quincy spoke with "wonder & some horror at the thought of *Christians* enjoying *Heathen Greeks*" and expressed the opinion that Greek myths were "gross & harmful superstitions." Margaret was forced to clarify: "She had no desire to go *back*," but she refused to "look upon the expression of a great nation's intellect as a series of idle fancies." Greek culture had achieved maturity, whereas "Christian cultivation was *in its infancy*"—evidently an unfamiliar notion to Mary Jane Quincy, but one that seemed to convince. These "fables & forms of Gods," Margaret continued, represented the "universal sentiments of religion—aspiration—intellectual action of a people whose political & aesthetic life had become immortal." Margaret urged the class to approach Greek culture "with respect—& distrust our own contempt of it."

From then on, Margaret encountered little resistance. She steered the group toward talk of Apollo, "the embodiment of the element of genius," and outlined the "Greek idea" of the human mind, "its characteristics, its actions, its destiny." Near the end of the two-hour period, she posed questions, among them "how far the possession of genius was compatible with—or assistant to happiness & virtue." As one woman wrote afterward, "though these great questions were not *settled* it was useful to discuss them." The plan was taking effect.

The Conversations continued in succeeding weeks with Venus—discussed "not as the Goddess of Love but as the Goddess of Beauty"—and then the fable of Cupid and Psyche, which "Miss Fuller told . . . with a grace & beauty that was of itself an exquisite delight." Here was one of Ovid's more risqué tales, with deep resonance for women: beauty, love, sex, and marriage all come into question in the story of Venus's jealousy of Psyche, the most beautiful of three sisters, and Venus's efforts to interfere with her son Cupid's love for the mortal girl. Unmarried despite her beauty, Psyche is offered up to an invisible lover—a monster, she is told, whom she must never look at when he visits her at night in the palace where she is held captive. The unseen lover, whom Psyche comes to care for and accept as her husband, is the handsome Cupid, of course, and when Psyche, taunted by her jealous sisters who envy her the palace, opens her eyes one night and discovers the truth, Cupid and Psyche must separate. The angry Venus subjects Psyche to trials—a journey to the underworld, a box full of temptations—but Cupid returns to defy his mother and take Psyche as his wife, making her immortal.

Margaret played the story several ways for her audience, rendering it first as a proto-Christian fable. The myth of Cupid and Psyche, Margaret explained, "set forth the universal fact of the trial of the soul on earth, its purification by means of the sufferings its own mistakes bring upon it, & its final redemption & immortality." Then questions came from the class. "Why was it wrong in Psyche to wish to see & know her husband? Do we not wish to understand our happiness? . . . Is the *desire* of knowledge *sin?*" Then, "What do her sisters represent?" and what of "Venus' enmity"? And how much analysis "was inevitable, how much was desirable, what was excessive," in dealings with loved ones?

Now Margaret suggested a Romantic's version of the tale, as if it were a story line from a novel of Goethe about the unfolding of the soul: the myth traced Psyche's progress from "credulous simplicity," she suggested, to understanding and, finally, transcendence. Psyche's first "innocent" love failed its test, leading her on to further earthly trials and at last a "divine," enduring love founded on knowledge gained through experience. Still, one woman recorded later, "Many questions were started that were not answered." Just what Margaret hoped for: another success in provocation.

In later sessions, when discussion stalled or became diffuse, Margaret required papers on the topic, as when Maria Child proposed, on the Wednesday assigned to Minerva, goddess of wisdom, that "wisdom was the union of the affections & understanding." So many women argued that "the principle of Beauty" should be added to the definition that Margaret halted the conversation and declared, "We should never get along till we had defined Beauty." The earlier class on Venus as the embodiment of beauty had not sufficed; Margaret asked each woman to give her own definition on the spot. Caroline Sturgis answered that beauty was "the *attractive* power—the *central* unifying power." Marianne Jackson, a former student of Elizabeth Peabody and daughter of Judge Charles Jackson, said it was "*the Infinite apprehended*," and Anna Shaw, herself a noted beauty, replied that "it was the *Infinite revealed in the finite*." Margaret objected: Truth or love could be defined the same way. How was beauty different? Then Sophia Ripley suggested that beauty "was the *aspect of the all*. It was the *mode* in which truth appeared." In the end, "the conversation was left unfinished & deferred to the next time—each was asked to bring a written definition of Beauty."

The result was twenty essays that Margaret considered "rather little poems about Beauty (& every one good) than definitions of Beauty." As she wrote to Waldo Emerson, the women "kept clinging to details." The exercise inspired a new tack, a session devoted to "seeking out some sound principles of criticism" so the women could learn to build logical arguments in their essays. Conversation drifted to the difference between "imagination" and "fancy." "We found ourselves so vague in the use of these words," one woman recorded in her diary, that again Margaret assigned a paper. She read these aloud in the following session, commented on them, and then required "*all* of us" to comment as well. Increasingly now, Margaret set aside mythology for direct confrontation of the "great questions." The "value of suffering to the intellectual as well as the moral character" was debated in the tenth meeting, and later, "what is inspiration?" By the close of the first thirteen sessions in midwinter, no one wanted the class to end; a second series began immediately. "Woman" was on the agenda.

But how to speak of "woman"? Three sessions barely opened the subject. The conversation itself exposed a seemingly intractable conflict. Some class members tried to articulate the essential qualities of an "ideal" woman; others argued that woman could be known only by comparison to man—either superior or inferior, depending on the quality under examination. Margaret raised the question "what was the distinction of feminine & masculine when applied to character & mind"?

Ellen Hooper thought "women were instinctive—they had spontaneously what men have by study reflection & induction." Margaret took this as the cue to state her own views. Man and woman, she asserted, "had each every faculty & element of mind—but . . . they were combined in different proportions." Ellen pressed harder, asking if "there was any quality in the masculine or in the feminine mind that did not belong to the other." Margaret said no: there were no capabilities belonging exclusively to either man or woman. Perhaps Margaret herself was not aware of how bold her statement was. Had she been present at the first meeting of the Transcendental Club three years before, when Waldo Emerson complained to the six males present that even the best thinkers of the day were hobbled by a "*feminine* or receptive" frame of mind rather than a "masculine or creative" one, what might she have said? But of course she had not been invited.

Within her own circle she grew passionate: she wished to hear no more talk of "repressing or subduing faculties because they were not fit for women to cultivate. She desired that whatever faculty we felt to be moving within us, *that* we should consider a principle of our perfection, & cultivate it accordingly.—& not excuse ourselves from any duty on the ground that we had not the intellectual powers for it; that it was not for women to do." Margaret returned to the topic of wisdom, a capacity that women and men shared equally, she argued—"something higher than *prudence*" and "combining always" with "the idea of execution." Wisdom enabled action, for both women and men.

But what of woman's "want of isolation," someone asked, her duties to family that kept her in a daily crush of people, always answering to their demands—and what of the "physical inconveniences" that prevented her from taking up certain occupations? Margaret was firm: "Nothing I hate to hear of so much as *woman's lot*." She wished never to hear the word "*lot*" again. Why was there this "universal lamentation"? A woman's "youth"—even when occupied with children and household duties—"ought not to be mourned." Another way must be found. Still, Margaret allowed for differences in style, if not in quality or caliber, of intelligence in men and women: "Is not man's intellect the fire caught from heaven—woman's the flower called forth from earth by the ray?" She assigned more papers, this time "upon the intellectual differences between men & women."

The results were striking: carefully composed, well-reasoned arguments that showed the progress the women had made since their earlier "poems" to beauty. Margaret read aloud a paper by Sally Gardner, a friend of Elizabeth Peabody's who traveled from suburban Newton on Wednesdays for the class:

> Let men & women be gentle & firm; brave & tender; instinctive but confirming their instincts by reason . . . Scattered up & down in the world's history there are women who have set aside the accidents of position, & left their mark on the ages . . . They prove that reflection & the power of concentration which predominate in men exist in women, and only require a more earnest culture . . . How do we know that in the possible future woman's intellect may not manifest itself in forms beautiful as poetry & art, permanent as empires, all emanating from her home—created out of it, from her relations as daughter, sister, wife, & mother? Out of these relations may yet rise a beauty & a power which shall bless & heal the nations. Then the progress of the race will be harmonious & universal . . . [and] "Men shall learn war no more."

The possible future: a changed world, with women as powerful as men, resulting in peace among nations. This was the sort of vision Margaret had hoped her class might contemplate, before it was too late for them to reach for it. And there was something more. Waldo Emerson guessed that it was Margaret's "passionate wish for equal companions" that motivated her to begin the Conversations. She was finding them at last among these women. "There I have real society," she wrote of "my class in Boston" to a friend in Providence, "which I have not before looked for out of the pale of intimacy."

II

"The gospel of Transcendentalism"

JAMES CLARKE WAS MARRIED. HE HADN'T EVEN TOLD MAR-
garet about his engagement to Anna Huidekoper, the second daughter
of a wealthy Dutch land agent, Harm Jan Huidekoper, who had helped
to found a Unitarian church near his home in Meadville, Pennsylvania, a
stopping-off point for Clarke on his travels between Louisville and Boston. "It is true I was hurt to hear the news of circumstances so important
to you from a stranger," Margaret admitted to James when she finally felt
up to writing him again. She did not let him know just how much.

Maybe James had hoped to spare himself a direct reaction from the
"cousin" in whom he had confided all his previous romantic involve-
ments—in too great detail, and not always to good result. Whatever his
reasons, Margaret felt cast aside, at the very least as the confessor to her
age mate, the openhearted friend who had always seemed so much the
younger of the two. During her months of writing and recovery at Groton in the early winter of 1839, after she'd left the Greene Street School
and before she learned of James's wedding plans, she'd written asking
him to send his journals or "any other record you may have kept of you[r]
life" for her perusal; she "would like to live with you" for a time. As Margaret worked on her biography of Goethe, searching out the important
influences on his life, she may have featured herself as the duchess of
Weimar to Clarke's Goethe: in Duchess Amelia's "wise mind," Margaret
wrote, her literary hero "found that practical sagacity, large knowledge

of things as they are, active force, and genial feeling, which he had never before seen combined" in a woman.

But Margaret had no court to which she could lure James, and he had moved ahead and away from her, first in claiming a profession and now in establishing a domestic life. She promised James, equivocally, that "I shall love your Elect, if I can, and shall wish to win her regard"; she was more intent on preserving relations with James — "in no event need either of us be disturbed" — than on befriending his bride. She would not, this time, attempt to enter into his feelings for his beloved; the "finest qualities rarely display themselves except to the eye of love," she snipped. But Margaret did not begrudge James his chance to "have in the truest sense a home, a home where the thoughts may rest, and the affections be called out, and the noblest aspirations be quickened. Such a home, and work suited to the capacity are all that the best human beings should claim." When would Margaret herself achieve so happy a balance of love and work?

In truth, though, James felt he'd failed in his mission to the West. He was ready to give up his post at Louisville where his liberal message had won few converts, and that was one reason he'd married the younger dark-haired Anna, whose family fortune would ease him into a new way of life. Indeed, the Huidekopers held a kind of court in Meadville, presiding over one of the earliest Unitarian congregations to thrive outside New England. With the exception of Anna, the Huidekoper sons and daughters intermarried with other prosperous Meadville families, establishing an enclave of genteel enlightenment at the outer limits of the civilized Northeast, forty miles from the shores of Lake Erie. Soon the newlyweds were settled in Meadville themselves, awaiting the birth of a first child, with James poised for a return to Boston whenever the chance for a pulpit might arise.

James Clarke's one clear success in the West had been his role in founding and editing the *Western Messenger*, which some argued was misnamed, considering that the bulk of the articles were penned by easterners, Margaret among them. The venture owed its easy acceptance by western readers to what James had recognized early on as his constituents' openness to "all sorts of religious supernaturalism" — Transcendentalism — "only not under that name," as well as to their relative innocence of the turf wars that raged in the East over Trinitarianism,

Unitarianism, and outright irreligion. There "is no public opinion here," he'd written to Margaret: "You are throwing your ideas to help form one." But his magazine had siphoned off energy that might have led to the creation of a similar publication based in Boston. Once the pet idea of Henry Hedge, who had hoped to "enlist all the Germano-philosophico-literary talent in the country" for his "journal of spirit, not philosophy," it never saw the light of day. Now, with James Clarke's return to the East and the *Messenger's* demise imminent without his involvement, the Transcendental Club members renewed their discussions of beginning a quarterly journal that would "speak truth without fear or favor to all who desire to hear it." The project had become more urgent with each of Waldo Emerson's incendiary Harvard addresses—to the Phi Beta Kappa Society in 1837 and the Divinity School in 1838—as the former minister locked horns with the Unitarian "Pope," Andrews Norton, over Transcendentalist notions that, no matter how eloquently expressed, struck not just Norton but many strait-laced Bostonians as "dreamy, mystical, crazy, and infideleterious to religion."

The stakes were higher than the often bombastic war of words implied. Massachusetts law still provided for the imprisonment of criminal "blasphemers." The same year Waldo Emerson exhorted the Divinity School graduating class to "obey thyself," to trust "intuition" over "second hand" representations of God by worn-out churchmen, and argued that religion should become "one thing with Science, with Beauty, and with Joy," the Universalist preacher Abner Kneeland had spent sixty days in a Boston jail for the crime of publishing a letter in his own newspaper, the *Boston Investigator,* declaring God to be "nature itself," and any other deity to be "nothing more than a chimera." Kneeland's paper had frightened Boston with its promiscuous advocacy of controversial causes, from a woman's right to keep her own bank account to interracial marriage, divorce, and birth control: he had been locked up for his politics as much as his pantheism. This was to be the last such incarceration in the state's history, but no one knew that at the time. In scarcely over a decade there would be arrests of prominent Bostonians for their active opposition to the fugitive slave law; Boston would never resolve the contradiction on which it was founded, as both refuge for dissenters and new dominion for the righteous.

Waldo's penalty for publicly denouncing "the famine of our churches" wasn't prison but banishment from Harvard, where he would not be invited to speak again for thirty years. His friends watched as he coolly accepted the derision of Norton, who deemed his second speech an "incoherent rhapsody" and an "insult to religion," and others who accused him of the "foulest atheism." "As long as all that is said is said against me," Waldo confided in his journal, "I feel a certain sublime assurance of success." But success at what? Nothing less than preaching a new secular gospel, available to every man (Waldo still thought primarily in the masculine) by way of private inner communion with the divine: "They call it Christianity. I call it consciousness."

Waldo Emerson didn't need a platform or professorship at Harvard; he was an increasingly popular lecturer, and his second book, the collection of essays he worked over painstakingly when not on the lyceum circuit, was taking shape with every certainty of publication and brisk sales. But what of the others in the Transcendental Club who had pulpits to maintain — or resign, as some would choose to do, following Emerson's example — and, more important, ideas of their own to express? "I begin to be proud of my contemporaries," he had written to Margaret at the height of the Divinity School controversy, as their expressions of support reached him through the flurry of correspondence, "some of it emphatic & remarkable, love & wrath & catechism."

"If utterance is denied, the thought lies like a burden on the man," Waldo had told the assembled Divinity School graduates — and it was true. His partisans were restless to defend him and to articulate their own views. Yet there was no longer any place for their writings in the pages of Boston journals that fell under the purview of Norton and his cronies. Elizabeth Peabody, who in 1834 had been the first to experience Norton's censorious wrath when he rejected an essay originally slated for publication in his *Christian Examiner* because of her use of the term "Transcendentalism," had started a bimonthly publication in Salem after dissolving her teaching partnership with Alcott in 1836. The *Family School*, which aimed to bring a Transcendental spirituality into the home by way of children's stories, advice to parents ("Never forget that you have the care of an intelligent soul"), book reviews, and poetry by James Clarke and the eminent painter Washington Allston, had lasted only two issues. Something more ambitious was needed, Transcendental Club members believed, along the lines of the *North American Review*, the only serious cultural journal of the day with a national distribution, but from which Waldo Emerson heard only "the snore of the muses."

At two separate meetings of the Transcendental Club in September 1839, "the subject of a Journal designed as the organ of views more in accordance with the Soul" was raised. Theodore Parker, in attendance at the second, recorded afterward in his diary, "There will be a new journal I doubt not. Emerson Miss Fuller & Hedge alike are confident to the birth." Bronson Alcott suggested a title, "The Dial," taken from his daily register of the activities and sayings of his young daughters, Anna and Louisa. But Henry Hedge drew back from the enterprise, nervous about the extremism he sensed in Alcott, who argued that the new journal's contributors must have "entire freedom" to express "the purest thoughts and tastes." Alcott envisioned a "Dial" that would be unabashed in its promotion of the ethereal—it would be the oracle through which "we of the sublunary world are to be informed of the time of day in the transcendental regions."

Although Margaret had her differences with Bronson Alcott, she took his side on the matter of absolute freedom for the journal: "A perfectly free organ is to be offered for the expression of individual thought and character," she wrote to her friend William Henry Channing. Her tastes were not so otherworldly as her one-time teaching partner's, and "purity"—Alcott's increasingly peculiar asceticism—was not her concern. She simply argued that there should be neither a "spirit of dogmatism nor of compromise." *The Dial* would not be so much an opinion leader as a means of "stimulating" readers "to think more deeply and more nobly by letting them see how some minds"—those of *The Dial*'s writers—"are kept alive by a wise self-trust."

Waldo Emerson claimed to be too busy for the job of editor, and Bronson Alcott lacked the skills. At a hastily arranged meeting in Concord in late October—an "afternoon and evening of high talk" among Margaret, Waldo, and Bronson—the trio optimistically surveyed *The Dial*'s prospects. Subscribers would sign on; George Ripley, who agreed to handle the business side, had bargained with the publishers Weeks & Jordan to offer individual copies for sale in bookstores. Receipts would trickle, if not pour, in.

Margaret had the most to gain from the editorship. Emerson knew of her troubled finances and promised her a substantial portion of the proceeds. But when she volunteered that day in Concord and Emerson seconded her self-nomination, Margaret was looking for more than additional income, which she knew would not be immediately forthcoming. As she once complained to William Channing, commiserating with his own sense of "unemployed force": "I never, never in life have had the happy feeling of really doing anything." Here was her chance "really to feel the glow of action." The job became hers the week of her first Boston Conversation, and soon after, she began soliciting contributions for a first issue to appear in the spring. Writing again to Channing on New Year's Day, Margaret recalled a time when "you prophecied [*sic*] a new literature; shall it dawn on 1840."

It was entirely fitting that the title of the new journal derived from a record of two young girls' daily lives — their "unfolding" souls. *The Dial*, under the editorship of the leader of the Conversations, was a different publication than it would have been under the direction of Henry Hedge, James Clarke, or Waldo Emerson, despite his readiness to welcome certain women into the Transcendental Club cohort. Margaret's own soul would unfold in its pages.

She worried at first that *The Dial*'s chief supporters — those who "wish it to be, but do not wish to be in any way personally responsible for it," as Waldo had quipped — would be "looking for the gospel of Transcendentalism" in the publication, an agenda she had little capability or interest to follow. As she admitted to William Channing, who had lately come to replace his Harvard Divinity School friend James Clarke as Margaret's epistolary confidant, "My position as a woman, and the many private duties which have filled my life, have prevented my thinking deeply on several of the great subjects which these friends have at heart." It wasn't an excuse, it was an explanation: she had not been to divinity school, her gender had confined her to a more "private" life than theirs; absorbed as she was at times with matters of the spirit, Margaret simply didn't care about the future of organized religion as much as George Ripley, Theodore Parker, and Henry Hedge did. William Channing, who'd spent several years after graduation from the Divinity School ranging from Boston to Rome to New York City and now was settled as a Unitarian minister in Cincinnati with his wife and young child, shared her indifference to doctrinal argument, if for a different reason. The lanky, dark-haired nephew of the great Reverend William Ellery Channing, father-less since infancy and reared under the wing of his eminent uncle, also wished to take action in the world, to aid the urban poor.

Of course Margaret sympathized with this "small minority"—the "Transcendental party," she called them—who were the first "since the Revolution" to experience a "violent reaction" against the established "mode of culture," recognizing a half-century after the birth of American democracy that "political freedom does not necessarily produce liberality of mind, nor freedom in church institutions." New England was finally "old enough," Margaret understood, and "some there have leisure enough," she wrote to William in Cincinnati, to look around and decry the "vulgarity of a commercial aristocracy," to "quarrel with all that is, because it is not spiritual enough." She was troubled, however, that no motivating principle had emerged from the group other than a habitual negativism, as if it were "the duty of every good man . . . to utter a protest against what is done amiss." She would aid "these men" in *The Dial* by "enabling them to express their thoughts, whether I coincide with them or not." As with the Conversations, Margaret was most interested in promoting a practical, or "true utilitarian," philosophy, which she hoped to accomplish by providing a vibrant literature to "combat" the "sluggish-ness, or worldliness" of so many who were "more anxious to get a living than to live mentally and morally."

Margaret felt instinctively that "the public wants something positive." *The Dial*'s readers would respond to a "noble and full Yea"; and she believed she could deliver it, for "hearts beat so high, they must be full of something, and here is a way to breathe it out quite freely." More than any others in the Transcendentalist band—for she *was* one of them, though not one of "these men"—Margaret saw aesthetic culture as a means of personal transformation, even transcendence. This was her gospel. At first, the "something positive" she would offer up was fundamentally a journal of the arts that would speak on a high plane to those with sophisticated tastes, and educate others to an understanding and appreciation of the life-affirming, soul-uplifting aspects of music, art, and literature—the "everlasting yes" that "breathes from the life, from the work of the artist," as she would write in a *Dial* essay on the great composers.

Margaret may have felt alone with this plan within the Transcendentalist circle, but others outside the group saw the same need. The thirty-five-year-old author of *Twice-Told Tales,* Nathaniel Hawthorne, thought it was "intolerable that there should not be a single belles-lettres journal in New England." When Margaret met him at a party in Boston shortly after assuming editorship of *The Dial,* it was on music and sculpture that she held forth; the arrival in Boston of the German pianist Ludwig Rackemann and a show at the Boston Athenaeum gallery, the city's prime exhibition space, were her latest preoccupations. Hawthorne, who'd attended the party with Sophia Peabody, to whom he was secretly engaged, was as shy as he was handsome, and may have said nothing in return. Two months later, with Sophia out of town, he begged off an invitation to a party hosted by George Bancroft at which Margaret would be present, preferring to avoid the company of "literary lions and lionesses" without the diminutive yet sociable Sophia "in the front of the battle." But on this evening Sophia, an artist who, like Margaret, suffered from migraines, reported that the couple had "feasted" on quite "another species of fare" than the "Greek roses and oranges" served to the guests: Margaret spoke "like a sybil on the tripod" — one of the maidens at Delphi who seated themselves above a cleft in the Sibylline Rock to relay oracular messages from the deeps.

Margaret also had Waldo Emerson on her side, holding her to what became their shared mission of presenting a *Dial* "measuring no hours but those of sunshine." Waldo was no outsider with the Transcendentalists, but his recent trials had given him an aversion to conflict. And with his resignation from the pulpit and his public advocacy of a personally derived, "conscious" rather than "Christian" spirituality, he had moved more than "*a little beyond*" (a phrase by which a skeptic had dismissed the whole of Transcendentalism) the sectarian battles that occupied his younger friends in the ministry.

Initially Waldo promised Margaret only that he would "gladly contribute of my own ink" to help fill up "the book," as he referred to the first issue. While he'd refused the work of readying articles for the printer, Waldo cheered her on with extravagant praise in her task of recruiting other writers: "your labors shall introduce a new Age . . . & we shall think what you think." As Margaret's Conversations took up more of her time through the winter and she suggested delaying *The Dial*'s first issue until the fall of 1840, Waldo wrote Margaret of his dismay that "this flowing river of your speech is to sweep away so far the fine castle you began to build." Ultimately they compromised on a July start, and in late April, with her second session of Conversations drawing to a close and her thirtieth birthday just a few weeks off, Margaret started to craft an introductory essay laying out the journal's intentions to its readers.

But her nerves began to show. The essay Margaret drafted has not survived, but Waldo's letter of advice remains: she was too defensive, dwelled too long on *The Dial*'s merits in comparison to other publications. "We have nothing to do," Waldo argued, "with the old drowsy Public" that cares for such magazines. *The Dial*—"our bold Bible for The Young America"—will have "a public of its own," he felt sure, "a new-born class." She would do better to emphasize the journal's "Universal aims" and omit any "preparation for defence & anticipation of enemies": "Don't cry before you are hurt."

Margaret had already shown her introduction to George Ripley, she told Waldo, and "those parts you thought too fierce," Ripley "thought not sufficiently so." She despaired of finding "the golden mean between you." The criticism stung. "Every body finds fault with me just now, some in one way, some in another," she confided in her journal. Would "these gentlemen . . . lose faith" in her abilities? She would not "take for final what they say," she told herself. "I will write well yet; but never, I think, so well as I talk," she worried. "My voice excites me; my pen never." In the end, Waldo drafted his own version, speaking for all three as "The Editors to the Reader." Margaret accepted the piece, worn out from already having composed nearly a third of the entries in the issue herself. Too many of the Transcendental Club coterie were waiting to see which way the critical winds would blow before offering their work to the fledgling publication.

In his introduction, Waldo took up Margaret's theme of a second American "revolution," with "no badge, no creed, no name," yet "in every form a protest . . . and a search for principles." *The Dial* would take its place above the fray, to be heard as "one cheerful rational voice amidst the din of mourners and polemics." Its authors, for the most part, were not "practised writers," and the editors had filled the pages by rifling through "the portfolios which friendship has opened to us." Still, he concluded, from "the beautiful recesses of private thought . . . from the manuscripts of young poets; and from the records of youthful taste commenting on old works of art; we hope to draw thoughts and feelings, which being alive can impart life."

The lead article in the first issue was Margaret's "A Short Essay on Critics," announcing by way of its placement *The Dial*'s allegiance to the arts. Arguing for the establishment of a "standard of criticism," Margaret expanded on ideas that she'd tried out in her Conversation session on the same topic to produce a landmark essay for its time — her pen had not failed her. Yet Waldo, who praised Margaret's "power & skill" and her "serene" tone, noted a peculiarity. He wondered, was Margaret "designedly concealing the authorship"? Why hide behind "the writer" and "*he*" rather than employ the first person "*I*" — and *she*?

In the essay, Margaret wrote of the need to discover "the laws of criticism as a science, to settle its conditions as an art." The best criticism should be more than "mere . . . impressions" or reflexive thoughts "got up to order by the literary hack writer, for the literary mart." Critics must engage in "conscientious research" and make a practice of "going out of themselves to seek the motive, to trace the law of another nature" — to identify the distinctive gifts of the artist whose work was under consideration and the circumstances that inspired creation. In the young American "literary mart," Margaret's call for standards was unprecedented, a signal of *The Dial*'s high ambitions.

But when it came to gendered nouns and pronouns, Margaret was indeed in a bind. She cited the common misconception that "critics are poets cut down" and then refuted it: "in truth, they are men with the poetical temperament to apprehend, with the philosophical tendency to investigate." And, in truth, virtually all the critics Margaret could think of, except herself, *were* men. How could she generalize accurately beyond her own limited experience without using the masculine noun and pronoun? The problem was deeper than one of conventional usage. Not only the critics, but most of the writers, musicians, and artists she admired or had written about so far were men too. The critic, she wrote, is "the younger brother of genius" and "should be not merely a poet, not merely a philosopher, not merely an observer, but tempered of all three . . . He must have as good an eye and as fine a sense . . . He will teach us to love wisely what before we loved well."

Perhaps Waldo was right: she *did* want to be taken for a male writer — or didn't mind, for now, if she was. Margaret signed "A Short Essay on Critics" simply "F," in accordance with the single-initial policy she adopted for all contributors to the issue. Given her choice of words — "In books, in reviews," she had written, "we wish to meet thinking men" — readers would likely assume that "F" too was a "thinking" man. And by Margaret's own standards that might have been for the best. "True manliness," she wrote in the essay — a combination of "firmness in his own position" and the "power of appreciating the position of others" — "alone can make the critic our companion and friend."

Could a woman writer, a female critic, be manly? Margaret had argued to the women in her Conversation class that there was no "quality in the masculine or feminine mind that did not belong to the other." But it was one thing to hold forth on female equality in front of a group of sympathetic women, and another to take that line as the lone woman assuming leadership of "these men" — the Transcendental revolutionaries — by editing their journal. It was easier to fall back into the old habit of thinking of herself as *intellectually* male, to imagine herself into a man's role on life's stage. When Henry Hedge wrote to say he couldn't spare the time to provide copy for the first issue because of his low minister's wage and the burdens of raising a family, she replied, "I know you are plagued and it is hard to write, just so is it with me, for I also am a father." Margaret saw herself as father to her younger siblings and father to *The Dial*. She invited Hedge to "write, my friend, write" and "become a godfather" to the new publication.

Yet there were hints of a more expansive sensibility in this essay. "Nature is ever various, ever new, and so should be her daughters, art and literature." Art, literature, and all of nature were feminine. The "true manliness" she endorsed was not simply a matter of the critic's "firmness in his own position," but was balanced by a more conventionally feminine sympathy for "the position of others" and resulted in companionship with readers. Margaret's "true man" was a more complicated figure than Waldo Emerson's masculine ideal, the "self-reliant" loner. Later in the issue, in a lengthy review of an exhibition of Washington Allston's paintings, Margaret took Waldo's advice and wrote in the first person, in journal form. The result was an essay that was as "alive" as Waldo's introduction had promised *The Dial*'s writing would be: Margaret transferred her vibrant conversation to the page, giving a frank assessment of each painting (some were failures, in her estimation) and sympathizing with Allston's predicament as a gifted artist "in an unpoetical society" like Boston. She met her own high standards for criticism while addressing readers in an intimate, personal voice.

"When I look at my papers," she admitted to Waldo, "I feel as if I had never had a thought worthy the attention of any but myself, and some fond friend." Yet conversation persuaded her of the value of her ideas: "on talking to people I find I tell them what they did not know" and "my confidence returns." She also realized that conversation forced her to "adapt myself" to a particular audience; sensing firsthand either comprehension or a lack of it, she could tailor her talk to satisfy. When she wrote, it was "into another world"—the far-off land of the writers she thought of as her peers, the European intellectuals who *did* know what Margaret knew. She still hoped to accomplish "something worthily that belonged to the country where I was born," she confided in William Channing, yet "how much those of us who have been much formed by the European mind have to unlearn and lay aside if we would act here." *The Dial* gave her the opportunity to unify her gifts—her conversational style, her erudition, her bold ideas—and write in a new way to that "new-born" audience, "The Young America," as it was called into being by the publication itself.

The rest of the "book" conveyed as intimate and confiding a tone as Margaret's Washington Allston review, particularly to those who knew the writers. "We shall write constantly to our friends in print now," Margaret had announced to William Channing as she gathered material for the issue, a task that all too often required her to "urge on the laggards, and scold the lukewarm," she complained. But those friends made up "a large and brilliant circle." In this first issue she published, at Waldo's urging, a short essay and poem by his new Concord friend Henry David Thoreau, the young man he liked to call "my protestor" for his refusal to take up any profession for which his Harvard degree qualified him. She included essays by "party"-liners John Sullivan Dwight and Theodore Parker, "The Religion of Beauty" and "The Divine Spirit in Nature, and in the Soul," which stressed the aesthetic dimension of spiritual life. Margaret also coaxed Dwight, an accomplished flautist, to write a roundup review, "The Concerts of the Past Winter," covering performances of

Messiah and *The Creation* at the Handel and Haydn Society's new Melodeon theater on Washington Street, and Rackemann's recitals of Chopin and Liszt. It was the beginning of Dwight's career as a music critic, which would ultimately replace his profession as minister.

The strongest statement of Transcendentalist "revolution" was Waldo Emerson's poem "The Problem." A retelling in verse of his renunciation of the ministry, it was also one of his first poems to appear in print:

> *I like a church, I like a cowl,*
> *I love a prophet of the soul . . .*
> *Yet not for all his faith can see*
> *Would I that cowled churchman be.*

Perhaps less evident to outsiders because of the single-initial bylines was another message that carried strongly in Margaret's selection of *The Dial*'s poetry: a third of it was written by women. Margaret's former student Ellen Hooper, James Clarke's sister, Sarah, and Waldo Emerson's first wife, Ellen, whose writings Waldo had cherished through the years since her death in 1831, were all represented. Margaret provided several of her own verses, having gained confidence in their quality since James surprised her with publication only a year before. One of these was a sonnet she'd written in response to Washington Allston's *The Bride,* a painting of the young biblical Queen Esther. Margaret paired her sonnet with another on the same subject by her friend Sam Ward, back now from Europe. She quoted Sam's description of the painting as "the story of the lamp of love, lighted, even burning with full force in a being that cannot yet comprehend it." For her part, Margaret had seen in the painting "a type of pure feminine beauty" and the vision of a "Woman's heaven": "Where Thought and Love beam."

The one exception to Margaret's single-initial rule was Bronson Alcott's "Orphic Sayings," the self-taught philosopher's catalogue of inspirational directives on topics from "Aspiration" to "Valor." He'd borrowed the title from James Freeman Clarke's *Western Messenger* translation of a five-stanza poem by Goethe ("Destiny," "Chance," "Love," "Necessity," and "Hope" were Goethe's headings) and spun out the conceit to fifty entries. Some were brief and gnomic: "Prudence is the footprint of wisdom"; others were long rhapsodic paragraphs, like "Vocation": "Engage in nothing that cripples or degrades you. Your first duty is self-culture, self-exaltation: you may not violate this high trust . . ."

Waldo had been the first to read the "Sayings" in manuscript, and he wrote to Margaret of his certainty that "you will not like Alcott's papers; that I do not like them; that Mr Ripley will not," yet "I think, on the whole, they ought to be printed pretty much as they stand, with his name in full." Waldo's idea was that readers who knew Bronson Alcott would "have his voice in their ear" and catch his "majestical sound." To others, he admitted, the "Sayings" might come off as "cold vague generalities," yet he liked their "Zoroastrian style." Margaret did too — they were "quite grand, though ofttimes too grandiloquent" — and after she'd coaxed Bronson to trim and clarify certain passages, she agreed with Waldo that nothing else they'd been offered spoke so much "in a new spirit." As the issue went to press, Waldo had been mildly dissatisfied, and needled Margaret. "O queen of the American Parnassus," he addressed her, "I hope our Dial will get to be a little *bad*. This first number is not enough so to scare the tenderest bantling of Conformity."

But with Alcott's "Orphic Sayings" at its center, "pleading . . . affinity with the celestial orbs," *The Dial* proved to be quite "bad" enough. One reviewer after another targeted Alcott's list of aphorisms as emblematic of the journal's all too free spirit — "infidelity in its higher branches," as a writer for the *Boston Times* charged. Waldo's plan of granting the "Sayings" a full byline left *The Dial* vulnerable to attack as the "ravings of Alcott, and his fellow-zanies." Failing to notice Margaret's opening essay on criticism or the journal's distinctive reporting on the arts, reviewers instead focused on and reviled what they'd expected to find in *The Dial*: "its *religion*," which, "if not all moonshine, is something worse." A "sickly, fungous literature" was how one reviewer described what the *Boston Times* concluded was an "unintelligible" and "grossly compounded mixture of Swedenborgianism, German mysticism . . . [and] Pantheism."

Still others charged that the journal prized "imagination" over "cool, substantial deduction of ratiocination" and served as nothing more than a vent for its writers' "inappeasable longings." A reviewer for the *Providence Daily Journal* ferreted out the identities of the issue's unnamed contributors and then lobbed predictable insults: Waldo Emerson had betrayed his calling, and Margaret Fuller was "a woman of extraordinary application and industry," yet with "no genuine love of knowledge . . . for its own sake, but for the eclat with which it is attended." This brilliant, willful female had once again overstepped the boundaries of decorum simply to feed her vanity. A lone note of approval came from Horace Greeley's *New-Yorker:* here, at last, was a "really *new* Magazine."

But private voices told of a more grateful response. *The Dial*, Margaret began to hear, "brings meat and drink to sundry famishing men and women at a distance from these tables"—the fractious dinner party of Boston doctrinal dispute. As John Sullivan Dwight later wrote, *The Dial* succeeded in telling "the time of days so far ahead" it could not help but invite scorn. If the journal was, in the eyes of its critics, "one of the most . . . ridiculous productions of the age," that meant it had managed to "explode," as Waldo Emerson had hoped, "all the established rules of Grub Street or Washington Street," Boston's own publishers' row. "Our community begin to stand in some terror of Transcendentalism," Waldo was pleased to report to his friend Thomas Carlyle in England. *The Dial*—"poor little thing"—had been "honoured by attacks from almost every newspaper & magazine." Waldo's chief request of Margaret for the succeeding issue was to alter the typeface on the cover so that "the word *Dial*" would appear in "strong black letters that can be seen in the sunshine . . . Can we not print it a little large & glorious . . . ?"

Margaret postponed a second installment of Alcott's "Sayings" to a later issue (she refused to scuttle the project), but otherwise the core writers remained the same, and others joined in: Henry Hedge, with the essay "The Art of Life—The Scholar's Calling," and Cary Sturgis, with a sheaf of poems that she elected to publish under the initial "Z." Waldo wrote a flattering introduction to a selection of poetry—"honest, great, but crude"—by another new young friend, Ellery Channing, cousin to William but of an altogether different temperament. As erratic as William was earnest, Ellery scribbled verses by the ream, but cared little whether they appeared in print, leaving it to Waldo to choose the best and then refusing his editorial advice. Persuaded by Margaret to support her aesthetic agenda, Waldo contributed a substantial essay of his own, "Thoughts on Modern Literature," and tolerated her editorial nudging on a difficult passage: "I think when you look again you will think you have not said what you meant to say." Margaret reviewed the Athenaeum gallery's latest exhibition, recognizing in particular two landscapes by Sarah Clarke that "deserve greater attention than from their size and position [in the gallery] they are likely to receive."

As the second *Dial* appeared in October 1840, Margaret took over the lease on the Willow Brook property in Jamaica Plain, to live for the first time in "my own hired house." The two oldest Fuller brothers, William Henry and Eugene, had recently married and settled in New Orleans, where their mother planned to spend the winter. Ellen left for Louisville to look for work as a schoolteacher; Arthur was at Harvard; and Richard, now sixteen, had taken a job with a dry-goods firm in Boston. Margaret had given up the three boarding students she'd been supervising through the previous year and now had only fourteen-year-old Lloyd to look after, assigning herself "the task of civilizing" the still restive boy "this winter." Her newfound independence and near solitude brought a feeling of "peace" and "almost happiness," Margaret wrote to Waldo Emerson in November.

Expecting soon to be earning a salary for her work on *The Dial*—Waldo predicted that the journal would become "better and perhaps next year bigger"—Margaret also put her faith in a new series of Conversations. A smaller but "truly interested" group of women began meeting in Elizabeth Peabody's recently established "Foreign Library," a bookstore and subscription library specializing in imported books and magazines, which occupied the first floor of a rented brick row house on West Street, a half-block from the Common and around the corner from Washington Street. The Peabody family lived upstairs, where Mary taught school and Sophia painted and sculpted in her bedroom-studio. The bookroom itself had quickly become a meeting place for Transcendental Club members, who gathered there in new configurations after a contentious last session at West Street in September. At the end of four years of haphazardly scheduled meetings, the group had disbanded to pursue separate aims: Margaret, Waldo, and Bronson Alcott were committed to *The Dial;* others to the reform of the Unitarian Church from within; and still others, in particular George Ripley, who'd dramatically resigned his Boston pulpit the previous spring, to found new freethinking congregations.

Elizabeth Peabody had also begun a publishing business, starting off with the Reverend William Ellery Channing's anti-slavery tract *Eman-*

cipation and then engaging Nathaniel Hawthorne for a series of historical tales for children. Elizabeth promised Margaret publication too, of
a translation Margaret contemplated of Bettine Brentano von Arnim's
fervid correspondence as a teenager with the somewhat older poet Karoline von Günderode, *Die Günderode*—a work that displayed, Margaret
thought, "all that is lovely between woman and woman."

Elizabeth's offer represented another potential source of income, and
the project gave Margaret the excuse to correspond with "Bettine," as
she thought of her already, having read von Arnim's *Correspondence with
a Child*—letters Bettine exchanged with Goethe in girlhood—in hopes
of gathering more information for her biography. Margaret would learn
that both the teenage letters and the Goethe correspondence had been
substantially rewritten or even fabricated, and she ultimately discounted
von Arnim as a source on Goethe. But the illumination of two distinct
yet complementary souls in *Die Günderode* seemed an authentic repre-
sentation of the worth of friendship, and the possibility that the letters
were embroidered for effect hardly mattered. "Our communion was
sweet—it was the epoch in which I first became conscious of myself,"
ran its epigraph. The suicide of the older Karoline some years after the
correspondence, in a period of melancholy after having been jilted by her
married lover, while not treated in the book, lent poignance to the earthly
"Woman's heaven" conjured in the letters.

Some of Margaret's biographical thoughts on Goethe found their way
into the third issue of *The Dial*, published in January 1841. Responding to the recent publication in English of an attack on Goethe by the
German literary critic Wolfgang Menzel, Margaret defended her hero as
"a prophet of our own age, as well as a representative of his own." She
might as well have been describing her own ambitions as she assessed
the accomplishments of this "agent in history" who had inspired her for
over a decade. Goethe, she wrote, was "just enough of an idealist, just
enough of a realist, for his peculiar task"—that is, to perform the "office
of artist-critic to the then chaotic world of thought in his country." He
deserved to be judged apart from the "private gossip" or even the "well-
authenticated versions" of his irregular domestic arrangements, which
critics like Menzel held against him. Goethe might not meet "the standard
of ideal manhood," Margaret allowed, but it was important to "consider
his life as a whole." His writings alone offered "sufficient evidence of

a life of severe labor, steadfast forbearance, and an intellectual growth almost unparalleled."

Margaret's commitment to showcasing the "new spirit" in this third and so far strongest issue of *The Dial* showed in her decision to reject an essay by Henry Thoreau, "The Service," that Waldo urged her to print. Margaret wrote to the twenty-three-year-old Thoreau that she hoped to publish the essay eventually, but while it was "rich in thoughts," in its present form those thoughts "seem to me so out of their natural order, that I cannot read it through without *pain*." Still, she recognized that his "tone" was far superior to the "air of quiet good-breeding" of much of the material submitted to the magazine: "Yours is so rugged that it ought to be commanding." She pressed him to revise and accepted, instead, another of Thoreau's poems and three of Waldo's, including the enigmatic "Sphinx."

Alcott's "Orphic Sayings" were defiantly back: "A man's idea of God corresponds to his ideal of himself. The nobler he is, the more exalted his God." And once again Alcott took the brunt of the criticism for the publication, which was otherwise gaining a modicum of acceptance as an "exponent of Literary Liberty." One reviewer allowed that Alcott's mystical dicta "need not frighten any body."

Margaret invited Theodore Parker to augment her defense of Goethe with a general article on the "most original, fresh, and religious literature of all modern times," that of the German Romantics; and Sam Ward wrote on Boccaccio and classic Italian literature. Margaret herself reviewed Nathaniel Hawthorne's first volume of children's stories, *Grandfather's Chair*, published by Elizabeth Peabody, taking the opportunity to mete out more general praise: "No one of all our imaginative writers has indicated a genius at once so fine and rich." She singled out his "power" of "making present the past scenes of our own history" and expressed the hope that Hawthorne would write again for "older and sadder" readers.

For those readers — *The Dial*'s readers — Margaret offered still more challenging fare: Sophia Ripley's essay titled "Woman," revised after its first presentation to Margaret's Conversation class the previous year. A searing indictment as closely reasoned as Alcott's "Sayings" were cryptic, the essay charged that "in our present state of society woman possesses not; she is under possession," referring to laws that barred married women from owning or inheriting property. From girlhood, "woman is educated with the tacit understanding, that she is only half a being, and an appendage." Once married, she "spends life in conforming to" her husband's wishes "instead of moulding herself to her own ideal. Thus she loses her individuality, and never gains his respect." After becoming a mother, "she is only the upper nurse," whereas the father is "the oracle. His wish is law, hers only the unavailing sigh uttered in secret." Through it all, "she looks out into life, finds nothing there but confusion, and congratulates herself that it is man's business, not hers."

"Is this woman's destiny?" Sophia Ripley demanded in exasperation, seemingly as ready to abandon the role of conventional wife as her husband, George, had been to shed his minister's robes. Restricting the entire female sex to "a sphere is vain, for no two persons naturally have the same," she argued. "Character, intellect creates the sphere of each," not sex, "and this separation is ruinous to the highest improvement of both" men and women. She proposed instead that every woman be "encouraged to question . . . gradually forming her own ideal." A woman "should still be herself" after marriage, and "her own individuality should be as precious to her" as her husband's love. She closed provocatively: "Is this the ideal of a perfect woman, and if so, how does it differ from a perfect man?"

Margaret approached the same subject — a new feminine ideal — from a different perspective in a prose meditation she called "The Magnolia of Lake Pontchartrain." She improvised on a story she'd heard from a neighbor in Jamaica Plain, Dr. William Eustis, a lonely bachelor in his fifties and an avid amateur horticulturalist, who had stopped in to see Margaret's mother shortly before Margarett Crane traveled south in October. Nearly dozing on the couch while Eustis droned on, Margaret nevertheless found herself intrigued by the man's excessively detailed description — "not like a botanist, but a lover" — of his "interview" with a flowering magnolia tree on the shores of Lake Pontchartrain, not far from where her mother would soon be living. The tale seemed almost "romantic," and Margaret began to think of shaping it into a "true poem," an allegory of an encounter between male and female. What might a female become if allowed by an adoring male to bloom on her own? What might that man learn from her?

Margaret's Magnolia has a history to relate when a nameless male traveler follows a strange fragrance and finds her "singing to herself in her lonely bower," though she scarcely deigns to speak to him. Her wisdom derives from "a being of another order from thee"—"Secret, radiant, profound . . . feminine," the Magnolia explains, and may not be communicated "in any language now possible betwixt us." Yet she recalls for him her former life when she was, instead, an orange tree, blooming in "endless profusion," offering up her fruit to merchants for sale and her blossoms to brides as ornamental garlands, but suffering inwardly: "I had no mine or thine, I belonged to all, I could never rest, I was never at one." As a bounteous orange tree, hers was the conventional woman's fate, so well described by Sophia Ripley. It was also Margaret's, as family caretaker, schoolteacher, Conversation instigator, and nursemaid to *The Dial*'s sometimes "laggard and lukewarm" contributors.

But chill weather and exhaustion bring the orange tree's death—and subsequent rebirth under the influence of that higher feminine power, "the queen and guardian of the flowers." "Take a step inward . . . become a vestal priestess and bide thy time in the Magnolia," the frozen tree is told. "I was driven back upon the centre of my being, and there found all being," the Magnolia concludes her tale. Contrary to Margaret's long-ago Thanksgiving Day epiphany, that burst of self-renunciation while still under her father's command, here it was possible to find both self and "All." In Margaret's story, the nameless man rides on after the flower bids him "farewell, to meet again in prayer, in destiny, in harmony, in elemental power." The Magnolia instructs him: "All the secret powers are 'Mothers' . . . Man never creates, he only recombines the lines and colors of his own existence."

Here was a radical shift from Margaret's "Essay on Critics," in which creative artists are all men. Perhaps the new living situation she had established for herself, independent and "almost happy," had helped her achieve the Magnolia's self-sustaining wisdom. "I cannot plunge into myself enough," she had written to Cary Sturgis in late October as her family scattered and she took possession of Willow Brook. She described then a sense of personal "transformation," borrowing her metaphor from nature: "The leaf became a stem, a bud, is now in flower." The nameless rider learns a similar lesson from the Magnolia: that he must "prize the monitions of my nature" and that "sometimes what is not for sale in the market-place" is of the highest value.

But in Boston in 1841, on the banks of the busy Charles River rather than the serene, idealized Lake Pontchartrain, could men learn from women? Margaret would soon find out. Her Conversations had attracted the interest of the men in her circle, and she'd invited several of them to join the women for a ten-week series meeting on Monday nights, to begin the first week of March. The class filled immediately, netting her six hundred dollars in ticket fees.

Waldo, to whom she had not at first revealed her authorship of "The Magnolia"—she'd published it without an identifying initial—would be among those attending. He'd admired the third issue: "the good Public ought to be humbly thankful," he'd written to her. As long as Margaret could "hold [her] volatile regiment together," the future of *The Dial* was secure, he believed. But he prodded her: "I . . . cannot settle the authorship of the Magnolia."

When Margaret admitted the piece was hers, Waldo was unsurprised, admiring its "fervid Southern eloquence" and predicting its "permanent value." Her fable caused him to wonder, however, as he had so often before, "how you fell into the Massachusetts." The tale was "rich and sad," yet "it should not be—if one could only show why not!" Waldo had had more than one opportunity to "show why not": to ease Margaret's sadness. His apparently heartless vacillations would ultimately force her departure from "the Massachusetts" and the "large and brilliant circle" she had helped him gather there. Margaret could play both characters in her allegory, female and male. She would flower, and then ride on.

Communities and Covenants

WALDO EMERSON WAS AMONG THE FIRST TO RECEIVE AN invitation to Margaret's evening Conversation series, and she should have taken his response as a sign of trouble to come. He would be glad, he told her, "to hear you talk *from the tripod*" on classical myth "or any other topic" — Waldo was playing on the now widespread notion of Margaret as sibyl. But he did not "anticipate any reciprocal illumination of my own." He would come to "the Mythology class" to listen to Margaret, but he could not promise to converse and did not expect enlightenment. That was in December. By late February, with the first meeting less than a week away, he feigned ignorance of the plan. He would bring Lidian along for what "I thought . . . was a party," he wrote to Cary Sturgis, who had also enrolled. "That it is a class is new." Then he missed the opening session, claiming to have received notice of the gathering a day too late.

In the end, Lidian may not have joined her husband at George and Sophia Ripley's house in Bedford Place, where the Conversations were held during the early spring months of 1841, before the Ripleys decamped to Brook Farm in West Roxbury. The renegade minister and his dissident wife had acquired a 170-acre property eight miles from Boston and attracted a small band of like-minded investors to join them in forming a "Community" to promote "a more simple and wholesome life, than can be led amidst the pressure of our competitive institutions." There, labor and profits would be shared equally; art and reform would thrive along with corn and potatoes. Nathaniel Hawthorne had been among the first to sign on, purchasing two shares at five hundred dollars each in hopes of making a home at Brook Farm for himself and his fiancée, Sophia Peabody.

But equality was not the watchword at Margaret's Monday-night class. If Lidian Emerson was there, she never spoke. Margaret was hard-pressed to bring together the two contingents she had cultivated for more than a decade. Her friendships with men could be sincere and confiding, particularly in correspondence, but in social settings she easily adapted to their banter and disputation, frequently besting them at it. With the women of her Conversations, however, she had deliberately fostered a "simple earnestness," a spirit of collaborative inquiry. As one woman later recalled of the group experience, "I was no longer the limitation of myself." Margaret led the women collectively into "a new world of thought"; she "opened the book of life and helped us to read it for ourselves." Her male friends were not so willing to follow.

It had been one thing for Margaret and a few other women to be invited occasionally as guests to meetings of "the club of clubs," as Waldo once wrote magnanimously to Margaret, urging her to attend an otherwise all-male Transcendental Club meeting in order to "inspire our reptile wits," but quite another for a man to join an ongoing conversation among women based in "simple earnestness," especially with other men looking on. Waldo, in whom Margaret had confided her certainty that the women's minds, "when once awakened," could not "cease to vibrate," must have wondered what place, if any, there was for him in such a gathering. There had been "more Greek than Bostonian spoken at the meetings," Margaret assured him of her first series, "& we may have pure honey of Hymettus" — the Athenian mountain noted for its thyme-covered foothills — "to give you yet." But was this a "Greek" that men could speak and understand? Or was it the Magnolia's "secret, radiant, profound . . . feminine" language: "of another order" and incommunicable to men?

Like the stranger in Margaret's fable, Waldo would never find out. From the start, as might have been expected, the men more often took the floor — and held it. Among these were Henry Hedge, Bronson Alcott, and James Freeman Clarke, who had returned to Boston despite being refused George Ripley's recently vacated pulpit to found his own Church of the Disciples. And, on those Monday nights when he could manage the trip from Concord, Waldo Emerson appeared and quickly forgot his promise to offer no "reciprocal illumination."

On March 1, the opening session that Waldo missed, Margaret commenced by advising all in attendance to "denationalize" themselves, to forget their American prejudices and "throw the mind back" to the Greek golden age. The Greeks, she explained, had likely "borrowed" their deities from the Egyptians and the Hindus—who "dwelt in the All, the infinite"—and then "analyzed" and "to some degree humanized" them as personifications of distinct qualities. She conjured up Rhea, the mother of all gods and goddesses, representing "Productive Energy," like the Egyptian fertility goddess Isis. Then she offered brief sketches of Rhea's progeny: Jupiter, Juno, Minerva, Neptune, Diana, Apollo, Mercury, Venus, all "embodiments of Absolute Ideas"—Will, Wisdom, Thought, Purity, Genius, Beauty.

Frank Shaw broke in to ask how these personifications had "suggested themselves in that barbarous age." Unfazed, Margaret responded as she had the year before to Mary Jane Quincy, countering that "the word *barbarous*" simply did not apply to "the age of Plato," a time when "the human intellect reached a point as elevated in some respects as any it had ever touched."

But Frank Shaw was not so easily convinced. Just retired at age thirty from one of the great Boston mercantile firms, repulsed by the greed and exploitation he'd witnessed in the family business and at slave-trading ports in the West Indies and the American South, Frank Shaw was a prime backer of the Ripleys' communal experiment at Brook Farm. His objection now was altogether different from Mrs. Quincy's. He argued that the Hindus must have had the superior belief system: wasn't the "infinity" of the Hindus "impaired" when the Greeks assigned to their gods "the duties, passions, and criminal indulgences of men"? By "bringing their deities to the human level," Frank thought, "the Greeks had taken one step down."

William White, a young reform-minded journalist, took another tack: What of the "North American Indian's worship of the Manitou," a god with "no passion that had degraded humanity"? Wasn't that "purer than the Greek worship"? Soon Henry Hedge was chiming in with an erudite gloss. "Nobody could show a purely Greek mythos," he pointed out, whereupon William White insisted that "culture," no matter how advanced, could not bring about spiritual enlightenment. Christian "revelation" was needed to "complete the work." The men had brought the conversation back around to church matters.

Sophia Ripley and Elizabeth Peabody managed an occasional interjection—Sophia to clarify that for the Hindus, "virtue lay in contemplation" rather than good works; Elizabeth to grumble that she'd always considered the Greeks to have taken "a step *up*." Elizabeth had studied Greek with her father as a girl and later in a yearlong tutorial with Waldo Emerson shortly after he'd graduated from Harvard; he'd refused to accept any pay, pronouncing her as proficient in the language as he. Still, Elizabeth's opinion counted for little on this evening. The teenage Caroline Healey, a newcomer among the women, taking notes as rapidly as she could, recorded her own frustration: "I thought a good deal, but did not speak." Margaret did not silence her own exasperation.

By Caroline Healey's account, Margaret attempted to steer the conversation back to the Greeks, remarking that she "was sorry we had wandered from our subject so far as to doubt her very premises!" But digression and dispute on the part of the men continued. "Would not Plato have been greater had he been born into the nineteenth century?" William White speculated. At last Margaret observed drily that she had hoped "the presence of gentlemen" would prevent such "desultory prattling" and "keep us free from prejudice." She asked the group to choose a subject for the next session and agree to keep to it. "Rhea," the mother of all gods, and her "Productive Energy," was voted in, perhaps by the otherwise mostly silent women. Margaret closed, Caroline Healey recorded, "with a gentle reproof to our wandering wits": "I thought she was rightly disappointed."

As a newcomer, Caroline could not have guessed at the extent of that disappointment. By the time she'd closed the latest series of Conversations for women only, Margaret had written to William Channing, the group had "seemed melted into one love." The women had established a "relation" that was "perfectly true": "We have time, patience, mutual reverence and fearlessness eno[ugh] to get at one another's thoughts." Margaret's beloved Anna Barker had been "all kindled," speaking freely from the outset and telling Margaret that "none there could be strangers to her more." Now most of these women had turned bystanders to the men's rambling disquisitions. How far short the class fell from her ideal was exemplified by the Greek gods and goddesses themselves: male and female "distinct in expression, but equal in beauty, strength and calmness."

A week later, Waldo Emerson was on hand. Caroline Healey was fascinated by the matchup: Waldo and Margaret "met as Pyramus and Thisbe," she observed, referring to the characters in Shakespeare's *A Midsummer Night's Dream,* "with a blank wall between," each unable to comprehend the other's views. Caroline had neatly intuited the "perpetual wall" that Margaret had once complained to Cary Sturgis "is always grieving me" when attempting to converse with Waldo face to face. On this evening, Margaret's introductory speech on the *"bounteous giver"* — Ceres, Persephone, Isis, Rhea, or Diana, who served as "modifications of one enfolding idea . . . accepted by all nations"—only prompted Waldo to propose Napoleon as a contemporary man of "will" who could "easily have suggested" a pantheon of gods. "Let us pray for scores of such," echoed Charles Wheeler, a newly appointed instructor of history at Harvard, "that a new and superior mythos may arise for us!"

"Margaret retorted indignantly," Caroline Healey wrote, that such a fraternity would more likely leave us "nothing better than . . . memoirs of their hats, coats, and swords," certainly no valuable "lesson." Margaret urged the class to "take the beautiful Greek mythi as they were, without troubling ourselves about those which might arise for us!" But, as Caroline wrote of a later session, "there were too many clergymen in the company. Everybody was interested in somebody nearer at hand." Worse still, for much of the evening Waldo Emerson "pursued his own train of thought. He seemed to forget that we had come together to pursue Margaret's."

Margaret postponed the next week's meeting, overcome by headache, and Waldo's attendance at later sessions was spotty. By the final class in May, there were "few present," Caroline Healey noted, and "we were all dull." Several had departed for Brook Farm, with Margaret privately expressing doubt that "they will get free from all they deprecate in society." Caroline herself was set to leave Boston for a teaching position in Baltimore. She concluded that Margaret "never enjoyed this mixed class, and considered it a failure so far as her own power was concerned." Yet the eighteen-year-old had been inspired to speak on occasion, perhaps after witnessing Margaret's refusal to conceal her impatience or to give up on her "theme." Caroline left the last class sorrowing that she might never see Margaret Fuller again — "I love her so much!" — and certain that "in no way was Margaret's supremacy so evident as in the impulse she gave to the minds of younger women."

At the sixth session, Waldo had clashed again with Margaret over the myth of Cupid and Psyche, and Psyche's "blunder," as Waldo saw it, in daring to look at her lover, the error that launched her into a life of trial. "It was a duty not to look!" he declared, "to resist the evil, to strive triumphantly" — and "to recognise it — never!" Good, he claimed, "was always present to the soul"; there was no reason not to follow "the good." But Margaret objected that evil itself was "a good in the grand scheme of things." Psyche's violation of the ban was no "blunder." It brought her new knowledge of the world and set her on a "pilgrimage of [the] soul." This was the grand theme of all the goddess myths, she asserted: the painful struggle toward self-knowledge and a means of exerting "the Productive Energy" after the loss of innocence, or "what is dear in childhood." Margaret herself "would not accept the world," she vowed, if she could not "believe evil [was] working in it for good! Man had gained more than he lost by his fall."

"Are we better then, than God?" Cary Sturgis asked. It was the kind of impertinent yet pithy question that she loved to ask and that in recent months had brought her even closer than Margaret to Waldo Emerson.

For the past eighteen months, Waldo and Margaret had played not Pyramus and Thisbe but Oberon and Titania, Shakespeare's meddlesome fairy king and queen, in a drama of rapidly shifting "elective affinities" among a cast of young lovers — Anna Barker, Sam Ward, Cary Sturgis, Ellery Channing, and Margaret's sister, Ellen — with some of its most poignant scenes set in the many-chambered Emerson home or the nearby Concord woods, a territory of both transcendence and treachery. The odd number of players ensured that there would be no symmetry, no satisfactory pairing off for all. And in the end it was Margaret, the one who "bound in the belt of her sympathy & friendship all whom I know & love," as Waldo would later write, who was left out, bravely attempting to live "more alone and less lonely" when so many around her were bent on establishing communal—or connubial—relations.

The year of mostly amicable work on *The Dial*, conducted largely through the mail, had covered over a succession of flare-ups between Margaret and Waldo that erupted again when they were in the same room together during the Conversations, with Waldo now publicly refusing to admit the "good" of suffering or to recognize and respond to Margaret's, as he had so often failed to do in private. For the pageant of fluctuating affections was as much about Margaret and Waldo's "connexion"—what could it be?—as about their ability, as polestars, to attract and influence the others in what Margaret called their "constellation." When "the young people"—in this case, Anna, Sam, and Cary, all members of the "Mythology class"—chided Waldo for his behavior, "wish[ing] to know what possessed me to tease you with so much prose, & becloud the fine conversation," as Waldo wrote to Margaret in a letter of apology for returning her fair "eastern pearls with chuckstones of granite," it was as a signal to Waldo that Margaret needed, and deserved, not just the financial support of their ticket fees, but also a cessation of strife after a long season of disappointment.

Waldo saw it too, if belatedly, and in his letter he asked Margaret's forgiveness not just for his performance in the "game of wits & fashionists," but also "for all the years of dereliction" in his duty toward her, signing himself "with joy & hope Your friend." The letter was proof of the truth, for Waldo at least, of the peculiar opening sentence of the essay "Friendship," which he had composed during these months of evolving alliances: "We have a great deal more kindness than is ever spoken." Waldo's reserve had been an obstacle to intimacy for as long as the two eminences had known each other, yet now, as he attempted to smooth Margaret's ruffled feathers, he offered only the pale assurance that "our friendship . . . should adjourn its fulness of communion into pure eternity." As Margaret had grown more certain of the range of her powers, what she called "my need of manifold being," Waldo's deficiency—his "most unfriendly friendliness"—became increasingly evident, and the contrast between the two more stark. Margaret knew all about the "masculine obligations of all-sufficingness"; she felt them herself in her role as family provider. But Waldo's self-sovereignty was extreme, a form of blindness. As Margaret phrased it, "this light will never understand my fire."

Yet she strove to be understood. Part of that effort had been introducing to Waldo her younger friends, the talented former pupils and budding "Genii" she had recognized in her circuit, announcing their excellences to the Concord "sage," only to have him affirm and expand on her initial approbation. This pleased her: the more friends Margaret and Waldo shared, particularly if they had been hers to start with, the more secure she felt in his friendship. On his side, Waldo may have sensed he could indirectly satisfy Margaret—"the much that calls for more," in her self-description—by tending to her flock. All were more monied and more beautiful than Margaret—or than Waldo had been at their age—and their greater ease in the world, their "gipsy" freedom of movement, tantalized Margaret and Waldo, both of whom "belong[ed] to the bread-winning tribe who serve the clock," in Margaret's phrase, despite their disparate natures, fire and light.

She had begun by sending Waldo one of Cary Sturgis's "good letters" and suggesting he invite the two of them for a stay in Concord. Waldo swiftly obliged, for "guests so queenly & poetic." Cary's unscheduled days permitted a visit before Margaret could break from her teaching, however, and in the end she went on her own. Waldo reported immediately to Margaret that Cary had "surprised me into very pleasant thoughts by her questions." There had been an instant affinity. "I shall see her hereafter as an old acquaintance," he wrote in June of 1838.

And in fact she was. Waldo and Cary Sturgis had crossed paths before at social gatherings in Boston; the previous year, he'd noted her in his journal as "the fair girl whom I saw in town expressing so decided & proud choice of influences, so careless of pleasing, so willful & so lofty a will." Perhaps Waldo knew the story of Cary's expulsion from the tiresome Dorothea Dix's Boston school before she found her way to Margaret's more liberal tutelage. Cary Sturgis "inspires the wish to come nearer & to speak to this nobleness," Waldo confessed in his journal. Margaret had managed the introduction that Waldo, the married householder sixteen years Cary's senior, had not been able to press for himself. Now Cary had "engaged my cold pedantic self," Waldo wrote, "into a fine surprise of thought & hope."

Nineteen years old and beyond the reach of her father's prohibitions, Cary had the self-possession as well to make her way to Waldo Emerson's house without Margaret as chaperone. She had already chosen

Waldo as an "influence." After hearing his lecture "The Heart" several months earlier, Cary had written to Waldo requesting a manuscript copy to read to her friends. The same age, at this Concord visit, as Waldo's first wife when she died after less than two years of marriage, Cary was a sturdier, braver version of the enchanting tubercular Ellen Emerson. Like Ellen she wrote poetry, the best of which Waldo called admiringly "her blasphemies." In Cary's "lofty" willfulness, Waldo detected a singularly uninhibited will to live as she pleased. One of Cary's first poems published in *The Dial* was called "Life" and began with these lines:

> *Greatly to Be*
> *Is enough for me,*
> *Is enough for thee.*

But Cary was drawn equally, if not more, to Ellery Channing, her age mate and companion from the prosperous shore town of Newburyport, north of Boston, where her family summered. Although Cary's and Ellery's poems had much in common — Waldo termed both their verse "the right poetry of hope" — she could hardly have made a more imprudent romantic choice. Ellery's poetry, which Margaret sent to Cary in manuscript, perhaps as an advisory, was his own best and worst advertisement: "Be not afraid to utter what thou art / 'T is no disgrace to keep an open heart." The footloose and feckless Ellery was not about to make a commitment to Cary Sturgis, despite her family wealth and kindred "gipsy" spirit. Waldo applauded Ellery as a "good vagabond," admired his "daredevil originality," and worried lest "irresistible custom brings him plump down, and he finds himself instead of odes, writing gazettes & leases." He was another of the young men, like Henry Thoreau, whose rebellions Waldo enjoyed vicariously. More practical and anxious to protect Cary's feelings, Margaret told Waldo that Ellery, so "full of indirections," as even Waldo had to admit, reminded her of "a great genius with a little wretched boy — trotting beside him." When, during the summer of *The Dial*'s first publication, as Ellery casually presented her with a sheaf of his poems for consideration and then announced his plans to leave for Illinois and take up farming, Margaret wrote to Cary approving the move: "I think he might as well be in one place as another, since he will not avail himself of the most precious friendships."

She had in mind not just Cary's infatuation, but also Ellery's long-time friendship with Sam Ward, his classmate at the progressive Round Hill School in Northampton, Massachusetts, and then for a semester at Harvard before the "good vagabond" Ellery dropped out, protesting the college's dull curriculum and compulsory chapel services. Leaving college for such reasons was understandable, perhaps noble, but how could anyone give up a close friendship with Sam, the boy-man whom Margaret and Waldo had taken to calling "Raphael" for his precocious talent as a painter and his connoisseurship in the visual arts?

In hindsight, Margaret would come to admit that she had a tendency to think she had "gone so much further with a friend than I really have." But for a time during the summer of 1839, as she was approaching thirty and Sam just twenty-one, Margaret had grieved as profoundly and self-righteously over a loss of connection with the fledgling artist as she had over her doomed passion for George Davis years earlier. The few days she'd spent with Sam Ward in Newport on their way home from the Farrars' Hudson River excursion the summer before Timothy's death had deepened in Margaret's memory into a true meeting of minds and hearts, one that had made her sing "a joyful song," which, to her consternation, "found no echo" from Sam on his much-anticipated return from Europe.

"How did you pray me to draw near to you! . . . I poured out my heart to you," she stormed, as Sam patiently assured her of his wish to remain friends. "You would not be so irreverent as to dare tamper with a nature like mine, you could not treat so generous a person with levity," she chastised Sam in disbelief when he appeared to be avoiding her company: "if you love me as I deserve to be loved, you cannot dispense with seeing me." She had learned the "bitterness of checked affections" from George Davis and believed herself to be "incapable of feeling or being content to inspire an ordinary attachment." With Sam, something extraordinary seemed possible: "We knew long ago that age, position, and pursuits being so different, nothing but love bound us together." Yet what sort of love?

Now Sam told Margaret she had never been his inamorata. He had reverenced her all along as he would a mother. Anything else, he told her humbly, would "spoil" him for his "part on life's dull scene," or— she must have been shocked to hear—"call up the woman" in him. Sam

Ward would not play the role she envisioned for him: the young aesthete, her fond follower, her chivalric lover. In fact, he had given up thoughts of becoming a painter, always more Margaret's idea than his, to work for Baring Brothers, the English banking firm for which his father served as American representative, and he had moved to New York City to oversee the office there. Margaret struggled to accept Sam's career decision and his verdict on their "love": "You have given me the sacred name of Mother, and I will be so indulgent, as tender, as delicate (if possible) in my vigilance, as if I had borne you beneath my heart instead of in it." However else the blow affected her, like other setbacks it prompted some of her most florid prose.

And then she learned, along with Waldo, that the year before, Sam had fallen in love with Anna Barker, Margaret's "star of stars," while the two were traveling in Europe. It was in order to establish himself on solid financial ground, to win Anna's hand, that Sam had settled in New York. Now Margaret wrote to him, "I understand all perfectly." To save her dignity, she delivered to Sam a Waldo-like pronouncement: "though I might grieve that you should put me from you in your highest hour and find yourself unable to meet me on the very ground where you had taught me most to expect it . . . the knowledge I have of your nature has become a part of mine, the love it has excited will accompany me through eternity."

But Waldo also loved, in his way, both Anna and Sam—and Cary Sturgis. Waldo admired Anna Barker as extravagantly as Margaret did. He met her on a rare visit to Willow Brook in Jamaica Plain where Anna was staying with Margaret in the early fall of 1839. On his return home, Waldo could only complain of the flimsy "strip of paper" in his journal that "remains to me to record my introduction to Anna Barker." "Few days of my quiet life," he wrote, "are so illustrated & cheered as were these two in which I enjoyed the frank & generous confidence of a being so lovely, so fortunate, & so remote from my own experiences." Once again Margaret had shown him that a "new person is to me ever a great event," as he wrote not just in his journal that evening, but also in "Friendship." In the essay, though, which he revised through the fall and winter, he continued the sentence enticingly: "A new person is to me a great event, and hinders me from sleep. I have often had fine fancies about persons which have given me delicious hours." And then, pulling back: "But the joy ends in the day; it yields no fruit. Thought is not born of it; my action is very little modified."

The news of Anna and Sam's attachment, not yet an engagement, had followed fast on that first meeting. Two weeks later, after a visit to Concord from Margaret and Bronson Alcott—"Cold as I am," Waldo wrote in his journal, "they are almost dear"—the story was out. Margaret had confided "to my private ear a chronicle of sweet romance, of love & nobleness which have inspired the beautiful & brave." But he added a qualification: Margaret's portrayal of her own role in the tale "mingled a shade of discontent" with "my joy" in "that which thou toldest me O eloquent lady, of thy friends & mine." Privately he speculated that Margaret's professed eternal, selfless love for Sam could not survive the "wear & tear of years" and would "be succeeded by another & another & the new will sport with the old." Still, he guessed, knowing Margaret, "it will never be nothing." And he had yet to become thoroughly acquainted with Sam Ward, the "young man of promising character and prosperous fortunes" who had so captivated Margaret, who seemingly had won the heart of the matchless Anna Barker ("The wind is not purer than she is," Waldo still believed), and who, perhaps intentionally, had managed to evade Waldo at every opportunity until they met by chance in the White Mountains on holiday in late summer, when Sam was fending off Margaret's ardent letters.

Now, as may have happened several years earlier with Margaret, Sam fell under Waldo Emerson's spell. With the cooling fall weather, the "chill wind and rain" that matched Margaret's mood of despond, Anna traveled south for the winter to her family's new home in New Orleans, and Sam quit his job with Baring Brothers to stay on in Boston, entering into long conversations with Waldo by his fireside while together they studied Sam's portfolio of prints from Italy—and, with Margaret's encouragement, writing poetry for *The Dial*. Sam felt he had made his point after a year's servitude in New York; Anna had given him permission to open a private correspondence, a strong indicator of her eventual acceptance of his suit. He was ready to give up the "vexation" of business, the "life that is rather my death," as he had written to Eliza Farrar while laboring in New York City. Maybe, with his family's wealth to rely on,

Sam could live as Waldo Emerson did, keeping morning hours in his study, tending a vegetable garden in the afternoons, entertaining a parade of high-minded guests with an enchanting wife and children to ornament the scene — without the onerous lecture engagements or publishers' deadlines. When he traveled to New Orleans the following spring, it was to announce these new plans to Anna as he asked her to marry him.

Her answer — or her father's — was no. She must marry a man with a steady income of his own or remain in the family circle to serve her aging parents. Stunned but unwilling to settle into the harness once more, Sam traveled north, stopping to see Ellery Channing in Illinois, only to discover the "bird has flown" again, back to Boston. By June of 1840, Sam was in Boston too, sick with the "ague" — "emaciated," by Margaret's account when she saw him in recovery in early July, but all "the more dear" and in a "gentle, celestial, not hopeful, but faithful" mood. Anna would return soon as well.

With their own hearts aimed high — at fervid, spiritualized friendship — Waldo and Margaret imagined Anna's refusal of Sam "implied another resolution," as Waldo later phrased it in a letter to Cary Sturgis, to the promiscuous desires among the band of five. In Margaret, the news revived the hope, crushed by Sam's rejection, of an intimate pentangle. Writing to Cary Sturgis in the wake of her disappointment the previous summer, Margaret had described Anna as her "eldest and divinest love" and explained to Cary that "I thought of all women but you two as my children, my pupils, my play things . . . You two alone I would have held by the hand." With "Mr E for the representative of religious aspiration" and "one other of Earth's beauty" — Sam Ward — "I thought my circle would be as complete as friendship could make it." Perhaps it was still to be.

Waldo's expectations were similar, if revolving around himself rather than Margaret, and he did his best to realize them. Margaret detected his growing enthusiasm as Anna's arrival drew near. She had received two letters from Waldo by midsummer, Margaret wrote to Cary, in which he was "soaring like an eagle, skimming like a swallow," although, she added sardonically, "never with me, nor in the depths." Margaret took the opportunity to press her case with Waldo for at least a tripartite bond, declaring herself and Cary "willing" to be his "friends in the full & sacred sense," but charging Waldo with "a certain inhospitality of soul," a tendency to "remain apart critical, & after many interviews still a stranger." She had put him on notice.

Waldo recognized the accusation: "I count & weigh, but do not love." He was willing to "confess to the fact of cold & imperfect intercourse" — conversation, he meant — "but not," he defended himself in a letter to Cary, "the deficiency of my affection. If I count & weigh, I love also." He continued, almost gushing: "I cannot tell you how warm & glad the naming of your names" — Margaret's and Cary's — "makes my solitude ... With all my heart I would live in your society I would gladly spend the remainder of my days in the holy society of the best the wisest & the most beautiful[.] Come and live near me whenever it suits your pleasure."

When Anna reached Boston in August, Waldo invited all three women — Margaret, Anna, and Cary — for a long weekend stay in Concord, traveling to Cambridge himself with "a good horse" and "caryall" to escort the trio back to his home. What followed were "three golden days," he wrote afterward to Cary, acknowledging "the debt of so much love to you all & severally." What transpired on those three days? Waldo left clues in a poem titled simply "The Visit," suggesting a kind of conversational convergence of souls:

> *More fleet than waves or whirlwinds go . . .*
> *Hearts to hearts their meaning show . . .*
> *Single look has drained the breast,*
> *Single moment years confessed.*

"I thought she had looked the world through for a man as universal as herself," he wrote of Anna Barker to Cary, "& finding none, had said, 'I will compensate myself for my great renunciation as a woman by establishing ideal relations: Not only Raphael shall be my brother, but that Puritan at concord who is reputed at some time to have seen the mighty Gods, I will elect him also.' And so thinking, she came & covenanted with me that we two should speak the truth to each other." By the time he'd written the letter, however, Waldo had heard the "strange news" from Anna, the astonishing "new fact," that she'd changed her mind and accepted Sam Ward's proposal. The two would marry in a month: Sam had acquiesced to her father's offer of a banking job in Boston and a home on fashionable Louisburg Square to go with it. Anna had stopped Waldo "at the church door in Cambridge," in the "midst of the Phi Beta crowd" at Harvard's summer's end commencement, to tell him. Anna, whose "angel has appeared at all the doors melted my reserves & prepared me to say things never before spoken," Waldo sorrowed.

The duration of a glance
Is the term of convenance . . .

Waldo registered the news "with a certain terror." The scene of his own inspirational address three years earlier was now also the setting of his baffled hopes. "She does not feel any fall," Waldo marveled of Anna's reversal, her betrayal of this Concord Puritan. "There was no compunction written on either of their brows," he noted of the couple. He could only confide in his "dear sister" Cary his regret that Sam and Anna, "these shining examples of Denial," had not "kept that starry road" of covenanted celibacy, "ideal relations," transcendent friendship: "I think we should all have worshipped them with weeping eyes." In his distress, he turned now to Cary alone, asking her to "be my saint & purify me wholly."

Left suddenly on the margins of the court she herself had assembled, Margaret had no choice but to parley with Waldo Emerson. Indeed there had been, as he wrote in his letter of apology after disrupting Margaret's Conversations, "years of dereliction." Certainly there were times when Margaret's friendship with Waldo had warranted effusions. During her first spring at Willow Brook, after she had passed up Waldo's offer to help her settle nearby in Concord, or even to board in the Emerson house, she had written to him of the wild geranium and hawthorn blooming in the countryside at Jamaica Plain, a Shakespearean dithyramb: "If you will come this week I will crown you with something prettier than willow, or any sallow . . . You can have a garland of what fashion you will[.] Do but come." But more often than not, Waldo did not come. He preferred to meet Margaret on his own ground. And there too she confounded him.

"Persons were her game," Waldo knew, but Margaret played the game of friendship by different rules than his. "The higher the style we demand of friendship," Waldo proposed in his essay, "the less easy to establish it with flesh and blood. We walk alone in the world." For Waldo, when all was said and done, friendship and its benefits accrued in the solitary mind, not in company at the common table or fireside—or in playful floral coronations. At times he found Margaret devious: "What a spendthrift you are, o beautiful Corinne! What needless webs you weave, what busy arts you ply." Yet he also knew her desire for connection to be sincere, if beyond his capacity to meet. She wanted an "absolute all-confiding intimacy between her & another." He was wary of being caught in her web of interdependence.

As early as Margaret's first summer of teaching in Providence, when the tone of their letters turned comradely, Waldo had been alarmed by her "flesh and blood" demands on his sympathy when she paid him a visit in Concord at the end of her summer term and readily opened her full emotional burden to him. Margaret was then still reconciling herself to the change of circumstances brought on by her father's sudden death. "Life is a pretty tragedy especially for women," Waldo had written in his journal at the time. "On comes a gay dame of manners & tone so fine & haughty that all defer to her as to a countess, & she seems the dictator of society. Sit down by her, & talk of her own life in earnest, & she is some stricken soul with care & sorrow at her vitals." Of Margaret's "care & sorrow" he did not wish to know. "We are armed all over with these subtle antagonisms," he wrote to her afterward, attempting to explain what he knew had turned out to be a disappointing visit, "which, as soon as we meet, begin to play, & translate all poetry into such stale prose."

Even more distasteful to him was the way he saw Margaret and other women conversing with each other as they gathered in his parlor: no sooner had the "stricken soul" confessed her woes than her companion "in return . . . disburdens into her ear the story of *her* misery, as deep & hopeless as her own." Such an exchange was about as far from the ideal of friendship Waldo espoused as could be imagined, yet it was what Margaret sought from him—a connection through mutual understanding and sympathy—and that, at times, unwilling as he was to admit it, Waldo coveted for himself. For Margaret knew Waldo suffered too, though he presented a "cold pedantic self" to his parlor guests or argued for a *Dial* "measuring no hours but those of sunshine." After age thirty, "a man wakes up sad every morning," he had written in his journal, for no one else to read; but Margaret sensed his melancholy. She had published his beloved Ellen's poems in *The Dial*, as well as poetry and essays written by his two favorite brothers, Charles and Edward, once his closest friends, both lost to tuberculosis within five years of Ellen's death in 1831. Margaret had enabled his mourning, sustained Waldo in his loss. Why wouldn't he meet her in the same way, allow her into his heart?

Margaret had "taxed" Waldo for his coldness before the summer of broken covenants. In a journal passage of the previous winter, Waldo recorded that Margaret told him she'd rather go to his lectures — "the best of me is there" — than talk with him in Concord. "It is even so," he admitted to himself. "Most of the persons whom I see in my own house I see across a gulf. I cannot go to them nor they come to me." When "friendship of the noble-minded is offered me, I am made sensible of my disunion with myself. The head is of gold, the feet are of clay." He could "see the ludicrousness of the plight," yet he would not put aside "my churl's mask." This "privation," his diffidence at close range even in his own home, he believed, "has certain rich compensations inasmuch as it makes my solitude dearer." Although he courted friendship, when guests arrived, all too often "in my heart I beseech them to begone & I flee to the secretest hemlock shade in Walden Woods to recover my selfrespect. *Patimur quisque Suos Manes!*" (*We each must bear our own destiny!*)

But Margaret would not give up on him, and instead learned to hold back, knowing that an open expression of emotion "might destroy relations, and I might not be able to be calm and chip marble with you any more," she teased. If she spoke to Waldo of her need, it was in code. Filling out the final blank pages of the first issue of *The Dial*, Margaret dropped in several poems of her own and one of Sarah Clarke's, and a few lines of prose ending, "Wise man, you never knew what it is to love." Then she wrote Waldo, asking him to "admire the winding up, the concluding sentence!!" He did not respond.

The expansion of their dyad to include the "young people" gave both Margaret and Waldo hope of more: "of being often & often shined on & rained on by these influences of being steeped in this light & so ripened to power whereof I yet dreamed not," Waldo rhapsodized, "suddenly uplifted" by the notion, foreign to him since Ellen's death, that "nobleness is loving, & delights in sharing itself." He "dared" to entertain "unlimited hopes" of "the four persons who seemed to offer me love at the same time and draw to me & draw me to them." Of the intimate conclave at Concord, Waldo wrote to Margaret, "I have lived one day." She had won him to her side.

But now she was bereft. Anna and Sam had not invited her to their wedding, where Waldo would appear as honored guest. A powerfully emotive single woman might have unsettled the celebrants, whereas a noted former minister—a married man—would seem to pose no threat. A week went by, and finally Margaret wrote Cary to "tell you how I fare,—yet it seems impossible. Rivers of life flow, seas surge between me and you[.] I cannot look back, nor remember how I passed them . . . I have no future, as no past." The best she could say was "I live, I am." She would remember her promise, made to Cary at midsummer, to find out Ellery Channing's address.

Margaret had received a letter from Waldo, thanking her "for the joy I have drawn & do still draw from these flying days," and pledging, "I shall never go quite back to my old arctic habits." He acknowledged his own hurt—"a flash of lightning shivers my castle in the air"—and the far greater "bereavement" that was Margaret's, "whose heart unceasingly demands all, & is a sea that hates an ebb." He urged her to "write to me from any mood: I would not lose any ray from this particular house of heaven in which we have lately abode."

And there was her mistake. She believed he wanted to hear all. She would write to him now of the "love" that animated her passions for their young friends, but that had at its source her love for Waldo, her desire to win his special regard—"I need to be recognized," she would tell him. Only one of her many letters to Waldo has survived from the several weeks leading up to and immediately following Anna and Sam's wedding on October 3, Sam's twenty-third birthday, also the fifth anniversary of Timothy Fuller's death. But Margaret saved all of Waldo's, each one marking a steady decline in his willingness to hear from her in "any mood," his weakening belief in "love . . . sharing itself," until finally: "I ought never to have suffered you to lead me into . . . writing on our relation."

He wished instead to turn the clock back, to "live as we have always done": "I was content & happy to meet on a human footing a woman of sense & sentiment with whom one could exchange reasonable words." A temperate connection was the "foundation of everlasting friendship," and "the slower & with the more intervals the better." Why couldn't theirs be a "relation" like that "of brothers who are intimate & perfect friends without having ever spoken of the fact"? But "ask me what I think of you & me,—& I am put to confusion . . . Do not expect it of me again for a very long time."

Along the way Waldo had let Margaret know that it was to Cary "I write my letters lately," receiving "golden epistles" in return: "I have agreed that we are brother & sister by divine invisible parentage." Waldo's only sister, Mary Caroline, had been born the year he was eight, the same year his father died; she lived until age three. Waldo told Margaret that "I have dreamed dreams concerning or with our radiant pair of lovers," but did not mention that "these extraordinary enlargements of my little heart" included a "new covenant" with Anna and Sam, now also too "my brother, my sister!" In his journal Waldo wrote "gladly" of recent scientific discoveries that seemed to open the possibility that "we have these subterranean, or rather, these supersensuous channels of communication, and that spirits can meet in their pure upper sky without the help of organs." Supersensuous channels: electric affinities.

By contrast, in response to Margaret's assertion, quoted by Waldo from one of her lost letters, that "I am yours & yours shall be," Waldo objected that "you & I are not inhabitants of one thought of the Divine Mind, but of two thoughts . . . we meet & treat like foreign states, one maritime, one inland, whose trade & laws are essentially unlike." In another letter, he doubted that he and Margaret could ever "reconcile our wide sights," that Margaret could "give me a look through your telescope or you one through mine;—an all explaining look." Finally, bluntly, he stated outright, "Sometimes you appeal to sympathies I have not." The concluding couplet of "The Visit" went further still:

> *If Love his moment overstay,*
> *Hatred's swift repulsions play.*

Having been party to the original covenant—present for the "three golden days," the "one day"—Margaret knew now it wasn't so much emotion Waldo resisted. He had welcomed the feeling natures of Cary, of Anna, and of Sam. It was *her* emotions, the unceasing sea of them, that overwhelmed, even repulsed him. Margaret's pining for "a life more intense," as she wrote once to a female friend, threatened Waldo's hard-won equanimity as she sought to make him the partner of her passionate intensity. "O these tedious, tedious attempts to learn the universe by thought alone," she complained of Waldo. One day she would taunt him: "You are intellect, I am life."

Waldo acknowledged Margaret's sovereignty, but her magnetic personality unsettled him, and he accused her of a will to power that she both conceded and denied. In her one surviving letter to Waldo from this time, which began, defensively, "I have felt the impossibility of meeting far more than you," she asked Waldo to "misunderstand me less" on this one point: "I do not love power other than every vigorous nature delights to feel itself living." She would not dispute her need to exert a "deep living force." But, she admonished Waldo, she did not "violate the sanctity of relations" any more than he had in their association with Anna, Cary, and Sam: "Could I lead the highest Angel captive by a look, that look I would not give, unless prompted by true love. I am no usurper. I ask only mine own inheritance."

That inheritance, she believed, was her right to the "highest office of friendship": that Waldo should offer to her "the clue of the labyrinth of my own being." That he should remain "faithful through the dark hours to the bright." Instead, when Margaret wrote to him from her heart, Waldo's response had been "I know not what this means; perhaps this will trouble me; the time will come when I shall hide my eyes from this mood." His incomprehension, his refusals, had taught her, finally, that "you are not the friend I seek."

And what did Waldo seek? "Did not you ask for a 'foe' in your friend?" she pressed him. "Did not you ask for a 'large formidable nature'?" Margaret could easily oblige. But "a beautiful foe, I am not yet, to you. Shall I ever be?"

Forced to accept the limitations of Waldo's "higher" style of friendship, Margaret now had to reckon with the awareness that, as she wrote to him later, "I value you more than I do myself." It was almost true, and she would have to change this in herself. For Margaret, unlike all the others, there was "no mortal, who, if I laid down my burden, would take care of it while I slept." She must learn to be "my own priest, pupil, parent, child, husband, and wife"—the "destiny" she had once foreseen and now would accept and fulfill.

In the weeks after their wedding, Anna and Sam welcomed Margaret too into a "new alliance," hoping to ease her hurt feelings. They spent an evening at Willow Brook, speaking little, but "all three meeting in one joy." After the couple left, however, Margaret realized she no longer envied their happiness. "Is it that whatever seems complete sinks at once into the finite?" she wondered. Anna's "strongest expression of pleasure," which she repeated over and over, Margaret noticed, was "I feel as if I had been married twenty years." How could an already too familiar marriage compare to Margaret's hazily imagined possibilities among the celestial five? Anna told Margaret she was her "Priestess," and "that name made me perfectly happy," Margaret reported to William Channing. "Long has been my consecration; may I not meet those I hold dear at the altar?" Let happiness again be deferred to a distant eternity.

What helped most was turning inward, cultivating "the deepest privacy," Margaret wrote to William Channing: "Where can I hide till I am given to myself?" In her journal she confessed, "I grow more and more what they will call a mystic. Nothing interests me except listening to the secret harmonies of nature." She composed the story of the Magnolia, who had died and was reborn into a "Woman's heaven." She dreamed of establishing an ideal "community" on the banks of the Merrimack River at Curzon's Mill in Newburyport, where she spent several warm October days with Cary. The "fair company" she numbered, aiming to "lie more at ease" together "in the lap of Nature," did not include Waldo or Cary—only Anna, Sam, William Channing, and his wife and child.

Margaret's thoughts began to turn away from Concord and the "tangled wood-walks" she had taken there alone and with Waldo. "Waldo is . . . only a small and secluded part of Nature," she wrote to Cary, playing on the title of his first book, "secluded by a doubt, secluded by a sneer." The "harmonies of nature" Margaret heard were different, wilder and more subversive than the hymns Waldo—"that Puritan at concord"— had sung. To William Channing, well out of the fray in Cincinnati, she fumed, "I wish I were a man, and then there would be one. I weary in this playground of boys, proud and happy in their balls and marbles." There were "women much less unworthy to love" than the men she knew: "The best are so unripe, the wisest so ignoble, the truest so cold!" Her short vacation on the banks of the Merrimack had provoked not just the fantasy of a community without Waldo, but the desire, she told William, "to sail downward along an unknown stream, seeking not a home, but a ship upon the ocean."

As Margaret may have hoped, Waldo was startled by her retreat into what he called "a sort of ecstatic solitude," her renunciation of "all things . . . myself, you also," as Margaret wrote to him. "After this"—the failure of the covenant, and of her entreaties to Waldo—"I shall be claimed, rather than claim."

Inevitably, Waldo found himself on the outside of Sam and Anna's marriage too, yearning for Cary, who, cannily, kept him at a distance. "To you I can speak coldly and austerely as well as gently & poetically," he wrote to Cary, who did not protest the few guises he was prepared to show. "Will you not hear me, will you not so reply?" Sometimes she did, sometimes she did not. "Friendship," Waldo would conclude in his essay, "like the immortality of the soul, is too good to be believed."

And so Margaret and Waldo squared off in the Conversations—that "fine war of the Olympians," in Elizabeth Peabody's recollection—quarreled, then called a truce; the pattern would not change. When the Monday evenings came to an end, Margaret made plans to move to Boston in the fall, having decided that even the "purest ideal natures" need "the contact of society . . . to temper them and keep them large and sure." She looked forward to attending concerts, plays, art exhibitions, the stuff of life for her. She vowed, "I will never do as Waldo does"—flee to the woods. She enrolled Lloyd, who had proved more difficult to reform than she'd expected, as a boarder in the new school at Brook Farm. Margaret sent the family cow as well to the "fledglings of Community," where Nathaniel Hawthorne quickly dubbed the animal the "transcendental heifer," a creature inclined, like her "mistress," to be "fractious," kicking over the bucket at milkings, he wrote to his fiancée, Sophia Peabody.

Waldo, meanwhile, invited Cary for an early-June stay in Concord, timed for Lidian's departure on vacation with the children to her hometown in Plymouth. The quicksilver Cary moved him at his depths; as his elected "sister," she required less of him than Margaret did. If Margaret was to be his friend, it was as a brother—yet how could that be?

It was not just her unusual intellect and outsized personality that made

Margaret seem to Waldo more manly than feminine, but also her anomalous position as a woman "of the bread-winning tribe" who earned her keep as a writer and public speaker, her rate of pay approaching his own. Margaret was Waldo's female double, not his feminine muse, as Cary was now. Margaret felt this too; it was why she thought she would make a better man than he. And why she rarely looked at men "with common womanly eyes," as she once wrote to George Davis, but rather with an eye to friendship—yet on her own more womanly terms. If Waldo wished she would befriend him as a brother, she willed him to befriend her as a sister. The disjunction perplexed and saddened them both.

Not surprisingly, it was in a poem on the subject of friendship between two men, his literary idol the French essayist Montaigne and his friend Étienne de la Boéce, that Waldo inadvertently wrote the history of his complicated "relation" with Margaret:

> *I serve you not, if you I follow,*
> *Shadowlike, o'er hill and hollow;*
> *And bend my fancy to your leading,*
> *All too nimble for my treading.*
> *When the pilgrimage is done,*
> *And we've the landscape overrun,*
> *I am bitter, vacant, thwarted,*
> *And your heart is unsupported.*

"Now all seems fermenting to a new state," Margaret had boasted to Cary Sturgis of her Conversations for women early in 1840. The same could be said of numerous schemes for reform or innovation that gained momentum in Boston during the century's fourth decade. The city of nearly 100,000 residents had been quick to recover from the 1837 financial panic and had suffered less than other mercantile centers on the eastern seaboard, its conservative banking industry reaping a rare reward in comparison to financial institutions in New York and Philadelphia, and securing Boston's place for the moment as the leading port of its size in the Union. The new prosperity seemed only to abet visionary plans born of the darker days when Waldo had asked in his journal, shortly after delivering his incendiary Divinity School Address, "Is it not better to live in Revolution than to live in dead times?" Boston in the 1840s was, in Margaret's view, a locus of "dissonance, of transition, of aspiration" where "no three persons think alike."

The fall of 1840 brought dreamers of all stripes together at Boston's Chardon Street Chapel, a plain-timbered steeple-less house of worship newly built by Millerite Adventists at the foot of Beacon Hill, for a November meeting of the Friends of Universal Reform. The abolitionists William Lloyd Garrison and Maria Chapman were there, along with liberal religion's gray eminence Reverend Channing, the young firebrand Theodore Parker, Waldo, and Margaret. Chagrined when a turbulent discussion snagged once again on a question of church reform—how best to observe the Sabbath?—Margaret declared the meeting "a total failure" in a letter to William Channing, who'd resigned his pulpit in Cincinnati and was contemplating a move to Brook Farm or possibly to an "association" of his own design in western Massachusetts. "I will not write to you of these Conventions and Communities unless they bear better fruit," she promised him; "we are not ripe to reconstruct society yet." Still, like William and others at the convention, Margaret believed that "one thing seems sure": "many persons will soon, somehow, somewhere, throw off a part, at least, of these terrible weights of the social contract."

Just what Margaret's role in the rebellion would be, if any, remained unclear. She was as capable as any of the communitarians at arguing the difference between "Living and 'getting a living.'" To William she confessed that if she had "a firmer hold on life"—that is, had the money to invest in a share of a communal property—she might be inclined to sign on. But when George and Sarah Ripley traveled to Concord in a campaign to enroll Waldo in their experiment at Brook Farm, inviting Margaret and Bronson Alcott along for a hearing, Margaret held back. "The Phalanx talk was useless," she reported afterward to Cary, except in helping her make up her mind to abstain.

Margaret published two long essays endorsing the Brook Farmers' aims in successive issues of *The Dial*, written by Elizabeth Peabody, who shared Margaret's preference for city life over rural confraternity, yet had opened her bookroom at West Street for the planning sessions of the Ripleys and their friends—men and women "who have dared to say to one another . . . Why not begin to move the mountain of custom and convention?" Margaret sent Lloyd to school at Brook Farm and recommended the community to William Channing and to her Rhode Island friend Charles Newcomb, who boarded there for several months. She visited often enough to have a room in the communal "Hive" designated as her own. But given what she'd learned of the "limitations of human nature" from one particular group of individuals, Margaret had come to believe that "Utopia is impossible to build up" on earth. She never joined the cause.

She was not surprised, either, to hear that Waldo had refused the Ripleys' offer of a founder's share in their enterprise. "At the name of a society all my repulsions play, all my quills rise & sharpen," he wrote to Margaret after the meeting. The *idea* of "Community" had some appeal: he thought "perhaps old towns & old houses," such as his own, might be turned to a similar purpose "under the kingdom of the New Spirit." If only Margaret "lived within a mile," Waldo wrote, tempting her closer once again (but not too close), "I should have many many things to say to you."

Waldo's utopian fancy turned instead to plotting with Bronson Alcott to establish a free or pay-as-you-please "University" as an alternative to Harvard, the alma mater that had rejected him and that Bronson, with his rudimentary schooling, could never have attended. Waldo admitted that the plan, which would enlist Parker, Ripley, and Hedge to give "lectures or conversations to classes of young persons on subjects which we study," was "built out of straws" but nonetheless seemed to have "very goodly" prospects, for "a college built as readily as a mushroom." Margaret might also "join in such a work"—becoming a female university instructor! Again, Waldo's Concord would be the base of operations: "What society shall we not have! What Sundays shall we not have! We shall sleep no more & we shall concert better houses, economies, & social modes than any we have seen." The idea lasted only long enough to excuse him from involvement in Brook Farm.

Margaret also found herself turning down Maria Chapman, sometime editor of William Lloyd Garrison's abolitionist newspaper *The Liberator*, when she tried to draft Margaret into the Boston Female Anti-Slavery Society. In mid-December 1840, Maria delivered a parcel of papers to Margaret, advertising the Massachusetts Anti-Slavery Fair, a fundraising bazaar to be held three days before Christmas, and asked Margaret to give over her next Conversation to the subject of abolition. Margaret distributed the pamphlets at the opening of class but, acknowledging that her "indifference" might "seem incredible or even culpable" to Maria, "whose heart is so engaged . . . in particular measures," refused to change the topic of the day: "my own path leads a different course."

"The Abolition cause commands my respect," she wrote to Maria Chapman, "as do all efforts to relieve and raise suffering human nature." But she was more interested in the Female Anti-Slavery Society's recent move to expand "their object" beyond "the enfranchisement of the African only" and to include women. Yet here too the society's plans for improving "the social position of woman" were poorly articulated and seemed "quite wrong" to Margaret. She had made the observation several years before to a startled Waldo Emerson that "women are Slaves." Married women in particular — and that meant most American women — were, in countless legal and emotional respects, the property of their husbands. Their liberation, however, was not to be found in a political movement, Margaret believed, but in reform of themselves as individuals, a process her Conversations had already set in motion.

What of Margaret's own self-reform, the revitalization born of personal crisis following the breakup of the "constellation, not a phalanx" she had belonged to all too briefly? She had written to William Channing of the change: "Once I was almost all intellect; now I am almost all feeling." The wrangle with Waldo had clarified this; her early ideal of Roman valor had been rekindled: "I feel all Italy glowing beneath the Saxon crust . . . I shall burn to ashes if all this smoulders here much longer. I must die if I do not burst forth in genius or heroism."

Margaret's candid reappraisal of Waldo's capacity for friendship was mirrored in changed feelings for her longtime literary hero Goethe — or at least for the biographical project that had represented her highest ambition for so long. She had once written to Waldo that the book would require five years of solid work to meet her high standards. Margaret didn't have five years, and now too she saw the danger in "living so long in the shadow of one mind." It was time to part with Goethe, and she did so by way of a nine-thousand-word essay in *The Dial*, published as the lead article in July 1841, the month after Cary and Waldo's Concord rendezvous.

The epigraph she chose, from the concluding lines of Goethe's poem "Nature and Art," reflected the urgency she felt in her own life: "He who would do great things must quickly draw together his forces." She opened her appreciation of the great man by recounting what she called "the hour of turning tide in his life," the moment of "choice" that Goethe himself termed the "Parting of the Ways." Rejected by his beloved Lili, "apparently the truest love he ever knew," Margaret wrote, Goethe abandoned a life dedicated to literature in order to join the court at Weimar, where he would enjoy "favor, wealth, celebrity." Like his Faust, as Margaret saw it, Goethe left "the heights of his own mind" to enter "the trodden ways of the world." Margaret measured the losses and gains: Goethe's writing was never again as "pure," yet he felt, for the first time, his power and influence. Was Margaret's choice this stark? Would she ever have the opportunity or the means to make a similar decision?

Margaret had once written to Cary of her desire to "do something frivolous to go on a journey or plunge into externals somehow." Yet, with so few resources and so many obligations, "I never can, my wheel whirls round again." As Margaret's ambition intensified, it was Waldo who seemed ready to frolic. He brought Cary to his home, with wife and children away and only his aging mother in residence as chaperone, to indulge a chaste romantic fantasy they both shared. Margaret had published Cary's poem "Love and Insight" in *The Dial* several months before:

> *The two were wandering mid the bursting spring;*
> *They loved each other with a lofty love;*
> *So holy was their love that now no thing*
> *To them seemed strange . . .*

Margaret had some idea of what transpired between "the two"—the walks to Walden Pond and to the Cliffs near Fairhaven Bay on the Sudbury River, stopping along the way in "field[s] of outsight & upsight" to find symbolic images in the high-flying clouds. Cary often showed Waldo's letters to Margaret, who would have known, in any case, that the pair had "never declined a jot from the truth"—never violated Waldo's marriage vows or Cary's innocence. She could, though, guess at Waldo's powerful attraction to the "insatiate maiden" of twenty-one, his "great needs," as he wrote to Cary, for "a new partnership of unprecedented terms & conditions" with this "angel friendly to my life."

Waldo's letters to Margaret, written a month later while on a solitary seaside vacation at Nantasket, a stretch of beach fronting the Atlantic southeast of Boston Harbor, sounded the exuberant tones of the boy-men she had derided: "I have walked & ridden & swum & rowed & fished — yea with these hands I have caught two haddocks, a cod, a pollock, & a flounder!" Waldo asked Margaret to send along "a sheaf" of Cary's letters, which presumably he would not entrust to Lidian to forward from Concord, and to tell Cary to look for a letter from him when she reached her own coastal retreat at Newburyport. "I gaze and listen by day, I gaze & listen by night," the spellbound thirty-eight-year-old confessed to Margaret, "and the sea & I shall be good friends all the rest of my life."

But Cary held Waldo at arm's length and was as stricken as Margaret when they both learned at summer's end that Ellery Channing and Ellen Fuller, Margaret's pretty twenty-one-year-old sister, had fallen in love out west and were engaged to be married. Ellery had drifted from farming in Illinois to newspaper journalism in Cincinnati and now into a romantic entanglement that, for the first time, he had no immediate wish to escape.

This was not the propitious match that Margaret had envisioned for her little sister, and Ellen's readiness to throw caution to the winds and accept the marriage proposal of a man with no steady means of support seemed to make a mockery of Margaret's own sacrifices to sponsor Ellen's education and entrance into society. Yet Margaret knew the impulse that drove Ellen. In the Conversations of the previous spring, speaking of the marriage of Venus to the lusty warrior god Mars, Margaret had compared the more serene Olympian deities, who had been shocked by Venus's impulsive marital choice, to "modern men" who expected beautiful women to fall in love with "their softness and delicacy," only to find that "the girl elopes with a red coat."

In the earnest, high-minded Transcendentalist "Coterie," the roguish Ellery Channing was the red coat. The only man who could hold a candle to him — in fact outshone him considerably — was the coolly handsome Nathaniel Hawthorne, who'd left the Custom House post procured for him by Elizabeth Peabody to make a go of it selling stories to magazines. Byronic in his looks if not in his shy manner, Nathaniel Hawthorne had won Sophia Peabody's heart, and after he'd tired of a season of manual labor at Brook Farm, the couple had made plans to set up housekeeping in Concord, where Waldo had secured them the Old Manse at a low rent. When news of the Hawthornes' long-delayed nuptials reached Margaret, she had written to Sophia in congratulation, "If ever I saw a man who combined delicate tenderness to understand the heart of a woman, with quiet depths and manliness enough to satisfy her, it is Mr. Hawthorne."

The installation of the newlyweds at the hulking gray Manse on the Concord River, vacant since the recent death of Waldo's step-grandfather, the Reverend Ezra Ripley, was part of Waldo's grand scheme to build up "Community" in Concord — or at least "a good neighborhood" providing "a solid social satisfaction." He'd first tried expanding his own household, inviting the entire Alcott family — Bronson, Abba, and their four little girls — to board. A summertime visit to Brook Farm had persuaded Waldo that only "living in the house with them for years . . . permits the association of friends without any compromise." Then he'd requested his cook and housekeeper to join the family in the dining room at mealtimes to promote an egalitarian spirit. Both offers were refused. In the end only Henry Thoreau, now twenty-three and "an earnest thinker" with "a great deal of practical sense," in Margaret's estimation, came to live with the Emerson family and eat at their table. He would earn his keep as a handyman and gardener, and Margaret approved — "*that* seems feasible." Now when she stayed in Concord — sometimes with Waldo, sometimes with the Hawthornes — Margaret could look forward to evening rides on the river or nearby ponds, propelled by Thoreau in the *Musketaquid*, the small rowboat he had built himself and given the Indian name for the town's languid waterway.

Waldo's project to muster his comrades in his own Concord neighborhood had achieved new seriousness in the wake of domestic tragedy. Early in 1842, his five-year-old son and namesake fell ill with scarlet fever and died in a matter of days — "fled out of my arms like a dream," Waldo wrote. "Nature . . . has crushed her sweetest creation." Lidian, nursing the infant Edith, born two months earlier in November, and tending to three-year-old Ellen, who was suffering a milder case of the disease, joined Waldo in the sharp apprehension of just "how bad is the worst." From his study, where "our fair boy" had played happily on the carpet, Waldo wrote despairing letters to Margaret and Cary, recalling that the child had been a part of "every cherished friendship of my life." "Margaret Fuller & Caroline Sturgis," he recorded in a journal passage commemorating Little Waldo, had "caressed & conversed with him whenever they were here." Now he asked Margaret, "Shall I ever dare to love any thing again?" And Cary: "Must every experience—those that promised to be dearest & most penetrative,—only kiss my cheek like the wind & pass away?"

The child's death did not, as sometimes happens, ruin the parents' marriage. Waldo and Lidian's attachment was already tenuous, as Waldo's efforts at "covenant" and "new partnership" betrayed. He had remarried too soon after his beloved Ellen's death, choosing an older woman who was his first wife's opposite—decorous, erudite, more conventionally pious, and, as years went on, with Waldo's heart inclining elsewhere, prone to illness and depression. To Margaret, Lidian was "saintly," her "holiness . . . very fragrant," a not entirely favorable judgment. Margaret would never carry "a bible in my hand," as she once wrote to Waldo, contrasting her own personality to Lidian's, and she considered herself "no saint, no anything, but a great soul born to know all, before it can return to the creative fount." Nothing made her feel "so anti-Christian, & so anti-marriage" as talking to Lidian, whose company she avoided almost to the point of rudeness on visits to the Emerson household, often leaving the house just before dinner in order to miss the family meal.

In the months Waldo spent working out his philosophy of friendship—in person and on the page—he had puzzled over the marriage bond as well, propounding a more eccentric and self-serving theory. "Marriage should be a temporary relation," he wrote in his journal during the summer of his chaste tryst with Cary. "When each of two souls ha[ve] exhausted the other of that good which each held for the other, they should part in the same peace in which they met, not parting from each other, but drawn to new society. The new love is the balm to prevent a wound from forming where the old love was detached." It was an apt description of his own marriage at the time, at least on his side. Cary had become Waldo's "new love," yet he debated the subject of marriage more often with Margaret, his spiritual brother. She took a darker view, remarking to him on one occasion that "all the marriages she knew were a mutual degradation."

As an outsider to the institution of marriage, Margaret had little reason to defend it. She had argued with Elizabeth Peabody during the first series of Conversations that for unmarried women there came a time when "every one *must give up*" and plan for a single life. Now in her early thirties, Margaret half believed she had reached that point. Sometimes she reasoned that her "ruined health," brought on by the shock of her father's death and the years of overwork that followed, resulting in a "lack of vital energy," would have prevented her from marrying anyway, even as she "mourned that I never should have a thorough experience of life, never know the full riches of my being"—never experience a sexual union. From opposite vantage points and for different reasons, both Margaret and Waldo yearned for a "supersensuous" connection with "perfect" friends, above and beyond the physical realm, that would provide relief from the strictures of their particular domestic lives.

On behalf of the married women in her classes, Margaret held out the hope of reforming the flawed institution from the inside, whereas Waldo, for all his theorizing, believed nothing could be changed: "We cannot rectify marriage because it would introduce such carnage into our social relations." The "boundless liberty" he dreamed of, the freedom to move from one love to the next, could not be trusted to "even saints & sages." Waldo would not knowingly hurt Lidian, yet he wounded her grievously anyway when he restlessly wandered the outermost shores of the marriage, falling in love with the sea.

The "saintly" Lidian issued her own complaint, not against marriage but against the philosophy that to her seemed to have robbed her husband of his humanity. In a handful of manuscript pages she called her "Transcendental Bible," Lidian inscribed a list of ironic commandments, which Waldo claimed to find amusing when he read them and which almost certainly would have aroused Margaret's sympathy for Lidian, had she known of the document's existence. Although phrased in the language of an embittered catechist, Lidian's lament was also Margaret's:

Never confess a fault. You should not have committed it and who cares whether you are sorry? . . .

Loathe and shun the sick. They are in bad taste, and may untune us for writing the poem floating through our mind . . .

It is mean and weak to seek for sympathy; it is mean and weak to give it . . .

Never wish to be loved. Who are you to expect that? Besides, the great never value being loved . . .

Let us all aspire after this Perfection! So be it.

Waldo now lured the newlywed Channings, Ellen and Ellery, to Concord, promising to find them inexpensive lodging after the Hawthornes refused Margaret's suggestion that the two couples share the rambling former rectory. "Let there be society again," Waldo declared, eager for distraction from his sorrows: "we shall have poets & the friends of poets & see the golden bees of Pindus swarming on our plain cottages and apple trees." Ellery would join the Emerson household in September for house hunting while Ellen packed up their belongings in Cincinnati for the move east.

Margaret was spending a month in Concord herself at the end of the summer, having reached the difficult decision to relinquish editorship of *The Dial*. After two years of publication to the same mixed reviews — satirical responses in the press, enthusiastic letters from a handful of dedicated readers — the magazine was never to be a fiscal success. As with her teaching for Bronson Alcott, Margaret could not afford to continue without pay. Unwilling to let "our poor Dial . . . perish without an effort," Waldo stepped into the breach, admitting the need for a "rotation in martyrdom." The chaotic business of editing the journal enlivened his too quiet study, but now it was Waldo's turn to press Margaret for copy. He summoned her to Concord, where he promised to supply "desk & inkhorn" for her use in composing an essay on European folk ballads to open the October 1842 issue.

"I began at once to write for him," Margaret recorded in her journal after settling into the "red room," the guest room across the hall from Waldo's first-floor study, in mid-August. For Margaret it was an inwardly satisfying reprise of the early days of her writing career, when her father had bidden her to compose an essay in defense of Brutus and she had readily obliged. Late-afternoon rambles with Waldo to Walden Pond to watch the sunset, and even "long word walk[s]" in the parlor, were peaceful now that their "questioning season" was past. Although "we go but little way on our topics, just touch & taste and leave the cup not visibly shallower," Margaret felt "more at home," noting, however, with a tinge of regret that "my expectations" of Waldo "are moderate now," and "we do not act powerfully on one another."

If this was so, the change was lost on Lidian. Suffering from a low-grade fever and looking ahead to the sad inevitability of Little Waldo's birthday in October, she could no longer maintain her composure in the face of her husband's obvious engagement with a female houseguest. She retreated to the bedroom. When Margaret knocked on the door after two days to inquire about her health, Lidian "burst into tears, at sight of me." Through her tears, Lidian apologized, blaming the outburst on her nerves and the stimulant medication—opium—she was taking for the fever. But, Margaret wrote in her journal afterward, "a painful feeling flashed across me," a sudden perception that Lidian was jealous of the time she spent with Waldo, though, in Margaret's view, "I never keep him from any such duties"—to his wife and family—"any more than a book would." Margaret had learned from her own painful disappointments that "he lives in his own way." Waldo would never "soothe the illness, or morbid feelings of a friend, because he would not wish any one to do it *for him*. It is useless to expect it." She might have been quoting from Lidian's Transcendental Bible. In the end, Margaret rationalized, "what does it signify whether he is with me or at his writing"? She "dismissed" the eruption as "a mere sick moment of L's."

Yet the next day, when Lidian appeared for the noon meal and proposed that Margaret take a walk with *her* afterward, and Margaret answered that she'd already made plans to walk with Waldo, Lidian was in tears again. The assembled family fell silent and "looked at their plates." Margaret offered to change her plans, but Lidian, saint and martyr, answered, "No! . . . I do not want you to make any sacrifice," even as she admitted to feeling "perfectly desolate, and forlorn," and to having hoped that Margaret might take her outdoors, where "fresh air would do me good." Still, Lidian bravely insisted, "Go with Mr E. I will not go." Waldo maintained his silence, smiling through the commotion, remaining "true to himself"—as Margaret saw it. In the end, Margaret walked twice, first with Lidian, next with Waldo.

Now she heard from Lidian—not a philosophy of marriage, but the simple "lurking hope" that Waldo's "character will alter, and that he will be capable of an intimate union," the reciprocal exchange of affection and sympathy she'd expected from marriage. Lidian's confession only served to convince Margaret that "it will never be more perfect"; no improvement was likely in relations between the two. There was so much Margaret had schooled herself to accept — and by now had forgiven — in Waldo, but Lidian, as his partner in daily life, evidently could not excuse. Margaret advised Lidian to "take him for what he is," at the same time congratulating herself that she was not in Lidian's place. Margaret did not "have fortitude" to live in "a more intimate relation" with Waldo, yet "nothing could be nobler, nor more consoling than to be his wife, if one's mind were only thoroughly made up to the truth" of his limited capacity for emotional give-and-take. It seemed inevitable to Margaret, in fact, that *she* would be "more his companion" than Lidian, for "his life is in the intellect not the affections." Waldo "has affection for me," Margaret believed, but only "because I quicken his intellect."

The walk brought an understanding, on Margaret's side at least, that Lidian's "magnanimity" had "led her to deceive me" into a belief that "she was happy to have me in the house solely for Waldo's sake, and my own." Margaret realized now that "there are pains of every day" in Lidian's life "which I am apt to neglect." But Margaret's own position as great friend to a great — but married — man had its own pains. The wives of her close male friends "don't see the whole truth about one like me," she wrote in her journal, and yet "on my side I don't remember them enough. They have so much that I have not, I cant conceive of their wishing for what I have."

What Margaret had with Waldo was still considerable, and perhaps what she was best suited for all along. As Timothy Fuller's "plain" but brilliant elder daughter, Margaret had won her father's attentions away from a beautiful mother, becoming Timothy's intellectual consort. It was a role she knew and could play to the hilt. In the best of times, Waldo saw Margaret as Timothy had — as a "wonderful sleepless working loving child, with such aspiration!" as Waldo had written earlier that summer, praising Margaret for a lengthy essay on musical performances in Boston that she'd provided for the first issue of *The Dial* that he edited. Extracting Lidian from the equation, becoming "more his companion" than she, was a simple reenactment with Waldo of the original family drama. For his own reasons, Waldo didn't hesitate to play along. Margaret's mistake with both Timothy and Waldo came when she positioned herself as a needy child — "when my soul, in its childish agony of prayer," as she'd written to Waldo during the "questioning" times, "stretched out its arms to you as a father." Then Waldo disappointed her, just as Timothy had.

In his angriest moments, Waldo had railed at Margaret in his journal: "You would have me love you. What shall I love? Your body? The supposition disgusts you." Both Waldo and Margaret understood—as father and daughter would—that theirs was never to be a physical "connexion." It was Margaret's emotional need of him—"the holy man, the confessor," as she once described Waldo—that he found impossible to fill, even as he adopted a paternal style of proud admiration and nurturing: "I see no possibility of loving any thing but what now is, & is becoming; your courage, your enterprize, your budding affection, your opening thought, your prayer, I can love,—but what else?"

When Margaret stopped asking, all was well. Then she became to him "my long suffering and generous friend," and Waldo could write to thank her for providing a "fine *manly*" production for his *Dial*, restating the masculinist approbation that Timothy had taught Margaret—his anomalous daughter—was her due. Then they could walk in Walden Woods—"interrogating, interrogating"—and get to "talking, as we almost always do, on Man and Woman, and Marriage."

But Margaret was tending away. Perhaps she no longer needed a father-confessor—or at any rate, not this one. The disappointments had taken their toll. She listened to Waldo expound: "Man," he told her, "is man and woman by turns. The soul knows nothing of marriage, in the sense of a permanent union between two personal existences." For Waldo, the marriage of two *people* was a spiritual impossibility. Instead, "the soul is married to each new thought as it enters into it." The result: "at last you find yourself lonely." Margaret had originated her own unified theory of the soul as both male and female, but it was not one that left a person stranded in lonely self-sufficiency. Rather, fulfilling one's dual nature made the soul complete, an active agent in society, ready to answer the question "What were we born to *do?*"

When Waldo turned to Margaret and complained that all wives "claim a devotion day by day that will be injurious" to the "genius" of a man "if he yields," she kept her thoughts to herself—"for it is not worthwhile" to argue with Waldo. Margaret, he insinuated "with a satirical side glance," would "do no better" than any other woman "if [she] were tried"—if she were wife to a man of genius. For once Margaret had no "*words*" with which to respond to this unconsciously rendered insult. "There seems to be no end to these conversations," she wrote, exasperated. "They always leave us both where they found us": happy, perhaps, to have gotten off "a good expression," but at an unbridgeable distance. Waldo may be a "Great Sage," Margaret would privately conclude, but he was an "Undeveloped Man!"

Ellery Channing's arrival in Concord brought even greater disruption—"it has not been pleasant," Margaret recorded in her journal. After an evening's conversation in the Emerson parlor, Ellery followed Margaret to her room and accused her of being "too ideal": "you converse, you have treasured thoughts to tell, you are disciplined, artificial"; and then, "I shall not like you the better for your excellence." Had Margaret asked to be liked? It was her sister, Ellen, he had married. Still she tormented herself: could Ellery not recognize her "seeking heart"? Perhaps he was right: "my continuity of thought or earnestness of character" may have offended or overwhelmed the assembled "angels and geniuses," Waldo and his guests. Yet "I must take my own path," Margaret vowed, while still making an effort to "learn from them all": "these fine people with whom I live at swords points."

And now Ellery asked her advice. Cary Sturgis had written him a "capital" letter urging him to visit her on Naushon Island, another family retreat off the Massachusetts coast near New Bedford. Should he go? He had never "done any thing" for Cary before, "never come when she wished him to." Now was his "last chance" to answer her call, he pleaded with Margaret, before "I am once united to E. again"—Ellen, who was expected in Concord on Wednesday, less than a week away. Ellery swore his love for Ellen and "showed a clearness as to his relations with the two [women] that satisfied and surprised me." Margaret gave her blessing to the visit, never thinking Ellery would forget to come back in time.

Tuesday passed with no Ellery—and then Wednesday. Mercifully, no Ellen either. Margaret began to worry that "some ill has happened to him" and to imagine with horror the scene if "Ellen arrives & finds him absent on such an errand, when she has come all this way to him alone." Margaret could only think "it will deal a death blow to their peace." Too distraught to work, Margaret wrote letters to New Bedford and Boston, hoping for news, receiving none. Waldo wandered out of his study and into her room to read more thoughts on marriage from his journal, listening to Margaret's rebuttals, but "nowise convinced" by them. Nor was she persuaded by his arguments for "the nuptials of minds" or his rephrasing of the wedding vow: "I marry you for better, not for worse, I marry impersonally."

On Friday evening, Ellen — "my poor little prodigal" — arrived in a pouring rain, asking, "Is Mr Channing here"? He was not. Margaret thought she or her sister might faint. But Ellen "behaved sweetly, though so disappointed." Waldo was now "distressed *for me*," wrote an astonished Margaret. He beckoned her from the room with a whispered offer to drive into Boston "this very evening, & bring me back news." Margaret insisted he stay, but "I shall never forget the tender sympathy he showed me." It did not occur to her that Waldo might have had his own interests in the matter — that the unexpected length of Ellery's stay with Cary Sturgis might have disturbed her host as well and fueled his ruminations on the elastic potential of the marriage bond.

In her enjoyment of Waldo's rare offer of solace, Margaret had "left Ellen too long alone." Her sister grew agitated, concerned that Ellery might be ill. Why else would he not be there waiting for her? Should she go to Boston to find him? Margaret could say only, "He may not be there." But "Where else could he be?" was Ellen's unanswered question. Ellen began unpacking her trunk. She took out Ellery's picture and placed it on the mantelpiece, then asked Margaret directly: had Ellery been to see Cary? "He reads her letters a great deal . . . [and] needs the stimulus of such minds." Margaret would leave it to Ellery to answer this question — if he would.

The next day brought clear skies and the vagabond Ellery, in fine health and happy to explain to Ellen his errand to Naushon. She "took it just as she ought," with calm acceptance, thought Margaret, who through the long "wretched" night had reasoned with herself: "If I were Waldo's wife, or Ellery's wife, I should acquiesce in all these relations" — the dalliances with Anna Barker and Cary Sturgis — "since they needed them." Margaret would, of course, "expect the same" tolerance "from my husband" in return. Sleepless with worry, she had nonetheless decided, "I should never repent of advising Ellery to go whatever happened."

And in the end there had been "no tragedy." Indeed, as Margaret and Waldo had watched and waited together like anxious parents, she had gained his "tender sympathy" at last. Margaret's "great mistake" this time, she realized, was in thinking that Ellery—men—"will surely do as they intend."

Ellery never spoke of what had kept him longer on Naushon than he'd "intended," but later he admitted to Margaret that he had always supposed marriage would "be impossible for him." By earning Ellen's love, he had been "snatched from the wreck" of an ill-spent youth. Finally a "simple" life beckoned, the opportunity for "connexion with realities." But the realities of marriage had yet to descend on him, Margaret knew, and as she read through a collection of his poetry that Waldo was bringing to press—once again, Ellery left publication to his mentor—Margaret realized that despite her desire to safeguard Ellen's happiness, what she most admired in her brother-in-law was his tendency to avoid "connexion." Although Waldo's poetical handyman Thoreau, possibly envious that his age mate had published a book first, dismissed Ellery's verse as "sublimo-slipshod," and Waldo himself considered his protégé to have gone "to the very end of poetic license," the young man's *life*, as revealed in his poetry, seemed to Margaret "a succession of ideal loves, and moods pursued to their utmost." Wasn't that Margaret's tendency as well?

As Margaret was preparing to leave Concord, her essay on folk ballads completed, Henry Hedge paid a call, then rode by stage with Margaret on to Cambridge, where she planned to live for the coming winter. Taking leave of "the true community life at Concord"—a tarnished truth, she knew by now—Margaret felt once again her own rootlessness, but found the freedom invigorating. In the coach with Henry Hedge, the two friends debated "all the great themes"—Hedge steadfastly arguing the cause of church reform. But "I have my church," Margaret thought. "What is done here at home in my heart is my religion." Finally she was content to say, "I belong nowhere. I have pledged myself to nothing." And to no one.

Margaret left Concord to compose another first-page *Dial* essay, "The Great Lawsuit. Man *versus* Men. Woman *versus* Women," drawing on her talks with Waldo on "Man and Woman, and Marriage" as well as the many conversations, both formal and informal, on "woman's place in society" that she'd engaged in since first addressing the topic with her advanced class in Providence. Ideas flowed until the work reached nearly fifty pages, among the longest published in *The Dial*. The following spring she would journey west with the prospect of writing a book on her travels, as Harriet Martineau had done after her visit to America. Margaret had reached her own "parting of the ways," and she would soon leave behind high-minded New England to enter the "trodden ways of the world."

It was Waldo Emerson who would stay, bound to his "imperfect" marriage "because he dont believe in any thing better," and unable to forget Margaret, who, he would realize with increasing gratitude in later years, with her "radiant genius & fiery heart was perhaps the real centre that drew so many & so various individuals to a seeming union." But for Waldo, after the loss of his first wife, an unassuageable grief that was compounded by the deaths of his brothers and son, there would never be more than a "seeming" union. In the same issue of *The Dial* in which Margaret's "Lawsuit" appeared—arguing that "woman, self-centred, would never be absorbed by any relation"—as she journeyed by covered "lumber waggon" through the Rock River Valley in northern Illinois, Waldo published his poem "To Rhea," using the name of the goddess he had associated with Margaret since the days of the disputatious Conversations, and uttering a plaint that spoke for them both of their "questioning season" and their several lost or never-to-be-realized loves:

> *THEE, dear friend, a brother soothes*
> *Not with flatteries but truths,*
> . . .
>
> *If with love thy heart has burned,*
> *If thy love is unreturned,*
> *Hide thy grief within thy breast,*
> *Though it tear thee unexpressed.*

· 13 ·

"The newest new world"

I T WASN'T THE JOURNEY SHE HAD TRACED SO OFTEN IN HER mind's eye—by sailing ship or Cunard Line from Boston to Liverpool to be greeted by Harriet Martineau, then by train and stagecoach to London to meet Waldo's friend Thomas Carlyle, perhaps an excursion to the Lake District for an audience with Wordsworth before crossing the Channel to France, Germany, Italy. But it was the only means of travel Margaret could afford with what she'd saved from the past year's Conversations, augmented by last-minute gifts from Sarah Shaw, one of her language students, and James Freeman Clarke. James would lead the expedition in its first stage, serving as chaperone to his mother and sister on a visit to his younger brother William in Chicago, a family errand on which Margaret had been invited to tag along. Margaret had an uncle William Fuller to visit as well, in northern Illinois, the second youngest of her father's four lawyer brothers—the only one to move west.

It wasn't the *Wanderjahr* she longed for either; there would be only four months of travel. Margaret's "summer on the lakes," as she would title the book about her trip, meant Lakes Erie, Huron, and Michigan, not Rydal Water, Grasmere, and Windermere, where Coleridge and the Wordsworths had rambled. But the journey to the edge of the American West, traveling over rutted wagon tracks through the prairie, by canoe and "fire winged" steamboat on restless waters, was in tune with the originating mood that had driven her to write "The Great Lawsuit."

Margaret would tell a friend afterward that Europe "lost its interest" as she "looked upon these dawnings of a vast future" in an open landscape whose unfamiliar terrain and peoples alternately overwhelmed and inspired her. She had beheld "the newest new world," and the experience would bring about what she'd hoped for in putting New England behind her, if only for a season—"the birth of a soul."

Beginning with the first overnight train ride from New York City to Albany through a "dripping" rain, during which Margaret was awoken frequently by the conversation of fellow passengers or her own fragments of dreams, the journey would retain an "effect of phantasmagoria" that never quite dissipated. Cary Sturgis traveled with the party as far as Niagara, only to turn back after a week at the falls, claiming indifference to them and any sights farther west—she had "known it all before" through travel books. But on returning to Concord, her recollected impressions apparently became more vivid. A giddy Waldo Emerson noted in his journal that Cary arrived "with eyes full" of Niagara, "dreaming by day & night of canoes, & lightning, & deer-parks, & silver waves."

On the riverbank overlooking the falls, Margaret had also struggled to "woo the mighty meaning of the scene," to determine "the Americanisms of the spectacle." But the thundering torrent resisted her efforts to ascribe meaning. Rather than respond to the great wall of water, the rising mists and churning rapids, with the expected wonderment—female tourists were known to burst into tears, their hands turn icy in shock—Margaret found the "continual stress of sight and sound" oppressive, "so much water in all ways and forms." There was "no escape from the weight of a perpetual creation," no escape, whether "awake or asleep," from "this rushing round you and through you."

As with Cary, it took moving on—in Margaret's case westward—to recognize that these confounding first impressions *were* the "Americanisms" she sought. The West itself was a "perpetual creation," its young cities doubling or tripling in population every year, its prairie lands sprouting sod huts, log cabins, and the occasional elegant frame house. As Margaret reached Buffalo and then Chicago, traveling in company with "hordes" of immigrants from as far away as Ireland, Germany, and Scandinavia, who "crowd[ed] the landings" and swarmed the decks of riverboats, the sense of a great force "rushing round you and through you" would not abate. The nation's "life-blood rushes from east to west, and back again from west to east," she would write in *Summer on the Lakes, in 1843.*

Another vision from Niagara would haunt her as well, more specter than spectacle: the sight of an eagle taken captive and chained "for a plaything." Rude tourists taunted the pinioned bird with "vulgar" language, verbal "thrusts and blows" that, with "his head averted," the silent creature "ignored." In words recalling her translation from Goethe's "Eagles and Doves" — the "inly-mourning bird" who had "lost the power to soar" — Margaret imagined that the Niagara eagle "listened to the voice of the cataract" and heard "congenial powers flow[ing] free," feeling "consoled, though his own wing was broken." The eagle's struggle in Goethe's verse to resign ambition was a lesson Margaret also read in the extravagant futility of the falls themselves: "the conspiring waters rushing against the rocky ledge to overthrow it at one mad plunge, till, like topping ambition, o'erleaping themselves, they fall on t'other side, expanding into foam ere they reach the deep channel where they creep submissively away."

But the captive eagle at Niagara, heckled by curiosity seekers, symbolized something more American than a figure in a German lyric, and more tragic than frustrated ambition: the broken race of Indians, the nation's harassed and abused "aboriginal population," in the phrase Waldo Emerson had used in an 1838 letter to President Van Buren protesting the infamous Cherokee removal by "sham treaty," the exodus that came to be known as the Trail of Tears, warning that "the last howl and wailing of these tormented villages and tribes shall afflict the ear of the world." Waldo knew firsthand only the itinerant Penobscot bands who camped each fall on the Concord River to sell baskets, Indians long disconnected from their "aboriginal" way of life — not the Cherokee of Georgia whose fate he protested, nor the Chippewa and Ottawa peoples of Michigan and Wisconsin whom Margaret would soon meet on her travels, only recently ousted from their homelands by more sham treaties to make room for the "hordes" of immigrant homesteaders. In his letter, Waldo had argued that surely these "savage" tribes would prove their "worth and civility" if "duly cared for": all the Indian needed to "redeem" himself from the "doom of eternal inferiority" was an education in "the arts and customs of the Caucasian race." Margaret would see more — the "worth and civility" of Indian culture itself, the compelling beauty of Indian "arts and customs"—and ultimately hope for less, observing at close range the eagle pinioned.

At every turn she found these strands intertwined—creation and destruction, creation out of destruction. Margaret had looked forward to viewing stands of virgin forest in the Michigan woods, but when the ferry docked at the Manitou Islands to refuel, she found instead crews of Indians at work chopping down "real old monarch trees" to "glut the steamboat" and feed its fires. She was horrified by the Indians' role, perforce, in defacing their wilderness. The "rudeness of conquest" necessary to support "the needs of the day" was "scarce less wanton than that of warlike invasion." Who could possibly "make amends to nature for the present violation of her majestic charms?"

For two weeks in Chicago, Margaret walked the sandy shores of Lake Michigan or kept to her boarding house, reading books on the Indians, while the Clarkes enjoyed their family reunion. The city of nearly eight thousand seemed to Margaret to have been founded solely "for business and for nothing else," yet there was an integrity to the Chicagoans' single-minded pursuit of "*material* realities." The women, she noticed, "do not ape fashions, talk jargon or burn out life as a tallow candle for a tawdry show." Here James Clarke's younger brothers Abraham and William had opened a drugstore, now firmly established after eight years in operation, a feat that would have been virtually impossible, she knew, in the congested shopping districts of Cambridge and Boston.

Margaret was on the alert too for employment opportunities for her brother Arthur, soon to receive his degree from Harvard. Arthur planned to become a minister, and founding a western school of his own, Margaret thought, would turn a better profit than filling a mere schoolmaster's post back east, the usual next step for a would-be divinity scholar with no family money. Although she had initially been repelled to hear the homesteaders she encountered on the docks "talking not of what they should do, but of what they should get in the new scene," when Margaret thought of her brothers struggling to make their way in cramped New England she began to warm to the expansive "new scene." Later that summer she would write from Milwaukee to her brother Richard, offering consolation after he'd been passed over for an essay prize in his third year at Harvard: "I say that the award of Cambridge is no test of what the world's will be."

The two-week excursion she took by covered wagon, led now by thirty-one-year-old William Clarke, with Sarah Clarke and her mother, Rebecca, riding along, to seek out Uncle William Fuller, seventy miles northwest through the Rock River Valley to Oregon, Illinois, almost persuaded Margaret to make the move herself. It was mid-June when they set out on a meandering course through prairie grasses studded with wildflowers and the occasional "oak shaded knoll," ideal for picnicking. To Margaret there seemed "room enough to wander on forever" in this "country [where] it is as pleasant to stop as to go on, to lose your way as to find it." Accustomed to moving from house to house since childhood and reliant on lengthy stays as a guest in her friends' homes, Margaret was reconciled to her vagrant existence as "one of the band who know not where to lay their heads." But now, as the group stopped for lodging along their way at a series of farmhouses selected in advance by William Clarke, it seemed to Margaret that there was no "pleasant or natural mode of life except travelling." She proudly counted herself a Yankee "born to rove."

William Clarke himself provided much of the satisfaction of this journey. The two slipped into an easy intimacy, sharing the driver's bench as William regaled Margaret with "every anecdote of the country whether of man or deer" and Margaret responded with her impressions of the prairie's "blissful seclusion." As James's brother, William was familiar to her, yet his western life had given him a jocular confidence that James lacked — "we do not see such people in the east," Margaret wrote later. William "drove admirably, with a coolness and self-possession in all little difficulties": "He knows his path as a man, and follows it with the gay spirit of a boy." During the years of their most intense friendship, James had never quite managed to be either — and, in any case, he was married now. William was not.

If, by the end of her summer on the lakes, Margaret would dismiss westerners as "so all life and no thought," it would also be on account of William; as the party circled back toward Chicago, the younger man began to clam up in the face of her ardor. But on the trail to Oregon, Illinois, all seemed hopeful. Margaret felt, she wrote to her brother Richard, "overpaid for coming here." She envisioned settling on a farm with him in the Rock River Valley — in June a fresh green canyon with fertile plains extending on either side — after his graduation from Harvard.

Farm labor would be "a twentieth part" what it had been in Groton, she guessed, recalling the long days in the fields that had worn down, possibly even killed, their father, and "would pay twenty times as much." The siblings would "have our books and our pens, and a little boat on the river," and find themselves "at least *as* happy as fate permits mortals to be." She had begun to sound like a handbill advertising the benefits of western migration.

Margaret's health improved with the "free careless life" in the open air. She didn't even mind stretching out for sleep one night on the supper table in the barroom of a boarding house from which its "drinking visiters" had been "ejected" for the sake of the traveling women, who took over the parlor couches as well. She spent the Fourth of July, 1843, with her uncle William, who promised to help select a parcel of land in nearby Belvidere suitable for Arthur's school. The townspeople of Oregon, Illinois, put on a homespun celebration with ice cream and fireworks, but what made Margaret think afterward, "I had never felt so happy I was born in America," wasn't the "puffs of Ameriky" from the orator and fife-and-drum band. Instead it was the morning hike up a bluff overlooking the Rock River, where she found open pastures "decked with great bunches of a scarlet variety of the milkweed, like cut coral, and all starred with a mysterious-looking dark flower, whose cup rose lonely on a tall stem." The purple flower claimed Margaret's imagination: "My companions disliked, I liked it." Her habit of personifying flowers caused her to fancy that the blossom sprang "from the blood of the Indians, as the hyacinth did from that of Apollo's darling."

Everywhere she was alert to the plight of the Indians. Her delight in the landscape deepened her understanding of their loss, and she collected anecdotes from the Yankee newcomers she stayed with to use later in her book. Her uncle's family had dug into a grassy mound on their property to discover three corpses "seated in the Indian fashion." In her letter to Richard, she told of a homesteader finding "the body of an Indian woman, in a canoe, elevated on high poles, with all her ornaments on." Another settler told Margaret of looking up one day to see a tall Indian "standing at gaze," arms folded, on a knoll above his house, surveying the land until, catching sight of the white farmer, he "gave a wild, snorting sound of indignation and pain, and strode away." Margaret wondered how the Indian could "forbear to shoot the white man where he stands."

Rather than express "compassion" or "remorse," the homesteaders complained bitterly about the occasional return of Indians to hunt game the newcomers considered rightfully theirs. Sensitive herself to slights from the "white man," Margaret heard in her informants' callous recitals "the aversion of the injurer for him he has degraded."

After William Clarke had seen them safely back to Chicago, with Margaret's feelings for him rekindled by a last intimate conversation, spurring her to ponder, as she wrote to James, whether his younger brother was "most engaging as a companion, or most to be loved as a man," the women set off on their own into Michigan and Wisconsin. There, encounters with Indians became more frequent. Margaret was drawn to such sights as a statuesque "Roman figure" of an Indian draped in a red blanket, "sullenly observing" his fellows dancing for handouts in front of the taverns in Milwaukee, his expression implying "he felt it was no use to strive or resist"; and a "beautiful looking, wild-eyed boy, perfectly naked, except a large gold bracelet on one arm" at an Indian encampment near Silver Lake. But Margaret engaged directly with the women: a girl who explained to her the "medicinal virtues" of wildflowers, another who expertly ferried the party across the Kishwaukee River. At Silver Lake, where Sarah Clarke took out her sketchbook to render the scene, an Indian woman of "sweet melancholy eye" welcomed the Yankee women to take shelter in her tent during a sudden violent thunderstorm. It was here that Margaret began to observe the "worth and civility" of America's true first families: their consideration and tact amid living conditions radically different from any she had known, a "delicacy of manners" from which "the educated white man, proud of his superior civilization, might learn a useful lesson."

Later, traveling alone to Mackinac Island while Sarah and Rebecca Clarke recuperated from summer colds, Margaret witnessed the gathering of the Chippewa and Ottawa tribes — several thousand displaced Indians — to receive the fifth of twenty annual payments, primarily in tobacco, blankets, and other provisions, guaranteed under the 1837 Treaty of St. Peters governing the sale of their lands. The natural beauty of the island, a heavily wooded American Capri with its own fabled arched rock, could not compete with the human drama. Fleets of canoes arrived from all over the Great Lakes; a city of wigwams rose on the beach, illuminated by campfires at night; sonorous Indian flutes penetrated the humid air. During the day, Margaret walked the sun-baked shore, stopping to demonstrate her collapsible parasol to curious Indians, conversing in improvised sign language, kneeling one morning to join the women in pounding their breakfast cornmeal.

None of this gave Margaret any more hope for the Indian peoples or their land. By the end of her tour, she knew that if she returned to the West another year, she would not find the same "*fair rich* EARTH"; the "vast flowery plains" would be "broken up for tillage," the "real old monarch trees" gone forever, "converted into logs and boards." She considered it an unalterable fact that within twenty years, or maybe just ten, the Yankee "mode of cultivation" would "obliterate the natural expression of the country." She had been fortunate to catch a fleeting glimpse of "the harmony of the first design"—primeval nature—which the Indians, the region's "rightful lords," had preserved since before the era of the Egyptian and Greek myths Margaret had taught in her Conversations. The West was, or had been until recently, "new, boundless, limitless." Here, as in Eden, she would write later in *Summer on the Lakes,* there was "neither wall nor road." The only "gain from the Fall" was "a wagon to ride in"—the wagon, also, of the "omnivorous traveler," the "white settler [who] pursues the Indian, and is victor in the chase."

Frontier wives did not fare well either, Margaret observed. They had followed their husbands west "for affection's sake," only to find "a great deal to war with" in their "new lot." Their "unfitness" for farm life was evident in fatigue and melancholy, the result of strenuous labor and an absence of "resources" for pleasure: "they have not learnt to ride, to drive, to row, alone." Margaret could only hope that the homesteaders' daughters might gain an education in "the language of nature," allowing "the little girls [to] grow up strong, resolute, able" like those "students of the soil," the Indian girls who could tell the secrets of western wildflowers.

Pressing farther on to Sault Sainte Marie, Margaret hired two Indian "canoe-men in pink calico shirts" to shoot the famous rapids that ran between Lakes Superior and Huron, an experience that, like her confrontation with Niagara, left her disappointed. Seated on a woven mat in the middle of the canoe, Margaret hoped for at least "one gasp of terror and delight, some sensation entirely new to me." But the rapids were so swift and the canoe men so expert at fending off jagged rocks that "I found myself in smooth water, before I had time to feel anything but the buoyant pleasure" of the four-minute ride. Not even "the silliest person" could have been frightened. Better was the trip by ferry back to Mackinac in the company of the frontiersmen she so often reviled. The lone woman traveler in the company, Margaret let herself be entertained by their "sportsman stories": "How pleasant it was to sit and hear rough men tell pieces out of their own common lives, in place of the frippery talk of some fine circle . . . Free blew the wind, and boldly flowed the stream."

And then, to her surprise, she was greeted at the landing by Sarah Clarke: "such childish joy I felt, to see . . . the face of one whom I called friend."

Looking back on her early thirties, Margaret would realize that "I have given almost all my young energies to personal relations." The time had not been wasted. Out of her sometimes thwarted desire for connection had emerged the Conversations, *The Dial*—the enterprise that had so often seemed a matter of "writ[ing] constantly to our friends in print"— and, most important, "The Great Lawsuit," Margaret's critique of "personal relations" among men and women, with its demand that "every arbitrary barrier" to women's progress "be thrown down," its prediction that the liberation of "many incarcerated souls," both female and male, would bring "an era of freedom . . . and new revelations" when "new individualities shall be developed in the actual world." Derived in large part from private observation and buttressed with historical and literary examples, the essay would prove to be *The Dial*'s most enduring contribution to American thought. But the time had come to "look abroad into the wide circle" for new mentors and friends, new subjects and ambitions.

Margaret had long believed a "noble career" awaited her, "if I can be unimpeded by cares." Returning from the West, she felt more capable of realizing that destiny—as if "the language of nature" had educated Margaret to become "strong, resolute, and able." Experiencing such powerful reactions to other people's suffering, as she had years earlier when visiting the cottages of her sick and elderly neighbors in Groton, fueled a passion now to "take share in more public life," to write on large questions for a broad audience.

Her journey back to New England was a different sort of "phantasmagoria," this time of familiar scenes and faces. Traveling alone again, she chose a route that took her down the Hudson River to New York City, retracing in early autumn the voyage on which she had first met Sam Ward in summer nearly a decade before. This time William Channing, who'd settled with his young family in Manhattan rather than Massachusetts, greeted her on the dock, guiding her to the City Hotel and, the next morning, to Sunday services at his newly formed Society of Christian Union church—a haven for communitarian thinkers—where, to her surprise, Bronson Alcott and an English friend, Charles Lane, were in attendance, seeking support for Fruitlands, their planned utopian settlement on a farm fifteen miles west of Concord. Henry Thoreau was there too, in a back pew. The young Concordian Margaret had come to think of as "the man to be with in the woods" had taken a job as tutor for the children of Waldo's lawyer brother William on Staten Island.

Margaret stayed long enough among what she had once referred to as "those dim New Yorkers" to meet a few luminaries, including Horace Greeley, the founding editor, in 1841, of the *New-York Tribune*, who had excerpted long portions of "The Great Lawsuit" for his newspaper, and Henry James Sr., a new acquaintance of Waldo's who was soon to leave the city for Europe with his wife and young sons, William and Harry. An old hand at travel now, Margaret sympathized with the elder Henry James's decision: "the student (of books) should see Europe; on its own theatre he better understands the life whence the literature sprang."

Margaret wrote to Henry James Sr. from the "poor shady little nook" of New England, where, after a stretch of "splendid October days," she was feeling at home again. Indeed, her quarters on Ellery Street in Cambridge, with a view of the Charles River similar to the one she'd enjoyed from the upper floors of the Dana mansion as a girl, felt to her surprise "as good a place as any in the world." The chief reason: Margaret had talked her way into desk privileges at Harvard's library in palatial Gore Hall, then the most extensive collection of books in the nation, yet never before opened to a woman for anything more than an impromptu tour. Each morning Margaret could walk a short way down the road from the little house she shared with her mother to the turreted stone edifice and "have sweets at will," like the Harvard men she had once envied. Over the course of the next several months, she completed the research for *Summer on the Lakes, in 1843*, not caring that she was an object of curiosity to young collegians who "had never before looked upon a woman reading within those sacred precincts."

Announcing the plan of her travelogue to Waldo, Margaret wrote apologetically that her new project meant there would be "no lives of Goethe, no romances"—the biography and novels she had once dreamed of writing—only this "little book," which might amount at best to "a kind of letter box," drawn from her correspondence during the months away. But as she worked on the manuscript, which grew to include not just revised excerpts from her journal-letters, but poetry, passages of "romance," and invented dialogues, Margaret began to develop a theory that "in addressing the public at large, it is *not* best to express a thought in as few words as possible." Instead, she argued, "there is much classic authority for diffuseness." She had not written her book on Goethe, but she could follow the example of his entertainingly discursive *Italian Journey*, as well as Lydia Maria Child's more recent *Letters from New-York*, which combined historical anecdote with contemporary observation, and Harriet Martineau's politically charged commentary on her tour of the New World, *Society in America*.

While Margaret would not defend the improvisational form of *Summer on the Lakes* to Waldo Emerson—in fact, she continued to worry up until publication that "my mind does not act" on the disparate portions of the book "enough to fuse them"—she sparred with him over his editorship of *The Dial*, which was foundering under his leadership. She objected that "you would have every thing in it good according to your taste," which she considered "far too narrow in its range." As editor, and now as writer, Margaret took the opposite tack: "I wish my tastes and sympathies still more expansive than they are, instead of more severe." Literally covering new ground with *Summer on the Lakes*, she could revel in that expansive sensibility.

Margaret consulted Waldo about a publisher for the book and relied on him to act as her representative—the "friend at once efficient and sympathizing" she had lacked only a few years earlier, as she'd complained to James Clarke—but she followed Horace Greeley's advice instead. Rather than publish with the Bostonian James Munroe, who had brought out all of Waldo's books so far, she accepted royalties of ten percent from Little and Brown, a new Boston firm that would share the title page with Charles S. Francis and Company of New York, giving the book a foothold beyond New England.

Henry Thoreau had recommended self-publishing, with production costs to be covered by subscription from *The Dial* circle; Margaret would take all the profit once expenses were repaid. But she sensed the folly of such a venture in light of the group's failure to make money on *The Dial*. Still, she looked toward publication warily, having grown accustomed to confronting "the Public at large" from *The Dial*'s pages, "amid a group of 'liberally educated and respectable gentlemen'"—never before on her own. When she signed her *Dial* articles at all, Margaret still used the relatively anonymous byline "F." For her book she used "S. M. Fuller," stopping short of announcing her feminine first names to those who didn't recognize her initials. But could she count on any who were not already her friends to buy and read the book?

Little and Brown typeset her copy in installments, so that Margaret was proofreading galleys while she continued to compose, writing the final lines on her thirty-fourth birthday, five years after a similarly exhausting effort brought her Eckermann translation to completion. The finished book appeared two weeks later, just a year after she'd set out on the journey west. A second, illustrated edition, with seven of Sarah Clarke's sketches transferred to etching plates, followed soon after. Despite her anxieties, Margaret hoped publication would usher in "an important era in my life," and she was not disappointed.

Summer on the Lakes sold better than any single issue of *The Dial*—seven hundred copies of the more expensive illustrated edition were gone within the year—and better than Waldo's first book, *Nature*. But equally important to Margaret was the book's reception by readers and reviewers. The New York City imprint persuaded the mainstream press that Margaret had distanced herself from that "literary sect" the critics so loved to despise, the Transcendentalists with their distasteful "excellencies and oddities," as the reviewer for *Graham's Magazine* in Philadelphia wrote. Edgar Allan Poe, whose reviews carried substantial weight, admired the book's "graphicality"—its vivid pictures of the West; Horace Greeley announced in his *New-York Tribune* that *Summer on the Lakes* provided proof that Margaret was "one of the most original as well as intellectual of American Women." The New York editor and critic Evert Duyckinck's admiration ran even deeper: he considered Margaret's to be "the only genuine American book . . . published this season." While her old friend Maria Child was put off by the book's conglomerate form, advising Margaret that "your house is too full; there is too much furniture in your rooms," Waldo Emerson found virtue in what Child identified as a root problem — Margaret's "higher education than popular writers usually have." Waldo wrote to Cary Sturgis that the book had exceeded his expectations and "has a fine superior tone which is the native voice of that extraordinary Margaret."

In Boston, Margaret was predictably faulted by the *Christian Examiner* for her "reflective tendency." A former ally, Orestes Brownson, whose Transcendentalism had recently transmuted into a stringent Catholicism, offered the most severe critique, labeling Margaret in his *Quarterly Review* "a heathen priestess, though of what god or goddess we will not pretend to say." Before addressing the merits of the book itself, Brownson attacked Margaret ad hominem as "deficient in a pure, correct taste . . . and especially in that tidiness we always look for in woman." Still, Brownson allowed that *Summer on the Lakes* was "marked by flashes of a rare genius, by uncommon and versatile powers, by sentiments at times almost devout." If she was damned by one erratic former Transcendentalist and dismissed by the Unitarian establishment at home, Margaret had been praised in magazines and newspapers from New Orleans to New York City and approved by her closest friends. The book was not in the end "assailed" by reviewers, as she had feared, but instead, she noted gleefully, it "seems to be selling very well" and was "much read."

In one short season, the town of Concord had become a "world of infants." Ellen and Ellery Channing's first child, a girl named Margaret and nicknamed "Greta," was born the same day that Margaret finished writing *Summer on the Lakes* — her birthday. Earlier that spring, Sophia Hawthorne had carried her first child to term after a disheartening miscarriage the year before. The Hawthornes' little girl was named Una, after one of Edmund Spenser's chaste heroines, the representative of pure faith in his allegorical verse epic *The Faerie Queene*. In June of 1844, Sophia generously took a second baby to breast, nourishing the hungry Greta when Ellen's milk failed. In July, Lidian Emerson gave birth to a second son, Edward, the day before Margaret arrived for her summer visit; Margaret stayed first with the Hawthornes, taking turns with Sophia at minding little Una, and then stole a solitary week in the Channings' empty house. In an early sign that the couple's marital strains would not diminish, El-

len had taken Greta to stay with Margarett Crane in Cambridge while Ellery set out with Henry Thoreau to the Catskills for vagabonding.

Although Margaret had written to Waldo the previous winter that she
hoped his next child would be a son, to help ease the loss of his firstborn — "men do not feel themselves represented to the next generation
by *daughters,*" she had learned from her own father — she decided that on
the whole it was fortunate that her sister's baby was a girl. "Girls are to
have a better chance now I think," she prophesied. But that better chance
still lay in the future. Margaret was as uncertain as ever of the merits of
being an adult female in her own time and place, which still meant leading a primarily private life. While she never wished herself a man — "I
love best to be a woman" — Margaret felt that "womanhood is at present
too straitly-bounded to give me scope." She resented the need to choose
to be "either private or public," a choice men did not face, even with the
advent of parenthood.

When she considered the lives of her sister, Ellen, of Sophia Hawthorne and Lidian Emerson, Margaret felt at times that she might manage
to "live truly as a woman; at others, I should stifle." The bare truth was
that "I have no child," she wrote in her journal, though "the woman in
me has so craved this experience that it has seemed the want of it must
paralyze me." That same paralyzing "want" was also, she understood, "a
great privilege . . . [to] have no way tied my hands or feet." These young
and not-so-young mothers, she could see, "feel withdrawn by sweet duties from Reality." Yet while a public life might provide wider "scope,"
the prospect was daunting, inducing "palsy" when Margaret imagined
herself "play[ing] the artist," like her idols Madame de Staël and George
Sand. These were European women of means; how could she manage
such a life in New England?

In February 1844, before the publication of *Summer on the Lakes,* before the births of Una, Greta, and Edward, Margaret had considered
renting a house in Concord across the street from Waldo's. The rent was
just sixty dollars a year, and Richard could join Margaret and her mother
there, once he graduated from Harvard in August. The Conversations,
which had provided Margaret's chief support while living in or near Boston, were dwindling in popularity; perhaps the time had come to with-
draw to an inexpensive house in the country and attempt to "play the

artist," to write more books. In March she also faced the certainty that William Clarke, for whom she'd entertained an infatuation the summer before, simply had no interest in forming a lasting connection, either as "companion" or "to be loved." William had arrived in Boston to visit his family and avoided Margaret at every turn. Worse, like other men before him, he was smitten with Cary Sturgis, who did not return the westerner's interest. Margaret hated the reminder of her relative plainness—that "I am such a shabby plant, of such coarse tissue." With spring in the air, it was painful "not to be beautiful, when all around is so." Margaret was momentarily undone by these "keen pangs" of "disappointment" and resolved to "wean myself" from "close habits of personal relations."

The Conversations had allowed Margaret to tread a fine line between public and private life, offering her the means to develop and express provocative ideas within the relative safety of a domestic parlor—or Elizabeth Peabody's communal bookroom—just as the near anonymity of her articles in the "poor little" *Dial*, in Waldo's phrase, had dulled the impact of her incisive critiques and allegorical fiction. Conversation topics in recent years had strayed ever farther from Greek myth, allowing Margaret to make "wide digressions" into "autobiographic illustration" on "Culture, Ignorance, Vanity, Prudence, Patience," and "Health." But in 1843–44, only sixteen women purchased tickets—"there is no persuading people to be interested in one always or long even," she sighed to Waldo. Margaret decided this series would be the last. It had been six years "of such relations . . . with so many, & so various minds!" At one time, the classes had swelled to include Julia Ward, a New York City socialite engaged to marry the Boston reformer Samuel Gridley Howe, and Elizabeth Cady Stanton, who lived with her lawyer husband in Boston before moving to Seneca Falls. Now the closing session in late April brought tears from the sixteen stalwarts, as well as bouquets of purple heliotrope and passionflowers. "Life *is* worth living—is it not?" Margaret asked, and collapsed on Cary Sturgis's couch afterward for a rest.

The final issue of *The Dial* appeared the same month. Margaret's single contribution was a fictional dialogue between two old friends over their weakening bond. "Our intercourse no longer ministers to my thoughts, to my hopes," declares one. "Ah! you have become indifferent to me," cries the other, only to be admonished that "reason seems cold because it is calm." Margaret's dialogue was framed by two of Sam Ward's poems, "The Twin Loves" and "The Consolers." The issue was thick with poetry—by Thoreau, Ellery Channing, and Waldo, including his own verse commentary on a fading friendship, "The Visit."

Margaret had been right. *The Dial* under Waldo Emerson was more than ever a matter of friends writing for one another—and, in this farewell issue at least, quite often *about* friendship. The circle had contracted, become suffocating, stifling, small. Now that both of her professional outlets in Boston were gone, Margaret saw that these intellectual proving grounds had finally come to limit her range of influence. She had reason to "doubt whether this climate will ripen my fruit."

In early June, Cary came to stay with her in Cambridge while Margaret's mother spent two weeks in Concord helping Ellen with the new baby. Margaret would always find reasons to envy Cary, through whom "the stream of love flows full & free enough to upbear your life." Waldo's love for Cary, Margaret knew, though unspoken and never to be acted upon, was balm. For Cary, "The keel does not grate against the rocky bottom," the painful depths of rejection Margaret had experienced. Yet if Cary could not have Waldo as a partner in "Reality," how different was Cary's situation from Margaret's own intensifying belief that "I am not fitted to be loved"? Margaret now prepared herself to be "as much alone as possible," to accept that a solitary life "is best for me." The two friends managed a happy coexistence this summer, an "independent life in the still house." It was a way of life she might try again, but never again in Cambridge, she decided. With Richard graduating in August, Margaret longed to "get beyond reach" of the college bell's "clang." When the lease on the Ellery Street house expired in September, she would give it up.

Idling in the nursery at Concord was not the answer either. Talking with Waldo again in July, taking the measure of his "transcendental fatalism," helped her see this. She understood fully now that her "disappointments" in Waldo, as she wrote to him in a letter that must have felt like a parting handshake, were the result of "a youthful ignorance in me which asked of you what was not in your nature to give." Her last *Dial* contribution had said much the same. "Life here slumbers and steals on like the river," she added, thinking of the lazy afternoons she'd spent basking in the sun on a favorite boulder beside the Concord River at the Old Manse. "A very good place for a sage, but not for the lyrist or orator." If

Margaret would sing or speak, and be heard, it must be from elsewhere. Perhaps, her words hinted, Waldo himself would do well to shift his own base of operations. Margaret would not rent the house across the road.

She knew that "deep yearnings of the heart" such as those she had experienced in years past at Concord would be "felt again, & then I shall long for some dear hand to hold." But she embraced "the blessings of my comparative freedom. I stand in no false relations." Concord was not just a nursery, but a village made up of those "who only *seem* husbands wives, & friends." Margaret's own "curse" — to be "much alone" — was "nothing compared with that of those who have entered into those relations, but not made them real."

A young friend she'd met the year before at Brook Farm, Georgiana Bruce, urged Margaret to write an expansive novel on womanhood — a bildungsroman like Goethe's *Wilhelm Meister's Apprenticeship*. Georgiana's own "adventurous course" in life had come to fascinate Margaret. Tired of the intrigues of sylvan fellowship at the West Roxbury community, Georgiana had taken a job as assistant to the reform-minded Quaker Eliza Farnham, newly installed as matron of the women's prison at Sing Sing on the Hudson River, thirty miles upstream from New York City. Margaret told Georgiana she would not write the *Apprenticeship;* she doubted her capabilities as a writer of fiction. But she had accepted a suggestion from Horace Greeley that she expand "The Great Lawsuit" into a book — or "pamphlet," as she persisted in referring to the volume through most of her work on the project — which Greeley, who admired the essay's "remarkable justness" and "brilliancy," promised to shepherd into print. When Georgiana Bruce sent Margaret some of the journals that the female inmates at Sing Sing had written under Eliza Farnham's program of rehabilitation, Margaret felt certain these women's stories had a place in her new book.

William Channing, a founding member of the New York Prison Association and an occasional visiting preacher to the men at Sing Sing, encouraged Margaret's new interest in female "moral reform" — most of the women prisoners were prostitutes. But Margaret insisted their "degradation" had less to do with personal moral failings than with the plight of women in general. The prisoners' diaries, she believed, "express[ed] most powerfully the present wants of the sex at large." As for the incarcerated women, "What blasphemes in them must fret and murmur in the perfumed boudoir." There was no separating one woman's disgrace—or deliverance—from another's, "for a society beats with one great heart." Margaret decided to take lodgings for the fall in the small town of Fishkill Landing, thirty miles upriver from Sing Sing, to make her own mercy call at the prison—she wished to meet these women as she had the Chippewa and Ottawa Indians at Mackinac—and to complete her "pamphlet." She would bring along Cary Sturgis, with whom she knew she could live "so pleasantly together and apart." Cary was writing and illustrating her own book, a collection of children's tales.

After this departure, Margaret would scarcely ever return to New England. She had decided to accept another of Horace Greeley's offers, this one to become literary editor of the *New-York Tribune*. Greeley had closed his literary magazine, *The New-Yorker*, to found the *Tribune* shortly after *The Dial* came into existence, and his daily paper had achieved a success well beyond that of the Transcendentalists' high-minded quarterly he so admired, with more than thirty thousand subscribers in the city and many more readers of its weekly edition throughout the northern states and the western territories where Margaret had traveled. For Margaret, accepting the assignment meant moving to the city in order to write regular columns—not just book reviews—on all the arts. Greeley considered Margaret "already eminent in the higher walks of Literature" and believed her contributions would "render this paper inferior to no other in the extent and character of its Literary matter," as he wrote when he announced she would take over the editorship in December 1844. Not only would Margaret's reviews and reportage bring distinction to the *Tribune*, but the attention she gave to the city's burgeoning performing arts would help make New York America's first city, as it was fast becoming, leaving Boston, with its inward-looking philosophers and single-minded reformers, far behind. Margaret always retained her New England–bred, spiritually based intellectualism, her belief that "the wiser mind rejoices that it can no way be excused from constant thought, from an ever springing life." But it was time to "at least try" to make her way in "the busy rushing world" of New York City.

For seven weeks in October and November of 1844, Margaret wrote and revised at Fishkill Landing, the manuscript "spinning out beneath my hand." Once again she produced an amalgam, introducing into her original critique of "personal relations" (inspired to a large extent by

Conversations at West Street and conversations with Waldo) her new ideas on the women of Sing Sing, an extended catalogue of influential women in the past and present, further thoughts on woman's essential nature and the possibilities and impossibilities of marriage, and a culminating argument that women should take up the anti-slavery cause. "When it comes to casting my thought into form," Margaret reflected now, "no old one suits me." She preferred instead to "invent one," which allowed "the pleasure of creation" to spur her on. When she had completed her "pamphlet" — *Woman in the Nineteenth Century* would be its title at publication in February 1845 — she felt "a delightful glow as if I had put a good deal of my true life in it." So closely identified was she with the work that, she wrote to William Channing, she expected to continue to revise it with future editions — "to be able to make it constantly better," the same wish Margaret had always had for herself.

· V ·

NEW YORK

City Hall Park, near the offices of the *New-York Tribune*

14

"I stand in the sunny noon of life"

MARGARET, WHO HAD ALWAYS ADMIRED THE MARRIAGE OF her friends Sophia Peabody and Nathaniel Hawthorne, and covertly acknowledged their "holy and equal" union in "The Great Lawsuit" as a model partnership of two creative minds, would have been surprised to hear Sophia's private condemnation of the treatise that became *Woman in the Nineteenth Century*. "What do you think of the speech which Queen Margaret has made from the throne?" Sophia wrote to her mother after reading the original *Dial* essay. "It seems to me that if she were married truly, she would no longer be puzzled about the rights of woman." In the newlywed Sophia's view, Margaret had no right to comment on the sacred "relation." Marriage, for Sophia, was a "revelation of woman's true destiny and place," which could not be "imagined" by anyone who had never experienced it.

When the book appeared, Sophia's opinion did not change. "A wife only" can understand the dynamics of marriage, she complained again to her mother, and, in expanding her subject to take in the plight of prostitutes, Margaret had given voice to thoughts that "should not be spoken." Other critics echoed in print Sophia's private reservations. "No unmarried woman has any right to say any thing on the subject" would be a recurrent theme with reviewers who dismissed the book — which, nevertheless, swiftly found an audience, as booksellers snatched up the first printing of fifteen hundred copies within a week to meet customer demand.

But Margaret's "disinterested" vantage point was precisely what enabled her to render so discerning a critique in a book that reviewers, whether favorably inclined or not, agreed was the first significant work to take "the liberal side in the question of 'Woman's Rights' since the days of Mary Wollstonecraft." Margaret wasn't married; she had no personal stake in defending the institution and plenty of experience in discovering that "woman's true destiny and place" could be found elsewhere. She was free to observe and free to say what she had witnessed — if she dared.

Other married friends, such as the writer Lydia Maria Child, whose difficult marriage may have made her especially sympathetic, found *Woman in the Nineteenth Century* to be "a *bold* book." Child had readily braved public outrage over her abolitionist writings, but she confessed to a friend that she would "not have dared to have written some things" in Margaret's book, "though it would have been safer for me, being married." Still, "they need to have been said," and Margaret was "brave" to have done it. Margaret was "a woman of more powerful intellect, comprehensive thought, and thorough education than any other American authoress," Child wrote in the *Broadway Journal*, and it took more courage and intelligence to speak up for women, one-half the people, than for enslaved blacks. And it took even more courage to connect the two forms of servitude and place them within a far-reaching system of oppression that cheated everyone of their humanity, as Margaret had done with this book. "There exists in the minds of men a tone of feeling toward women as toward slaves," Margaret had written. "While any one is base, none can be entirely free and noble."

Although Margaret's additions to the original essay almost tripled its length, its core arguments remained those laid out in "The Great Lawsuit," whose subtitle, "Man *versus* Men. Woman *versus* Women," alerted readers to the comprehensive nature of her inquiry. Man and woman, she asserted, were two halves of "the same thought." Neither "idea" could be fully realized as long as man failed to see that woman's "interests were identical with his; and that, by the law of their common being, he could never reach his true proportions while she remained in any wise shorn of hers." Conventional modes of behavior and patterns of development — the separate "spheres," private and public, in which women and men were expected to conduct their lives—prevented *individual* women and men from attaining their "true proportions." A house is "no home" for a woman "unless it contain food and fire for the mind as well as for the body." Every human being, woman as well as man, must be allowed "as a nature to grow, as an intellect to discern, as a soul to live freely."

Posing man's and woman's fates as linked, and emphasizing that neither man nor woman could "live without expansion" as individuals, had earned Margaret partisans among the male Transcendentalists. Henry Thoreau praised "The Great Lawsuit" as "a noble piece, rich extempore writing, talking with pen in hand." Waldo Emerson counted the essay "quite an important fact in the history of Woman: good for its wit, excellent for its character." But the events of the past year—the births in discordant Concord, the visit to Sing Sing, the favorable reception of her book on the West, with its explicit condemnation of the white man's abuse of the Indian, and perhaps most of all the "independent life" she maintained for several productive weeks spent "so pleasantly together and apart" with Cary Sturgis—pushed her both to strengthen her indictment of male culpability in female suppression and to adopt an impassioned rhetoric of uplift directed to women readers. "The world, at large, is readier to let Woman learn and manifest the capacities of her nature," Margaret declared, as if she could will her own recent soul-expanding experiences to extend to all women. She would not hear from Waldo Emerson about her new book.

Working at her desk in Fishkill Landing, Margaret had surrounded herself with volumes of Spinoza, Confucius, and Plato, spread open for reference—and she made use of them. But the extraordinary power and enduring appeal of *Woman in the Nineteenth Century* lay in Margaret's prescient readings of women's lives, related in anecdote and biographical summary with the same expansive sympathy she had applied as a critic to texts by her favorite writers. Many women—if not Sophia Hawthorne—found their own simmering frustrations acknowledged, and their secret hopes affirmed, in the book. For, extraordinary as she was, Margaret had plenty of "sisters," as she now addressed her readers, who had experienced similar cruel slights and crushing disappointments and could thrill to Margaret's recitals of them, as well as to her promise of a better day to come, if only women would "rouse their latent powers" and "assume [their] inheritance."

Margaret pointed to the beginnings of woman's suppression in child-hood, when, "instead of calling out, like a good brother, 'you can do it, if you only think so,'" boys instead taunted their sisters: "'Girls can't do that; girls can't play ball.'" When girls showed themselves the equals of boys in schoolwork, their accomplishments were robbed from them by being labeled "masculine." "Let it not be said," Margaret admonished, "wherever there is energy or creative genius, 'She has a masculine mind.'" And too few girls had the opportunity to face intellectual challenges and succeed at them. "If she knows too much, she will never find a husband" was a sad and self-perpetuating prejudice maintained by all too many parents. The corresponding practice of limiting the education of girls to subjects that would make them "better companions and moth-ers *for men*" was a pernicious one: "a being of infinite scope must not be treated with an exclusive view to any one relation." Instead, "give the soul free course" and "the being will be fit for any and every relation to which it may be called."

And what of that "relation"—marriage? Margaret lamented the fact that woman "must marry, if it be only to find a protector, and a home of her own." The security marriage offered was illusory, for in truth a woman had fewer rights when married than when single: she gave up all her property to her husband, forfeited her right to appear in court or to raise her children in the event of divorce, and became a possession or, at best, "an adopted child" in her husband's household. The marriage con-tract was a "seal of degradation" under these circumstances: the woman "belong[s] to the man, instead of forming a whole with him." Margaret invoked the eighteenth-century mystic and theologian Emanuel Sweden-borg's vision of a heaven in which "there is no marrying nor giving in marriage, each is a purified intelligence, an enfranchised soul,—no less!" and she applauded his imagined paradise as an entirely natural response to the legal and spiritual bondage of conventional marriage.

Yet Margaret held out hope for the reform of earthly marriages. She identified four types, each of which enabled wife and husband to function as equal partners, and evaluated them according to the degree of nourish-ment they provided for the "enfranchised soul." First was the "household partnership," based in "mutual esteem," in which the husband serves as provider, the wife as housekeeper. While such marriages were marred by a "mutual dependence" and an adherence to the separation of spheres, each partner respects the other's contribution, grateful that "life goes more smoothly and cheerfully." The second type represented a "closer tie," but a more dangerous dependence: this was marriage based on "mutual idolatry," in which "the parties weaken and narrow one another," living as if "in a cell together," believing that they alone are "wise."

The inverse of "mutual idolatry" was a third, far more positive type: the outward-looking "intellectual companionship" of partners who "work together for a common purpose." Such marriages were most often made by men "in public life"—artists, writers, politicians—whose wives become their "companions and confidants." And increasingly, as "the intellectual development of Woman has spread wider and risen higher," both husband and wife have "shared the same employment." Provocatively, Margaret cited as a prime example the extramarital union of Mary Wollstonecraft and William Godwin: two writers who married only when Wollstonecraft became pregnant, "two minds . . . wed by the only contract that can permanently avail, that of a common faith and a common purpose." Such unions, Margaret wrote, "express an onward tendency": "They speak of aspiration of soul, of energy of mind, seeking clearness and freedom." Margaret also endorsed the French novelist George Sand's extramarital liaisons as Sand's only means of "seeking clearness and freedom" in a love "relation" available to Sand after an unhappy early marriage arranged by her parents. Margaret deplored arranged marriages, or any marriage made for the sake of shoring up the parties' finances, and she looked forward to the day when "such beings as these"—Wollstonecraft and Sand—"rich in genius, of most tender sympathies, capable of high virtue," would not "find themselves . . . in a place so narrow, that, in breaking bonds, they become outlaws."

And there was a fourth, "highest grade" of marriage, which included the best features of the others, "home sympathies" and "intellectual communion," but added to these a "religious" dimension, "expressed as a pilgrimage towards a common shrine." Margaret was careful to specify that by "religion" she meant "the thirst for truth and good, not the love of sect and dogma." She also had in mind a particular style of devotion: a "reverent love," a sense that one's partner is the "only true" companion, the only other one "of all human beings" who can "understand and interpret . . . my inner and outer being." There was an echo here of the bond Margaret had hoped to form with Waldo Emerson, her "need to be recognized" by him, to receive from him the "highest office of friendship": "the clue of the labyrinth of my own being." And of the far from "ordinary attachment" she had felt for Sam Ward, her belief that "age, position, and pursuits being so different, nothing but love bound us together." Margaret had sought this highest relation from all the men she loved so far, inaccessible as they were or had made themselves to her. A "mutual visionary life," she had termed it the summer before when pondering in her journal the diverse attributes of the men she knew — the "deep polished intellect" of one, the "pure & passionate beauty" of another. That day she had allowed herself to imagine the perfect masculine amalgam: "I seem to want them all."

Not surprisingly, the marriages Margaret cited as examples of this fourth type were also unconventional ones: the Count and Countess Zinzendorf, Saxon royalty of the previous century who gave their fortune to support a religious community founded on principles of equality, only to endure long periods of separation as a result of religious persecution. And even more shocking than her approving passages on Mary Wollstonecraft and George Sand was Margaret's account of "The Flying Pigeon" — one of seven wives of an American Indian chief, but "his only true wife," who "inspired a veneration" because of her active generosity and the "quick decision and vivacity of her mind."

Margaret's examples of "onward"-spirited, egalitarian marriages all featured unorthodox, at times scandalous living arrangements. Yet her analysis dwelled exclusively on "supersensuous" connections — emotional, spiritual, intellectual. Indeed, she praised the "chastity and equality of genuine marriage." What did she mean by "chastity" within marriage? Margaret wasn't championing marital celibacy. Her critics, offended by her praise of Wollstonecraft and Sand and her sympathy for prostitutes, assumed she favored sexual license, but instead of license or celibacy, she was advocating something more radical: the personal integrity of the self-reliant female. "Woman, self-centred, would never be absorbed by any relation." The "excessive devotion" that results when women live "so entirely for men," when a woman makes marriage "her whole existence" — or, as Sophia Hawthorne had phrased it, her "true destiny" — Margaret argued, has "cooled love, degraded marriage, and prevented either sex from being what it should be to itself or the other."

Woman "must be able to stand alone." Marriage should be to woman, as it is to man, "only an experience."

While women sometimes wished to be men in order to partake of their freedoms and opportunities, "men never," Margaret observed, "in any extreme of despair, wished to be women." There was nothing for man to envy in woman's "lot," and the imbalance was too great to be tolerated. Margaret knew the aspirations stifled in little girls; she'd seen "the ennui that haunts grown women." She'd watched her mother and her friends become "absorbed" in marriage, their "self-reliance and self-impulse" degenerate into "compromise" and "helplessness." She'd witnessed Sophia Hawthorne's marriage of "intellectual companionship"—two creative artists working side by side—become transformed with Una's birth in the spring of 1844. Out of "obedient goodness," Sophia had abandoned her studio to tend to her daughter, and then to Margaret's niece, the hungry infant Greta.

Yet Margaret saw it as an encouraging "sign of the times" that *unmarried* women, once considered "despised auxiliaries," were no longer so immediately and "contemptuously designated as old maids." Single women could now strive to "gain, undistracted by other relationships," a greater "fulness of being." For them, and for men who might also choose not to marry, "celibacy is the great fact of the time": "now the rowers are pausing on their oars; they wait a change before they can pull together." Did she have in mind, with this metaphor, the rowing race from the *Aeneid* and the line she had taken for her long-ago theme, "They can conquer who believe they can"?

Margaret herself had become one of those women who "know too much," whom men were disinclined to marry. But in *Woman in the Nineteenth Century*, by way of an autobiographical sketch of a character she called "Miranda" (borrowing the name from Shakespeare's independent-minded castaway of *The Tempest*), Margaret offered belated thanks to her father for having raised her to become just such a woman. The fictional Miranda had been educated by a father who, like Timothy in his early years as Margaret's teacher, "cherished no sentimental reverence for Woman," but rather held "a firm belief in the equality of the sexes": he treated his daughter "not as a plaything, but as a living mind." Miranda had come to cherish the "self dependence" so often "deprecated as a fault" in women, but "honored in me" by her father. Although Miranda ultimately discovered, as Margaret had, that "I must depend on myself as the only constant friend," she was proud that she had "taken a course of her own, and no man stood in her way."

"Saints and geniuses," Margaret wrote, "have often chosen a lonely position," believing that, "undisturbed by the pressure of near ties," they might "understand and reproduce life better" than by direct experience. This was the "high stand" that Margaret took in writing *Woman in the Nineteenth Century*—the role of prophetic sibyl that Sophia Hawthorne had once admired in her friend but now privately objected to. From her "lonely" vantage point, Margaret envisioned a noble future for women. They required, first, "much greater range of occupation . . . to rouse their latent powers." She called on men to "remove arbitrary barriers": "We would have every path laid open to Woman as freely as to Man." Because "men do *not* look at both sides," women themselves must become "the best helpers of one another": "Let them think; let them act; till they know what they need." Then, "if you ask me what offices they may fill, I reply—any." In what would become the most quoted line she ever wrote, Margaret exhorted her readers to "let them be sea-captains, if you will."

During her last summer visit to the Emerson house in Concord, simultaneously exasperated and inspired by her as he so often was, Waldo had told Margaret that her personal emblem ought to be "a ship at sea in a gale," with the "Motto: 'Let all drive.'" The half-teasing, half-admiring remark was one of several derived from Margaret's conversations or correspondence with Waldo that found their way, improved upon, into *Woman in the Nineteenth Century*. More subtle than her rallying cry of "let them be sea-captains," but more profound in its implications, was Margaret's assertion of the "common being" of man and woman, her rebuttal to Waldo's isolationist statement that "man . . . is man and woman by turns" and so "knows nothing of marriage, in the sense of a permanent union between two personal existences."

Margaret's "law" of "common being" was also her ultimate challenge to the rigid demarcation of separate spheres. While "male and female represent the two sides of the great radical dualism," she wrote, "in fact, they are perpetually passing into one another. Fluid hardens to solid, solid rushes to fluid." The divide was not fixed or impermeable between men and women, or within the individual human soul. As Margaret had told the women who attended her Conversations, women and men shared "every faculty & element of mind," but these faculties were "combined in different proportions." Here she stated it outright: "There is no wholly masculine man, no purely feminine woman." If each human soul was permitted to achieve its "fulness of being," its unique combination of male and female qualities allowed free play, then at last there would be "no discordant collision," and a "ravishing harmony of the spheres, would ensue."

In the journal Margaret kept while revising *Woman in the Nineteenth Century*, she had sketched two overlapping equilateral triangles to form a six-pointed star, encircled by a snake biting its own tail—the Greek *ouroboros*, or symbol of eternity. Rays of light emanated from the emblem—her own, not Waldo's storm-tossed driving ship—and she explained the image with these lines in verse:

> *Patient serpent, circle round*
> *Till in death thy life is found,*
> *Double form of godly prime*
> *Holding the whole thought of time,*
> *When the perfect two embrace,*
> *Male and female, black and white*
> *Soul is justified in space,*
> *Dark made fruitful by the light,*
> *And centred in the diamond Sun*
> *Time, eternity, are one.*

Margaret transferred the symbol to the frontispiece of her book, one triangle white, the other shaded black. Whether or not readers understood the image, which appeared without the explanatory poem, its message of radiant unity galvanized Margaret's narrative and worked its way into her closing paragraphs, in which she invited women to follow her own example by turning away from regrets, resentments, all that bound and fettered them. "I stand in the sunny noon of life," she wrote, and "what concerns me now is, that my life be a beautiful, powerful, in a word, a complete life."

· · ·

Woman in the Nineteenth Century did its work. Readers felt "their wounds probed, and healing promised by it," Margaret wrote to Cary Sturgis, marveling at the "ardent interest" the book "excites in those who have never known me." Advertisements dubbed it the "Great Book of the Age," claiming: "The thousands who have perused this book speak of it as being the only one which has been written, in which WOMAN is portrayed in her real and true character." As for reviewers, "the opposition and sympathy it excites are both great," Margaret reported to Cary, exhilarated by the attention. Whether she was faulted for "loose" doctrine or praised for upholding a "chaste ideal," Margaret knew she had been "heard," and the brisk sales, along with the eighty-five dollars she earned from the book during its first week, were the "speaking fact[s]" that proved it.

Although Cary had been writing in an adjoining room at Fishkill Landing as Margaret revised the book, the two women were worlds apart four months later when it was published. Cary wrote of her reaction to the "pamphlet," as she continued to refer to *Woman in the Nineteenth Century* even after learning it had been declared the "Great Book of the Age," from her father's echoing mansion on Summer Street in "demure Boston." There, as the only one of four older sisters not yet married off, she was supervising her twenty-year-old youngest sister Susie's entrance into society and paying visits to their mentally unstable mother in nearby Brookline. Cary's letter reached Margaret in early March 1845 at Horace Greeley's ramshackle rented mansion on Turtle Bay—where 49th Street would one day end at the rocky banks of the East River—and brought with it the chill of New England, or of a friend suffering abandonment.

"The style troubles me very much," Cary complained of the book, which reads "as if you had gathered flowers and planted them in a garden but had left the roots in their own soil." The volume was "full of suggestions," she granted, "but one living child is worth a whole series of tableaux. It is not a book to take to heart and that is what a book upon women should be." Cary's blunt criticism was not hard to interpret. The success of *Woman in the Nineteenth Century* represented Margaret's New York City flowering, but where were her roots? At ages twenty-six and thirty-four, both Cary and Margaret inwardly sorrowed over their lack of "one living child" while their sisters had taken infants to breast. And, capricious as Cary was in her affections for Margaret, she missed her former teacher, and more than ever wished Margaret might take *her* to heart. Shortly after they'd parted in the fall, Cary had written Margaret a rare letter of distress, confiding that her mother had slipped into one of her "trances," pacing the darkened rooms of her Brookline home, "her gaze bent upon the floor as if fixed there by all the swords that ever fought in Jerusalem." And, frighteningly, "She depends upon me more than upon any-one."

"It makes me sad that it is necessary such [a book] should be written," Cary added now in her letter to Margaret, searching for some way to retrieve the situation and offer praise, "but since it is so[,] it cannot but do good to lift the veil as you have done." Still, Margaret was stung, writing to her brother Richard, "I have found the stranger more sympathizing and . . . intelligent than some of my private friends." But the weeks spent with Cary in June and October had helped Margaret to forgive her younger friend for having captured Waldo's fancy, for the material advantages that had seemed like liberty. For the "first time," Margaret admitted in her diary, she could understand Cary's "position": "What a paradise is my degree of freedom compared with her life." Eventually Cary would be constrained to marry a man who was not Waldo, or Ellery Channing, or William Clarke—or, if she remained single, to continue serving in the "prison" of Captain Sturgis's several homes as an "auxiliary" to her mother and sisters, perhaps not despised, but nonetheless consigned to a life that could not be characterized as less than "beautiful, powerful, in a word, complete." No amount of visits to or from Waldo Emerson, whose appearances at Summer Street Cary faithfully reported to Margaret, would make a difference.

Margaret simply chose to overlook Cary's churlishness. Her own life was moving forward too rapidly to pause for recriminations. Margaret's need to earn a living, that ceaseless burden, had finally turned blessing. She'd known, since the day she rose from Timothy's bed in Groton, that her father's death had meant her life, his end her beginning—the *ouroboros*. Not only did she sign her second book, into which she had put "a good deal of my true life," with her true name, S. Margaret Fuller, she also marked it with her emblem. And she would retain the star, in the form of an asterisk, as byline for the front-page *New-York Tribune* articles she began to write as soon as she'd delivered the manuscript of *Woman in the Nineteenth Century* to Horace Greeley's pressmen, ensuring that her own column would be distinguished from Greeley's unsigned editorials.

Choosing to work as a journalist for a prominent New York City daily was scarcely less ambitious for an American woman in the nineteenth century than becoming a sea captain. Although in her book Margaret had proposed that women serve as "the best helpers of one another," she had accepted a job that made her the lone female in an office of streetwise newspapermen in the Great Metropolis—for so the city was beginning to be known in 1845—which must have seemed, after "demure Boston," like a roiling sea of humanity. While Margaret had an enlightened supporter in her employer, she might have done well to heed the skeptical response of Eliza Peabody, Sophia Hawthorne's mother, to *Woman in the Nineteenth Century*—if she'd heard it. Unlike her daughter, Mrs. Peabody didn't object to Margaret's critique of marriage; rather, she thought Margaret too optimistic. As long as man "has the physical power, as well as the conventional" to treat a woman "like a play-thing or a slave," she'd written portentously to Sophia, "woman must wait until the lion shall lie down with the lamb, before she can hope to be the friend and companion of man."

15

"Flying on the paper wings of every day"

T HE MID-MARCH DAY WAS "DULL AND DUBIOUS," THE SKY "leaden and lowering," the birds silent in the chill air that had brought a swift end that morning to one of New York's unseasonable warm spells. But the dour weather seemed "suitable" for the outing, a visit to the "pauper establishments": first the old Bellevue Alms House on the outer limits of the city, on the East River at the foot of 26th Street, and then, by open boat to Blackwell's Island, a quarter-mile offshore, for tours of the recently constructed Farm School for orphans, the Asylum for the Insane, and the massive crenellated fortress of the Penitentiary, filled already with twelve hundred inmates. All four were institutions that "admonish us of stern realities," the chill winds of misfortune that could so readily effect the "blight of Nature's bloom," Margaret would write in "Our City Charities," her most comprehensive front-page *Tribune* editorial to date on societal ills.

These and other similar establishments she had visited since beginning to write for the *Tribune* in December — the privately run Bloomingdale Insane Asylum in rural upper Manhattan, the dank overcrowded jail in the heart of the city known as the "Tombs" — "should be looked at by all," Margaret instructed, repeating the imperative twice in her opening paragraph. She urged her readers not to "sink listlessly into selfish ease," now that the city had completed the three facilities on former pastureland on Blackwell's Island — the paupers' new Arcadia. The ambitious building plan was part of a wave of publicly funded social reforms that had swept the young nation since the establishment of the Worcester State Lunatic Hospital in Massachusetts a decade earlier in 1833, an initiative that had gathered the impoverished mentally ill from local jails across the commonwealth, where they were normally held alongside convicted criminals, and provided them with medical treatment in healthful surroundings at the centrally located hospital. As the population of needy citizens, criminals, and other outcasts swelled in big cities, the notion of providing enlightened care and remediation took hold elsewhere, and by 1845 few would have disagreed with Margaret's statement that "parsimony" was "the worst prodigality" when it came to the treatment of the poor man or the prisoner—though just what should be done inside the new buildings continued to be a matter of debate.

Margaret argued that New Yorkers should play an active role as visitors, both to monitor progress and, more important, to extend a representative hand of care to the inmates so that their benefactors' "intelligent sympathy" would be felt directly. The "acceptance of public charity," she wrote, can be "injurious" to the recipient in an atmosphere devoid of human kindness. "Men treated with respect are reminded of self-respect" was the reform doctrine Margaret preached, allying herself with progressives like Eliza Farnham, the matron at Sing Sing who had the female prisoners under her care keeping journals, tending gardens, and rehearsing for choral concerts.

Yet Margaret knew that few of her readers would heed her advice and follow the route she took on that dreary March day. Few would witness the "vagrant, degraded air" of the men residing in the Alms House, who lacked any employment "except to raise vegetables for the establishment, and prepare clothing for themselves." There were no books, no classes, no opportunities to learn a trade, no "openings to a better" way of life. Few would see the young mothers next door in Bellevue Hospital exposed to the "careless scrutiny of male visitors" as they nursed their newborns and echo Margaret's plea to allow them privacy. Few would be greeted on entry to the hospital yard by the little Dutch girl, a misshapen dwarf child abandoned in the city by "some showman," or notice, along with Margaret, how the poor "gnome" ran expectantly to the gate every time it was opened to search the face of each new visitor.

Out on Blackwell's Island, the Farm School—which, to Margaret's eye, was nothing more than "a school upon a small farm"—also failed to provide any vocational training for its young charges, even though, as Margaret noted, children "have vital energy enough for many things at once, and learn more from books when their attention is quickened" by a variety of pursuits. She admired the well-ventilated dormitories and the way the school's infants were arranged in a circle at mealtimes "like a nest full of birds" to be spoon-fed by affectionate nurses. But she worried about how the older students, who were required to leave the school at age twelve, would find work. Many of these "show[ed] by their unformed features and mechanical movements" the ill effects of having been "treated by wholesale"; they were not accorded the respect that engenders "self-respect."

The Asylum for the Insane too, despite its location on the island's grassy headlands and its ingenious design—two three-story neoclassical dormitory wings with a row of columns marking their separate entrances, one for women and the other for men, extended at a right angle from a central octagonal structure containing the doctors' rooms—appeared to serve as little more than a warehouse. Here Margaret found the inmates crouching in the corners of their rooms. They had "no eye for the stranger, no heart for hope," in stark contrast to patients in the privately run Bloomingdale, where "the shades of character and feeling were nicely kept up, decorum of manners preserved, and the insane showed in every way that they felt no violent separation betwixt them and the rest of the world, and might easily return to it."

The Penitentiary was gloomier still—in fact "one of the gloomiest scenes that deforms this great metropolis." There, seven hundred women, more than half the prison's population, were incarcerated "simply as a social convenience, without regard to pure right, or a hope of reformation," in Margaret's view, and they lacked even a single matron. As at Sing Sing, most of the imprisoned women had been prostitutes, and "I have always felt great interest in those women, who are trampled in the mud to gratify the brute appetites of men," Margaret wrote afterward to a friend, "and wished I might be brought, naturally, into contact with them." She was convinced, as she told Horace Greeley, they were "women like myself, save that they are victims of wrong and misfortune." Writing for the *Tribune* gave her the opportunity to test her intuition, and the chance to speak out, as she had in *Woman in the Nineteenth*

Century, against the hypocritical laws that made a woman pay for a man's crime. Why should women "receive the punishment due to the vices of so large a portion of the rest"?

Acute firsthand observation enlivened by "intelligent sympathy" had quickly become Margaret's distinctive style as a critic and, increasingly, as an advocate for social reform: to read, to hear, to see what the *Tribune*'s many subscribers could or would not, and then to shape an instructive message from her experience, was the means she chose "to aid in the great work of mutual education," as she summed up her ambitions as a journalist in a letter to James Freeman Clarke. To her relief, James had emerged, perhaps in an effort to make amends for his younger brother's indifference, as the chief—sometimes, it seemed, the sole—supporter of Margaret's new vocation among her old Boston friends. Cary might offer only slighting praise—"for those who like introductions[,] your criticisms must be of value"—and Waldo complain that the job, "made acceptable" only "by good pay" (ten dollars per week, two dollars higher than Greeley had paid his previous literary editor), was "honourable" to Margaret, but "not satisfactory to me." But James understood Margaret best now, as he had so many years earlier, and recognized that the *New-York Tribune* was "an excellent organ through which to speak to the public." Her *Tribune* articles, which had "more ease, grace, freedom and point to them," he told her, were "better written than anything of yours I have read."

It *was* the perfect job for Margaret, who always had an opinion on almost any subject as well as the verbal facility and the compulsion to express it. The "rich extempore writing" that Thoreau had admired in "The Great Lawsuit," her gift of "talking with pen in hand," enabled her to turn out three or four articles per week, more than 250 in eighteen months. The goal of "mutual education," as well as the space constraints and frequent deadlines, forced a clarity and efficiency of expression that she had not submitted to previously. Margaret was aware that her "old friends . . . think I ought to produce something excellent"—another book—yet, as she wrote to James, she had spent all of her writing life so far in "*the depths.*" She expected that "an abode of some length in *the shallows* may do me no harm." Like James, Margaret was already pleased with the results: in the shallows, writing about vitally important surface realities, "the sun comes full upon me."

Her success was attributable to more than the new compression, how-ever, or to the fluent delivery of swift perceptions for which she'd always had a talent in conversation. Margaret's eye for the telling detail and the poignant image, developed over many years of immersion in the great Romantic novels, in Shakespeare and the classics, allowed an easy transi-tion to the new style of literary journalism of which she promptly became a leading practitioner. Waldo Emerson was wrong to see the newspa-pers of the mid-1840s as cheapening their writers. In fact, the rise of the "penny press," papers like Horace Greeley's *Tribune*, which relied on subscriptions, newsstand sales, and paid advertisements rather than the financial backing of religious sects or political parties, put greater pres-sure on writers to provide compelling copy.

Seventy newspapers were listed in the 1845 New York City directory; the *Tribune* vied with the *New York Sun* and the *New York Herald* for top circulation figures in a battle that took place on the page. Unwilling to stoop to publishing lurid accounts of murder and mayhem, the stories that sold the lesser publications, Greeley nevertheless valued the human interest reporting at which Margaret instinctively excelled. The charac-ters and incidents she'd habitually recorded in her journals, noting they might make "scenes for a drama" or "materials for romance," now found their way into her journalism, as in the case of the little Dutch girl at Bel-levue, who, Margaret wrote, "would have suggested a thousand poetical images and fictions to the mind of Victor Hugo or Sir Walter Scott." She exhorted her readers: "Do you want to link these fictions, which have made you weep, with facts around you where your pity might be of use? Go to the Penitentiary at Blackwell's Island." Her readers might not go, but Margaret did, turning her fact-finding missions into emotionally charged narratives in order to "be of use."

It took some time for Margaret to write as a New Yorker, however. The early news she delivered came from New England and betrayed a predisposition to think of Boston as a "chief mental focus to the New World," as she wrote in her first article, a review of Waldo Emerson's second collection of essays—which privately she had concluded were "more fine than searching." On Thanksgiving in 1844, celebrated in early December, she applauded Massachusetts, where "the old spirit which hallowed the day still lingers, and forbids that it should be entirely de-voted to play and plum-pudding." At Christmastime, she reviewed *The*

Liberty Bell for 1845, an anthology sold to benefit the annual Massachusetts Anti-Slavery Fair, praising "the contributions of the men of color," in particular the work of a new writer named Frederick Douglass, only six years out of bondage. She even gave an account of the dispute among Boston's Unitarian clergy over Theodore Parker's radical views on the "nature of inspiration, and the facts of Bible history," which had come to a head in late January 1845, when James Clarke granted the "excommunicated" Parker the opportunity to preach in his Church of the Disciples. The incident spawned outrage in the local press and inspired Margaret to respond from New York with "regret that, in the nineteenth century, 'liberal Christians' should not be liberal enough cheerfully to allow an honorable mind free course."

But by the time of "Our City Charities," Margaret had experienced enough of the city to begin addressing her readers as one among them. She had attended concerts of the New York Philharmonic Society, where she heard symphonies by Beethoven, Haydn, and Spohr "performed with a degree of perfection worthy a great metropolis"; she had walked or ridden the city's cobblestone streets by horse-drawn omnibus, discovering the manicured parks at Washington Square and Union Place as well as the bustling commercial blocks of Nassau Street near the *Tribune* offices, where two dozen of Greeley's competitors printed and hawked their wares. "There is no reason why New-York should not become a model for other States" in social reform, she concluded. "We trust that interest on this subject will not slumber," for "there is wealth enough, intelligence, and good desire enough, and *surely, need enough.*"

What did it mean to be a New Yorker anyway? Between 1840 and 1850, the city's population, already three times that of Boston, would nearly double, jumping from 300,000 to over 500,000, with most of the growth in newcomers. More than eighteen hundred ships from foreign ports reached New York Harbor each year, many of them carrying passengers with no intention of making the return trip. Margaret experienced New York's cosmopolitan nature first through its music, which she found to be "worthy the admiration of any mind," the highest praise she could give. Here she found an audience of "persons educated where the Fine Arts have already attained their perfection" — enough listeners who had emigrated from or traveled in Europe — and "also an influx of well-educated musicians." Opera singers from Italy and Germany, and the great violinist Ole Bull from Norway, passed through on tour during Margaret's first months as reviewer for the *Tribune*, and many more well trained if lesser virtuosi had taken up residence to staff the philharmonic and other New York orchestras.

But there were far larger numbers of poor Irish immigrants new to the city as well, whose plight Margaret took up in a series of articles on "The Irish Character," both out of principle and because of fellow feeling. Margaret was an immigrant to New York herself, along with most everyone else she knew, lured to a city whose half-million residents had "needs enough" to fuel an urban economy unlike any other in the New World. Margaret's old friend from Boston Lydia Maria Child was here now, writing for the weekly *Broadway Journal*, edited by a Virginian, Edgar Allan Poe. Waldo's older brother William had settled on Staten Island to work as a lawyer; William Channing was in Manhattan preaching to his Society of Christian Union, and in the fall before her own arrival, Margaret's brother-in-law Ellery Channing had left Ellen and little Greta in Concord once again to try his hand at writing for the *Tribune* as well — where their employer, Horace Greeley, was himself a New Hampshire man.

It was in Horace Greeley that Margaret recognized a "go-ahead, fearless adroitness" that was simply "American." Waldo's deprecatory assessment that Greeley was "no scholar," but rather a "mother of men . . . an abettor," captured the very reasons Margaret quickly warmed to the tall, unkempt newspaperman, whose thick wire-rimmed glasses, settled unsteadily on his ruddy baby face, were the only hint of erudition in a carelessly rustic ensemble that usually included an old white coat of Irish linen, heavy boots, and baggy black trousers. The "go-ahead" Greeley had traveled all the way to Cambridge the previous September to press for Margaret's acceptance as she deliberated over his offer of a job, and his proposal that she take a room in his home on Turtle Bay, the former summer residence of New York banker Isaac Lawrence, had helped make up her mind. Margaret had already met Greeley's wife, Mary, a sometime invalid who'd suffered numerous miscarriages and stillbirths, during one of Mary's summer residences at Brook Farm, an enterprise that husband and wife supported as ardent "associationists." Margaret had found Mary to be a witty conversational partner. She may even have proposed Margaret for the *Tribune* literary editorship, and she welcomed Margaret to the isolated Turtle Bay homestead, two miles beyond the more "thickly settled parts of New York," where, as Margaret learned, her hostess had insisted on settling in the tumbledown waterfront mansion for the sake of their one surviving child, two-year-old Arthur, whose health was a lingering concern.

Horace and Mary Greeley were "Grahamites and Hydropaths," according to Margaret, followers of the latest health and dietary fads, and they were temperance-minded teetotalers as well. Margaret was chided for taking "strong potations"—her daily cup of coffee or tea—and for wearing leather gloves ("Skin of a beast!" Mary Greeley would exclaim), but otherwise she enjoyed the remote residence. Maria Child described the route she took to visit her friend: exiting the Harlem omnibus at 49th Street, as Margaret had instructed, then following "a winding, zig-zag cart-track . . . as rural as you can imagine, with moss-covered rocks, scraggly bushes, and a brook that came tumbling over a little dam." Finally, after passing through three swinging gates, Child reached the house, overgrown with vines and climbing roses, and "so old and picturesque" she could scarcely believe it had been "allowed to remain standing near New York so long." There were gazebos "dropping to pieces," and a "piazza" at the back of the house, "almost *on* the East river, with Blackwell's Island in full view." Margaret's room looked out over "a little woody knoll, that runs down into the water, and boats and ships are passing her window all the time."

Margaret simply felt that "I like living here," where "all flows freely." In New York City she had discovered "I don't dislike wickedness and wretchedness"—the squalor of the more "thickly-settled parts" and the houses of reform she could see across the water on Blackwell's Island—any more than the "pettiness and coldness" of Boston and Concord. Although the Greeleys squabbled at times—the more intellectual Mary suffered from the "ennui" Margaret had identified in *Woman in the Nineteenth Century*—Margaret sometimes overheard Horace and Mary singing duets in the evening, and their son, Arthur, loved to swing in the hammock on the piazza with Margaret as she read books for review. She was not missing her New England friends and planned not to visit Boston until at least July.

As they became better acquainted, both at home and in the *Tribune* offices, where her host-and-employer often worked late into the night, Margaret decided Horace Greeley was "in his habits, a slattern and plebeian," but "in his heart, a nobleman." Maybe best of all he allowed Margaret to write as she chose, never minding "what turmoil it might excite, nor what odium it might draw down on her own head." He was the rare man who felt no challenge to his own authority from Margaret's strong will; instead, he admired her for it. "She never asked how this would sound," Greeley marveled, "nor whether that would do, nor what would be the effect of saying anything; but simply, 'Is it the truth? Is it such as the public should know?'" As literary editor, Margaret was more partner than employee. Together they were "flying on the paper wings of every day," as Margaret wrote of the news business in her New Year's Day column at the start of 1845. Both were ever on the lookout for "the new knowledge, the new thought, the new hope" that might bring "the clear morning of a better day." Although the willfully unrefined Greeley delighted in teasing Margaret on occasion for what he considered her "entirely inconsistent" requirement that men display an attitude of "courtesy and protection" toward women in public with a mocking cry of "LET THEM BE SEA-CAPTAINS IF THEY WILL!" —the joke itself marked the vast difference between the two *patresfamilias* in her life, in Concord and New York City.

16

"A human secret, like my own"

The trek from Turtle Bay to the *New-York Tribune* offices was a long one, and Margaret sometimes preferred to write at home when reviewing books. But her material was the city itself, and points beyond. Even so slight an incident as a wealthy woman's officious treatment of an Irish boy on an East River ferry could make a column: "Prevalent Idea that Politeness is too great a Luxury to be given to the Poor." One day William Channing took her on a tour of the notorious Five Points slum. On another, he escorted her up the Hudson to Sing Sing, where she'd been invited to address the women prisoners, her first formal public-speaking appearance.

It was Christmas Day, among the most sorrowful of the year for the prison's inmates. The chairman of Sing Sing's Board of Inspectors escorted Margaret to her seat at a desk in the front of the prison chapel—should a woman stand to speak, especially on a holy day in a house of worship? But then she rose "like an inspired person before these women," recalled her new friend Rebecca Spring, a Quaker philanthropist and supporter of William Channing's New York Prison Association, and "spoke to them not as to criminals, but friends." Margaret told her hundred female listeners, most of them convicted as prostitutes, they weren't "fallen" women. "It is not so!" she exclaimed. "I know my sex better." She proceeded to outline a program of self-reflection and mutual introspection they might pursue while at Sing Sing—like her Conversations, and in keeping with the originating ideals of the "penitentiary" movement—that would turn their "defying spirit[s]" into "better selves" and supply them with the courage to prevail in "the struggle when you leave this shelter!"

And so, most weekdays, Margaret left her own shelter at Turtle Bay, made her way past the three swinging gates and down the zigzag path to ride the Harlem line along rural Fourth Avenue into the city, entering the thicket of four- and five-story commercial and apartment blocks that began just north of Union Place at 14th Street and extended all the way south to Castle Garden and the Battery promenade. Exiting the omnibus near City Hall Park for a glimpse of greenery and municipal grandeur before ducking inside the "dismal inky" doorway of the *Tribune* building at the corner of Spruce and Nassau, Margaret climbed to the third-floor editorial rooms, passing the massive steam-powered cylinder presses on the first floor, quiet now after a night of whirling out the morning edition, dispensed to waiting newsboys and -girls at five A.M. Upstairs among carelessly arranged sofas and bookcases stuffed with reference texts were stationed several pine tables for reporters to use as writing desks. Margaret had her own, easily identified by the piles of books waiting for review stacked beneath it on the floor.

During Margaret's first months on the job, Ellery Channing was often on hand as one of the scribbling men in shirtsleeves at the other writing tables. But by April, Greeley had discovered Ellery's inability "to make his own work," and Margaret's brother-in-law was fired. She was angry at Ellery for wasting the opportunity, but she was also relieved. His presence, reminding her of the old family obligations, had put a crimp in the freedom she'd anticipated in choosing to pursue a profession in New York. She welcomed the excuse to travel into the city and follow her own whims, whether to attend concerts or lectures in the evening or to visit the houses of friends like Maria Child, on Third Street in Greenwich Village, or to the literary salon in the home of Anne Charlotte Lynch, on Waverly Place at Washington Square.

The success of *Woman in the Nineteenth Century* made Margaret a celebrity even at Waverly Place, at these regular Saturday-evening gatherings of New York's elite writers and editors—Poe, Sedgwick, Duyckinck, O'Sullivan—where the admiring Elizabeth Oakes Smith noticed that, in the overfull rooms, Margaret's "fine head and spiritual expression at once marked her out from the crowd." Anne Lynch's soiree held the Saturday after St. Valentine's Day in 1845 made the newspaper, with Margaret depicted sitting at table, "her large gray eyes lamping inspiration and her thin quivering lip prophesying like a Pythoness." Shortly after, Poe's *Broadway Journal* ran an unflattering review of Margaret's book, accompanied by an even less flattering cartoon, captioned "Portrait of a Distinguished Authoress," featuring a haughty, mannish, ringleted creature at her writing desk, holding a book and peering at it nearsightedly. Misogynist envy jostled with sisterly admiration for Margaret among New York's literati.

Margaret, who found the Lynch salon "not pleasant" and inclined toward the transmission of "second hand literary gossip," had already spent that same Valentine's Day—the "merry season of light jokes and lighter love-tokens," as she observed in her *Tribune* report—touring the Bloomingdale Insane Asylum, then under the enlightened supervision of the Paris-trained physician Pliny Earle. The dancing party held on a Friday evening for the patients, so differently cared for than the cowering inmates Margaret would later encounter on Blackwell's Island, demonstrated that "even those who are troublesome and subject to violent excitement" had "the power of self-control" if given "an impulse strong enough" and "favorable circumstances." While one member of Margaret's touring group remarked "how very little our partialities, undue emotions, and manias need to be exaggerated to entitle us to rank among madmen," Margaret took an opposite view in concluding her *Tribune* account: "that, with all our faults and follies, there is still a sound spot, a presentiment of eventual health in the inmost nature." The excursion to Bloomingdale had "embolden[ed]" her "to hope—*to know* it is the same with all." That hope surely extended to her youngest brother, Lloyd, the sibling for whom she still felt most responsibility in her newly carefree New York days. The nineteen-year-old's "partial inferiority," as she now described Lloyd's mental disability, had so far prevented him from learning a trade or settling into a stable living arrangement. Yet Margaret continued to find him situations—as a boarding student at Brook Farm, as a clerk in Elizabeth Peabody's bookstore—always expecting to locate that "sound spot" in her brother's troubled nature.

This season Margaret's personal "presentiment of eventual health" derived from her acquaintance with another doctor in the city whose skills had been developed in France, a native Frenchman named Theodore Leger, who practiced the "supersensual" science of mesmerism in an office near the *Tribune* building. The troubles Margaret sought help for were more physical than psychic, "material" rather than "spiritual," by the terms of a book she reviewed in the *Tribune* the week before her visit to Bloomingdale — *Etherology; or, The Philosophy of Mesmerism and Phrenology*. Margaret had long suffered from pain and fatigue caused by spinal curvature — the lazy "S" that supported her back, leaving one shoulder lower than the other and contributing to the awkward "swan-like" (or pythonesque) extension of her neck so often noted in physical descriptions. She customarily wore a horsehair shoulder pad inside her dress to compensate for her uneven posture. But no matter how well the trick worked in social settings, Margaret's weak, ill-formed spine added to the shameful sense of homeliness she'd felt all her life in comparison to her pretty mother and sister, and that had overcome her the year before in springtime when she'd felt burdened by "this ugly cumbrous mass of flesh." She'd hated "not to be beautiful, when all around is so" — when William Clarke was so evidently not in love with her. If there was "a prospect of *cure*" she would "do almost any thing to ensure it," Margaret wrote to her friend Rebecca Spring's husband, Marcus, who knew Dr. Leger and offered an introduction. Nothing "that could now happen" would "make me so happy."

Mesmeric healing — Dr. Leger's science, or art — operated on the principle that there *was* a connection between the spiritual and the material and, further, that properties of mind could penetrate physical boundaries to effect cures. At a time when new discoveries about electricity and chemistry, invisible forces with properties that could be proved empirically, were altering the "rule of life," as Margaret wrote in her review of *Etherology,* showing that "old limits become fluid beneath the fire of thought," the probability that there existed an *ethereal* "means by which influence and thought may be communicated from one being to another, independent of the usual organs, and with a completeness and precision rarely attained through these," seemed plausible even to a habitual skeptic like Margaret. And she had long harbored a fancy that women were particularly receptive to such "magnetic" influences, as they were also called. Woman's "intuitions," she'd noted in *Woman in the Nineteenth Century*, "are more rapid and more correct"; surely this pointed to the predominance of the "electrical, the magnetic element in Woman." Although, as Margaret would write in a later review, "we do not yet know the origin, or even clearly the features" of the medium, and "patience and exactness in experiment" would be required to discover and prove them, she nevertheless believed that "victories in the realm of the mind" were inevitable. Within fifty years, Margaret predicted, there would be "more rapid and complete modes of intercourse between mind and mind."

Margaret considered herself "free from prejudice" on the subject of mesmeric healing, though not precisely an advocate, and was well aware of the many quack physicians preying on the credulous public. But she had heard persuasive accounts of Dr. Leger's "decisive cures." At her first appointment she received so much "entertainment" from the "*insouciant* robust Frenchman," who chatted through the twenty-minute treatment about his adventures during a ten-year stint as professor at a medical college in Mexico, that she began to visit him almost daily on her way to work. Margaret experienced "no sleep, no trance," she wrote to Cary Sturgis, but the "accessions of strength" she received from Dr. Leger's "local action on the distended bones is obvious." According to reports from friends who saw Margaret that spring, her posture improved markedly. By one account, her spine gained two to four inches over five months of treatment, and she was able to abandon her shoulder pad. In pleasant weather now, she walked the four miles to work, all the way from Turtle Bay to City Hall Park.

The process was certainly magical, if not actually magnetic. According to Georgiana Bruce, who attended one of the sessions, Margaret sat on a stool with the back of her dress unbuttoned while the doctor, standing behind her, "held his right hand horizontally, close against the vertebral column, the fingers pointing towards but never touching it. Slowly he moved his hand from the very end of the spine to the base of the brain, charging it with his vigorous magnetism. There was a slight trembling of his arm as he *willed* that power should flow from him to the patient." Afterward, Margaret told Georgiana that Dr. Leger's ministrations were so forceful it had felt "like having a rod of iron worked into her poor spine."

In a review of Leger's own book, *Animal Magnetism*, published the year after the treatments were completed, Margaret added her personal impressions to a favorable assessment of his text: the French doctor had "a power of transmitting vital energy to those who need soothing or strengthening." In the spring of 1845, Margaret explained tantalizingly to Cary Sturgis, "what I meet at the Mesmeric apartments affords a new view of life."

Why do women love bad men? Margaret had asked the question herself, and answered it, in *Woman in the Nineteenth Century*. The belief that men have "stronger passions," Margaret theorized, has been "inculcated" in women for centuries, and "the preference often shown by women for bad men arises . . . from a confused idea that they are bold and adventurous, acquainted with regions which women are forbidden to explore." But Margaret's awareness of this "confused idea" didn't stop her from falling in love with such a man herself the same winter that her book appeared in print. Her canny insight did not help her to recognize what was happening as she found herself in thrall to a man of just her own age, dark-haired and blue-eyed, a German Jewish banker with literary aspirations who sang and played the guitar and had already made his fortune in the big city, planning to retire soon to his native Germany after traveling in Italy and Egypt—but who also, as Margaret would learn after she'd already let herself believe theirs might become "a truly happy intercourse," kept a mistress in his downtown Manhattan rooms.

Margaret met James Nathan, a textile wholesaler turned Wall Street banker, at Anne Lynch's New Year's Eve party, just as she'd issued her *Tribune* editorial heralding "the new knowledge, the new thought, the new hope . . . of a better day." Nathan himself later claimed, building up his connection with the famous newspaper editor, that the meeting had taken place at the Greeleys' home in Turtle Bay. Perhaps to exonerate himself, James Nathan—who by then had changed his name to James Gotendorf—preferred to place their first meeting in a tamer setting than the unchaperoned soiree. Or perhaps his fuzzy memory retrieved an emotional truth, that all along his chief aim had been to reach Horace Greeley through Margaret. This was to be the only wish consummated by either of the two: near the end of an affair that played out inconclusively over more than a year, Margaret finally persuaded her employer to publish a half-dozen of her "beloved" James Nathan's travel letters, heavily edited by herself, in the *Tribune*.

Such was the progress of the "nameless relation," as Margaret would defensively label her tumultuous romance with James Nathan, "which cannot be violated and may grow to what it will." Incongruent desires ran on parallel tracks, which Margaret persisted in hoping might one day bear the couple on a shared journey, the "religious" union "expressed as a pilgrimage towards a common shrine" that she had described in *Woman in the Nineteenth Century* as the highest form of marriage. It was not to be. Still, the connection advanced well beyond any Margaret had previously experienced with a man. Margaret was now a woman of certifiable influence in the Great Metropolis, a woman from whom James Nathan believed he could gain something; he would not readily sever the tie.

And James Nathan was no Puritan of Concord, no child-man of the near West. A self-made man of the world, who had arrived penniless in New York fifteen years before and was about to leave it as a man of leisure, James Nathan must have taken Margaret for a woman cast in the mold of her publicly avowed models, Mary Wollstonecraft and George Sand: women "rich in genius" and "of most tender sympathies" who, "in breaking bonds," had knowingly "become outlaws," as he read in the copy of *Woman in the Nineteenth Century* that Margaret gave him as an early token of her affection.

Their first private rendezvous, a month after the meeting at Anne Lynch's party, took them to exhibition rooms for a viewing of a panoramic painting of Jerusalem. Margaret had proposed to James Nathan by letter that "some day when you are not bound to buying and selling, and I, too, am free . . . you will perhaps take me from Dr. Leger's in the morning, and show me some one of those beautiful places which I do not yet know." After receiving an invitation so enticingly phrased, so clearly designed to draw them both into a covert alliance initiated on the French doctor's doorstep, could James Nathan be blamed for not taking to heart a different line from *Woman in the Nineteenth Century,* one that expressed more accurately Margaret's private views on romance — "the utmost ardor is coincident with the utmost purity"?

The same week that he received Margaret's suggestive invitation, James Nathan would have read in the *Tribune* her further biographical remarks on George Sand, who, Margaret argued in her essay "French Novelists of the Day," should be "prized . . . both as a warning and a leader." Sand, Margaret wrote, had "not only broken the marriage bond," but "since that, [had] formed other connections independent of the civil or ecclesiastical sanction"; "loudly called by passion: she yielded." James Nathan could have easily—or willfully—overlooked Margaret's corollary judgment of Sand, her "warning" that if only this woman of "genius," so "free" and "bold," had held herself "pure from even the suspicion of error"—had *not* yielded to sexual passion—then she might have become more than a "leader"; she "might have filled an apostolic station among her people."

At the close of the essay, Margaret printed two sonnets by the English poet Elizabeth Barrett addressed to George Sand, "A Desire" and "A Recognition." Would it have changed Margaret's response to James Nathan's overtures in the coming months if she had known that in London, this same spring of 1845, Barrett was being courted in secret by the younger, lesser-known Robert Browning, with whom she would elope to Italy in defiance of her father? Or would Margaret even then have held herself to an exacting standard of purity, explaining to James Nathan, in rebuffing his advances, her belief that "there are . . . in every age *a few* in whose lot the meaning of that age is concentrated"? "I feel that I am one of those persons in my age and sex," she told him. "I feel *chosen among women*." Margaret would preserve her right to fill an apostolic station, if called. Or, at least, her declaration revealed the extremity of self-justification she had reached in arguing the merits of chaste love with a man of "boldness, simplicity and fervor" to whom, she readily admitted, she had "felt a strong attraction . . . since we first met."

In the beginning there were outings to concerts and lectures, to which Margaret had free entry as a reviewer, arranged in person following her "soothing and strengthening" sessions with Dr. Leger, or with notes conveyed by errand boys running between their two offices. Eventually Margaret won Mary Greeley's permission for James Nathan to visit her at Turtle Bay, where he brought his guitar and entertained both women with German lieder on days when Horace stayed late at the office. Later he brought his dog, Josey, an enormous male Newfoundland whose rambles provided convenient cover for Margaret and her gentleman caller to tramp the rocky shoreline of the East River together. She permitted James Nathan to take her in his arms and lift her across fences, to sit with her alone on the bank in the moonlight.

Over these days, although James Nathan warned Margaret she might "never know" him "wholly" and seemed reluctant to respond to Margaret's "wish to hear more" of his "life and position," Margaret felt certain she had "seen [his] inmost heart" and would never "misunderstand what is deepest" in him. She loved this man whose first language was Goethe's: an exotic Jew, perhaps the first she had met, who could "show me how the sun of to-day shines upon the ancient Temple" even as he squired her to Sunday services at William Channing's Society of Christian Union, a man with whom she never felt "restless sad or weary." And as they talked, James Nathan listening more than he spoke, Margaret felt loved by him, as if "my mind has been enfolded in your thought as a branch with flame."

Suddenly, "twenty four hours are a great many," she complained, when a full day passed without seeing *"my dear friend"* or receiving a letter from him, without being able to confide "these little things" — the jubilant songbirds she heard outside her bedroom window at Turtle Bay, called forth by "the sunshine of this beautiful world." To a former student, Anna Loring, in Boston, Margaret wrote obliquely that despite the sorrows of "last Winter's frost" and her vow "to wean myself from . . . close habits of personal relations" — "still hopes will spring up." Margaret now felt "exceedingly happy, really like the Spring." Dr. Leger's magnetic magic, James Nathan's enfolding arms and enflaming mental embrace, had squared her shoulders, made her feel part of "this beautiful world." To James Nathan she confided that on days such as those they spent together at Turtle Bay, "one feels at home on the earth." She could not believe her new hopes would "suffer an untimely blight."

But her revelatory intuition that "there is to be so quick a bound to intercourse," as she announced in a letter to James Nathan, was really not so new for Margaret. She had entertained premonitions of deep connections rapidly formed with George Davis, Sam Ward, William Clarke. What was new was the rumor she heard near the end of March from the proprietress of a boarding house in his neighborhood: James Nathan had a young woman living with him in his apartments. When confronted, he did not deny the charge, only promised a letter of explanation, which Margaret received from his errand boy on the street a day later. With "a cold faintness" she removed the fragrant flowers she had pinned to her dress that morning in an effort to cheer herself, handing them to a blind beggar girl on the corner, almost envying the child "for being in her shut up state less subject to the sudden shocks of feeling," and opened the letter.

Yet hadn't Margaret welcomed this too? "I love sadness," she had written in her journal the year before, sorrowing over William Clarke's indifference. "But let it be a grand a tragic sadness." Here was grand tragedy—or was it farce? In his letter, James Nathan told Margaret he had done nothing worse than take in "an injured woman," hoping to reform her. He had "broken through the conventions of this world" in doing so—all for the sake of rescuing the poor "English maiden," as Margaret ever after referred to her. And although Margaret's friend Rebecca Spring, doing her own detective work, would discover that before sailing "penniless" to America, James Nathan had loved and then "deserted" a woman in England named Louise, who followed him to New York and lived as his mistress through his fifteen years of "buying and selling" (Margaret, in a less vulnerable frame of mind, might have read this more likely story between the lines of James Nathan's letter, as he may have expected her to do), Margaret chose to take him at his word. "I have elected to abide by you," Margaret wrote in answer to the letter she had received with "cold faintness."

"Could the heart of woman refuse its sympathy to this earnestness in behalf of an injured woman?" Margaret asked in an effort to reassure him that she had been persuaded his motives were "honorable nay heroic." Then she insisted, "We will act, as if these clouds were not in the sky." She claimed not even to understand why James Nathan would have used the word "*atonement*" in his letter—"I know all, and surely all is well." Wasn't James Nathan doing the good work that Margaret had so often exhorted her *Tribune* readers to take up themselves?

As for flouting convention, she told him, "*That* I know a generous and ardent nature may do." Once again she voiced her approval of those who "break bonds." Now, despite the probability that rumors of his scandalous living arrangement would circulate farther, Margaret was willing to join him on "the path of intrigue," to continue meeting James Nathan in private or public: "I have no fear nor care. I am myself exposed to misconstruction constantly from what I write." Provocatively, she alluded to "circumstances in *my* life, which if made known to the world, would [if] judged by conventional rules, subject me as probably to general blame as these could you." These facts, she believed, would "never be made known," but "I am well prepared for the chance." James Nathan read an invitation in her decisive words: "*as to you* I *have* judged and have chosen."

Having won the reprieve — and perhaps more — James Nathan had another confession to make. He planned to leave New York City for Europe in June — alone, he implied — to travel and write. "The golden time is passed," Margaret mourned. The revelation of James Nathan's "maiden" had not turned her away, but gone was that "feeling of childhood" when Margaret would "creep close to the side of my companion listening long to his stories of things unfamiliar to my thoughts." Now the news of his imminent departure had "awakened" a "deeper strain" — "an unison," she hoped. James Nathan visited Turtle Bay to leave Josey and his guitar with Margaret — he would return for them both within the year, perhaps as early as next autumn — and the gift of a white veil. Surely once, at least, she wrapped herself in the gauzy mantle, which later she draped over the precious bundle of his letters. She wrote to him, "I am with you as never with any other one. I like to be quite still and have you the actor and the voice . . . I *will* trust you deeply." She confessed a "timidity" along with the wish to "see you now and borrow courage from your eyes." She urged him to visit her freely in the days before his departure, to "come unannounced, and depart informally as if *at home*." Were they to be married — in all but name? And if so, what kind of marriage?

A return visit to Turtle Bay — announced or not — in mid-April: James Nathan "approached" Margaret "so nearly." Too near: "I was exceedingly agitated." In the crisis, Margaret felt his "powerful magnetic effect on me," but "I had always attached importance to such an act." And when "it was asked of me" — "I could not." James Nathan had propositioned Margaret, pressed himself on her, and "I could not." The next day she wrote to him, "Yesterday was, perhaps, a sadder day than I have had in all my life. It did not seem to me an act of 'providence,' but of some ill demon that had exposed [me] to what was to every worldly and womanly feeling so insulting. Neither could I reconcile myself to your having such thoughts, and just when you had induced me to trust you so absolutely. I know you could not help it, but why had fate drawn me so near you?"

She walked the city streets in tears. It seemed to her, she wrote to James Nathan, as if "the sweet little garden, with which my mind had surrounded your image lies all desecrated and trampled." How might the "earth-stain" ever be washed away? Yet even now she equivocated. She would not blame him: "It seemed the work of an evil angel making you misread a word in my letter." The James Nathan of yesterday's trespass, the man of "force" who said he saw "'*the dame*' in me," was not the same man whose "inmost heart" Margaret knew so well—the man of "so much of feminine sweetness and sensibility," conforming to her law of "common being." She wrote to him of herself distantly now, in the third person: an "ill demon" or "evil angel" had prevented James Nathan from understanding "that if Margaret dared express herself more frankly than another it is because she has been in her way a queen and received her guests as also of royal blood." A queen not to be "approached so nearly."

Yet the incident—was it an assault?—made her "crave" all the more "sweet content with thee." Margaret pleaded with James Nathan to be "noble enough to be willing to take me as I am"—to love her as a virgin. Abjectly, she offered to assume all blame—it was "myself who have caused all the ill. It is I who by flattering myself and letting others flatter me that I must ever act nobly and nobler than others, have forgot that pure humility which is our only safeguard." She had, after all, "not been good and pure and sweet enough." Indeed, James Nathan, his transgression, was "the instrument of good to me." And "I have now taken the kernel of your life and planted it in mine." She quoted Novalis—

> *No angel can ascend to heaven*
> *till the whole heart has fallen*
> *to the earth in ashes*—

And she implored him to "come tomorrow morng without fail." Loudly called by passion, she would not "yield"—but she would not yield up James Nathan either.

The year before, as Margaret had struggled to "wean" herself from "close habits of personal relations," she had reread an old letter from Sam Ward and copied a portion of it into her journal—a passage that had struck her so powerfully on first reading, the sentences had imprinted themselves on her memory almost word for word. The subject was "Platonic affection," which Margaret had advocated in those earlier days of covenants and constellations—and that Sam Ward admitted he also had once "recognized" as a "possibility" before he'd fallen in love with and married Anna Barker. But, Sam informed Margaret, for "those whose personal experience of passion has been thorough," who "*have* passed that line" to discover "the existence of a new, vast, and tumultuous class of human emotions," the physical passions — for these "more experienced" people, "the higher emotions and the passions are apt to be always afterward inextricably commingled." Platonic affection "is possible," Sam explained, only "to those who have never passed the line," whose "personal experience of passion . . . remain[s] comparatively undeveloped."

"Your views of life and affection are perfectly true to *you*," Sam had conceded; they may give "brightness to the fancy and earnestness to the thoughts." Yet "Platonic affection" can only seem "sublimated and idealized to the more experienced." It was a painful message for Margaret, an unmarried woman with no romantic prospects but with a deep need for connection with men. Yet there it was: there could be no turning back to the Platonic after a "thorough" experience of passion. Worse, her quest for Platonic affection, for connections or covenants that dwelled only in "the higher emotions," marked her as "undeveloped" — a notion that Margaret, with her credo of self-expansion, could scarcely tolerate. Sam's words made so profound an impression, she had paraphrased them in "The Great Lawsuit," writing in her defense of "the class contemptuously designated old maids" that "those, who have a complete experience of the human instincts" often maintain a "distrust" as to whether those who do not "can be thoroughly human." A year ago Margaret had read Sam's letter once more, copied out the passage, and then sealed it up — to "read not again ever perhaps." Its contents were too disturbing, Sam's careful honesty too humiliating, even as Margaret sensed there was truth in his letter too vital to be forgotten.

And now James Nathan had appeared to force the question. Margaret longed for "childish rest and play, instead of all the depths," she wrote to him; "can it not be again?" Was the problem that Margaret "was not enough a child at the right time," had been "called on for wisdom and dignity long before my leading strings were off" — "and now am too childish"?

The "new, vast, and tumultuous" carnal emotions, those of an earthier life — should she claim them now? The tulips were blooming in the garden at Turtle Bay, she wrote to James Nathan in early May as he prepared for his voyage, and "the crimson ones seem to me like you. They fill gloriously with the sunlight, and the petals glow like gems, while the black stamens in the cup of the flower look so rich and mystical." She had gathered two crimson tulips and put them in a vase in her room, but the scent was "almost overpowering." Margaret was fascinated by two others that she left growing in the garden, "golden ones that have rooted themselves on the edge of a grassy bank." How had they gotten there? "It was a strange elopement from the regular flower bed": these flowers "so *vornehm*" — she used the German word for "noble" — so "willing to be wild."

Was Margaret willing to be *vornehm* in this way, to be wild? In her public life she had followed George Sand's lead, producing "works which systematically assailed the present institution of marriage and the social bonds which are connected with it," as Margaret had written approvingly of Sand's novels in the *Tribune*. But would she follow Sand's example of breaking bonds in her private life? Margaret argued with herself, back and forth, but could not "get out of the labyrinth," she wrote to James Nathan. "Your voice awakens a longer echo through the subterranean chambers, yet not long enough to teach me where to go."

She thought of Psyche, whose story she had recited in the Conversations and recalled now in a letter to James Nathan. Psyche was "but a mortal woman, yet as the bride of Love, she became a daughter of the Gods too." There had been no "other way" Psyche could learn "this secret of herself." Had she *not* accepted her lover, "all had been lost, the plant and flower and fruit." Was James Nathan godly — was he "Love"? Could Margaret reverse her decision — "I could not" — and become immortal by way of a "thorough" experience of the passions? Margaret herself had just written, in *Woman in the Nineteenth Century*, that once a woman is "able to stand alone" — as certainly the *Tribune*'s star, healed by Dr. Leger, could boast — "then she will not make an imperfect man her god . . . Then, if she finds what she needs in Man embodied, she will know how to love, and be worthy of being loved."

At times, "life seems so ful[l] so creative; every hour an infinite promise, — I cannot keep in mind prohibitions or barriers or fates," she wrote to James Nathan. Yet there was "so much for me to assimilate and absorb." Could she not simply "let it rest in me till I grow to the stature of what I feel"? It was different for James Nathan—"*mein liebste*," as she addressed him now—"since you have the secret of this vital energy." He revealed to Margaret that he had "carried . . . many poor women across the mire," not just the English girl. He "must know" how this vital energy "works in all forms of life, especially in mine"; "you must always instruct me very clearly"—carry Margaret too across the mire. But "take it gently, and take me near your heart." Then again, no. No. "You have touched my heart, and it thrilled at the centre, but that is all."

Margaret had become so rattled, she realized, that she'd been address-ing James Nathan incorrectly in the feminine. The phrase wasn't "*mein liebste*," but "*mein liebster*"—my beloved. Perhaps this was no "mistake," but rather "an instinct": Margaret had been "seeking the woman" in him, she proposed. She resorted to her theory of the "common being": if both Margaret and James Nathan were beings in which male and female were "perpetually passing into one another," why need they meet in body? She offered herself to him as "your moon," your "pure reflection . . . in a serene sky." And she copied out for him a verse she had composed at Fishkill Landing, while living peaceably "together and apart" with Cary Sturgis, "To the Face Seen in the Moon":

> . . . if I steadfast gaze upon thy face
> A human secret, like my own, I trace,
> For through the woman's smile looks the male eye.

Was this Margaret's secret, as well as the source of her rallying cry in *Woman in the Nineteenth Century*, that male and female were united in her? Would carnal love for either man or woman lead to personal dis-union, dis-integration? Was this her fear?

When Margaret read through her 1844 journal in search of the poem, she might have found this entry too, which so accurately described her current crisis: "The Woman in me kneels and weeps in tender rapture; the Man in me rushes forth, but only to be baffled." The previous fall, as Margaret wrote the final pages of *Woman in the Nineteenth Century*, she had been more certain of the result she desired: "the time will come, when, from the union of this tragic king and queen, shall be born a radiant sovereign self." She was not yet ready to take back her "no" to James Nathan, but she was no longer certain she wanted to become a "radiant sovereign self," a "queenly" moon, as she referred to the luminous orb that seemed to watch her so closely at night, "to bless so purely."

For James Nathan she altered the second line of her verse: "A human secret, like *our* own, I trace." And Margaret made him promise to keep their secret—"have no confidant as to our relationship! I have had and shall have none. I wish to be alone with you in strict communion."

Margaret was not as inexperienced as Sam Ward believed. She knew that "we improve most by being loved and trusted and by loving and trusting." But Margaret's own experience warned her of complications, dire ones, that could result from "loving and trusting." She had made bold claims for women's equal capabilities in *Woman in the Nineteenth Century,* yet in the realm of sexual experience, only "men have the privilege of boldness," she observed to James Nathan. Women took on all the risk; pregnancy made their private choices public, altered their lives. She had not forgotten the day a young woman died in her arms in a wretched cottage in Groton, the victim of a botched abortion. She had not forgotten her mother's many pregnancies, albeit in grander homes, or the two that had resulted in deaths of beloved infants. And Margaret herself had only just been released from care for the six siblings who survived childhood. There was life in carnal relations, but also risk of tragedy, of never-ending encumbrance—of relegation to a shadow world in which women like James Nathan's "English maiden" or the female prisoners at Sing Sing lived.

Margaret gathered farewell gifts—the pen with which she wrote a "last letter" before his departure, a book of poems by Shelley, the short-lived Romantic renegade whose "magnetic power of genius" she'd extolled in her early *American Monthly* essay "Modern British Poets." She offered to secure letters of introduction for James Nathan on his travels—from George Bancroft, Edward Everett, Samuel Gridley Howe. She tried not to be "too sensitive," as he'd accused her of being when she complained that he'd missed a visit—"it is well we are to separate now," she attempted to convince herself. And perhaps it was so. James Nathan would not let her come to the docks to say goodbye—"May we meet as we feel!" she wrote instead, looking forward to his return. Did she suspect what soon turned out to be true, that he had sailed with the "English maiden" at his side? Yet he'd left *her*, Margaret, the white veil.

So she kept on believing him — "I cannot do other than love and most deeply trust you." James Nathan had brought the "poor maiden" on board only to deliver her to her parents in England, he explained, to finish the good work he had begun. Margaret forced herself to sympathize with the "fair girl," regretting that she had never met her, offering to ask Harriet Martineau's help in finding the girl "friends and employment" if her parents didn't welcome her home. "She must suffer greatly to part from you," Margaret wrote to James Nathan, "you who have been a friend to her such as it has been given few mortals to find *once* in this world and surely none could hope to find twice!"

Margaret felt much the same way. She had finally found a man "who combined force with tenderness and delicacy," the same words of praise she had once ascribed to Sophia Peabody's fiancé, Nathaniel Hawthorne. This was now a "certainty": "Yes there *is* one who understands . . . and when we are separated and I can no longer tell [him] the impulse or the want of the moment, still I will not forget that there *has been* one." Margaret had been loved — desired.

In the days of the "beautiful summer when we might have been so happy together" — "happy in a way that neither of us ever will be with any other person" — Margaret wrote letter after letter to James Nathan, handing them to errand boys to deliver to ships waiting at the docks. She put on her "prettiest dresses" to sit on *their* rocks at Turtle Bay, watching Josey sport in the water below. One hot night she climbed down the boulders to bathe in the river, "the waters rippling up so gentle, the ships gliding full sailed and dreamy white over a silver sea, the crags above me with their dewey garlands, and the little path stealing away in shadow. Ah! it was almost *too* beautiful to bear and live."

On nights like this Margaret "concentrated on our relation as never before." "It seems to me not only peculiar but *original*," she wrote to James Nathan, feeling more certain that "indeed there *are* soul realities," with "*mein liebster*" at a safe distance. "I have never had one at all like it, and I do not read things in the poets or anywhere that more than glance at it." She could feel James Nathan's thoughts "growing in my mind . . . your stronger organization has at times almost transfused mine." There had been "moments when our minds were blended in one," and this "unison" beat "like a heart within me." She had given him Shelley to read, but there is "no poem like the poem we can make for ourselves": "is it not by living such relations that we bring a new religion, establishing nobler freedom for all?" How hard Margaret worked to persuade herself—and James Nathan—of their disembodied "unison." As she wrote in a *Tribune* essay that July, titled "Clairvoyance," on the "wonderful powers" of the mind, "time and space" may yet be "annihilated" so that "lovers may be happy."

In late July, Margaret finally received a packet of letters from James Nathan, only to learn that "the affair that has troubled you so long" had found no "definitive and peaceful issue"—the "poor maiden" was yet to be settled elsewhere. Worse, James Nathan appeared to have no thought of coming back to America. Margaret struggled to temper the language of her return letters. "*Now* is the crisis," she informed him; he must "find a clear path" out of his entanglement. She appreciated, at least, the "tender and elevated" tone of his letters, which allowed her to hope "we [may] ever keep pure and sweet the joys that have been given." Adopting Margaret's own theory for the moment, James Nathan had assured her that "the precious certainty of spiritual connexion" was "worth great sacrifices," and theirs would "bear the test of absence." If she was indeed so much in his thoughts, Margaret responded, he must make note of the precise dates and times. Then they would compare notes and see whether there was a simultaneous "rush of our souls to meet . . . as used to be the case." Yet, in retrospect, James Nathan's sudden departure now seemed to her "sad and of evil omen."

Margaret begged him to have his portrait taken for her as a keepsake, preferably "a good miniature on ivory" — "but do not have it taken at all unless it can be excellent." If he didn't return, what would she do with Josey, who shook salt water all over Margaret's pretty dresses and whose eyes seemed to be infected? The dog would need someone else to walk him. Margaret had not tramped in the woods since James Nathan left; she refused to climb the low wall that he had always lifted her across. Would he never return to take her in his arms again?

Rather than walk in the woods, Margaret had been visiting the new Female Refuge in the city, established by Rebecca Spring and other women of the Prison Association to help former prisoners find work after their release. "I like them better than most women I meet," Margaret wrote darkly to James Nathan of the inmates. "They m[ake] no false pretensions, nor cling to shadows," though she suspected they hid from her the "painful images that must haunt their lonely hours." When she wrote in her journal several months later that the year 1845 "has rent from me all I cherished, but . . . I have lived at last not only in rapture but in fact," Margaret had in mind both her love for James Nathan and her encounters as journalist and volunteer with lives harder than her own.

Margaret had delayed her New England vacation, once planned for July, in order to receive her first letters from James Nathan as soon as they reached New York. But when only one "cold and scanty" missive followed the July packet in late August, she made arrangements to travel north to Cambridge and Concord in early fall. Waldo had made a short but satisfactory visit to Margaret in Turtle Bay in June while staying with his brother on Staten Island. That autumn at Concord, however, "our moods did not match." Waldo was "with Plato"—preparing his lectures on "Representative Men"—Margaret wrote afterward to Anna Ward, and "I was with the instincts." Did she have Sam's letter on Platonic affection still in mind?

Cary Sturgis was increasingly occupied with a new beau—William Aspinwall Tappan, a wealthy New Yorker who had caught Waldo's fancy two years earlier. Waldo had published a poem by Tappan in one of the last issues of *The Dial*, but mostly he enjoyed the young man's company. Tappan spoke "seldom but easily & strongly," Waldo approved, and he "moves like a deer." Cary had taken an interest simply "because he is the greatest unknown to me now." She would marry Tappan in 1847 and move with him to Highwood, a country estate on property owned by Sam Ward in the Berkshires; they were still mysterious to each other, but the match satisfied Waldo, who had done everything he could to push them together, no longer able to tolerate the fascination Cary held for him at close range.

Over the summer, Henry Thoreau had built a small log cabin on land Waldo Emerson had recently purchased at Walden Pond to preserve the wooded acreage, and he had been living alone there since July. Ellen and Ellery Channing had moved into a new house on the outskirts of town at Punkatasset, leaving Ellen "very lonely and unhelped," and Margaret worrying, "for she is to have another little one in Spring." Two-year-old

Margaret Fuller Channing—Greta—would soon be joined by a sister, the infant Caroline Sturgis Channing.

The presence most palpable to Margaret that fall was Timothy Fuller's. On the tenth anniversary of her father's death, she wrote to James Nathan at "just about [the] time he left us and my hand closed his eyes." Sitting at her writing desk, Margaret stared at that hand, which since that day "has done so much": edited a literary journal for which she had supplied more articles than anyone else, written two books and nearly one hundred newspaper pieces. Her writing hand seemed "almost a separate mind."

"It is a pure hand thus far from evil," Margaret was glad to say, and "it has given no false tokens of any kind," unlike (she grew more certain of it by the day) James Nathan's hand. "My father," she asked, "from that home of higher life you now inhabit, does not your blessing still accompany the hand that hid the sad sights of this world from your eyes"?

A decade earlier, before his death, Margaret had suffered under Timothy's stern authority, so accustomed to his failure to express his affection that—until the fortunate moment when she had been so ill, just before his sudden last sickness—she had burst into tears over the unexpected benediction. Perhaps this history with her living father, rather than Timothy's premature death, was the source of the "childishness" that drove her to seek Platonic relations with men whose affection flickered just beyond her reach.

But now she wondered whether her father's blessing did "still accompany" her. Margaret asked the question of "my friend" James Nathan—no longer *mein liebster*. She gave the answer herself: "I think it does. I think he thus far would bless his child."

· VI ·

EUROPE

Giuseppe Mazzini

George Sand

Adam Mickiewicz

Giovanni Angelo Ossoli

17

Lost on Ben Lomond

W HEREVER SHE WENT, HE FAILED TO APPEAR. THAT WAS the troubling undercurrent of Margaret's first weeks traveling abroad with her New York friend Rebecca Spring and her husband, Marcus, both reform-minded Quakers, and their nine-year-old son, Eddie, for whom Margaret served as tutor. (The Springs' younger child, Jeanie, had been left behind with relatives.) Margaret could not have made the trip without accepting the generous terms of the governess position, which covered meals and lodging as well as her fare on the Cunard steamer *Cambria* in a record-setting Atlantic crossing of ten and a half days in early August 1846. Horace Greeley helped support the venture too, paying Margaret his highest rates and advancing her $120 on fifteen dispatches, which she initially titled breezily, "Things and Thoughts in Europe." With no fanfare, she had become America's first female foreign correspondent. Margaret continued to sign her columns with the distinctive yet anonymous star, intent simply on writing up the best material she could find and branding it with her own increasingly "radical" sensibility — a term she began to use as a badge of honor as she established bonds with Europe's freethinking exiles and activists.

Margaret no longer expected dramatic personal gains from spending a year in Great Britain and the Continent. She'd given up her dream of the life-altering grand tour she had envisioned a decade earlier in the company of young Sam Ward and the cosmopolitan Farrars, which "would have given my genius wings." At thirty-six, Margaret believed her "mind and character" were already "too much formed" through "a liberal communion with the woful struggling crowd of fellow men." She had instead worked for a living and reaped the "fruits of spiritual knowledge" these past ten years, seeking common cause with the laborer, the immigrant, the prostitute. Still, traveling with the Springs, who were comrades as well as companions, to survey the Old World's prisons, manufactories, shipyards, and schools as well as museums, monuments, castles, and cathedrals, would "add to my stores of knowledge" and allow Margaret to expand her role as conductor of information and ideas in the "great mutual system of interpretation" she had joined two years earlier as a columnist for the *New-York Tribune*. "If I persevere, there is nothing to hinder my having an important career even now," she wrote to Sam and Anna Ward, describing her travel plans and looking back on the old missed opportunity. "But it must be in the capacity of a journalist, and for that I need this new field of observation."

The one romantic notion about the journey that Margaret permitted herself was the hope of reestablishing ties with James Nathan, who had not returned to New York as originally promised. Even before the Springs made their offer, Margaret had begun looking for ways to cross the Atlantic to search him out. Despite his infrequent and sometimes indifferent correspondence, she still felt, for days at a time, "a desire for you that amount[s] almost to anguish," she wrote to him in the spring of 1846, when four months had passed without a letter. She recalled their "reconciliation" after the breach of the previous April and sent him a sprig of the flowering myrtle she had given him that dreadful day when "we seemed to be separated for ever. But we were not." Now she begged to know, "Where are you? What are you doing?" Margaret had done all she could to prove her constancy—"retouching" several of his travelogues to meet the *Tribune*'s standards and mailing them back to him once they were in print, supplying more letters of introduction, even monitoring Josey's care from afar as she moved into boarding-house rooms in the city during the winter of 1845–46 to escape the increasingly fractious Greeley marriage and the riverbank scenery that reminded her so vividly of James Nathan. Josey, she mourned in one letter, would "never be the intelligent and fine creature he might, if you had not left him." Should she find a way to ship the dog to his master?

But with her travel plans in place, Margaret let Josey go to the new oc-cupants of the Greeleys' Turtle Bay house when Mary Greeley left with Arthur for a curative stay in Brattleboro, Vermont, and Horace moved into town for the summer. Indeed, as she wrote to Cary Sturgis, with whom she managed to be both forthright and self-dramatizing, "I am go-ing to let everything go in this world and scud where the wind drives." She would not let even Ellery Channing's most recent abandonment of Ellen worry her too much. Ellery, who seemed to step out ahead of Margaret at every turn, had set off for Rome in early March, well before Ellen's sec-ond pregnancy had come to term, claiming his peace of mind depended on reaching the Eternal City in time for Easter and asking Margaret to ar-range for him to print his commentaries in the *Tribune;* he would stay for just sixteen days before turning back to Concord, "full of distaste for all things foreign." Still, Ellery felt he'd gathered enough material to write a book, a fanciful dialogue called *Conversations in Rome: Between an Artist, a Catholic, and a Critic,* published a year later and scarcely noticed by any but his ever faithful partisan Waldo Emerson.

Although Margaret was careful to keep her desires a secret, she had reason to believe that her own winds of fortune might drive her into James Nathan's arms once more. In July, a month before her departure on the *Cambria,* she received a letter written from Hamburg in which James Nathan promised to leave word in London as to his where-abouts — perhaps even travel there himself — "and then thanks to god! in all probability shall we meet either there or here." He also asked her help in finding a publisher for a book based on his recent travels in the Near East. Eagerly, Margaret consulted with Horace Greeley and reported her employer's willingness to consider a manuscript, if "brief and vivid" and "repeat[ing] no information" from other travel books. She passed along Greeley's warning that Nathan could expect little remuneration, "as your name is not known as a writer," then closed her letter with the advisory "I will expect to find a good letter, if not yourself in London, early in September."

Margaret's own standing as an author had risen even higher in the year since James Nathan left New York City. *Woman in the Nineteenth Century* appeared in a London edition in England, she was delighted to learn, when she received a copy of the finished book, handsomely bound as a volume in the Clarke's Cabinet Library series. No international copyright laws protected American authors, so she would gain nothing from sales of this pirated edition, but Margaret was nonetheless "very glad to find it will be read by women there," she wrote to her brother Richard—all the more so, once she decided to follow her book to England. To her frustration, Greeley's business partner Thomas McElrath—narrowminded and known to be a "close calculator"—was stalling on a second edition of the book in the United States, but the impasse helped Margaret decide to accept the offer of her friend Evert Duyckinck to publish a selection of her *Dial* and *Tribune* essays with the New York firm Wiley and Putnam.

In the last hectic days before boarding the *Cambria*, she haggled with John Wiley about which essays to include. Wiley deemed several of her choices too controversial on religious grounds, particularly her favorable review of a volume by Shelley, a known atheist. Margaret shot back: "The attractive force of my mind consists in its energy, clearness and I dare to say it, its catholic liberality and fearless honor. Where I make an impression it must be by being most myself." Holding to her own views would draw a "sufficient and always growing sympathy" in her readers, she insisted. Margaret had discovered this by writing ever more biting editorials—arguing in favor of suffrage for black New Yorkers in "What Fits a Man to Be a Voter?" and against capital punishment in "Darkness Visible"—without costing the *Tribune* any readers. Yet because of time and space constraints, *Papers on Literature and Art* was shorter and less fully representative of Margaret's "catholic" interests than she would have liked, though it appeared in print just in time to serve as a calling card in literary drawing rooms on the other side of the Atlantic.

The harbor at Liverpool, where most commercial as well as passenger vessels like the *Cambria* docked after an Atlantic crossing, dwarfed even New York City's teeming waterfront. Margaret found the miles of piers "slower, solider," but no "less truly active . . . than at home," she wrote in her first *Tribune* letter from abroad, searching from the outset for signs of both difference and commonality to support her comparative observations. The problems of industrialization had gripped the Old World in advance of the New, she understood, and sending home "packages of seed"—ideas ripe for transplant to American soil—would be a large part of her self-appointed mission as correspondent, as she'd written in her "Farewell" column for the *Tribune*. Margaret and the Springs merged their literary and reform agendas to devise a schedule that included, in their first "nine days of wonder," tours of the Mechanics Institutes at Liverpool and Manchester—adult education centers providing night classes and libraries for working men and women—as well as audiences with Harriet Martineau, the young Matthew Arnold, and the aged William Wordsworth in their Lake District retreats.

Wordsworth, in his "florid, fair old age," was more beloved by his neighbors for his kindness than for his poetry, Margaret learned by quizzing her innkeeper, and Wordsworth himself seemed to value the pastoral environs of Ambleside and Grasmere as much for their distance from "the real wants of England and the world . . . the cry of men in the jaws of destruction"—the mill and mine workers of the English Midlands, the beggars of London and Glasgow—as for the rugged landscape that had drawn him there decades earlier. Even the peaceable Lake District shopkeepers, Margaret reported, wished the seventy-six-year-old poet laureate would take a stand in the parliamentary debates on the protectionist Corn Laws or on the Factories Act, which aimed to limit working hours of women and children to ten per day. Disappointed that Wordsworth was no crusading Byron—nor, for that matter, an Emerson, who had, when prevailed upon, written his 1838 letter to President Van Buren decrying the Cherokee removal and spoken against slavery in an 1844 address in Concord—Margaret wished that he had at least settled in a "more romantic" setting than his Rydal Mount cottage, with its neat avenue of hollyhocks. The house and grounds seemed to her "merely the retirement of a gentleman, rather than the haunt of a Poet."

Wild nature was on the itinerary as well, and Margaret had written to James Nathan, inviting him to join her and the Springs for a tour of the Trossachs in Scotland—the Highlands region of deep-water lochs and towering bens she knew so well from reading Scott and Burns. Instead she received a letter from him stating bluntly that he would not meet her anywhere in Europe. Possibly he was miffed by her stark assessment of his literary prospects, but that no longer mattered. James Nathan told her the main reason outright: he was engaged to marry a young German woman.

"I care not," Margaret forced herself to write in her journal. "I am resolved to take such disappointments more lightly than I have" — more lightly than surprise announcements in the past from George Davis, James Freeman Clarke, and Sam and Anna Ward. But this betrayal was of an altogether different order. "I ought not to regret having thought other of 'humans' than they deserve," she told herself, acknowledging at last that an inhumane James Nathan had played her for a fool, and she ripped the offending letter to shreds. Perhaps she could turn the episode "to account in a literary way"; then at least something productive would come of what otherwise seemed such a waste of "affections and ideal hopes." But that impulse was an old one too — what had she gained from the silly tale she'd spun and published anonymously in reaction to the news of George Davis's engagement?

On the journey from Edinburgh into the Highlands, Margaret insisted on riding in the open air, alone among the baggage on top of the coach, even through an entire day of "drenching" equinoctial rain. Margaret told Rebecca Spring, who had guessed at James Nathan's treachery long before, that she was enjoying the view and the speed of travel over Scotland's uncommonly smooth roads. But Rebecca recognized that her headstrong, overqualified governess was also in a reckless, despairing mood.

Margaret's love for James Nathan had blossomed at a time of unusual productivity, of both professional and physical well-being, and she had very nearly accepted his challenge to establish a "thorough" relation. "Life seems so full so creative; every hour an infinite promise," she had written to him in the days after their April reconciliation, as she debated with herself — "I cannot keep in mind prohibitions or barriers or fates." Would things have turned out differently if she'd given in to impulse and responded favorably to James Nathan's advance? But she had let him go, only to endure another solitary year, attending a second Valentine's Day soiree at Anne Lynch's Washington Square mansion "alone, as usual," she'd commented dejectedly to the sympathetic Elizabeth Oakes Smith as she left the party. In her diary that winter Margaret described an oppressive awareness that "I have no real hold on life, — no real, permanent connection with any soul." She felt disembodied, like "a wandering Intelligence, driven from spot to spot." Perhaps her fate *was* this: to live alone, to "learn all secrets, and fulfil a circle of knowledge," but never to experience full communion with another being. The prospect "envelopes me as a cold atmosphere. I do not see how I shall go through this destiny. I can, if it is mine; but I do not feel that I can."

Now she had gone through yet another cycle of raised hopes and disillusionment. How fitting that her betrayer was a German gentleman of means. When Margaret researched her biography of Goethe, she had studied the correspondence of his young friend Bettine von Arnim, her letters to Goethe as well as those to her friend and mentor, the canoness Karoline von Günderode. Margaret had made a partial translation of these last, published by Elizabeth Peabody as a testament to women's friendships. Margaret had always fancied herself more like the energetic younger Bettine, a would-be writer and acolyte of the great man Goethe; her intuitive grasp of spiritual matters earned Bettine the nickname "Sibyl." But perhaps it was the older doomed Karoline whose fate Margaret was destined to follow: deserted by her lover, a married university professor of high rank, Karoline had fallen into a depression. Bettine tried to cheer her—the young woman even delivered to her friend a handsome French soldier, an "Officer of Hussars" wearing a high bearskin cap, "the handsomest of all youths," who offered himself as a lover. Heedless of these efforts, Karoline committed suicide on the banks of the Rhine, stabbing herself in the heart with a silver dagger, having earlier showed Bettine the precise spot just below her breast where she planned to drive the blade home. Such events had once seemed to Margaret unthinkably—safely—distant: women of intellect taking married men as lovers, a young woman procuring a handsome soldier as gigolo for her sorrowing friend, a carefully premeditated suicide. But the enveloping despair Karoline von Günderode felt was not now at all foreign to Margaret.

Trekking up Ben Lomond on a cool September afternoon with Marcus Spring and no guide, Margaret reached the summit and proceeded to "drink in . . . the heavens." On every side were foothills covered in purple heather, lakes gleaming "like eyes that tell the secrets of the earth," and in the distance "peak beyond peak" catching "all the colors of the prism" from the shifting light as clouds flew by overhead. On their descent, the path that wound among so many rills and ridges petered out, and Margaret sent Marcus ahead to scout for a bridge she remembered crossing over a spring on the way up. Within minutes the two Americans had become separated, their shouts lost in the twilight. Had Margaret willed herself into this dangerous solitude? Now each headed down the mountain, aiming for the inn far below on the banks of Loch Lomond, but only Marcus reached safety that night.

Darkness fell, and with it a mist obscuring any lights below. Margaret tramped down hillsides, only to turn back after sinking knee-deep into bogs. She lowered herself down rock walls, clinging to heather. Soaking wet and with only a light shawl for warmth, Margaret found herself stranded on a high promontory, hemmed in on three sides by roaring streams. She could go no farther that night, but how would she survive, "all fevered and exhausted"? How escape the fate of a child lost on the same mountain earlier that summer, dead long before his small body was discovered five days later?

For the *Tribune* letter Margaret composed several days after the ordeal, she framed her "hair-breadth 'scape" as a triumph of Yankee vigor and Transcendental self-reliance. "My only chance," Margaret decided, "lay in motion . . . my only help in myself." She paced her rocky perch, refusing to succumb to cold or fatigue, supported by a "feverish strength." The "mental experience"—which she did not report—was "most precious and profound." Yet she admitted to having been visited by "visionary shapes" unfurling from "the great body of mist," doubtless to "come upon me with a kiss pervasively cold as that of Death . . . if I had but resigned myself more passively to that cold, spirit-like breathing!" When the moon rose at two A.M., Margaret permitted herself a few hours' rest, then rose at first light to battle her way through swarms of biting flies up the hill and across the top of a waterfall, stopping to drink its waters, "good at that time as ambrosia." She scrambled down more slopes on the other side, mercifully "in the right direction," until one of a band of twenty shepherds with their dogs in a search party dispatched by the Springs found her.

"I had had my grand solitude," Margaret announced to her *Tribune* readers. And the Springs, relieved of their "doubt amounting to anguish," arranged for a dinner party that evening in the barn behind the inn for all the searchers, with talk of Robert Burns and narrations of other close calls on the majestic peak. "It was sublime indeed—a never-to-be-forgotten presentation of stern, serene realities," Margaret wrote of the escapade. In a more introspective letter to her brother Richard, she underscored her certainty that she would not have lived "*if* I had not tried." She was "glad of the experience, for it was quite a deep one." Whatever transpired in her "mental experience" when enveloped by "the great body of mist" that night, Margaret now had the self-assurance—the stern serenity—to ask for a "cessation of intercourse" with James Nathan and to request the return of her love letters. All this time she had been testing her own faith, not his. She would not enter into so unequal a "relation" again.

Despite her pride in what she called "my Yankee method" of survival on Ben Lomond, Margaret had grown impatient with her own country, where "life rushes wide and free," and all too often headlong down blind alleys. The black suffrage measure she supported in New York had been soundly defeated soon after her editorial appeared, and national politics boded even worse, as President James Polk led the country into an expansionist war with Mexico in hopes of annexing Texas as a slave state. It was all backward, Margaret wrote in one of her last *Tribune* columns before leaving for Europe: "the *feeble* Mexicans" were "fighting in defense of their rights," and "we" Americans "for liberty to do our pleasure." Her hopes "as to National honor and goodness" were "almost wearied out"; she could only "turn to the Individual and to the Future for consolation." The few signs of advance she saw were in the "heightening and deepening" of "the cultivation of individual minds," Margaret told her readers in her "Farewell" column, and in "the part which is [to be] assigned to Woman in the next stage of human progress." Precisely what indicators she found of woman's progress Margaret did not say—although she could well have cited her own front-page editorials, themselves a remarkable advance for women in public discourse.

As for individuals, a large measure of Margaret's purpose in traveling to Europe was to meet the writers and radicals whose work she'd admired from afar and test their minds in conversation. Margaret told Sam Ward, who reported the exchange to Waldo Emerson, that "she had seen all the people worth seeing in America" and was ready to extend her circle of acquaintance. This might have sounded like a compliment to Waldo and Sam, except for an additional remark Sam recalled: Margaret's boast that "there was no intellect comparable to her own" in the United States, and she would have to look elsewhere to find her equal. Perhaps Margaret had known Sam would pass along the comment, intending to prick Waldo

for his failure to acknowledge the worth of her move into journalism—
"making some good strokes in a good cause," as she thought of it. But
others shared what might have seemed an inflated self-opinion. Maria
Child was "glad Margaret Fuller has gone to Europe," she wrote to their
mutual friend the Brook Farm investor Frank Shaw. "She is a woman of
the most remarkable intellect I ever met with."

Arriving in London in early October, at what turned out to be the
off-season for literary socializing, was discouraging at first. Many of the
writers to whom she'd been carrying letters of introduction were out of
town; Elizabeth Barrett had just "*eloped*" with Robert Browning to Italy,
escaping from "a severe hard father," Margaret learned. En route from
Scotland in late September, Margaret had glimpsed enough of Glasgow's
poor in several hours—"especially women, dressed in dirty, wretched
tatters, worse than none"—to report that the city "more resembles an *In-
ferno* than any other we have yet visited"; she had been lowered by bucket
into the mouth of a mineshaft at Newcastle, finding deplorable conditions, not just for the coal miners but for their cart horses, permanently
quartered below ground. Ferreting out the literati of London was more
difficult than conducting humanitarian field research, yet tremendously
rewarding once she succeeded.

"I found how true for me was the lure that always drew me towards
Europe," Margaret wrote as soon as she could make the time to pen a letter to Cary Sturgis, "how right we were in supposing there was elsewhere
a greater range of interesting character among the men." Although she
had found "no Waldo"—Margaret may have hoped Cary would pass
along this estimation as a corrective—and "none so beautiful" as William Channing or Sam Ward, she had met numerous "persons of celebrity and others that will attain it ere long." These included the playwright
and poet Richard Henry Horne; the associationist editor of the *London
Phalanx*, Hugh Doherty; and the Swedenborgian philosopher and friend
of Henry James Sr., James John Garth Wilkinson. It helped that most
had read her *Dial* essays or *Woman in the Nineteenth Century*, and all had
a "preconceived strong desire to know me." Favorable reviews of *Papers
on Literature and Art* had begun to appear in London journals, and while
Margaret regretted that Wiley's timidity had meant the omission of all
her essays on Continental literature and "others of a radical stamp," their
absence seemed to have cost her nothing.

English "habits of conversation" were "so superior to those of Americans," Margaret wrote to her brother Richard, that she felt able to "come out a great deal more" here "than I can at home"—and her eloquence was returned "proportionately" with interest. Six years earlier, as she commenced her Conversation classes, Margaret had written in her journal about the discomfort that her verbal superiority sometimes brought her, when "a woman of tact & brilliancy like me, has an undue advantage in conversation with men." Men "are astonished at our instincts. They do not see where we get our knowledge, &, while they tramp on in their clumsy way, we wheel, & fly, & dart hither & thither, & seize with ready eye all the weak points, like Saladin"—the legendary swordsman—"in the desert." Back then in Boston, Margaret had failed to rouse her women students to spar with men in mixed conversation, and the men, tramping on in their pedantry, had held the group to an impasse. But in "European society," Margaret wrote in a letter to Waldo Emerson summarizing her experiences, she felt entirely "in my element": "so many of the encumbrances are cleared away that used to weary me in America, that I can enjoy a freer play of faculty, and feel, if not like a bird in the air, at least as easy as a fish in water."

Margaret spent many of her London evenings with William and Mary Howitt, married writers who shared the editorship of the *People's Journal*. At their home she met a trio of young women, including the Howitts' oldest daughter, Anna, all of whom had "chosen the profession of an artist." The watercolor portraitist Margaret Gillies explained to Margaret the difficulty of mastering the craft when "men *will not* teach girls drawing with any care" and rules of propriety prevented female students from sketching live models in the nude, so essential to rendering the human form with accuracy. Margaret particularly admired the twenty-five-year-old Eliza Fox, daughter of the "celebrated" editor of the *Monthly Repository* William J. Fox, who had determined not to marry in favor of leading a "noble independent life" devoted to art. In her letter to Cary Sturgis, Margaret "lamented" that Cary had not made a similar decision to "embark on the wide stream of the world" as an artist, making the most of her own talent and setting an example for other women "who needed it so much." Margaret suspected rightly that Cary, then on the eve of her marriage to William Tappan, would soon join the expanding group of friends and former students who had made "the miserable mistake" of marrying impulsively out of a desire to settle into domestic life. One Concord friend had confided in Margaret her conviction that if women "waited long enough to think about it they would never marry."

The Howitts, contented with their partnership as writers and reformers, seemed a different kind of couple, but Thomas and Jane Carlyle offered a daunting example of a marital mismatch along the lines of Waldo and Lidian Emerson, although Jane Carlyle — "full of grace, sweetness and talent" — provided a much more sympathetic example to Margaret of a misunderstood wife, and Thomas Carlyle — "very Titanic, and anticelestial" in his oppressive bluster — a far less attractive sage. Margaret had been prepared to find the author, whose brilliant novel of ideas *Sartor Resartus* Waldo Emerson had shepherded into print in the United States, intimidating — but not to see him talk over every one of his guests, "haranguing" both Margaret (despite Waldo's testimony in a letter of introduction that she was "full of all nobleness . . . an exotic in New England . . . our citizen of the world") and the man who became the hero of her six-week stay in London, the exiled Italian activist Giuseppe Mazzini.

The Genovese patriot had been so long in exile that he introduced himself to Margaret as "Joseph" in fluent English. Nearly two decades earlier, Mazzini had served a jail term in Savona for his insurrectionist writings. While in prison, he had conceived the Young Italy movement, an underground society that counted as many as sixty thousand members on the peninsula and in exile, united in the goal of making "One, Independent, Free Republic" of the country's several states and kingdoms, most of them under the control of the pope or an Austrian, Spanish, or French sovereign. A contemporary of Waldo Emerson's, but the psychological opposite of Margaret's stay-at-home mentor, the gaunt, eagle-eyed man of ideas — *and* action — was eluding a death sentence for his role as leader of a failed uprising in northern Italy in 1833, resulting in the execution of a dozen of his comrades. Margaret had already praised Mazzini's political writings in the *Tribune,* and she had learned his story from a novel she reviewed by the Danish revolutionary Harro Harring, who had joined Mazzini in the fighting and later turned the charismatic leader into a character in his novel. She was well prepared, as an American politician's daughter, to admire this man who dedicated himself to restoring the republican principles she had cherished since childhood to the country that had initiated them in its long-lost golden age. For Margaret, Mazzini represented both heroic Individual and hoped-for Future.

Joseph Mazzini seemed drawn to Margaret as well. He invited her to attend the fifth anniversary exhibition at a school he'd founded for poor Italian boys rescued from the streets of London, where they had been forced to work as organ grinders, and he asked her to speak to the assembled students and dignitaries. After just a few conversations with the exiled patriot, Margaret had mastered his rhetoric of "one nation, one republic" well enough to deliver it with an American slant to an English audience. "Beyond any other country, save ancient Greece," Margaret declared, Italy had done more to "awaken the love of the beautiful and the good, and thus refine the human soul." How could anyone "capable of thought on the subject, be indifferent to the emancipation of this fair land from present degradation?"

If Thomas Carlyle didn't see the use of the American citizen of the world, Mazzini—who had conscripted not only his fellow Italians but Danes and Poles and Englishmen into a movement that he hoped would one day draw all European countries into an alliance of republican nations—clearly did. As Margaret and the Springs prepared for their departure to Paris and then to Italy, Mazzini entrusted his new friends with a letter to deliver to his mother in Genoa, containing, they were led to believe, secret instructions. Mazzini hinted that he might consider traveling with them incognito, on an American passport if one could be obtained, back to his troubled homeland.

On one of Margaret's last nights in London, Mazzini—a man of "beauteous and pure music" when they talked alone—arrived at the Springs' rented rooms for conversation, only to be joined unexpectedly by the Carlyles. Although Mazzini was "a dear friend of Mrs. C.," his presence "gave the conversation a turn to 'progress' and ideal subjects," which inspired in the cranky Thomas Carlyle a stream of "invectives on all our 'rose-water imbecilities.'" After making a futile effort to "remonstrate," Mazzini withdrew, turning visibly "sad." Jane Carlyle whispered into Margaret's ear what she already knew: "These are but opinions to Carlyle; but to Mazzini, who has given his all, and helped bring his friends to the scaffold, in pursuit of such subjects, it is a matter of life and death."

· 18 ·

"Rome has grown up in my soul"

I N PARIS — "THE CITY OF PLEASURES," MARGARET WAS QUICK to say—the women devoted their first days to *getting dressed*," choosing not to send out their calling cards right away and instead keeping to the new Hôtel Rougement on the Boulevard Poissonnière, in their rooms furnished with "thick, flowered" carpets, marbled walls, canopied bedsteads, and the "inevitable large mirror," to be fitted for new clothes. The Springs decreed this was no time to economize, as they had in London by moving after two days from a fine hotel overlooking the fountains in Trafalgar Square to rented rooms "in a little narrow street." Margaret had instantly noticed "the devotion of a French woman to her *mise*" — her attire—and the money she used to buy her French wardrobe, a portion of her *Tribune* advance, was well spent. The dresses would last for the next three years.

Margaret had begun to mention in letters home the possibility of staying on in Europe for at least another season, if she could find the means. The Howitts had invited her to publish in their journal, and other "openings were made for me to write" on topics she wished to comment on in England. But while Margaret sequestered herself in the Hôtel Rougement for dress fittings and tutoring sessions to improve her spoken French, she was also looking backward, writing the dispatches she owed to the *Tribune* covering the weeks in London when she had been too busy to write, both harried and pleased by receiving so much company that the "only way of escape is *to hide*."

It was not simply in conversation that Margaret felt more in her element in Europe, but in her writing as well, now that she could reach past the boundaries of even America's Great Metropolis for subject matter. One of Margaret's last columns for the *New-York Tribune* before leaving, titled "Mistress of Herself, Though China Fall," had addressed the American housewife's "besetting danger . . . of littleness," the tendency of women to cry over broken china or "spots on the table cloth," fearing that "other women will laugh at them" for their sloppy housekeeping. Instead, Margaret advised her female readers to "see how much you need a great object in all your little actions." Cooking and cleaning should be "a means to an end," that of creating a "home" filled with "good spirits," not a "work-house." But Margaret's horizons had always stretched beyond the home. In England she had observed women in truly oppressive working conditions and confronted hard facts, such as the "habit of feeding children on opium" among mothers in Manchester to pacify hungry babies through long workdays. She had left America in search of both great objects *and* great actions — in writing, in life.

Once stylishly dressed and with several *Tribune* letters filed, Margaret began attending the opera and theatrical performances, museum exhibitions, and debates in the Chamber of Deputies; her French was now good enough for her to take in the arguments of the verbal "sharpshooters" who held the floor. She was presented at Louis Philippe's court but preferred her audience with the "true kings" of France: the socialists Félicité-Robert Lamennais and Pierre Jean de Béranger, the first a renegade priest whose internationally known *Words of a Believer* and *Book of the People* espoused a return to the democratic principles of the early Christian church, the second a poet whose verse satirized both church and monarchy and who had spent time in prison for it. Mazzini's good word had brought about the meeting and also served as entrée to the editors of *La Revue Indépendante*, who swiftly accepted Margaret's essay on American literature from *Papers on Literature and Art* for publication and asked her to become the journal's American correspondent when she returned to the United States.

Margaret's translator for the article, Pauline Roland, an intimate of *La*

Revue Indépendante's founders, the socialist philosopher Pierre Leroux and Margaret's heroine George Sand, had been mistress of a household that would have been scarcely imaginable to the American wives Margaret conjured up in her *Tribune* article as weeping into their broken teacups. For twelve years Pauline had lived in a "free union" with the father of two of her three children, declaring her firm opposition to marriage; more recently she had moved with the children to Pierre Leroux's experimental commune at Broussac, near George Sand's country house, and taken the job of teacher in the community's school. By way of Pauline's example, Margaret came to understand that Charles Fourier, the French originator of the international communal movement—called Associationism by its American popularizer, Albert Brisbane—had advocated social reforms far more revolutionary than the model *phalanstères* he'd outlined in his writings, which had inspired the formation of egalitarian working communities such as Broussac and Brook Farm. Horace Greeley was now helping to found the North American Phalanx in New Jersey, which the Springs planned to join on their return to the United States.

Taking up the cause of women—"*le feminisme*" in his terminology—Fourier had argued not just for a fair distribution of labor between men and women in his ideal communities (Margaret, in *Woman in the Nineteenth Century*, had cited Fourier's estimate that a third of men were likely to prefer traditionally male labor, and a third of men would prefer women's work). He also advocated the full emancipation of women through the abolition of marriage, which he viewed as a form of enslavement or legalized prostitution. French Fourierist *phalanstères* like Leroux's at Broussac, Margaret learned, supported free love, or "passional attraction," among communards, with the children born of such unions, whether temporary or enduring, to be raised collectively in infant *crèches*, liberating all parents to pursue their chosen occupations.

The Springs must have wondered how, with so much visiting, Margaret would ever fulfill her obligations as governess, yet Eddie's health was precarious and he was not always able to study. One of his illnesses held the Springs in Paris longer than they'd intended, to Margaret's relief. George Sand had been away for weeks at her country house, unable to respond to the letter Margaret directed to her home in the place d'Orléans. And though Margaret had attended the opera and seven performances by the celebrated dramatic artist Rachel, she had not yet had an opportunity to hear Sand's Polish lover, Frédéric Chopin, play the piano. At last, on Valentine's Day, 1847, rather than suffer another lonely call to the Lynch salon on Washington Square, Margaret spent an afternoon in Chopin's Paris atelier as the invited guest of the composer and one of his English piano students, listening to the man with whom Sand "lives on the footing of combined means, independent friendship!" as he expressed the "subtile secrets of the creative spirit" at the keyboard.

Margaret also met George Sand, who had returned to the city for the purpose of correcting galley proofs. Before the meeting, Margaret was impressed by what she heard of "Madame Sand," as she was called in Paris (Baroness Dudevant was her discarded married name) — "she takes rank in society like a man, for the weight of her thoughts." Yet when the novelist descended from her study to greet "*La dame Americaine*" — Margaret had simply dropped by in hopes of finding Sand at home — she was wearing not her famous black trousers and cape but a dark violet dress draped with a black mantle at the shoulders, her long dark hair brushed into curls, and her "lady-like dignity, presenting an almost ludicrous contrast to the vulgar caricature idea of George Sand." Margaret believed she would never forget the moment when Sand, her dark eyes shining with "truly human heart and nature," fixed those eyes upon her, asked "*C'est vous?*" and extended her hand. Sand explained afterward that Margaret appeared to have been summoned magically to her door: she had just been reading Margaret's letter, which she pronounced "*charmante,*" and begun to compose an invitation in return.

Despite Margaret's continuing struggle with spoken French, "a great trial to me, who am eloquent and free in my own tongue, to be forced to feel my thoughts struggling in vain for utterance," the two writers managed to communicate "as if we had always known one another." They did not take up the "personal or private matters" that may have been uppermost in Margaret's mind as she interviewed the social renegade, but the topics must have seemed urgent enough to Sand, who put aside her proof sheets to entertain Margaret for the rest of the day, explaining her decision in a phrase Margaret also committed to memory: "it is better to throw things aside, and seize the moment."

When Margaret called again a few days later, Sand's daughter and several friends, male and female, were on hand. She stayed long enough to see that Sand's "position" among the company was "of an intellectual woman and good friend,—the same as my own in the circle of my acquaintance." Although Margaret didn't draw the connection to her own conversational style, she noted too that Sand's "way of talking" was "just like her writing—lively, picturesque, with an undertone of deep feeling, and the same skill of striking the nail on the head every now and then with a blow."

Margaret quickly accustomed herself to Sand's habit of smoking a small cigarette while talking—now a "common practice among ladies abroad," which, Margaret believed, had "originated" with Sand. Writing against convention had long seemed a legitimate means of protest to Margaret, but in Paris both small and large *acts* of defiance began to seem acceptable as well. "She needs no defence," Margaret recorded after the two encounters with George Sand, "but only to be understood, for she has bravely acted out her nature, and always with good intentions." If Sand had found a man "who could interest and command her throughout her range," she might have loved that one man "permanently," Margaret speculated, "but there was hardly a possibility of that, for such a person." Margaret decided that Sand's having "changed the objects of her affection," not just once but "several times," was inevitable for a woman of her "range" and disposition: there may have been "something of the Bacchante in her," a "love of night and storm," a susceptibility to "free raptures" like those that had overcome "the followers of Cybele, the great goddess, the great mother." Unable any longer to disapprove of George Sand's "passional" prodigality now that she'd been welcomed by the novelist as an old friend and had confirmed their likeness in certain key respects, Margaret turned to mythology to find precedent, and perhaps a measure of propriety, in her heroine's transgressions—committed as a means of "acting out her nature."

Adam Mickiewicz, the great Polish poet and patriot, was another new acquaintance living a large life in Paris. Mickiewicz had been a professor of Slavic studies at the Collège de France until, shortly before Margaret arrived in Paris, he'd begun to attack the established church in his lectures and lost his job. Those same lectures had also introduced Emersonian Transcendentalism to the Paris intelligentsia, as Margaret found when she read them herself—and she sent Mickiewicz a copy of Waldo's newly published book of poems, guessing correctly that the gift would draw him swiftly to the Hôtel Rougement. If Waldo Emerson brought the two together, it was by stark contrast to her emotionally restrained American friend that Margaret knew she had found, in the handsome, exuberant forty-eight-year-old political exile Mickiewicz, "the man I had long wished to see, with the intellect and passions in due proportion for a full and healthy human being, with a soul constantly inspiring," as she wrote to Waldo a month after their first meeting, knowing he would take her meaning.

During her final ten days in Paris, Margaret spent most evenings in the company of Adam Mickiewicz, once attending a meeting of his "Circle of God," the group of ecstatic Christian radicals he was grooming for the fight for Polish independence from Prussia. George Sand probably had not read *Woman in the Nineteenth Century,* but Mickiewicz, who was fluent in English, had, finding himself in full agreement with Margaret's prediction that, as the Circle of God radicals put it, "the present is the era of the liberation of women." He announced as much at the meeting, impressing upon the assembled students and exiled Polish intellectuals his belief that Margaret would carry the cause to fruition. By one account, the intensely focused attention Margaret received from Mickiewicz that night caused her to faint.

Mickiewicz's enthusiasm for the cause of women's rights placed him closer to the Fourierists than to his Italian revolutionary counterpart Mazzini—and closer to Margaret as well. Whether Margaret was aware of Mickiewicz's troubled marriage is impossible to know. His wife had become mentally unstable during their years of exile, and recently the poet had transferred his affections, for a time at least, to the family's governess, with whom he had conceived a child. Perhaps Margaret knew and didn't care, or cared most of all about what Mickiewicz had suffered. As with so many of her previous attractions to powerful men, it was the "deep-founded mental connection" she experienced with Mickiewicz that anchored her in "this real and important relation." But the connection to this "full and healthy human being" was "real"—felt in her body, as the report of Margaret's fainting revealed.

Rebecca Spring, who had not followed Margaret to George Sand's house, refusing to enter the home of a woman who had broken her marriage vows, worried that Margaret was falling in love with Mickiewicz, or falling in with his Circle of God zealots. If Rebecca had read the letter Mickiewicz sent Margaret summing up his predictions at the evening meeting, she might have worried even more. Margaret, however, prized the letter above any she had received, as one of "the very few addresses to me to which I could respond." She felt *recognized*. And no wonder: Mickiewicz's words both echoed her highest aspirations and sounded her deepest self-doubt. Margaret was "the only one among women genuinely initiated into the antique world," Mickiewicz wrote, honoring Margaret's classical education, and "the only one to whom it has been given to touch that which is decisive in today's world and to comprehend in advance the world to come." He continued: "You have acquired the right to know and maintain the rights and obligations, the hopes and exigencies of virginity." Yet "the first step in your deliverance . . . is to know if it is permitted to you to remain virgin." Margaret had told the assembled members of the Circle of God that she had made a "vow never to marry." Did that vow require her to "remain virgin"?

To Rebecca Spring's blunt question—did she love Mickiewicz?— Margaret would answer, "He affected me like music or the richest landscape, my heart beat with joy that he at once felt beauty in me also." To Mickiewicz, Margaret was not simply, as Horace Greeley once observed, "an embodied intellect." She was body *and* mind. In Paris, Margaret lamented, "How much time had I wasted on others which I might have given" to Mickiewicz! But it was time to leave. Distraught, she packed her bags. In Rome Margaret would tell Rebecca Spring that "the attraction" she felt for Mickiewicz was "so strong that all the way from Paris"— through Arles to Marseille, stopping to view the working conditions of French silk weavers, by boat to Genoa, suffering "frightful" seasickness on the Mediterranean, and finally through a hurried tour of Pisa, Naples, Capri, and Pompeii to the Springs' rented rooms on the Corso—"I felt as if I had left my life behind." Margaret was powerfully tempted to return to Paris and leave the rest of Italy "unseen."

But she did not. Soon Margaret was leading Eddie Spring on walks in the Villa Borghese gardens, although she remained preoccupied. Once, while she sat nearby, deep in thought, the boy tumbled into the fountain and she had to fish him out. In Paris Margaret's French tutor had told her that with her naturally expressive voice and gestures, "I speak and act like an Italian." Margaret held out hope that in Italy "I shall find myself more at home." As for missing Mickiewicz, "I do not know but I might love still better tomorrow."

On April 1, Holy Thursday, six days after arriving in Rome and ten days before she wrote out her rueful plaint to Rebecca Spring, Margaret had met the man she would love still better—or differently—than Adam Mickiewicz. She'd ridden with the Springs by carriage to St. Peter's Basilica for evening services marking the Last Supper. As always, pilgrims from all over Europe—colorfully dressed in peasant costume, elegantly clad in silks—descended on Rome's most sacred church to celebrate the rituals of Easter week. The massive, echoing sanctuary was mobbed after a late mass as Margaret found her way into a side chapel for vespers. The daily escalation of pageantry, beginning on Palm Sunday, filled the air with expectation this year more than any in recent memory. Three days later, on April 4, Easter Sunday, the broad piazza in front of the cathedral would fill with a "prostrate multitude" kneeling to receive the first Easter blessing of the new pope, Pius IX, as he was borne high above their heads in his ornate pontifical chair into the cathedral. "Pio Nono," Margaret had already learned to call the man who since his election the previous June had swiftly, almost miraculously it seemed, brought liberalizing reforms to Rome, including amnesty for political refugees of the Papal States.

The mood in the city was heartening, and Margaret would soon be caught up in it herself, invited to attend an elegant open-air dinner in celebration of Rome's "natal day" two weeks later at the Baths of Titus, where writers just returned from exile stood among the ancient ruins to give speeches lauding Pio Nono as destined to become "a new and nobler founder for another State." Music wafted on the breeze as the guests, seated under an effigy of "the Roman wolf with her royal nursling," looked out toward the Colosseum and the arches of the Forum. "It was a new thing here, this popular dinner," Margaret wrote in her account for the *Tribune*, "and the Romans greeted it in an intoxication of hope and pleasure." Several days before, Margaret and the Springs had witnessed a torch-bearing procession—"a river of fire" streaming down the Corso from the Piazza del Popolo, past their apartment to the pope's Quirinal Palace—formed spontaneously in tribute to Pio Nono after he'd issued a circular granting the states under his control, Rome among them, the right to elect representative councils. Pio Nono's circular provided only a "limited" improvement, in Margaret's view, compared with a fully representative democracy like the United States, but it was "a great measure for Rome." Margaret had followed the parade, which advanced "slowly with a perpetual surge-like sound of voices" and torchlight flickering on "animated Italian faces" all the way to the Quirinal, where red and white "Bengal" flares were tossed into the night sky, lighting up the colossal statues of Castor and Pollux with their steeds. She watched as the pope stepped out on his balcony to shouts of "Viva!" from the crowd, which dispersed in an instant, torches extinguished, after receiving Pio Nono's open-armed blessing. Margaret had "never seen anything finer." Yet she worried that even Pio Nono was "not great enough"—how could he compare to Mazzini, who had risked his life and stirred an international movement?—or that the new pope lacked the temporal power to bring about "the liberty of Rome" that its people, with their "perpetual hurra, vivas, rockets," had now come to expect. Then what would happen?

At evening vespers on Maundy Thursday, Margaret had become separated from the Springs in a more subdued crowd of the worshipful, her thoughts still dwelling on the music—on the astonishing, transporting experience for a New Englander of a religious service that included no sermon. There had been simply a blending of male voices, "elaborate, expressive, and sacred," as her countryman George Hillard, traveling in Rome the following year, would describe vespers at St. Peter's, "weaving solemn airs" for nearly an hour "into a complicated tissue of harmony, such as tasked both the voice and the mind to unwind." At first Margaret hadn't noticed she was lost, and may have willed herself to become one of the multitude to test her self-sufficiency in the world's capital.

True to her French tutor's prediction, the Italian language Margaret had mastered as a reader came more easily to her tongue, and in any case, as she'd written to James Nathan two years earlier at a time when she expected never to see the inside of St. Peter's, "Rome has grown up in my soul in default of the bodily presence." Margaret arrived in Rome as much a native as was possible for someone who had never lived there. "We know every nook of St Peters, every statue, every villa, by heart almost," she'd admonished James Nathan from her desk at the *Tribune* when he contemplated writing about the city; "Rome is an all hacknied theme and by the most accomplished pens." For Margaret, who at age twenty-three had read Goethe's *Italian Journey* (the book that inspired "an earnest desire to live as he did") and countless other reminiscences of travel since, whose knowledge of the antique world was that of a "genuine initiate," as Mickiewicz easily saw, mere travelogue could never satisfy. Rather than "describe outward objects there in detail," she advised James Nathan, he should find what was "characteristic": analyze, interpret, and deliver "your own thoughts." Another sign that Margaret had estimated James Nathan too highly was her expectation that he could readily offer up the knowing, incisive commentary that came instinctively to her. Even after receiving her explicit instructions, he had failed.

But in the crowd of departing worshipers that Thursday night, with her Parisian clothes and American independence, Margaret did not blend in. When she couldn't find the Springs at their appointed meeting place and drew out her lorgnette to see better, she attracted the attention of a tall, slender, twenty-six-year-old Roman, Giovanni Angelo Ossoli. The young man inquired in Italian—he knew no English or French—was she lost, did she need guidance to her hotel, her rooms? Perhaps she enjoyed answering him in Italian.

Margaret never recorded the meeting herself, other than to say it was "singular, fateful." Or maybe she did, but the "little book" in which she inscribed her account was lost. According to the American publisher George Palmer Putnam, who had taken the same paddle steamer from Livorno to Naples with her several weeks earlier and claimed to have chanced upon the two at St. Peter's as she searched "bewildered" for the Springs, Margaret dropped Ossoli's arm as soon as Putnam recognized her and set off on the long walk back across the Tiber River to the Corso alone. But something must have struck him about the pair—the uncharacteristically flustered and fashionably dressed American literary celebrity with the attentive young Roman at her side—despite his assertion that Margaret "certainly did not give her address" to the Italian youth. In a letter to Evert Duyckinck written soon afterward, Putnam speculated suggestively that "within the precincts of the sanctuary" the *Tribune*'s star reporter had "received very singular suggestions from the young men of Rome which may afford instructive notes to a future edition of Woman in the Nineteenth Century."

Margaret's own testimony a few years later, reported by her friend and closest confidante in Rome, Emelyn Story, a Bostonian married to the expatriate sculptor William Wetmore Story, did not involve a surprise appearance by George Putnam. Rather, Margaret had kept hold of Ossoli's arm through a fruitless search of the cathedral's side chapels for the Springs, a vain foray into the streets surrounding the piazza looking for a carriage to hire, and then a stroll back to the Corso, where the kind young man left her, fully apprised of her address.

Yet the facts of that night remain irretrievable. Margaret wished to obscure them, always preferred to "say nothing" about the details of her early involvement with Giovanni Angelo Ossoli. Her version of events may have been contrived to mislead. Indeed, George Putnam was certain he'd spotted Margaret and the young Italian on a Wednesday evening, at the singing of the plaintive miserere. Could the two have parted quickly after a chance first encounter, arranging to meet again at Thursday vespers, giving Margaret a night to consider whether she truly wished to be escorted home by the young man with a touch of melancholy about the eyes—if only she could detach herself from her chaperones, the Springs? His evident "simplicity" and "unspoiled nature" may already have signaled to Margaret that Ossoli was "ignorant of great ideas, ignorant of books," a man whom most of her friends would consider "nothing." Yet perhaps she saw in him instantly, as well, his "excellent practical sense," his "native refinement" and "sweet temper," qualities she would remark on again and again to those same uncomprehending friends several years later. She might have sensed too in those early moments in the cathedral that Ossoli was, like her if from a less learned perspective, "a judicious observer" of the passing scene: he *had* noticed Margaret's distress and offered help. If all this had not been apparent in his manner, why else would she have taken the stranger's arm?

What happened next took place rapidly, for by April 10 Margaret was projecting a new and "better" love to Rebecca Spring and hinting that she might leave her traveling companions to make an independent tour of northern Italy in July and August, rather than follow the Springs into Switzerland and Germany and back to America. "I wish to be free and absolutely true to my nature," she informed Rebecca, who only grew further alarmed. Was Margaret planning an impulsive return to Mickiewicz? No, she was considering a return to Rome, rather than Paris, at the end of the summer.

A letter from Mickiewicz supported her choice—he was not yet free to see her under circumstances when "all of me could be with you." She "needed" more of Italy, the poet advised. Margaret thought so too, even though, when the young man who was paying such ardent suit stunningly "offered me his hand through life," she turned down his proposal of marriage. "I loved him," but the prospect of a permanent "connexion" to the twenty-six-year-old unlettered Giovanni Angelo Ossoli, no matter how sweet-tempered, "seemed so every way unfit."

Could this momentous exchange—"singular, fateful"—have taken place as early as April 4, Easter Sunday at St. Peter's, a date the two would later celebrate as an anniversary? Was it their first meeting, or the second, if Putnam is to be believed, or a third, at St. Peter's on Easter Sunday, that caused Margaret to associate the cathedral and its expansive piazza with "the splendidest part of my life"? "No spot on earth is worthier the sun light," she exulted; "on none does it fall so fondly."

But Margaret could still write honestly to her brother Richard in mid-April of her stay so far in Rome, "I have not yet formed any friendship of the mind, such as I had in London and Paris" with Mazzini and Mickiewicz. Giovanni Ossoli, she had discerned correctly, was "a person of no intellectual culture"—he may never have read a book all the way through. "Nature has been his book," Margaret would one day write to defend him, and "of that some lines he has spelled thoroughly." But he had never been to school, received only cursory tutoring in liturgical Latin from a parish priest. Despite his air of "refinement," Giovanni Ossoli was also very much "an obscure young man." The fourth and by far the youngest son in a family of faded nobility, a half-orphan who still mourned the mother who died when he was six, he shared with an older married sister the care of their elderly father, with whom he lived in an apartment near the Capitol, a short walk from the Springs' rooms on the Corso.

"Giovanni," as Margaret introduced her "gentle friend" to the Springs, who suspected no romantic involvement with so young a foreigner, could walk with Margaret the several blocks to the Church of Santa Maria Maddalena near the Piazza Colonna to show her the ornate Ossoli chapel, with its columns and panels of richly colored marbles, its seventeenth-century painting of the Virgin Mary and St. Nicholas, savior of the hungry and the destitute. Although Giovanni was descended from the same prosperous baker who had earned the title of marchese two centuries before—hence the family's choice of St. Nicholas, known for his miraculous multiplication of wheat—this was not truly *Giovanni's* sacred altar. This Margaret would never learn, or never reveal that she knew, if she did: Giovanni was not heir to the title marchese Ossoli. That title belonged to his oldest brother, and would pass to the first son of that brother—a nephew. Giovanni's correct title was Giovanni Angelo *dei Marchesi d'Ossoli*, of the marquises d'Ossoli, a mere member of the family. Still, he was honest about his prospects. The majestic Palazzo Ossoli in the Piazza Quercia had been sold a century earlier, and the Roman law of primogeniture meant he would gain little of what remained of the family fortune at his father's death. Giovanni had not made up his mind whether to enter papal service, as his older brothers had. His future in Rome was as uncertain as Margaret's.

Yet he affected her powerfully. When Margaret turned down his proposal—"never dream[ing] I should take it"—and, both eager and sorrowing, left Rome for Venice with the Springs, soon to part from them as well, Giovanni Ossoli told her he would wait. She would change her mind and come back to him.

Margaret wrote openly to Mickiewicz for advice, but to no one else. "Do not be too hasty about leaving places," he counseled by return mail. "Prolong your good moments. Do not leave lightly those who would like to remain near you. This is in reference to the little Italian you met in the Church." Even Mickiewicz shared the prejudice Margaret anticipated in other friends, terming Ossoli "the little Italian." But Poland's great national poet had taken up with his children's governess. Was he encouraging an extramarital involvement with Ossoli that he saw—that Margaret might see—as similar: a powerful literary personage loving and loved by a younger besotted "nothing"? Mickiewicz urged Margaret to come back to Paris, but first "try to bring away from Italy what you will be able to take of it in joy and in health." Could Mickiewicz have hoped to welcome a more "thoroughly" experienced Margaret at their next meeting, when he might be free to offer "all of me" in return?

She wrote to family and friends in America, asking Horace Greeley for further advances on columns, requesting loans from her brother Richard, her mother, even Waldo Emerson, so that she could stay on in Europe without the support of the Springs. "A single year is so entirely inadequate to see all which I wish to see," she wrote to Mary Rotch of Rhode Island, a wealthy friend to Waldo Emerson and the late Reverend Channing, and "I find myself better here." She explained to them all, however, that she had little time to write letters, that they must follow her progress now through her *Tribune* columns. The dispatches recorded a vital outward life: "I take interest in the state of the people," she wrote to William Channing. "I see the future dawning." She predicted it would be "in important aspects Fourier's future" — egalitarian, socialist.

To William she confided a little more: "Art is not important to me now." She would no longer write to him "of the famous people I see, of magnificent shows and places. All these things are only to me an illuminated margin on the text of my inward life" — an inward life she would not describe, but that now took precedence. She needed "a kind of springtime to renovate my faculties," she wrote to Mary Rotch. She would find it in Rome, in the fall.

So far as can be known, Margaret did not communicate with Giovanni Ossoli during the summer of 1847 as she traveled from Venice, where she spent an evening at Florian's on the Piazza San Marco after parting tearfully with the Springs, to Florence (too "busy and intellectual," Margaret complained, "more in its spirit like Boston, than like an Italian city"), and finally to Milan, where she fell in with "a circle of the aspiring youth," disciples of Mazzini. In letters to Marcus Spring and anyone she hoped might aid her materially, Margaret emphasized the difficulties of solo travel. She had become ill in Brescia after making a journey "very profitable to the mind" through Vicenza, Verona, Mantua, and Lago di Garda. Though she had lived alone "in our own country," it had been a frightening experience to fall sick "here where there is no one on whom I can call for aid in any case." Once recovered, she had "nearly killed myself finishing a letter for the Tribune" in hopes of meriting another advance from Greeley. Traveling briefly into Switzerland, she was overcharged by her guide, then pestered by a well-meaning traveler who assumed she wanted company when all she wished for was a "quiet room . . . in a place where I was unknown, and where there was nothing, except the mountains to distract my attention."

But writing to her mother, who promised to send one hundred dollars once she'd received the sum from brother Eugene in repayment of a loan, Margaret stressed the "advantage I derive from being alone": "if I feel the need of it, I can stop," and she had in fact made a detour to visit the Armenian monastery on an island near Venice frequented by Byron. In Tuscany she paused to watch women braiding one another's hair; in Assisi she mingled with a crowd of curious schoolgirls, inquired about their studies (reading, writing, and sewing), and chatted in Italian with a woman who called down to her from an upstairs window. "Who can ever be alone for a moment in Italy?" she asked her *Tribune* readers. To Richard, who finally extracted the hundred dollars from Eugene, Margaret wrote that since leaving the Springs, "I passed happier and more thoughtful hours than at all before in Europe."

The truth may have been somewhere in the middle—euphoric moments when she felt happy to be "alone with glorious Italy," mixed with anxious ones and even times when, after being away for so long, Margaret felt "a yearning for the loved familiar faces" and bravely vowed not to "yield to it." To one of those longed-for familiars, Cary Sturgis, Margaret confessed what she would never tell the Springs—she had begun to feel "a wicked irritation against them for being the persons who took me away from France." After floating as the sole passenger on a gondola that first week in Venice on her own, "I seemed to find myself again." At last, "I begin to be in Italy"; she wished to "drink deep of this cup."

Without the Springs in tow, Margaret could mingle freely with the community of expatriates and returning exiles whose fervor for the cause of independence she instinctively shared and her travels had affirmed: "In this Europe how much suffocated life!" Particularly in Italy, Margaret believed, "the signs have improved so much since I came." She felt "most fortunate to be here at this time," she wrote to Richard. In Milan she cultivated a friendship with the marchioness Costanza Arconati Visconti, whom she had met first at the open-air dinner in Rome, and again in Florence for a celebration of Grand Duke Leopold's relaxation of press censorship in Austrian-controlled Tuscany. But in Milan Margaret saw Arconati Visconti in her private residence, newly established after a twenty-five-year exile in Belgium and France, as well as at the marchioness's villa on Lake Como, where Margaret spent two weeks in August. Here she could scrutinize this "specimen of the really highbred lady," to Margaret a new breed entirely. Most striking was the way her hostess managed, "without any physical beauty," to employ "the grace and harmony of her manners [to] produce all the impression of beauty." An "intimate with many of the first men" of Italy—Mazzini, and the great poet Alessandro Manzoni, to whom Margaret gained an introduction in Milan—Costanza Arconati Visconti possessed a mind that was "strong clear, precise and much cultivated by intercourse both with books and men."

Although the vacation at Bellagio on Lake Como brought Margaret "into contact with . . . high society, duchesses, marquises and the like," as she wrote to Cary Sturgis, and the talk was often "of spheres so unlike mine," Margaret was reminded of nothing so much as the dreams she and Cary had once entertained of an ideal riverside community in Newburyport: "these people have charming villas and gardens on the lake, adorned with fine works of art; they go to see one another in boats; you can be all the time in a boat if you like." Margaret would later decide that there were few "women in Europe to compare with those of America"; she managed to establish "real intimacy" with only three, Arconati Visconti among them. But at Bellagio, during that summer in which "I seemed to find myself again," Margaret felt welcomed into an elite company of like-minded women. Arconati Visconti's friendship circle in exile had included Margaret's heroine Bettine von Arnim, and she introduced Margaret now to the "fair and brilliant" Polish countess Radzivill, another "one of the emancipated," Margaret judged. The countess "*envies me,*" Margaret marveled, for being "so free, so serene, so attractive, so self-possessed!" In her travels Margaret had unknowingly acquired the same poise she admired in the marchioness Arconati Visconti: the ability to project "without any physical beauty . . . all the impression of beauty." Certainly Giovanni Ossoli thought so—along with the "pretty girls of Bellagio," daughters of the Italian gentry, who "with their coral necklaces, all brought flowers to 'the American Countess' and 'hoped she would be as happy as she deserved.'" Their "cautious wish" seemed, for the moment, within her grasp.

If Margaret lost touch with Ossoli—she could not have written to his family residence in Rome without arousing suspicion of an attachment—she traveled with three powerful male epistolary companions: Mickiewicz, Mazzini, and Waldo Emerson. Waldo's periodic letters to "our queen of discourse," as he addressed Margaret in sympathy with her struggles in the French language, brought news of a world that must have seemed impossibly distant. Over the winter, Henry Thoreau had read an "account of his housekeeping at Walden" to a receptive audience at the Concord Lyceum, the lecture billed as "Subject—History of Himself." But despite Waldo's approval of the manuscript's "witty wisdom," the young memoirist was having trouble finding a publisher. A reception at Elizabeth Peabody's Boston bookroom following Waldo's own winter lecture, "Eloquence," had brought out the old Conversations crowd: Anna Ward, Sarah Clarke, Cary Sturgis and her two sisters, Ellen and Anna Hooper, along with William Henry Channing and Theodore Parker. Waldo joked that the gathering seemed "an Egyptian party; on this side of Styx too!" Without Margaret, the affair took on a "melancholy absurdity," and soon the guests "glided out like so many ghosts." Cary had teased Waldo that even his lecture "was old!!"

How could her one-time mentor in the "newness"—a man just forty-three years old—feel so ancient, mummified? Now Margaret had other heroes to compare him to, men who had given up home and country for a cause—to put an end to these "everlasting struggles" to bring freedom to "those who will come after us," as Mazzini had written to her before she left Paris.

Waldo wrote Margaret that he'd been invited to deliver a series of lectures in England; he viewed the prospect with alarm, as "one to whom almost every social influence [is] excessive & hurtful." He would rather they "send me into the mountains for protection," he admitted. Waldo had toured Europe the year after his first wife's death and returned to New England convinced that there was little to be learned from "these millennial cities"—London, Paris, Rome—with "their immense accumulations of human works," so dizzying to the beholder that "nothing but necessity & geometry" remained in retrospect. Yet once he learned that Margaret planned to stay on in Italy, he applauded her decision, understanding her quite different need to "run out of the coop of our bigoted societies . . . and find some members of your own expansive fellowship." Waldo longed to know, "O Sappho, Sappho, friend of mine"—identifying Margaret with the Greek love-poet at one time exiled in Italy—"the best of your Roman experiences," wishing he could somehow inhabit her mind, guessing that even the "faithfullest paragraph of your journal" would not reveal them.

Waldo did not tell Margaret that he had devoted many spare hours during the past year to refining a "rugged" translation he'd made years before of Dante's *Vita Nuova* (*New Life*), the medieval Italian poet's series of lyrics exploring his transfiguring love for the unreachable Beatrice — an account "almost unique in the literature of sentiment," in Waldo's opinion. Margaret had once held the text, among the earliest renderings of the chaste passions of courtly love, sacred herself. Nor did Waldo reveal to Margaret that he privately considered her own journal record that she'd once shown him of just "two of her days," perhaps covering the long-ago negotiations over the "covenant" of five, so much the equal in pitch and ardency of Dante's work that he'd labeled the passage "Nuovissima Vita" — *newest* life. No wonder Waldo longed to read whatever as-yet-unwritten record of the heart Margaret might keep in Rome; possibly he looked forward to further manifestations of her "deep-founded mental connection" with "the Polander," as he referred to Mickiewicz, the "full and healthy human being" with "intellect and passions in due proportion" whom Margaret had pointedly described in her letter from Paris.

Yet Margaret knew anyway that Waldo was still absorbed imaginatively, sentimentally, with his own Beatrice — Cary Sturgis — by way of a poem in his recent collection, "Give All to Love":

> *Obey thy heart;*
> *Friends, kindred, days,*
> *Estate, good-fame,*
> *Plans, credit, and the Muse, —*
> *Nothing refuse.*

The poem began as a hymn to Fourierist "passional attraction," yet in the end it sounded the notes of the Concord Puritan's *Vita Nuova* —

> *Cling with life to the maid;*
> *But when the surprise,*
> *First vague shadow of surmise*
> *Flits across her bosom young,*
> *Of a joy apart from thee,*
> *Free be she, fancy-free . . .*

Mickiewicz had read the poem too, and he quoted the first line to Margaret in a letter she received at Milan—"*give all for love*," Mickiewicz admonished her, "but this *love* must not be that of . . . schoolboys and German ladies."

In Paris, "I saw you, with all your knowledge and your imagination and all your literary reputation, living in bondage worse than that of a servant," the poet protested. "You have persuaded yourself that all you need is to express your ideas and feelings in books. You existed like a ghost that whispers to the living its plans and desires, no longer able to realize them itself." He might have been describing Waldo Emerson, Margaret knew, but it was to her that Mickiewicz addressed his appeal: "I tried to make you understand that you should not confine your life to books and reveries. You have pleaded the liberty of woman in a masculine and frank style. Live and act, as you write."

Margaret responded that his words were "*harsh.*" "Do not forget that even in your private life *as a woman* you have rights to maintain," Mickiewicz had scolded her. But his return letter stated his case more strongly: "Literature is not the whole life." Margaret must "try to get this inner life lodged and established in all your body . . . I tried to make you understand the purpose of your existence, to inspire manly sentiments in you. Your mind still does not wish to believe that a new epoch commences and that it has already begun. New for *woman* too." It was an argument she could scarcely dismiss; he was building on her own precepts to argue for her emancipation: "The relationships which suit you are those which develop and free your spirit, responding to the legitimate needs of your organism and leaving you free at all times. You are the sole judge of these needs."

But how could she act out this "manly" prescription with no money to live on? Maybe a new epoch had commenced, but it had not yet fully arrived. In Paris, Margaret had discovered that although George Sand was more influential than her male contemporaries Balzac and Dumas, she earned far less for her writings. Waldo Emerson had turned aside Margaret's request for funds, pleading debt, although his combined real-estate holdings and lecture fees were soon to make him one of the fifty wealthiest men in Massachusetts. Margaret knew full well that he had paid for Bronson Alcott's tour of England after the demise of the Temple School; now he was sponsoring both Thoreau and Alcott in the construction of a "summerhouse" of Alcott's own quixotic design. "Tumbledown-Hall," Waldo called the whimsical bungalow, outfitted with "peristyle gables, dormer windows, &c in the midst of my cornfield." Waldo's salvo to Margaret—"we all succeed in your success"—must have rung false in her ears.

Waldo knew in April what Margaret did not learn until June—that her uncle Abraham had died. Perhaps he assumed, like most who knew the family, that rich, childless Abraham Fuller, with an estate valued at $80,000, would make his fatherless nieces and nephews his chief beneficiaries. But Margaret would be disappointed in this too. The legacies had gone elsewhere, and Abraham had divided the remainder evenly among sixty-two near and distant relations, many of whom had no need for the "legal fraction" they received. Rather than the "ten or even five thousand dollars" she could well have expected, Margaret received less than $1,000, from which Abraham deducted $400 he had grudgingly doled out to her in years past, leaving her with scarcely $200. "My uncle died as he had lived, hard-hearted against me," Margaret concluded bitterly; "far from aiding, [he] wished to see me fall, because I acted against his opinion . . . and defended my mother against his rude tyranny." Soon she would grow "sore at being continually congratulated about my uncle's legacy," his death making it harder to ask for assistance—loans against the proceeds of a book she was beginning to plan about the independence movement in Italy.

She had already begun to exploit opportunities to write on the subject for European publications. Mazzini had enlisted her as his American exponent of Italian independence for the *People's Journal,* and she drew on the hopeful signs of the summer—Pio Nono had granted Rome and Bologna the right to establish Civic Guards to defend against imperial forces—to draft a short plea and an accompanying poem, published after her return to Rome in the fall.

Mazzini had stayed behind in London, deciding it was too risky to travel in disguise with Margaret and the Springs into Italy. And after her successful delivery of the packet of letters to his mother in Genoa— which provoked Maria Mazzini Drago's curiosity as to whether a romantic alliance had been formed between her son and the American journalist—Mazzini had limited his correspondence with Margaret, knowing that his mail would be intercepted and read by Italian authorities. But

Mazzini had, like Mickiewicz, made his appeal to Margaret by way of Emerson, in his case warning, in a last letter to her in Paris, against an Emersonian devotion to "the inward man": "Contemplation! no; there are too many sufferings, too many gross iniquities, too many sacred causes in this world of ours, for us to indulge in contemplation. Life is a march and a battle." Like Mickiewicz, Mazzini believed a too "inward" life to be dangerous, not to personal liberty, but to the liberty of humankind.

In her poem "To a Daughter of Italy," Margaret brought the rhetoric of *Woman in the Nineteenth Century* to the cause, summoning the figure of the vestal virgin from ancient Rome and calling on her "anew" to "rouse to fervent force the soul of man" in Italy's fight for a modern republic. She was not satisfied with her "poor text," Margaret wrote to the journal's editor, but until she could find a language for the new imperatives slowly forming in her heart and mind, she was left with reciting her customary list of idealized goddesses, among whom Isis alone stood for an earthy fertility:

> *Amid the prayers I hourly breathe for thee,*
> *Most beautiful, most injured Italy!*
> *None has a deeper root within the heart,*
> *Than to see woman duly play her part:*
> *To the advancing hours of this great day*
> *A morning Star be she, to point the way;*
> *The Virgin Mother of a blessed birth,*
> *The Isis of a fair regenerate earth,*
> *And, where its sons achieve their noblest fame,*
> *Still, Beatrice be the woman's name.*

Margaret's invocation of a vestal virgin consecrated to the republican cause must have pleased Mazzini, who had written to his mother in response to her query about his "American friend": "Don't worry! If I were a man to yield and grow soft in the midst of Capuan delights, I would have all possible opportunities to do so: there are at least half a dozen young women, who contend each other the privilege of surrounding me with loving care . . . but I cannot afford to grow soft in the midst of their attentions." When he'd written to Margaret as she left Paris for Rome, "You do not know how much I esteem and love you," Mazzini knew he could count on her to understand that the love he expressed was for a comrade—a citizen of the world. If Mickiewicz read the poem, however, he must have thought all his counsel had gone for naught. Waldo Emerson would have hailed his Beatrice.

Fortunately, the man uppermost in Margaret's thoughts was none of these. When Margaret returned to Rome in October, would it be to persuade her lover, Giovanni Ossoli, to accept her in the long-preferred role of unapproachable inamorata in a chaste *Vita Nuova,* or to join him in a "Vita Nuovissima," in which she claimed at last her "legitimate needs," her "right" to a "private life *as a woman*"? Would the *Tribune*'s "Star" descend to earth? Of one thing Margaret had become certain that summer, as she wrote to her brother Richard, who was suffering over a recent broken engagement: "I feel . . . such a conviction of the need in every human heart for love." But was love a feeling, or an act?

"It must be inhaled wholly, with the yielding of the whole heart," Margaret wrote of Rome to Cary Sturgis. "It is really something transcendent, both spirit and body." Margaret was describing "those last glorious nights" in the city three months earlier, before she left for the summer, "in which I wandered about amid the old walls and columns or sat by the fountains in the Piazza del Popolo, or by the river." Rome in the 1840s was still in the early stages of excavation, and access to ruins at the Forum and Colosseum, where "every stone has a voice, every grain of dust seems instinct with spirit from the Past, every step recalls some line, some legend," was easy. For Margaret, England, Scotland, and France had been "more attractive than I expected," but Rome "fulfills my hopes; it could not do more, it has been the dream of my life."

In her letter to Cary, Margaret omitted mention of her companion, Giovanni Ossoli, but she alluded obliquely to her predicament: those warm spring nights had seemed "worth an age of pain both after and before . . . only one hates pain in Italy." When Margaret returned in the fall, Giovanni helped her find an apartment on the Corso, this one nearer to the Piazza del Popolo and the entrance to the Borghese gardens at the Pincian Hill, across the busy main thoroughfare from the rooms Goethe had occupied over a half-century before, living under an assumed name to escape his adoring public. She could see his windows from hers, as well as "all the motions of Rome" in the street below, as every important parade or procession took the Corso for its route. With the hundred dollars from home and the prospect of two hundred more from Uncle Abrahame's estate, she engaged the rooms—"elegantly furnished" and "so neat, more like England than Italy," she wrote to her mother—for an anticipated six months "of quiet occupation" beginning in October. Anxious for privacy herself, Margaret was pleased to learn that it was the "custom of Rome," she explained, "to take your apartment and live entirely separately from the family"—so unlike American boarding houses with their communal meals and forced conviviality. Was she hinting to her mother of the step she was about to take?

In her upstairs rooms at 514 the Corso, Margaret had "my books, my flowers"—freshly cut on her writing table—a sitting room for entertaining guests, and "all the pleasures I most value, so rich and exalting . . . within my reach." Above her bed she had hung a print of Raphael's *Poesy,* the winged beauty with book in one hand and lyre in the other, which filled one of four famous ceiling medallions in the Vatican's Stanza della Segnatura, where the pope signed decrees of the ecclesiastical court. Margaret had purchased a second copy, which she planned to send to Cary; the much-reproduced engraving by Raimondi depicted the seated muse as an angelic sibyl—the medallion's motto, *numine afflatur (she is inspired by the divine force),* was adapted from lines in the *Aeneid* in which Apollo inspires the Cumaean prophetess to speak—flanked by two putti. But unlike Raphael's original in the Vatican, the print lacked the solemn stony face of a masculine god peering out from beneath her elbow. The image, which called up her many hours spent translating Virgil in girlhood and featured her personal avatar, the sibyl, expressed the feelings Margaret reported that fall to her brother Richard: "I find myself so happy here alone and free."

She was not truly dissembling when she wrote to Waldo Emerson that "I live alone, eat alone, walk alone, and enjoy unspeakably the stillness, after all the rush and excitement of the past year." She saw almost no "Amerns," as she dismissively abbreviated her countrymen, who tended to "lose the benefit of being abroad, by herding too much together," and in any case made up only a small percentage of Rome's English-speaking tourists, most of whom were British. "I have seen them standing three deep" in the Vatican, Margaret complained, "with Murray [guidebooks] sticking out of each pocket." "Since I have experienced the different atmosphere of the European mind," Margaret wrote to another friend, probably William Channing, "and been allied with it, nay, mingled in the bonds of love, I suffer more than ever from that which is peculiarly American or English. I should like to cease from hearing the language for a time." She was leaving hints again: "I am in a state of unnatural divorce from what I was most allied to."

To Waldo, who quickly gleaned that Margaret was "in a sort of beatitude of rest after years of hurry," as he wrote to Lidian from Manchester, England, where he'd journeyed in November after all, having received a guarantee of satisfactory lecture fees, Margaret described her plans for a winter "quite by myself": "I shall make no acquaintance from whom I do not hope a good deal, as my time will be like pure gold to me . . . and, just for happiness, Rome itself is sufficient." She painted the scene of the day on which she'd written, which was "the last of the October feasts of the Trasteverini," residents of the ancient riverside quarter near St. Peter's: "I have been, this afternoon, to see them dancing. This morning I was out, with half Rome, to see the Civic Guard manoeuvring in that great field near the tomb of Cecilia Metella, which is full of ruins. The effect was noble, as the band played the Bolognese march, and six thousand Romans passed in battle array amid these fragments of the great time."

She was "in a state of unnatural divorce," she was "mingled in the bonds of love," she was "alone and free"—all were possible now that Margaret was in "a full communion with the spirit of Rome," the multifarious city with its boisterous Trasteverini, who danced a saltarello that "heated" Margaret with enthusiasm and "carried me quite beyond myself" in "wickedly stolen" moments; with its seductive allegory of *Sacred and Profane Love* hanging in the Villa Borghese, Titian's painting of two strikingly beautiful women seated by a well, one fully clothed, the other nude, that "has developed my powers of gazing to an extent unknown before"; and with its massive, manly marble *Moses,* Michelangelo's sculpture lodged in the basilica of San Pietro in Vincolo (St. Peter in Chains), "the only thing in Europe, so far, which has entirely outgone my hopes." It was not quite true, as Margaret had written to William Channing, that "art is not important to me now." Loving and being loved by Giovanni Ossoli, soon to be commissioned a sergeant in the newly mustered Civic

Guard—the spirit of Rome—had intensified all sensory experience, the aspect of Italy, of life itself, as Mickiewicz had tried to tell her, that she could never learn from books.

In the end, the decision had not been painful—"one hates pain in Italy." There was no need for decision. The most Margaret would ever say in explanation, and this came some years later, was "I acted upon a strong impulse. I could not analyze what happened in my mind." But yielding to impulse did not mean abandoning principle. "I acted out my character," she would assert, borrowing the phrase she had used to approve George Sand's affairs. In discussions with Waldo Emerson years before, Margaret had made up her mind that marriage was a "corrupt social contract" that cheated wife far worse than husband. The question she had needed to resolve was not about loving a man outside the protective bonds of marriage, but about giving up her virginity, altering her view of chastity: that emblem of virtuous womanhood, of personal integrity, as she had long believed; the "lonely position" often chosen by "saints and geniuses," female and male, as she'd written in *Woman in the Nineteenth Century*, in order to leave themselves "undisturbed by the pressure of near ties."

Yet even this she had begun to doubt as early as her first encounters with the prostitutes imprisoned at Sing Sing. Margaret had asked Georgiana Bruce, her Brook Farm acolyte, how she thought prostitutes "viewed the whole concept of chastity." "Do they see any reality in it"? Or did they "look on it merely as a circumstance of condition, like the possession of fine clothes?" Margaret knew that "novelists are fond of representing" prostitutes "as if they looked up to their more protected sisters as saints and angels!" But Margaret had become a journalist, not a novelist, whose trademark was experiencing reality firsthand and recording the truth as she saw it. In Rome, in the fall of 1847, she chose as her icon not a saint or a genius, but Poesy, whose Greek name she knew was Erato, the muse of lyric and love poets. Margaret bought Cary a copy of the Raphael print as a wedding gift to hang over her marriage bed. "The union of two natures for a time is so great," Margaret wrote to Cary Sturgis Tappan, hinting that she too possessed new carnal knowledge.

Margaret had never forgotten the lines she copied from Sam Ward's letter into her journal. She *did* wish to discover "the existence of a new, vast, and tumultuous class of human emotions"—the physical passions.

She would not be left behind with "those who have never passed the line" that divided the "more experienced" from those whose "personal experience of passion . . . remain[s] comparatively undeveloped." "Had I never connected myself with any one," Margaret understood, "my development must have been partial." Her "thoughts of consecration," of a modern-day vestal virginity, which once seemed "true to the time," she now recognized as "false to the whole." After meeting Pauline Roland and George Sand in Paris, and in Rome this fall the "energetic and beneficent" Princess Belgioioso, another returned political exile—"a woman of gallantry" who "also has had several lovers, no doubt," she wrote offhandedly to her increasingly perplexed brother Richard—Margaret could think of no reason not to join their number. Sam Ward's words and her own thoughts now ran parallel to the "Polander's" advice: "The relationships which suit you are those which develop and free your spirit, responding to the legitimate needs of your organism . . . You are the sole judge of these needs."

But why choose to enter into "earthly union," as she termed sexual intercourse, with Giovanni Ossoli—a young Italian "nothing"—in Rome, and not with the German Jewish banker James Nathan in New York who serenaded her with lieder, or the eminent Adam Mickiewicz in Paris whose fervent attentions had caused her to swoon? "I wanted to forget myself in Italy," Margaret would later write. Forget how ill prepared she had been to meet James Nathan's advance, how painfully she'd suffered from disappointed hopes of men with whom she'd envisioned forming the "sacred" relation she had extolled as the highest form of marriage. Forget her aim to fill an "apostolic station" as the chaste high priestess of reform—never yielding to passion, "pure from even the suspicion of error." Forget even Mickiewicz's directive: "Live and act, as you write."

Giovanni Ossoli barely knew her, and he could not read the thousands of English words she'd written in books and newspapers and literary journals. In his love there could be no "mixture of fancy and enthusiasm excited by my talent" to confuse or taint his affections, as there had been with the duplicitous James Nathan. He felt, and showed Margaret with his tender "acts, not words," a "simple affinity." He had no expectations of her: "he loves to be with me." That was all, and for now that was balm and "inestimable blessing."

Margaret had seen enough of the "great faults" in men "of enthusiasm and genius." By contrast, Giovanni's "unspoiled instincts, affections pure and constant," were "of highest value." He was a man "wholly without vanity," without "the slightest tinge of self-love," qualities Margaret may never have found in a man of equal ambition or with genius comparable to her own. He was as far as possible from the type of man she had always fallen for, had once described in the fictional "Sylvain"—heedless of the "secret riches," the interior life of the woman he professed to love.

Giovanni Ossoli, as Margaret came to know, was nearly solitary, self-sufficient in a more authentic way than Waldo Emerson, with his talk of escaping from parlors, hiding in woods. In this Giovanni was "very unlike most Italians, but very unlike most Americans too," Margaret thought. His "affections are few but profound" and "thoroughly acted out"; he withheld nothing he could give to his sister, to his ailing father, to Margaret. His bond with his mother, "lost" when he was "very small"—six years old—was still powerful: "It has been a life-long want with him." These were the few to whom he found himself "spontaneously bound."

Perhaps his spontaneous move to rescue Margaret in St. Peter's, appearing at her elbow as she searched, flustered and anxious, had taken her breath away; certainly she felt with Giovanni, now, as if "something of the violet," in her private language of flowers a term for sweet seclusion, had "been breathed into my life"—*inspired*, as Apollo breathed his prophecy to the sibyl—"and will never pass away." Perhaps they both needed rescue: Margaret, lost from her traveling companions, Ossoli soon to lose his father. Margaret, a maternal thirty-seven, and Giovanni ten years younger, a boy of Rome, established a "mutual tenderness." No one, "except little children or mother, ever loved me as genuinely as he does," Margaret would say.

Besides, Margaret was "alone and free" in Rome. After all she'd done to gain what was more "precious" even than Giovanni's love—"the liberty of single life"—she had no interest in entering on the "jog-trot" of domesticity, with its "trifling business arrangements and various soporifics." She liked ordering her own days, seeing friends, and Giovanni, only when she chose: "I liked to see those I loved only in the best way." It was Giovanni who had wanted to marry, not Margaret. Perhaps she had to instruct him on her Fourierist views, her Mickiewiczian "manly sentiments"; their "tie" was not meant to bind, to be "permanent and full," should leave them both "mentally free" to form and maintain other connections. It would not be fair to hold Giovanni, so much the younger — "all human affections are frail, and I have experienced too great revulsions in my own not to know it." For her part, "the time was gone by when I could more than *prefer* any man." Margaret no longer looked to one man to satisfy her "need of manifold being," to suit her in more than "a part of my life." And she was glad to see that "when I am occupied" with the American expatriate artists she entertained on Monday evenings, with "no refreshment" but a brightly lit room full of fresh flowers, when she accepted invitations from Princess Belgioioso and others who "highly prize my intelligent sympathy," he "is happy in himself."

Yet this fall, both were happiest when together. "I have not been so well since I was a child, nor so happy ever," she wrote to her mother of her first six weeks in Rome, though she would not tell her why. She was not sure "how I can ever be willing to live anywhere else." In her Italian journal, Margaret had recorded her "first acquaintance with the fig and olive," tasted as she traveled from Naples to Rome in early spring of 1847. She did not record her first experience of "earthly union" with Giovanni Ossoli — where it took place, when, or how she felt.

Perhaps, although he was so much younger, Giovanni was more experienced than she, had already "crossed the line." He could guide her through any awkwardness, make her feel, with sure motions, beautiful, loved. Or perhaps the "pious" Catholic youth, with a strong "habitual attachment" to the "Roman ritual," crossed the line with her, and together they experienced "new, vast, and tumultuous" passions for the first time. The lean, lithe, dark-haired, mustachioed sergeant in the Civic Guard was "gentle," "tender," "sweet," "exceedingly delicate." These were words she used to describe his character — and his touch? He "loves . . . to serve and soothe me." Did the shade of melancholy in his eyes vanish when he looked into hers?

Whatever else Margaret might say, or not say, afterward, she had chosen Giovanni for pleasure, the most radical act of her life so far. This too delighted her — to find that "*I* am no longer young, yet still so often new and surprising to myself." Her life in "books and reveries" had not been wrong, had trained her spirit, her mind, her heart to achieve intensities of feeling that now could be matched and amplified by bodily sensation. She had postponed this pleasure so long, developed so keenly her emotions, believed so powerfully in the science of "supersensual" forces, how could she have experienced anything less than "full communion" in her love-making with Giovanni Ossoli—"transcendent, both spirit and body"—in this city of the "indolently joyous"?

And there was "this fantastic luxury of *incognito*," the thrilling yet strangely calming need to keep their love a secret. Giovanni could not openly court a woman who was not a Catholic, and Margaret could not afford the scandal that would come with discovery. She might choose to conduct herself as "one of the emancipated" women of Europe—George Sand, Princess Belgioioso—but she was still an American, and the readers her career depended on would judge her by American standards. Secrecy heightened passion—"I liked when no one knew of our relation, and we passed our days together in the mountains, or walked beautiful nights amid the ruins of Rome." These were the "blessed, quiet days, when I could yield myself to be soothed and instructed by the great thoughts and memories of the place," as she wrote obliquely to Waldo Emerson. The first "intoxicated" months of her affair with Giovanni Ossoli felt "like retiring to one of those gentle, lovely places in the woods"—"I should have wished to remain as we were."

"I now really live in Rome," Margaret announced in a *Tribune* column written the day after she'd reported her six weeks of good health to her mother, "and I begin to see and feel the real Rome." The city "reveals herself now; she tells me some of her life." Margaret described her habit of making daily excursions to no particular destination, always finding "some object of consummate interest to end a walk." Although it was mid-December, nearly the winter solstice, the evenings seemed long, and "I am at leisure to follow up the inquiries suggested by the day." She threw herself into a "nightly fever" of writing, she told one friend, after long days in which "I dissipate my thoughts on outward beauty . . . happiest moments."

In the *Tribune* column Margaret described one of those walks, taken in early November during the Octave of the Dead, the week following All Souls' Day. Giovanni was with her—"my attendant," as she discreetly referred to her lover—and they had crossed the Tiber to take the road up the Janiculum hill above St. Peter's to the Santo Spirito Cemetery, joining other pilgrims in ritual mourning. Their route was lined with "professional beggars" playing on the sympathy of the crowd, and Margaret could not help laughing at some of their tricks, "to the alarm of my attendant, who declared they would kill me, if ever they caught me alone." But "I was not afraid." Her mood changed when they entered the cemetery, "a sweet, tranquil place, lined with cypresses, and soft sunshine lying on the stone coverings." In a courtyard painted with murals depicting the stations of the cross, they watched as a Franciscan monk, a pregnant woman "uttering, doubtless, some tender aspiration for the welfare of the yet unborn dear one," and a cluster of chanting boys took turns kneeling to pray before the series of images marking each stage in "the Passion of Jesus."

Margaret knew that her American readers, mainly Protestants, would find the scene barbaric—worship before painted idols! Margaret herself felt "my own removal" from their "forms" of belief was "wide as pole from pole." On her travels through Europe, she had been exposed to the deeply held religious convictions of revolutionaries like Mazzini and Mickiewicz, reared in the Catholic Church, who fused their native faith with radicalism: "noble exiles, pining for their natural sphere; many of [whom] seek in Jesus the guide and friend." Margaret had not been influenced to alter her private belief in a pervasive, all-suffusing, ever-rejuvenating "Creative Spirit." But that day, among the kneeling Romans, "their spirit touched me," and she joined them:

> I prayed too—prayed for the distant, every way distant—for those who seem to have forgotten me, and with me all we had in common—prayed for the dead in spirit, if not in body—prayed for myself, that I might never walk the earth
>
> 'The tomb of my dead self,'
>
> and prayed in general for all unspoiled and loving hearts, no less for all who suffer and find yet no helper.

Then she rose and walked with Giovanni to the top of the Janiculum, where "before me lay Rome," a broad expanse of tiled roofs and cupolas, stucco walls and glowing domes, with the broad oaks of the Borghese gardens in the distance, "how exquisitely tranquil in the sunset!"

The *Tribune* account contained a coded message for anyone who knew the poems of Shelley as Margaret did. She had quoted from "The Sunset," a love poem that told of the "night [a] youth and lady mingled lay / In love and sleep":

> . . . *None may know*
>   *The sweetness of the joy which made his breath*
> *Fail, like the trances of the summer air,*
> *When, with the Lady of his love, who then*
> *First knew the unreserve of mingled being . . .*

Like the lovers in Shelley's lyric, Giovanni and Margaret had wandered a wooded hillside, watched a glorious sunset, and, a knowing reader might infer, spent a night together. In the poem, the lady wakes to find her young lover dead beside her, leaving her to a lifetime of mourning, to walk the earth as "the tomb of thy dead self"—the line Margaret adapted for her *Tribune* column. New to the blissful "unreserve of mingled being," Margaret had prayed that November afternoon, among kneeling pilgrims communing with their dead, that this would not be her fate—that her "Vita Nuovissima" would last. For the moment, with "unspoiled and loving" Giovanni Ossoli at her side, she "was not afraid."

But on December 20, three days after posting her *Tribune* column, Margaret guessed she might be pregnant. Could she not have expected this? Her health had never been steady, and at thirty-seven she was "no longer young." Perhaps she believed herself too frail, too old to conceive a child. Had Giovanni, young and pious, so "truly the gentleman," attempted any means to prevent conception? In America, where she had not—probably never would have—found her way into such a crisis, Margaret might have dared to employ an abortionist; the practice was legal there, a last resort elected, increasingly, even by married women who wished to limit family size. But here in Italy, with "none to help me," as Margaret wrote to Waldo Emerson that awful day, she could only wait to see what the "incubus of the future" might bring—whether "accident or angel" might guide her, as she wrote to Cary Sturgis Tappan three weeks later—whether the pregnancy would take hold in the body she again considered weak, though signs of health were unmistakable in her fatigue, nausea: "I am tired of keeping myself up in the water without corks, and without strength to swim." Just days before, she had rejoiced in her "surprizing" vigor. Now, she wrote Waldo, "nothing less than two or three years, free from care and forced labor, would heal all my hurts, and renew my life-blood at its source": the length of time it would take to bear, nurse, and wean an infant. She had longed for a child—she trusted Giovanni as a lover. But what would he say when she told him? Would the young man wish to be a father? And how arrange their lives if he did?

Margaret's anxious letter must have crossed with Waldo's of early December. Now she received his ill-timed counsel: "I rejoice in your beatitude . . . but you must not stay alone long." How many weeks had it been since she'd written to him of all the ways in which she was contentedly "alone" in Rome? He passed along recent news of "all the good people of that bog of ours"—Sam and Anna, the Channings, Cary. And then Waldo raised his own lament: "Shall we not yet—you, you, also,—as we used to talk, build up a reasonable society in that naked unatmospheric land"—in Concord—"and effectually serve one another?" Was there not still time to form the covenant of hearts and minds? In holding on to this hope, he told her, "I certainly do not grow old . . . All the persons who have been important to my—imagination . . . retain all their importance for me. I am their victim, & ready to be their victim, to the same extent as heretofore." Still delivering lectures in England, Waldo wished only to return to the company of those "persons who speak my native language, & love what I love. Few—few!" But his proposal, more nostalgic than practical, was no help to Margaret now. Although Waldo would stay in Europe for another six months, she could not suggest a meeting.

A letter arrived from Richard, describing more of his own romantic reversals and asking her to return and set up housekeeping with him and their mother. "God knows I have not myself been wise in life," she wrote to him on New Year's Day, 1848. Although "the first two months of my stay in Rome were the best time I have had abroad," the past two weeks had "quite destroyed me." Now she expected "my health will never be good for any thing to sustain me in any work of value." She was just thirty-seven years old, but her prospects seemed few. She imagined, almost hopefully, the end of her life: "I must content myself with doing very little and by and by comes Death to reorganize perhaps for a fuller freer life." In a second letter, Margaret explained that she could make no definite plans until autumn: "There are circumstances and influences now at work in my life, not likely to find their issue till then." Her child—if it lived, if she lived—would be born in September. For now, quite simply, "I am tired of life and feel unable to face the future."

Writing to Cary, who had sent news of her wedding, Margaret was even more despairing: "this year, I enter upon a sphere of my destiny so difficult, that I, at present, see no way out, except through the gate of death . . . I have no reason to hope I shall not reap what I have sown, and do not. Yet how I shall endure it I cannot guess; it is all a dark, sad enigma." She imagined Cary's days as a new bride: "you have really cast your lot with another person, live in a house I suppose; sleep and wake in unison with humanity; an island flowers in the river of your life." None of this could be Margaret's, although she too had "cast her lot" with another. Of "my present self," Margaret would say nothing, except that "a love, in which there is all fondness, but no help, flatters in vain. I am all alone; nobody around me sees any of this."

In Rome that January, the winter rains set in—ten days, sixteen, thirty—with no letup. To her sister Ellen, Margaret wrote, "Rome is Rome no more."

19

"A being born wholly of my being"

E VEN AT HER MOST DEJECTED, WRITING TO WALDO EMER-
son at her first suspicion of the pregnancy, Margaret had managed
to shift moods to express her intention to write for the British press on
"my view of the present position of things here" in Italy. She repeated to
Waldo what she had written to Cary Sturgis from Paris: "I find how true
was the lure that always drew me towards Europe. It was no false instinct
that said I might here find an atmosphere to develop me in ways I need."
Those ways were as much professional as personal.

Although Margaret couldn't write home about the specifics of her private life — she "made a law to myself to keep this secret as rigidly as possible" — her *Tribune* dispatches were a source of detailed news that her
American readers found not just absorbing but indispensable as a wave
of revolution swept across Europe in 1848. "God 'twas delicious," recalled the poet Walt Whitman of the time when, working as a New York
City newspaperman himself, he eagerly followed Margaret's accounts of
"That brief, tight, glorious grip / Upon the throats of kings" — the year
when it seemed that all of Europe might fight its way to freedom. The
style of reporting Margaret had developed, first in her travels in the West
and then on her forays into the netherworld of the Great Metropolis, personal in tone but visionary in scope, was a perfect match for the tumultuous world events of the next eighteen months. As Margaret would later
write, Europe had come to seem *"my* America," an unsettled territory

where liberty was at hand, while the New World she had left behind had grown "stupid with the lust of gain, soiled by crime in its willing perpetuation of slavery, shamed by an unjust war," the imperialist conflict with Mexico over the annexation of Texas.

Margaret had predicted revolution in a column, composed during her "happiest" days of October, that reached the *Tribune*'s pages on January 1, just as she sank into depression. "Still Europe toils and struggles with her idea," Margaret had observed of the forces gathering against the old regime, but "all things bode and declare a new outbreak of the fire, to destroy old palaces of crime!" Austria had sent troops to occupy Ferrara the previous summer in hopes of provoking resistance that would in turn justify an Austrian invasion of central Italy. In response Pius IX had armed the Civic Guards in Bologna and Rome and matched Tuscany in granting press freedoms. Mazzini, watching expectantly from London, exploited the moment by writing an open letter to the pope, widely circulated in Rome and even tossed into the pontiff's carriage by a conspirator, urging Pio Nono to take charge of all the Italian states under Austrian rule and lead them in a fight for independence and a national democracy. "Our age is one where all things tend to a great crisis," Margaret had written hopefully, "not merely to revolution but to radical reform."

January brought "the fortieth day of rain, and damp, and abominable reeking odors" to Rome, Margaret mustered the energy to write for the *Tribune*. "As to eating, that is a bygone thing; wine, coffee, meat, I have resigned; vegetables are few." The only food she could stomach was rice. But there was "authentic news" to report: "full insurrection" in Palermo and threatened uprisings in Apulia, Basilicata, Calabria, and Naples—where, she added in a last-minute postscript, "revolution has now broken out"—had forced the Sicilian king Ferdinand to grant a popular constitution to his lands in the south, more than half the Italian peninsula. By March, Margaret wrote to William Channing, "war is everywhere," but she was thrilled, not dismayed: "I have been engrossed, stunned almost, by the public events that have succeeded one another with such rapidity and grandeur." The ferment and frustration Margaret had witnessed firsthand in both Europe's workers and the intelligentsia could no longer be contained. Uprisings across the Continent brought a new French republic, the resignation of Austria's Prince Metternich in Vienna, the separation of Hungary from Austrian rule. There had been popular insurrections in all the states of Germany. Margaret was optimistic that democracy in Italy, where Milan was now "in the hands of my friends"—the young radicals she had met the previous summer—would be achieved without "need to spill much blood."

The turmoil meant "I cannot leave Rome"; it was simply too dangerous to travel, Margaret reported to William, with regiments forming and leaving the city to join the fight against Austria. To an acquaintance in Paris, from whom she hoped to gather a firsthand account of King Louis Philippe's "dethronement," she explained simply, "I am nailed here by want of money." But her physical safety, her straitened finances, even her pregnancy were surpassed by a more compelling reason for staying in Rome. "It is a time such as I always dreamed of, and for long secretly hoped to see," she wrote to William; she expected to "return possessed of a great history." The book for which she had been gathering material now seemed both urgent and epochal, destined to become the saga of "a great past and a *living* present."

Mickiewicz arrived in March with a small "squadron" of Polish exiles on their way home to make revolution, planning to recruit any of his countrymen living in Rome. He quartered his regiment on the Via della Pozzetto, not far from Margaret's rooms, but he may have stayed with her. "Mickiewicz is with me here, and will remain some time," Margaret wrote in a letter to Waldo explaining why she would not meet him in Paris, where he planned a respite from his lectures in May, "if bullets have ceased to sing on the Boulevards." She didn't hide from Waldo the fact that Mickiewicz had been her main object in considering a return trip to Paris, and "I have him much better here."

But there was no long-delayed tryst. Margaret was nearly three months pregnant. She had not been surprised to find that Giovanni proved himself "unswerving and most tender. I have never suffered a pain that he could relieve," she would later write. But her health was still poor. "At present, I am not able to leave the fire, or exert myself at all," she wrote to Waldo. A doctor she consulted gave the opinion that her health would "of itself revive," and she mentioned vaguely to Waldo a plan of "moving for the summer," making her recovery, as the doctor advised, "the first object." Perhaps as encouraging as the doctor's assurances, which she did not tell Waldo concerned a pregnancy, and Giovanni's steady attendance, was Mickiewicz's acceptance of her situation. Her mentor in "full and healthy" living saw nothing wrong in her unlooked-for pregnancy, and Margaret began to welcome, cautiously, the prospect of motherhood. Years ago she had given up hope of becoming "a bestower of life," but she had never given up longing for a child, "a being born wholly of my being." To Waldo, who had sent news of his second son, three-year-old Edward, she wrote, "Children, with all their faults, seem to me the best thing we have."

After confiding in Mickiewicz and finding relief, it was hard to keep her vow of silence. In a letter to Jane Tuckerman, a favorite pupil from Greene Street School days, Margaret came close to revealing her secret. "The Gods themselves walk on earth, here in the Italian Spring," she wrote as the weather improved and the wave of revolution swept onward. "But ah dearest, the drama of my fate is very deep, and the ship plunges deeper as it rises." Margaret expected that "my present phase of life" would "amaze" Jane, if only she could "know how different" it was, how her former teacher had "enlarg[ed] the circle of my experiences." All Margaret would say now was "I love Rome more every hour; but I do not like to write details, or really to let any one know any thing about it. I pretend to, perhaps, but in reality, I do not betray the secrets of my love." It had been a decade since Margaret taught a teenage Jane Tuckerman the myths of Aspasia, Daphne, and Atalanta, "who wished to live in the enjoyment of 'single blessedness.'" Now Margaret informed her one-time pupil, provocatively, "I have done, and may still do, things that may invoke censure." Yet "in the foundation of character, in my aims, I am always the same:—and I believe you will always have confidence that I act as I ought and must." Would Margaret marry Giovanni Ossoli now? Or wait to see if their child lived? Or, even then, retain her "single blessedness"?

In late March of 1848, she traveled, probably with Giovanni, to the coast at Ostia. "A million birds sang," Margaret wrote on April 1 in a dispatch for the *Tribune*, "the surf rushed in on a fair shore . . . the sea breezes burnt my face, but revived my heart; I felt the calm of thought, the sublime hopes of the Future, Nature, Man." It was the first column she had completed since late January. "Now this long dark dream—to me the most idle and most suffering season of my life—seems past," she wrote. "Nature seems in sympathy with the great events that are transpiring; with the emotions which are swelling the hearts of men." Returning to Rome, she learned the astonishing "official" news that, with the capitulation of the Hapsburg viceroy at Verona on March 22, all of Italy had become "free, independent, and One." She hoped this would "prove no April foolery, no premature news."

But of course it was. As quickly as revolution had forced concessions and abdications throughout Europe, reaction set in. Margaret had seen the Austrian coat of arms "dragged through the streets of Rome" and burned in the Piazza del Popolo to cries of "*Miracolo, Providenza!*" She had read accounts of the hero's welcome Mickiewicz received in Florence when he arrived with his regiment— "O, Dante of Poland!"—and she had given her *Tribune* readers his full address to the cheering crowds. She learned of Mazzini's triumphal return to Milan in April; until this month the target of a death warrant, this "most beauteous man," in Margaret's estimation, was now greeted as his country's true leader. But with Mickiewicz no longer in Rome, her spirits flagged. At Easter on April 22, in contrast to last year's blissful discoveries at St. Peter's, the "gorgeous shows" were "fatiguing beyond any thing I ever experienced," the "*benedicti* leave me unblest." And on April 29, the holy man who had celebrated his first Easter mass as pope only a year earlier turned traitor to the cause of Italian unification, withdrawing his support from the war against Austrian rule, taking the course opposite to the one Mazzini had urged in his open letter of six months before. Pressured by Catholic monarchies on the run in France, Austria, and Spain to retreat from civil leadership, Pio Nono now instructed the people of Italy to "abide in close attachment to their respective sovereigns." Angry mobs filled the Corso in front of Margaret's apartment on the morning of the pope's announcement, and the Civic Guard took control of the gates to the city. Demonstrations lasted well into May. "Italy was so happy," Margaret grieved along with the citizens of Rome, in "loving" this "one man high placed" who seemed willing to serve the people rather than distant, corrupt, and exploitive monarchs. "But it is all over." In mid-May, the ousted Ferdinand II, king of the Two Sicilies, regained Naples in a coup, and an Austrian counteroffensive led by the brilliant military strategist Count Joseph Radetzky began to systematically undo the work of the "radicals" in the north.

By now Margaret had made plans to spend the remaining months of her pregnancy in L'Aquila, a remote "bird's-nest village of the Middle Ages" in the Abruzzi Mountains, seventy miles northeast of Rome, where she would deliver the baby in secret. Although most foreign tourists avoided Rome in the summer for fear of contracting Roman fever — malaria — Margaret's body already revealed enough of her condition that she had hidden from a courier sent by Costanza Arconati Visconti to deliver a letter, and the American novelist Caroline Kirkland was expected to arrive soon and seek out Margaret. She could not settle in any of the closer spa towns — Ostia, Frascati, Tivoli — frequented by American tourists or wealthy Italians. And she would have to live alone. Giovanni must remain in the city so as not to arouse the suspicions of his family and to serve with his regiment; after the pope's defection, the Civic Guard had increasingly operated under its own leadership, readying to fight under the banner of a republic, if it was raised.

Margaret would not tell the name of the town — only "I am going into the country," or "into the mountains," as she wrote to her brother Richard, Waldo, and Costanza Arconati Visconti. At the urging of Mickiewicz, she allowed a young American artist with an atelier in Rome, Thomas Hicks, to paint her portrait before they both left the city at the end of May — Margaret for her "mountain solitude," Hicks to meet Waldo Emerson in London, bearing gifts of engravings for Margaret's friends and family and "a piece of the porphyry pavement of the Pantheon" for Waldo, which Margaret had acquired "by bribe" from workers mending the tiles. Hicks was the "only artist" Margaret had met in Europe as "deeply penetrated by the idea of social reform" as she, perhaps the result of his own poverty. Hicks's "struggles and privations" equaled Margaret's; he'd been similarly overlooked by rich relatives and was getting by on rare commissions. He was probably the man Margaret had in mind when she wrote to her former pupil Jane Tuckerman, "The artists' life is not what you fancy; poor, sordid, unsocially social, saving baiocchis [pennies] and planning orders." Hicks knew her secret too. In the portrait, Hicks seated Margaret fancifully on a red velvet bench in a Venetian portico, pale but full-bodied, swelling with her unborn child. A portrait bust of Eros on a pillar hovers in the background, just as the lyrical Erato had over her bed. The young socialist, enamored of Italian sacred art, had painted Margaret as an expectant, careworn Madonna, with Love as her god.

There were already rumors, perhaps sparked by the voluble Mickie-wicz, which Margaret did her best to quash. When she sent their mutual friend Costanza Arconati Visconti a letter like the one to Jane Tucker-man, or to the elderly Mary Rotch, a friend since her days of teaching in Rhode Island—"You must always love me whatever I do"—the Italian marchioness responded, to Margaret's alarm, with forthright questions: "What mystery lies in the last lines? Yes, I am faithful and capable of sympathy . . . but just what are you talking about?" Someone had told her "that you have had a lover in Rome, a member of the Civic Guard. I have not wanted to believe it, but your mysterious words arouse my doubts."

Margaret made the best case she could without divulging the truth, outlining her plans to "sit in my obscure corner, and watch the progress of events." She claimed it was "the position that pleases me best, and, I believe, the most favorable one." Margaret was "beginning to set down some of my impressions" of recent events, and "everything confirms me in my radicalism." She hoped that "going into the mountains" to find "pure, strengthening air, and tranquillity for so many days" would "al-low me to do something": to write her book. Margaret could only hope Costanza would accept her story.

She had to answer Waldo as well. Margaret's letters describing her "debility and pain" had prompted his invitation to "come live with me at Concord!" where he would "coax" her "into Mrs Brown's little house opposite to my gate." Waldo himself was answering to a despondent and increasingly invalid Lidian, who complained from Concord that he never wrote about his feelings for her. Waldo pleaded as an excuse "a poverty of nature": "the trick of solitariness never never can leave me." Besides, "am I not, O best Lidian, a most foolish affectionate goodman & papa, with a weak side toward apples & sugar and all domesticities, when I am once in Concord? Answer me that." But he had little difficulty express-ing urgent concern for Margaret. At the end of April he'd written again to Margaret in Rome, "You are imprudent to stay there any longer. Can you not safely take the first steamer to Marseilles, come to Paris, & go home with me"? Waldo accepted her excuse that she was occupied with Mickiewicz, but on the last night of his stay in Paris—where, a week after his arrival, "there was a revolution defeated, which came within an ace of succeeding"—he implored her a third time to "come to London immediately & sail home with me!" Margaret had learned quite enough of "the dwellers of the land of *si*," he thought, and must return to America to "be well & strong."

"I have much to do and learn in Europe yet," Margaret answered Waldo in a letter more emphatic than the one she'd written to Costanza. "I am deeply interested in this public drama, and wish to see it *played out*. Methinks I have *my part* therein, either as actor or historian." Margaret could only "marvel" at Waldo's "readiness to close the book of European society" just now. Among her old friends, there were "few indeed" she wished to see, and although "the simplest and most retired life would now please me," she "would not like to be confined to it" in Concord, "in case I grew weary, and now and then craved variety, for exhilaration." She must have mystified Waldo by then explaining her plan to move to the country outside Rome—"I want some scenes of natural beauty." And, still more enigmatic: "imperfect as love is, I want human beings to love, as I suffocate without." How could Waldo not wonder what she meant? Hadn't Margaret said she was alone? Wouldn't leaving Rome make her lonelier still? Margaret ended by chastising Waldo for missing the opening days of the Paris assembly in late April, the first experiment in direct universal suffrage in France. "There were elements worth scanning," she scolded. Having recovered enough to plan out her own defensive maneuvers, Margaret may have had Mazzini's critical words on Waldo Emerson in mind: "Contemplation! no . . . Life is a march and a battle."

But as Thomas Hicks completed her portrait, Margaret wrote a letter for him to convey to her family in America if she did not survive the summer. Margaret asked that he "say to those I leave behind that I was willing to die" and that "I have wished to be natural and true." But "the world was not in harmony with me—nothing came right for me." She was not without hope for a better life, but Margaret placed her faith in "the spirit that governs the Universe" to "reserve for me a sphere" in that supersensuous ether of the afterworld "where I can develope more freely, and be happier." She had little expectation that her "forces" would sustain her long enough to find that "better path" on earth.

"Fortune favors the brave," Margaret had written jauntily just three days before setting down her last wishes for Thomas Hicks. This time she was addressing a new American friend she'd met in Rome, Elizabeth De

Windt Cranch, wife of the artist Christopher Pearse Cranch, sometime member of the Transcendentalist circle in Boston; the Cranches were wealthy New Englanders making the grand tour. Elizabeth was frail, pregnant with her second child, and she'd just left Rome with her husband and one-year-old son for Sorrento, where oranges were said to be as big as New England pumpkins, in search of a more healthful location for the birth at a safe distance from Rome's factional strife. Margaret could not tell her new friend that she would be leaving Rome soon for the same reason. Instead she expressed hope that Elizabeth might have a daughter, "a girl that comes to help on the 19th century," she wrote, playing on the title of her own book—the one whose message Mickiewicz had exhorted her to live by. Margaret rejoiced that Elizabeth would have "two female friends," American traveling companions, "near when you are ill"—when labor began.

Margaret tried to be brave during the early weeks of summer in L'Aquila, but stiff winds blew up from the valleys below, and a hot sun blazed for forty days straight, even as snow lingered in the highest mountain passes. Not only did Margaret have no female friends near to help her, but also Giovanni could not think of making the three-day journey to visit her for at least a month. The ancient stone hill town with its surrounding pastureland and terraced vineyards lay just beyond the boundaries of the Papal States, and mail arrived unpredictably; weeks passed without the delivery of newspapers or Giovanni's bulletins of information gathered from cafés and comrades in the Civic Guard. Margaret wrote to Costanza Arconati Visconti that in her "lonely mountain home" she had begun "writing the narrative of my European experience," devoting a "great part" of each day to her book. Perhaps she would finish in three months' time: "It grows upon me."

In truth, as her child grew inside her, perhaps kicking and turning, Margaret was hardly sleeping, and she suffered from recurring headaches that twice required bloodlettings for relief. Before leaving Rome she had received a letter from Mickiewicz urging her not to be "frightened at a very natural, very common ailment"—her pregnancy. "You exaggerate it in an extravagant manner," he admonished her. If Margaret did not "have the courage to be happy about it," she must at least "accept the cross with courage." But Margaret's situation, even her "ailment," was not at all natural or common for a woman of thirty-eight. "All life that has been or could be natural to me, is invariably denied," she would later write to Cary Sturgis Tappan. First she had feared she might never experience love, never bear a child. Now she must endure the anxious wait for labor, with its many risks, in secret, far from friends and family who knew nothing of her plight, and a three-day journey from the baby's father, with whom she was falling more deeply in love.

She felt "lonely, imprisoned, too unhappy," Margaret wrote to Giovanni: "mi sento tutta sola, imprigionata, troppo infelice." Her jaw and teeth ached, but could she trust a midwife's assurance that this too was natural, common? "According to these women, one must think that this condition is really a martyrdom," Margaret wrote to her young lover, a boy almost, who had never tended a baby, whose mother had died when he was six, leaving him, her youngest child, unfamiliar with the "ailment" of a woman's pregnancy. Margaret cried after receiving letters from her family begging her to come home, knowing that she could provide only vague descriptions of her whereabouts, pretend to enjoy "hid[ing] thus in Italy," like the "great Goethe." She experienced "fits of deep longing to see persons and objects in America" and once again felt "*I* have no 'home,' no peaceful room to which I can return and repose in the love of my kindred from the friction of care and the world." Her money worries were greater than ever, as promised bank drafts from both her brother Richard and Horace Greeley failed to arrive.

Trying to be brave, she wrote to Charles King Newcomb, the protégé of her Rhode Island years, describing her landlady as "a lively Italian woman who makes me broth of turnips and gets my clothes washed in the stream." Her residence in the mountains was a "beautiful solitude," she told him, invoking the Transcendentalist virtues. Each day that she was well enough, Margaret walked or rode by donkey beyond the town limits, through wheat fields edged with red poppies and yellow cornflowers to ancient monasteries, entering churches to take shelter from the sun, where she found sacred paintings, "not by great masters, but sweetly domestic": "the Virgin offering the nipple to the child Jesus, his little hand is on her breast, but he only plays and turns away"; and "Santa Anna teaching the Virgin, a sweet girl of ten years old, with long curling auburn hair[,] to read, the Virgin leans on her mother's lap; her hair curls on the book." How long had it been since an auburn-haired Sarah Margaret Fuller sat with her mother, writing a letter to her absent father, and then, when asked to "hold the baby," exchanged pen for swaddled infant? She had been a daughter, a virgin with book in her lap; now she would be the mother.

As Margaret walked the roads of L'Aquila, she wrote to Charles Newcomb, "The country people say 'Povera, sola, soletta, poor one, alone, all alone! the saints keep her,' as I pass. They think me some stricken deer to stay so apart from the herd." She did not tell Charles Newcomb that the "povera, sola" walking, riding a donkey, was a lone woman swollen with child, six months pregnant. Another painting showed "the Marriage of the Virgin," in which "a beautiful young man, one of three suitors . . . looks sadly on while she gives her hand to Joseph." Had Margaret been inspired to write to Charles Newcomb, one of several handsome younger American men she had once fancied, as she was about to give her hand to Giovanni? Would Margaret marry? Giovanni addressed his letters to her at L'Aquila "Mrs. M. Ossoli." Was this a scheme to protect his lover, alone and pregnant in an Italian hill town, or had the couple already married in secret?

"I don't like this place at all," she wrote Giovanni, "non mi piace niente." "Si solamente era possibile venire più vicino a ti"—"If only it were possible to come closer to you." The only reason to stay was for "the good air and its safety"—"per buon aria e sicurezza." Here "I never see any English or Americans," she wrote to Waldo Emerson, still not disclosing her location; she now thought "wholly in Italian." Once it was too late to join him on his return to America, she confessed that "my courage has fairly given way, and the fatigue of life is beyond my strength." Worse: "I do not prize myself, or expect others to prize me." In her "mountain solitude," Margaret debated anew the choices she had already made and could not now unmake.

Then L'Aquila too was no longer safe. Close to Rome, yet within the boundaries of Ferdinand II's Sicilian kingdom, the windy mountain village was fast becoming a billeting post for Neapolitan soldiers who, by the end of July, had begun arresting republican sympathizers. Margaret quickly moved down the mountainside to Rieti, within the Papal States, a riverside "hive of very ancient dwellings" in a verdant plain cross-hatched with vineyards, just one day's ride from Rome. Giovanni could visit so reliably now that she had coffee waiting for the two of them to share when he arrived on Sunday mornings after a journey made under cover of darkness. Margaret was beginning to discover, as she would later write, that "we are of mutual solace and aid about the dish and spoon part"—the trivial pleasures of domestic life.

No sooner had Margaret settled in second-floor rooms overlooking the rapids of the Velino River, with rent and board cheaper than any she had found in Italy (quantities of "figs, grapes, peaches" and "the best salad enough for two persons for one cent a day," she wrote to her brother Richard, surely puzzling him about her living arrangements), than Giovanni found himself pressured to join a regiment that would leave Rome for Bologna to defend against the Austrians led by Count Radetzky, who had regained first Milan and then Ferrara by late July. Giovanni wanted to go, and after a time, Margaret agreed to the plan: "if it is necessary for your honor, leave and I will try to be strong." When she wrote to Richard in mid-August, "All goes wrong," she meant not only in the Italian city-states—where "the Demon with his cohort of traitors, prepares to rule anew," where "my dearest friends," the radicals of Milan, "are losing all"—but also in her hideaway in the "mountains of Southern Italy," the indeterminate address she used in writing to Richard. Margaret wrote to Giovanni that she would prefer to spare him the "ordeal" of the birth if she was "sure to do well," but she feared the possibility, if he went to Bologna, that she might "die alone without touching a dear hand."

As September approached, Margaret found it difficult to write; perhaps, with so many reversals, her chronicle would no longer "seem worth making such a fuss about," she worried. She had written to her friend Emelyn Story in mid-June, "If anything should occur to change my plans for the summer," she would certainly visit her and the Cranches in Sorrento. But there had been no "accident," as Margaret had once both feared and hoped, tormenting herself: "was I not cruel to bring another into this terrible world"? She could only wait, looking often at the daguerreotype Giovanni had given her—his dark hair, searching eyes, so young, so thin. She worried about him too.

Just as it seemed he would leave for Bologna, the Austrian forces withdrew, and Giovanni was free to join Margaret in Rieti, to wait with her for labor to begin. She brewed morning coffee on Sunday, August 27. He stayed until September 6, the day after the birth of Angelo Eugene Philip Ossoli.

The baby "still cries a lot," Margaret wrote a day later, addressing Giovanni for the first time as "Carissimo Consorte," the "dearest husband" to whom she could give kisses and hugs "in this dear baby I have in my arms" — "dandoti un abbraccio, ed un bagio in questo caro Pupo." Then soon Giovanni was again "mio caro," "mio amore" in the letters Margaret wrote every day, then every other day, until the end of September when he could make his next visit. She told him that her milk would not come in, that she'd had a fever; like her sister, Ellen, she could not nurse her child; "he refuses my breast." Then all was well; she had hired a wet nurse, Chiara Fiordiponte. Now she could write "I am delighted to see you in the baby who I have always close to me." He is "very beautiful, everybody says so"; he "has your mouth, hands, feet: I think his eyes will be turquoise. He is very naughty; understands well, is very obstinate to have his will." And "he is still so pretty; his gestures as delicate as a ballerina's."

They had named their son Angelo for his father, giving him Giovanni's middle name; for Eugene, the oldest of Margaret's brothers; and for Giovanni's father, Filippe, who had died in February, leaving Giovanni, who cared for him through his final illness, to war with his "odious brothers" over such inheritance as might be allowed a youngest child. The ancient law of primogeniture was one of the reasons Giovanni was so committed to the republican cause — the code favoring eldest sons in all things would be abolished. The wrangle over his modest share of his father's estate was Giovanni's motive too for hiding the child; to anger his brothers, all in the employ of the pope, with a connection — married or not — outside the church would ruin his chances of receiving even his meager allotment.

Giovanni was also determined to have the child baptized, which required Margaret and the baby to stay forty days in Rieti before the ritual could take place; Giovanni wished to establish the baby's paternity, to ensure his son's inheritance, one day, of Giovanni's tiny fortune — and, Margaret believed, of the title marchese. They must find a man to stand as godfather. Margaret proposed Mickiewicz: "He knows about the existence of the baby[,] he is a devout Catholic, he is a distinguished man who could be a help to him in his future life, and I want him to have some friend in case something happens to us." But Mickiewicz was on the march. Giovanni confided in his nephew Pietro, in line to become the true marchese Ossoli, who obliged with signature, seal, and family crest on the necessary documents and promised to keep Giovanni's secret from the "odious brothers" as long as needed.

When Giovanni left Rieti after his early-October visit, Nino, as they called the child, short for the affectionate Angelino, "seemed to look for you," Margaret wrote. "He woke up before sunrise, looked, refused his milk; cried very much and seemed to look for something that he could not find." Margaret missed Giovanni too. Would she miss Nino as much—more? She knew she must return to Rome, to resume writing *Tribune* columns, gathering material for her book; it was the only way to support herself and, now, beautiful, naughty, obstinate, delicate Nino—with his "exstatic smiles."

She spent, she would say afterward, "entire" nights "contriving every possible means by which, through resolution and energy on my part, I could avoid that one sacrifice"—leaving Nino. "It was impossible." Could she rent rooms for Chiara and Nino, separate from hers, in Rome? But Chiara would have to leave her husband and bring her own baby to the city as well. The plan was both too expensive and too risky, Giovanni argued, and Margaret knew it. Rebecca Spring had left her three-year-old daughter for more than a year with no qualms; Nino was only an infant, so young he might miss his mother less than an older child would, Margaret may have believed.

As the day of the baptism approached, the day when she could leave if she chose, as she must, Margaret wrote a confused letter to Giovanni, directing him to find her a room in Rome, but not for long. Nino "becomes more interesting every day," yet Margaret needed "to spend some time with you," to "go once again into the world from which I have been apart now for 5 months." But "I don't want to settle in Rome so as not to be able to leave if I am too unhappy away from the baby."

She would go. Still, Nino "has grown much fatter . . . he starts to play and dance . . . He bends his head toward me when I ask for a kiss." And Giovanni? "I love you much more than during the first days because I have proof of how good and pure your heart is." She could not now have them both—and Rome.

To a canny reader, Margaret's *Tribune* columns told the whole story, from her loss of appetite, reported in late January, to the "swelling" hopes of a republic in March, to the cessation of her dispatches for six months of "seclusion" in summer and fall. And when she resumed her column in early December of 1848, at the end of a year of "revolutions, tumults, panics, hopes," Margaret wrote of her return to the city by carriage after a weekend of torrential rains: "The rivers had burst their bounds, and beneath the moon the fields round Rome lay one sheet of silver." As she waited at the city gate for her bags to be inspected, Margaret strayed onto the grounds of a ruined villa, the gardens of the first-century Roman historian Sallust — "the scene of great revels, great splendors in the old time." Was a historian ever equal to the task of revelation? "Strange things have happened now," Margaret wrote, "the most attractive part of which — the secret heart — lies buried or has fled . . . Of that part historians have rarely given a hint." Yet here was Margaret's hint, her cry: although "I was very ready to return . . . I left what was most precious" — that, "I could not take with me."

"Were you here, I would confide in you fully," Margaret wrote to her mother from Rome in mid-November, "and have more than once, in the silence of the night, recited to you those most strange and romantic chapters in the story of my sad life." She had not been prepared for "this kind of pain," she wrote later to Cary Sturgis Tappan, "the position of a mother separated from her only child." This also was "too frightfully unnatural."

But neither was she prepared for the "strange and romantic chapters" that unfolded in Rome on her return, and quickly she became absorbed in recounting them for her *Tribune* readers, in playing her "*part* therein." By the time she returned to the city, nearly all of Europe's revolutions had failed or lost their momentum; the "springtime of nations" had passed. In France, the fragile coalition of socialists, workers, and shopkeepers that had formed so swiftly to depose King Louis Philippe in February had splintered during the terrible "June Days" of bloody street fighting in Paris. The ensuing election of the Imperialist party's Prince Louis Napoleon as president brought about only a sham Second Republic, which would turn Empire in little more than a year. Similar dissension among the leaders of uprisings in Germany, Hungary, and Vienna opened the way for the return of autocratic rule. But although Pio Nono had refused to support the radicals in Milan, Ferrara, and Naples in outright war with their sovereigns, the Papal States under his rule, a wide band at the center of the Italian peninsula that included Rome and the ancient university town of Bologna, remained the one portion of Italy, perhaps of the entire Continent, where a popular impetus toward the "radical reform" that Margaret favored remained strong.

Rome was "empty of foreigners" now, Margaret wrote to her *Tribune* readers in early December 1848: "most of the English have fled in affright—the Germans and French are wanted at home—the Czar has recalled many of his younger subjects; he does not like the schooling they get here." Giovanni had easily found Margaret a room in a central location, on the top floor of a high corner building overlooking the Piazza Barberini. From her windows she had views of the pope's palace at the Quirinal and, across the piazza with Bernini's immense travertine Triton Fountain as its centerpiece (the brawny kneeling sea god held an enormous conch to his lips and blew jets of water high into the air), of the Palazzo Barberini, the imposing residence of one of Rome's principal families, and beyond that, the dome of St. Peter's. The palazzo, also of Bernini's execution, dominated the square with its several stories of arched, leaded glass windows, speaking the message to the outside world of its baroque interior ceiling fresco, *Allegory of Divine Providence and Barberini Power*. At the foot of Margaret's own modest stucco building at 60 Piazza Barberini, on the opposite corner of the square from the palazzo, was nestled Bernini's more delicate Fountain of the Bees, another tribute to the Barberini family and a watering spot for passing wagon horses.

Just days after her return, Pio Nono's newly appointed prime minister, Count Pellegrino Rossi, whose forthright opposition to Italian unification many credited with the pope's disappointing concessions to Austria, was stabbed in the back as he climbed the steps to a meeting of the Chamber of Deputies and left for dead by his own troops, who "remained at their posts, and looked coolly on," Margaret wrote the following day in her letter to her mother. That evening the streets filled with soldiers and civilians united in singing "Happy the hand which rids the world of a tyrant!" Although she didn't join in, Margaret too felt the "terrible justice" of the deed. The same crowd stormed the Quirinal the next day, firing on Pius IX's residence when he refused to appear; the pope's Swiss Guard returned fire. From her room, Margaret heard gunshots followed by the drumbeat of the Civic Guard called to arms. Through her eagle's-nest window, she could see a wounded man carried by on a stretcher, followed soon after by Prince Barberini's carriage, which clattered to a halt in the palace courtyard while liverymen hurriedly barred the gates. "Thank Heaven, we are poor, we have nothing to fear!" exclaimed the servant of Margaret's landlady, who had joined Margaret at the window. It was a sentiment Margaret shared and, as she wrote to her mother, hoped would "soon be universal in Europe." Scarcely more than five years earlier, in rejecting a founding stake in the Brook Farm community, Margaret had scoffed, "Utopia is impossible to build up" on earth. In Europe, she had become a believer.

Although she'd begun her letter by admitting to a sadness she would not name and confessed that "at one time . . . I thought I might die," Margaret assured her mother that she was safe on the streets of Rome despite the civic unrest: "I am on the conquering side." Besides, as she'd written of the journey from Rieti over treacherously flooded roads, "I have never yet felt afraid when really in the presence of danger, though sometimes in its apprehension." This was the closest she could come to telling her mother about the anxious months awaiting Nino's birth, and her courage during labor.

Back in Rome, Margaret once again invited considerable risk by throwing in her lot with the revolutionaries, but the high stakes reinforced her difficult decision to leave Nino. This was a moment like no other — or rather, for Margaret, a time that recalled the uncertain beginnings of the American republic, a chapter in history she had glimpsed as a girl attending a reception for that revolution's hero, the marquis de Lafayette, whose arrival in Boston had made her painfully aware that "to a female . . . the avenues of glory are seldom accessible," even as she aspired to tread them. "These events have, to me, the deepest interest," she wrote to her mother now from Rome. "These days are what I always longed for, — were I only free from private care!" In response to her mother's urging that she come home, Margaret replied: "I wish to see America again; but in my own time, when I am ready, and not to weep over hopes destroyed and projects unfulfilled." In her thirty-eight years she had wept too often over disappointed hopes and abandoned plans.

In Margaret's *Tribune* account of the Rossi assassination and its aftermath, she implored "America" to send a "good Ambassador" to Rome in the crisis, "one that has experience of foreign life, that he may act with good judgment; and, if possible, a man that has knowledge and views which extend beyond the cause of party politics in the United States." In the spirit of *Woman in the Nineteenth Century* she continued, "Another century, and I might ask to be made Ambassador myself . . . But woman's day has not come yet." Margaret revealed that "these past months" of seclusion had "sharpened my perception as to the ills of Woman's condition and remedies that must be applied." She had hope for Rome, for Italy, and for her own effectiveness as advocate for the cause in the American press. But as for women, "I am very tired of the battle with giant wrongs, and would like to have some one younger and stronger arise to say what ought to be said, still more to do what ought to be done." To achieve "radical reform" of women's lives would require methods more sophisticated than armed revolt. "Enough!" she declared. As to the matter of an ambassador, in the end President Polk, whom Margaret so reviled for waging war with Mexico, would send the young, untried Lewis Cass Jr., son of Senator Cass, one of Polk's chief supporters on the Mexican War and an advocate of states' rights on the question of slavery.

"Rome has at last become the focus of the Italian revolution and I am here," Margaret wrote in her diary on January 1, 1849. She had traveled to Rieti at Christmastime, satisfying herself that Nino "seems to be well," although "not much bigger than when I left him," she wrote to Giovanni. Their son, now almost four months old, seemed much the same — "same gestures" and "very charming" — and his daily habits, sleeping, and fretting seemed "better than with me." The rooms where he stayed with Chiara's family were unheated, and Margaret caught cold, but "surely" Nino would be "stronger for having been so exposed in his first few months," she persuaded herself. She had been appalled to find his little body — though not his face — marked with scars and lingering pustules, the remainder of what she at first took to be smallpox, despite her successful efforts to have Nino inoculated against the disease before she left for Rome. The doctor she had asked to look in on him had never come — "I suppose he thought it wasn't worth saving our child," she wrote to Giovanni, but mercifully Nino had survived the illness, which was after all only chickenpox.

The baby "seemed to recognize me," Margaret wrote, relieved — and "when I picked him up he rested his dear head on my shoulder for so long." Nights were best: "I had so much pleasure in sleeping with him." During the day, "it doesn't go so well; there is hunger, cold." Mother and son listened to the church bells on Christmas Eve. "He seemed very excited . . . he did not want to sleep, nor let the others sleep." It would be painful to "leave our dear child" again. But "Rome is always Rome." She needed to return.

A week after Rossi's assassination, the pope had fled the city, departing the Vatican through a secret doorway and disguised as a priest, taking refuge with Sicily's King Ferdinand. Pio Nono appointed a council to govern in his absence, made up of "men of princely blood" but with "character so null that everybody laughed and said he chose those who could best be spared if they were killed," Margaret wrote in the *Tribune;* no one paid the council any attention. The way was clear for the meeting of the Constitutional Assembly, and in early February representatives from all over Italy began to fill the hotels in Rome, so recently abandoned by "the Murray guide book mob."

Margaret watched from a balcony on the Piazza di Venezia, for centuries the hub of Roman carnival festivities, as a grand procession of the delegates passed, led by regiments of soldiers, many of them wounded in the recent war with Austria, flying the banners of the Sicilies, Venice, and Bologna. The flag of Naples was "veiled with crape," in mourning for King Ferdinand's savage bombardment of the city the previous spring. The bands "struck up the *Marseillaise,*" the battle hymn of the first French republic, as the representatives entered the piazza, among them Giuseppe Garibaldi, the hero of the past summer's fighting in the north and Mazzini's confederate in the failed uprising of two decades before. Garibaldi had spent his own twenty-year exile in South America, first joining gaucho rebels in Brazil and then raising an "Italian legion" to fight in the Uruguayan civil war; he'd brought sixty of his most loyal soldiers, the core of his highly skilled regiment, back with him to Europe.

On this day, everyone "walked without other badge of distinction than the tricolored scarf" of a unified Italy, Margaret noted, in contrast to Pio Nono's council, which had first met "only fourteen months ago"; mostly men of noble rank, they arrived in "magnificent carriages lent by the Princes for the occasion," with "liveried attendants follow[ing], carrying their scutcheons." Now "Princes and Counselors have both fled or sunk into nothingness." In those former "Counselors was no Counsel," Margaret wrote for the *Tribune*. "Will it be found in the present? Let us hope it!"

On February 8 came the proclamation of a republic. An expectant crowd gathered in the same courtyard where Rossi had fallen, waiting late into the night for the assembly's decree, and at an hour past midnight the news was delivered. The jubilant multitude rushed away to "ring all the bells."

Reflecting on the rapid series of events, Margaret wrote to her American readers, "The revolution, like all genuine ones, has been instinctive, its results unexpected and surprising to the greater part of those who achieved them." In a subsequent session, the assembly voted to call Mazzini to Rome, where he would soon become the most powerful of three triumvirs selected to lead the young republic through its infancy, as the new government prepared to implement a program of drastic reform. A punitive tax on flour would be repealed, a national railway system constructed, church properties claimed for inexpensive housing, and papal lands outside Rome divided among the *contadini* (Italy's peasant class).

It had been a Roman winter unlike any other, even in terms of the weather, with each day as sunny as the previous one. In the middle of the excitement, Margaret received letters from both Sarah and James Clarke, Sarah asking advice in planning a European tour, James providing news of Boston friends and asking when she'd come home. Margaret had begun to worry that "people in U.S. are fast forgetting me," but her interest in the New Englanders who had once made up her "large and brilliant circle" was waning too. "O Jamie," she responded. "What come back for?" Certainly not for "Brownson [and] Alcott and other rusty fusty intel. and spiritual-ities." Here in Rome, "men live for something else beside money and systems, the voice of noble sentiment is understood." She had found in Italy "a sphere much more natural to me than what the old puritans or the modern bankers have made" in America, the now stagnant and degraded "new" world.

Margaret had not lost her affection for the Concord Puritan, Waldo Emerson, to whom she wrote a half-truth: "I am leading a lonely life here in Rome." She was missing Nino, and she saw Giovanni less often since he'd been quartered with his regiment of the Civic Guard, now army of the republic. But "the sun shines every day," and Rome "seems my Rome this winter"—"my spirits have risen again to concert pitch." To Emelyn Story, Margaret admitted that she had "screwed my expenses down to the lowest possible peg," but "nothing can be more tranquil than has been the state of Rome all Winter," she told her American readers, perhaps wishing to advertise the peaceful nature of this revolution.

But Margaret was not so blindered by optimism that she did not see threats to the stability of the fledgling Roman state. As she wrote to Sarah Clarke, "France is not to be depended on" despite its status as a republic, "and the Pope is now become decidedly a traitor, willing to make use of any means to recover his temporal power." She expected Pio Nono to "call the aid of the foreign armies. We shall know by April or May." Even if reports of the "Marseillaise" being played in the Piazza di Venezia reached Paris, little could be done to rouse French support of Italian unification in what Margaret suspected were the last days of Louis Napoleon's Second Republic. To her brother Richard, Margaret wrote of her determination to "accomplish at least one of my desires": "to see the end of the political struggle in Italy and write its history." She believed the republican cause would "come to its crisis within this year. But to complete my work as I have begun I must watch it to the end." If "written in the spirit which breathes through me," her book might record "a worthy chapter in the history of the world."

Margaret was keeping from Sarah and Jamie, Waldo and Richard, the pain of her separation from Nino, which deepened as weeks passed without seeing her son. She sent yet another letter of oblique disclosure to William Channing—"I am not what I should be on this earth . . . a kind of chastened libertine I rove, pensively, always, in deep sadness." Sometimes guilt over leaving Nino, perhaps over giving in to the passion that brought the boy to life, gripped her. "Nothing is left good of me, except at the bottom of the heart, a melting tenderness," she wrote, perhaps seeking absolution from the Unitarian minister, her comrade and friend. "She loves much," Margaret wrote, paraphrasing Luke's well-known account of the pardon of Mary Magdalene: "Her sins, which are many, are forgiven; for she loved much." But Margaret found no solace in so cryptic an admission: "Thus I now die daily."

Finally she made a frank confession to Cary Sturgis Tappan, requesting that Cary keep her secret and asking for help in paying for Nino's care. Margaret's letter does not survive, but two subsequent ones reveal the "true consolation" she experienced in communicating her feelings. Margaret had not even told Giovanni, as she did Cary, of the reproach she'd felt from Nino when she'd first taken him in her arms again at Christmastime: the "little swaddled child" had "made no sound but leaned his head against my bosom, and staid so," as if to ask, "how could you abandon me?" The wet nurse Chiara told Margaret that on the day she'd left for Rome, Nino "could not be comforted, always refusing the breast and looking at the door." The brief reunion with her son had been as heart-rending as it was gratifying.

Since she could not visit him, Margaret indulged herself in describing Nino to her friend, who was also a new mother. Nino had been "a strangely precocious infant," Margaret thought, "through sympathy with me." She tried to believe that it must be "a happiness for him to be with these more plebian, instinctive, joyous natures"—the family that cared for him in Rieti. Margaret herself had wished for a more ordinary upbringing. Yet "all the solid happiness I have known," she wrote to Cary, "has been at times when he went to sleep in my arms." She wished, "if I had a little money," to "go with him into strict retirement for a year or two and live for him alone"—for "it is *now* I want to be with him." But "this I cannot do."

To Cary she could admit that in Rome "I only live from day to day watching the signs of the times." Garibaldi's regiment—men known to be "desperadoes," even if they served the right cause—was stationed in Rieti, and King Ferdinand's troops were massing only six miles off, across the border of the Papal States, readying to strike on Pio Nono's behalf: "every day is to me one of mental doubt and conflict; how it will end, I do not know." Margaret was ever vigilant, trying to "hold myself ready every way body and mind for any necessity." It cannot be known whether Cary supplied the monetary assistance Margaret requested, but she agreed to keep Margaret's secret, though she expressed doubt that any "secret can be kept in the civilized world." Responding to Margaret's sense of danger at hand, Cary offered to act as guardian for Nino if anything should happen to his parents. The gesture brought Margaret's "profound gratitude," but provoked her old caginess with Cary; while she sought her friend's support and cherished her confidence, she disliked the feeling of dependence and wished to set the terms herself. "Should I live, I don't know whether I should wish him to be an Italian or American citizen," she answered Cary. "It depends on the course events take here politically." Margaret no longer worried as much that "I might die": "now I think I shall live and carry him round myself as I ride on my ass into Egypt," referring to Mary and Joseph's flight there. If Margaret was something of a Mary, whose son had been conceived mysteriously and born in rude surroundings, Giovanni figured as a kind of Joseph in search of vocation. Margaret had mentioned to Cary the title of marchese that she assumed was Giovanni's, but explained that "being a nobleman is a poor trade in a ruined despotism just turning into a Republic."

Margaret's pen earned what little the couple could raise for Nino's support. She had written two *Tribune* columns in late February of 1849 and completed a third in March, reporting: "The Roman Republic moves on better than could have been expected . . . Could Italy be left alone!" Instead, "treacherous, selfish men at home strive to betray, and foes threaten her from without on every side." Ferdinand of the Two Sicilies and Charles Albert of Piedmont-Sardinia, the despised "King Wobble" who had fought for Italian unification when he thought he might be crowned king of all Italy, had both declared their opposition to the young Roman Republic. The only good news was Mazzini's return. His rallying cry, "Dio e Popolo" ("God and the People"), encircling the Roman eagle, had already been minted on new coins; now he entered the Chamber of Deputies hailed as the champion of Italian unification who had fanned the flames of freedom into full blaze from abroad. Margaret reported on his speech from memory in her *Tribune* account: "Let us not hear of right, of left, of center . . . for us they have no meaning; the only divisions for us are of Republicans or non-Republicans." After watching the failure of one insurrection after the next across Europe, Mazzini knew his first task was to preserve unity among the republic's leadership if he hoped to sustain the revolutionary cause in Rome.

One night soon after his arrival, Mazzini answered a letter from Margaret with a surprise visit. "I heard a ring; then somebody speak my name," she wrote to Marcus Spring, who had met Mazzini at the same time as Margaret in London. Italy's hero looked "more divine than ever, after all his new, strange sufferings" — in the past year Mazzini had worked tirelessly to mediate a peaceful resolution to the northern Italian conflict, only to join the fighting along with Garibaldi's foot soldiers in the mountains above Turin when negotiations broke down. Mazzini stayed with Margaret for two hours that night, and "we talked, though rapidly, of everything." Margaret confided her own "new, strange sufferings," as she had to Mickiewicz. Mazzini promised to return as often as possible, but the "crisis is tremendous."

When Mazzini couldn't visit, he sent Margaret tickets to attend his speeches to the assembly. Margaret admired "the celestial fire" that fueled his oratory, but she was drawn as much to a quality they shared, a worldly pragmatism that could acknowledge, at least in private, the precarious state of the republic: "the foes are too many, too strong, too subtle." Margaret also recognized in Mazzini an exhaustion and sadness much like her own, if stemming from a different cause. After delivering each stirring speech in his "fine, commanding voice," Mazzini appeared drained of energy, "as if the great battle he had fought had been too much for his strength, and that he was only sustained by the fire of his soul." Neither would give up the cause, but only because of the hope that "Heaven helps sometimes."

As spring arrived, Rome remained "as tranquil as ever, despite the trouble that tugs at her heart-strings," Margaret wrote in the *Tribune*, ending her column with a rare digression from national politics to review the work of several American artists she had met in Italy. She paid special attention to Hicks, her portraitist, who was "struggling unaided to pursue the expensive studies of his art." Margaret hoped that when Hicks returned to the United States, "some competent patron of art—one of the few who has mind as well as purse" would become his benefactor. She left her readers with a glimpse of a typical evening in the piazza beneath her windows: *contadini* gambling at the hand-game called *morra*, priests returning home by way of the nearby Porta Pia, stone cutters emerging from the sculptor Tenerani's studio. High above all the activity in the square at day's end, "the setting sun has just lit up the magnificent range of windows in Palazzo Barberini, and then faded tenderly, sadly, away, and the mellow bells have chimed the Ave Maria." "O Stella!" Margaret called out to the evening star soon to rise in the night sky, to the star that marked the conclusion of her column, to Stella herself, the ideal beauty famously conjured up by Philip Sidney as the feminine embodiment of "sweet poesy"—"O Stella! woman's heart of love, send yet a ray of pure light on this troubled deep!"

Margaret left Rome at the end of March for two weeks in Rieti, traveling with papers probably furnished by Mazzini that identified her as "la cittadina Margherita Ossoli," a native of Rome twenty-nine years old; Mazzini had dropped ten years and made the American journalist an Italian by birth. At Rieti, she found Nino "in excellent health" and "so good that he sleeps in bed alone, day or night . . . sucking his little hand." Best, after Nino's momentary look of surprise, back in Margaret's arms and "alone with me, he seemed to recognize me and bent his head and frowned as he did in the first days." Nino was her own precociously sympathetic child again, now seven months old.

This time Margaret wondered in her letters to Giovanni whether it might be possible at last to "tell our secret." Perhaps disclosure was "necessary for him"—for Nino's sake—so the family could be united: "who knows if it will not be the best thing in the end?" Chiara was "good as always," though the men of the Fiordiponte family revealed themselves to be crude drunkards. One night Margaret rushed downstairs in response to Chiara's cries of "*aiiuto*" to find that Chiara's husband, Nicola, had drawn a knife against his brother, who threw a piece of stove wood, narrowly missing Margaret's head. She imagined that Nino might have been killed if she hadn't been there. Giovanni urged her to bring Nino to Rome if his life was at risk. But Margaret understood that "it is necessary to think of everything . . . because our whole future lives depend upon the discretion of this moment." Giovanni had angered his older brothers enough by serving as an officer in the Civic Guard, which, since the day of Rossi's assassination, considered the pope its enemy. His duties now included night watches, and he had not been able to join Margaret in Rieti for their April 4 anniversary: "We must pray to be happier another year." Even if Giovanni was willing to risk a complete rift with the Ossolis, he would not be able to live with Margaret and Nino as a family. And by mid-April 1849, it had become too dangerous—more so than leaving their child in a household headed by a violent drunk—to bring Nino to Rome, whether or not Margaret and Giovanni decided to "tell our secret."

Margaret returned to a city preparing for assault. Not only was France proving unsympathetic to its sister republic, but the retrograde French president, Prince Louis Napoleon, had dispatched a force of ten thousand men to regain the city for the pope. The French battalion took up a position thirty-five miles from Rome on the coast at Civitavecchia, flying the tricolor flags of both France and Italy, a deliberate ruse. Scarcely two months had passed since the morning when, as Margaret had written for the *Tribune* after the assembly's brave vote, "I rose and went forth to seek the Republic." That day the streets of Rome were filled with men wearing bright red liberty caps; a crowd had gathered in the Campidoglio, where Italy's tricolor was raised and senators read out the ambitious provisions of the new constitution to shouts of "*viva la Republica! viva Italia!*" Margaret's American companion that happy morning, unnamed in her *Tribune* account but possibly her friend Emelyn's husband, the sculptor and former judge William Wetmore Story, had predicted the new republic wouldn't last a month.

Now when she went for her morning walk the streets were quiet. The Borghese gardens, where she had fished Eddie Spring out of the fountain two years before, were empty even of their grand old oaks, cut down for use as fortifications. Giovanni's regiment was stationed in the gardens of the Vatican, where the white peacocks that supplied feathers for the pope's processional fans once strutted among scarlet poppies, fragrant orange trees, and rose hedges. The great birds, with tails "like golden ripples," were gone now, along with the pope and his cardinals, replaced by armed men and their campfires on the gardens' grassy banks. Margaret could still recall the "refreshment, keen and sweet," she'd received when walking in the Vatican gardens during the spring of her first meeting with Giovanni. Now he was quartered there, his presence allowing her important access as a journalist to the innermost workings of the republic's defense—and, as "wife," to her "Carissimo Consorte."

Alone in her room on the morning of April 28, after listing a series of recent betrayals—Charles Albert's declaration of war, his son Victor Emmanuel II's flight to Spain, Genoa's refusal to join the republic, a "reaction" in Florence, ending with "the infamy of France"—Margaret made a final entry in her Roman diary: "Rome is barricaded, the foe daily hourly expected. Will the Romans fight?" From her window she could see "they are bringing boards I suppose to make a support for cannon, and it seems to be such play for men and boys alike."

Did she remember writing long ago, from a small New England town where a revolution began, "I wish I were a man . . . I weary in this playground of boys, proud and happy in their balls and marbles"?

· · ·

Margaret had wondered if she would be "called to act." She did not fight, although she would hear of one brave woman, a mere girl of twenty-one and already a two-year veteran of the Italian campaigns, who "fought like a man, rather say a hero" alongside her husband, defending the walls of the city until struck by a cannonball in her side. She died crying "*Viva l'Italia.*" But as Rome fortified itself against invasion, Margaret was called by the "energetic and beneficent" Princess Belgioioso, who had already given a good portion of her fortune to fund a regiment at Milan, to direct one of the hospitals for the wounded in the expected attack.

On the morning of April 30, "Margherita Fuller" was named "Regolatrice" of the most ancient of Rome's hospitals, the Fate Bene Fratelli on Tiber Island, and requested to report there by noon "if the alarm bell does not ring before." She would be responsible for organizing the schedules of female nursing volunteers in order to staff the hospital "night and day," as well as for attending at the bedsides of the wounded herself. Princess Belgioioso's plan was a pioneering one; Florence Nightingale's mission to Crimea was five years in the future. Although the exit from Rome of many of its priests left the hospitals understaffed, the presence of Belgioioso's nurses was initially resisted at some of the nine hospitals she commandeered for the cause; doctors and medical students objected to the "female invasion" and specifically to the undignified sight of "a woman seated at a desk (exercising the greatest power in the hospital)." But the need for the volunteers became rapidly evident.

That same morning, a guard posted on the dome of St. Peter's sighted French troops advancing in columns. Garibaldi's regiment of "desperadoes," twelve hundred seasoned patriots and six hundred veterans of the Lombardy war, had already arrived to join the Roman army—the Civic Guard, augmented with volunteers, students, and defectors from the Papal Guard, under Mazzini's direction. France had expected an easy occupation, a merging of tricolors in the capital city of the religion both nations shared. But Mazzini and Garibaldi knew Louis Napoleon's aim was to return the pope to power once his legion took up residence in Rome. Soon the unthinkable was happening, as Margaret exclaimed in a May 6 column for the *Tribune*—"the soldiers of republican France, firing upon republican Rome!"—firing on St. Peter's, their cannonballs directly striking the Vatican.

Garibaldi led a fierce defense of the city walls, and on the afternoon

of April 30, the French expeditionary force beat a hasty retreat after losing five hundred men in battle. Margaret speculated that the "quick and
shameful" flight was the result of the French soldiers themselves feeling
"demoralized by a sense of what an infamous course they were pursuing"
in attempting to "destroy the last hope of Italian emancipation." Garibaldi had wanted to drive the French troops all the way back to their ships
on the coast, but Mazzini restrained him; there would be no reprisals, no
needless displays of military might, only a dignified defense signaling
to the outside world that the Roman republicans were reasonable men,
not vengeful revolutionaries like the French, with their guillotines of the
past century, their bloody "June Days" of last summer. Mazzini would
negotiate with the French; he had already secured a temporary armistice.
Besides, Garibaldi was needed to defend against King Ferdinand's Neapolitan army, which crossed the border into the Papal States at Frascati as
soon as the French withdrew.

And "Roman blood has flowed also," Margaret wrote. She had spent
the night of April 30 in the hospital on Tiber Island, where she had witnessed "the terrible agonies of those dying or who needed amputation
. . . their mental pains, and longing for the[ir] loved ones." Many were
university students who "threw themselves into the front of the engagement" with no previous experience of battle. Margaret moved from one
cot to the next in the large receiving hall, assisting in the flickering lamp-
light under the painted gaze of a flaxen-haired angel that filled an enormous canvas on one wall of the room, a beneficent feminine presence that
may have merged with Margaret's in the unsteady vision of injured and
dying men. Mercifully, Giovanni was not among them. Across the river,
the city was illuminated with celebratory bonfires and torchlight parades,
and Margaret herself felt the thrill of righteous victory. As she walked the
quiet streets at dawn on the first of May, she felt these had been "grand
and impassioned hours."

She met Giovanni in the Vatican gardens, and he showed her where
the cannon had been concealed amid the flowering shrubs: "we climbed
the wall to look out on the rich fields; the *contadini* were coming up with
little white flags of peace; figures with black flags were still searching for
dead bodies in the gully, and amid the tall canes." On the wall beside her,
Margaret noticed "a long red streak where a man's life-blood had run

down," a vivid reminder of the risk Giovanni faced. Climbing farther up into a tower "where charts and models had been kept," she found a few officers sleeping on straw. Margaret had wanted to "look through the windows, each of which presented a view of distinct beauty, a calm Roman landscape, calmest in the world." Gazing out on Italy's storied *campagna*, she wondered, "How *can* men feel" the enmity of war when beholding such vistas of pastoral harmony?

Leaving Giovanni's encampment, Margaret found the city had come to life again. In a later account for the *Tribune,* she reported finding the cardinals' ornate carriages burning in the streets, wooden confessionals dragged out of the churches, and men making "mock confessions" in the piazzas: "I have sinned, father . . . Well, my son, how much will you pay to the church for absolution?" On Mazzini's orders, the mayhem soon stopped, although not before six priests had been massacred. The "brotherly scope of Socialism" must be proven by maintaining order and showing respect for Rome's sacred spaces, Mazzini insisted, even if its highest religious leader, Pio Nono, was no longer welcome. *Dio e popolo.*

At the gates to the Vatican gardens, Margaret had met the new American chargé d'affaires, Lewis Cass Jr., and found him more sympathetic to the republic than she'd expected. Cass knew Margaret at once: a small woman with auburn hair, dressed in one of her now faded Parisian gowns, she was easily recognized as the sole American journalist remaining in Rome, the one whose *Tribune* letters had stirred widespread support for the republican side. By the end of June, as her accounts of the siege reached American shores, Margaret would be singled out for blame as "the female plenipotentiary who furnishes the *Tribune* with diplomatic correspondence" in an angry letter from New York's Bishop Hughes to the *New York Courier and Inquirer,* decrying the "reign of terror" instigated by the "revolutionists in Rome." Concerned for her safety, Cass urged Margaret to move from her perch on the Piazza Barberini, dangerously near to one of the city's gates, and into the more sheltered Casa Diez, a hotel near the Spanish Steps, now all but vacant of its usual English and American tourists and not far from Cass's own lodgings at the Hotel de Russie. Cass would see to it that an American flag was raised, offering a modicum of protection in the event that the French broke through the city walls. Margaret readily agreed. From the Casa Diez on the Via Gregoriana, she could reach Tiber Island more quickly, and a newly improvised convalescent hospital on the grounds of the pope's own Quirinal Palace was only blocks away.

Now came a longer wait, as lonely and suspenseful, as full of worry and fear, as the past summer's wait for Nino's birth. Would France honor the truce Mazzini had brokered? "The French seem to be amusing us with a pretence of treaties, while waiting for the Austrians to come up," Margaret wrote to her brother Richard. She closed her May 27 letter to the *Tribune* with these words: "I am alone in the ghostly silence of a great house, not long since full of gay faces and echoing with gay voices, now deserted by every one but me."

It was when she thought about Nino that Margaret lost her courage, "became a coward": "It seemed very wicked to have brought the little tender thing into the midst of cares and perplexities we had not feared in the least for ourselves." At night she "imagined every thing." Perhaps Nino would be killed by troops massing outside the city, as she had heard the Croatian soldiers fighting for Austria in Lombardy had massacred babies; they might set fire to Chiara's house and Margaret would not be there to save him. Giovanni could be killed in the fighting; Margaret herself might not survive the French assault. What would become of Nino then? Since Nino's birth, "my heart is bound to earth as never before." But she could not leave, she "could not see my little boy."

Garibaldi's desperadoes had repelled the Neapolitan army at Frascati, but Louis Napoleon had sent his own reinforcements to Italy rather than wait for Austria to join the offensive, tripling his army and supplying powerful siege artillery and a corps of engineers to dig trenches. In the early morning hours of June 2, violating the truce due to expire in two days, the advance guard of a force of thirty thousand French soldiers reached the outskirts of Rome, seized the strategic hillside villas Pamfili and Orsini, and began to fire at long range on the city.

"What shall I write of Rome in these sad but glorious days?" Margaret began a June 10 letter to the *Tribune*. "Plain facts are the best; for my feelings I could not find fit words." She had written out the plain facts in a letter to Emelyn Story immediately following that first "terrible" battle, a "real" one that Margaret witnessed from the top-floor loggia of the Casa Diez. Beginning at four in the morning, the fighting lasted "to the last gleam of light"—sixteen hours. "The musket-fire was almost uninter-mitted," punctuated by the "roll of the cannon" from Castel St. Angelo, the fortress near the Vatican gardens where she knew Giovanni and his men must have joined the fray. With a spyglass Margaret could see "the smoke of every discharge, the flash of the bayonets." She could see the men. "The Italians fought like lions," she would write later to Waldo Emerson.

Under clear skies and a full moon, the "cannonade" continued night and day until the morning of June 6. Margaret made her way to the hos-pital each day, arriving once just as a rocket, fired over the city walls, exploded in the Fate Bene Fratelli's venerable interior courtyard. The "poor sufferers" in their cots called out in fear: "they did not want to die like mice in a trap." But with an army half the size of the French legion, and most of its soldiers untrained, the citizens of the Roman Republic could hardly hope for any other fate.

Mazzini—and Margaret—had known the situation was hopeless, save for the unlikely "help" of heaven. If Louis Napoleon hadn't supplied his own reinforcements, the Austrians would have been next to lay siege to Rome, joined by King Ferdinand's Sicilian army at full force. Hope, if there was any, lay in holding out as long as possible, presenting to the eyes of the world a brave defense, and proving the French assault mor-ally indefensible. Margaret's dispatches to the *Tribune* and her projected book became key elements in a strategy that would outlast the immediate conflict. If the effort "fails this time," they both believed, it will succeed in the coming "age." But the cost to the city and its people would be enormous.

"Rome is being destroyed," Margaret wrote to Waldo Emerson in mid-June as the French advanced their trenches ever nearer to the city walls: "her glorious oaks; her villas, haunts of sacred beauty, that seemed the possession of the world forever," all these "must perish, lest a foe should level his musket from their shelter." Margaret pitied Mazzini as the leader of the republic's desperate stand: "to me it would be so dread-ful to cause all this bloodshed, to dig the graves of such martyrs . . . *I* could not, could not!"

Yet Margaret did, in her own way, help dig the graves by attending the injured and dying in the hospitals each day, learning firsthand "how terrible gunshot-wounds and wound-fever are," watching a brave university student kiss his arm goodbye after it had been cut off to save his life and reporting the moment to her readers. At such times Margaret began to "forget the great ideas" that propelled Mazzini, Garibaldi, and the Roman assembly, and instead to "sympathize with the poor mothers" who had nursed these "precious forms, only to see them all lopped and gashed." But the "beautiful young men" themselves would not forget the ideas that had sealed their fates. One crippled youth looked forward to wearing his uniform, tattered by gunshot, on festival days celebrating the founding of the republic. Another cheered Margaret by clasping her hand "as he saw me crying over the spasms I could not relieve, and faintly cried, 'Viva l'Italia.'" She watched another soldier "kissing the pieces of bone that were so painfully extracted from his arm, hanging them around his neck." He would wear them "as the true relics of to-day," mementos proving he had "done and borne something for his country and the hopes of humanity." In her work as a volunteer nurse, Margaret was also accomplishing a great deal in "the way of observation," as she wrote Waldo Emerson, playing her part in Mazzini's campaign of moral suasion. All these anecdotes would be shaped for publication in the *Tribune,* conveying with their pathos the power and righteousness of the Roman Republic's "great ideas."

But Margaret's private anguish, unexpressed in these weeks under siege to any beyond Giovanni and Lewis Cass, to whom she had at last confided her secret, was no use as propaganda, even as it was the true source of her sympathy with "the poor mothers" of the wounded soldiers. Margaret spent hot afternoons waiting in line at the post office, hoping for news of Nino. He "is perfectly well," Margaret finally reported to Giovanni on one of Rome's terrible June days. She told Giovanni she had given Nino's baptismal papers and other important documents to Lewis Cass for safekeeping, specifying that Emelyn Story should care for Nino if they both should die. Margaret had begun to think that Nino would be better off in America, but "if you live and I die," she wrote to Giovanni, he could take the papers back "as from your wife" and "do as you wish." She urged, "Be always very devoted to Nino. If you ever love another woman, always think first of him—io prego prego, amore—I beg you, beg you, love."

She wrote to Waldo in similar desperation, confiding her fear that she might never return to America. Even if she survived the war, "I am caught in such a net of ties here." Again she almost revealed her secret: "if ever you know of my life here, I think you will only wonder at the constancy with which I have sustained myself." But she would not. "Meanwhile, love me all you can; let me feel, that, amid the fearful agitations of the world, there are pure hands, with healthful, even pulse, stretched out toward me, if I claim their grasp."

Had she forgotten his coldness? Or had Margaret understood all along that there was love for her within Waldo's reserve, the love that had moved him to insist she come home with him? Could she have guessed, as Waldo had written in his private journal years before, his reluctant awareness that he had "underrated" his friend, a woman whose "sentiments are more blended with her life" than were his own, "so the expression of them has greater steadiness & greater clearness"? Could she have known that it was her own image that, Waldo wrote, "rose before me at times into heroical & godlike regions, and I could remember no superior women"? Indeed, to Waldo, who had once unkindly disrupted her Conversations on classical myth, Margaret was best compared to "Ceres, Minerva, Proserpine, and the august ideal forms of the Foreworld." He had not told her this, but perhaps somehow she knew.

Margaret's courage may have failed her "in apprehension," when she thought of Nino, but she could always act when required. She wrote two lengthy dispatches to the *Tribune*, on June 10 and 21, 1849, denouncing the French, "who pretend to be the advanced guard of civilization" yet "are bombarding Rome" in an "especially barbarous manner": aiming for the Capitoline Hill and Rome's "precious monuments," lobbing explosives at the hospitals marked with black flags. But "wounds and assaults," Margaret reported, only strengthened the resolve of Rome's "defenders," who by then included many more than the armed soldiers under Garibaldi's command. She wrote of the brave Trasteverines, women living near contested ground at the Palazzo Spada, who seized bombs as soon as they fell and extinguished their fuses, who gathered cannonballs and passed them to the republican army. But provisions in the city under siege were dwindling, and in the June heat many fell ill with Roman fever.

On June 20, the Casa Diez began to fill with residents fleeing the opposite bank of the Tiber, and in the early morning of the twenty-second, the city's outermost walls were breached. It was "the fatal hour," Margaret wrote. From then on, "the slaughter of the Romans became every day more fearful" as the French fired from the high ground of the Janiculum, where Margaret had once wandered with Giovanni, learning "the unreserve of mingled being." Now those gardens were "watered with the blood of the brave." Garibaldi himself led one last reckless charge up the hillside, only to find his daring band overpowered. Although "the balls and bombs began to fall round me also," Margaret could no longer "feel much for myself." The hospital scenes had become too grievous to describe.

Margaret would always treasure the handful of letters she received from Mazzini that June, letters written "for you only." But Mazzini was also accounting for his actions in anticipation of Margaret's book. "My soul is full of grief and bitterness, and still, I have never for a moment yielded to reactionary feelings," he wrote to her, refuting rumors spread by the French that he had ordered the placement of mines on the grounds of St. Peter's. He described settling disputes between officers and generals, nightlong strategy sessions, and watching at the bedside of a friend, "a young soldier and poet of promise," who could not be saved. On June 28, as bombs "whizzed and burst" near Margaret's Casa Diez, and thirty fell on Lewis Cass's residence at the Hotel de Russie, Mazzini wrote: "I don't know whether I am witnessing the agony of a Great Town or a successful resistance. But one thing I know, that resist we must, that we *shall* resist to the last, and that my name will never be appended to capitulation."

Mazzini argued before the assembly that the entire "Government, Army and all should walk out of Rome" to set up a government in exile in one of the mountain towns beyond the city. He sent Margaret a copy of his "protestation" to document his effort, but the assembly rejected the plan and Mazzini resigned his post as triumvir rather than concede defeat. Garibaldi appeared before the assembly too, in blood-spattered uniform, refusing to continue what had become a fight for each city block. Garibaldi also advocated relocating the government to the mountainsides — "Wherever we go, there will be Rome!" — but he could not gain enough support.

Garibaldi made the heroic gesture on his own, gathering what remained of his army — four thousand men — and marching out of Rome on the afternoon of July 2 as the French prepared for occupation the following day. Margaret followed the regiment along the Corso and on to the city's southern gates, beyond the broad piazza at the Basilica of St. John Lateran. She watched as the men, still "ready to dare, to do, to die," passed in waves, parted only by the ancient Egyptian obelisk at the center of the piazza, the oldest and tallest monument in Rome, scavenged fifteen centuries before from Karnak.

"Never have I seen a sight so beautiful, so romantic and so sad," Margaret wrote for the *Tribune*. "The sun was setting; the crescent moon rising, the flower of the Italian youth were marshaling in that solemn place." Wearing bright red tunics and carrying their possessions in kerchiefs, their long hair "blown back from resolute faces," Garibaldi's men marched behind their leader as, high on his horse and dressed in a brilliant white tunic, he took one glance back at the city, then ordered them onward through the gates. "Hard was the heart, stony and seared the eye," Margaret wrote, "that had no tear for that moment." Garibaldi's Brazilian wife, Anita, an expert horsewoman who had fought with the legion, rode beside him, pregnant—although Margaret mentioned nothing of it in her account—and suffering from malaria. On this quixotic last mission, chased by the armies of all the nations opposed to the Roman Republic, Garibaldi's legion would dwindle to a handful. Anita died in his arms within a month of their proud exodus.

On July 3, French troops claimed the city, marching "to and fro through Rome to inspire awe into the people," Margaret wrote, "but it has only created a disgust amounting to loathing." The assembly had not decamped to the mountains, but the deputies would not surrender easily. Instead they kept their seats, reading aloud once again the provisions of the new constitution, voting in measures to aid the families of the dead and awarding citizenship to any who had defended the city, until French soldiers entered the chamber and ordered the deputies' removal. Margaret had dreaded this day and "the holocaust of broken hearts, baffled lives that must attend it," as she'd written in the *Tribune*. But what she had seen was bravery.

"It is all over," Mazzini wrote in one of his last letters to Margaret. He wandered the streets of the city for most of a week, at liberty, it seemed, because the French did not want to make a martyr of the failed republic's greatest hero. Now it was Margaret's turn to procure a false American passport for a Roman citizen, asking the favor from Lewis Cass, so that

Mazzini could travel safely into exile once more. She would secure another for Giovanni; the couple would make a trip to their son's home, their first one together.

"But for my child, I would not go," Margaret told Lewis Cass. She worried about the Roman soldiers still in the hospitals, "left helpless in the power of a mean and vindictive foe." Margaret had not completed her "observations" either. One day in early July, soon after the fighting ceased, she walked the deserted battlefields outside the city, surveying the ruined villas. One of the *contadini* showed her where a wall had crumbled, burying thirty-seven republican soldiers, after just one cannon blast. "A marble nymph, with broken arm" looked on sadly from her fountain, empty of water. Farther on, Margaret studied the terrain held by the French, "hollowed like a honey-comb" with trenches. "A pair of skeleton legs protruded from a bank of one barricade," she reported, giving the "plain facts." A dog had scratched away the soil to uncover a man's body, fully dressed, lying face-up. How Margaret felt, she did not say: "the dog stood gazing on it with an air of stupid amazement." The dead had not yet been counted, but of the many soldiers who lost their lives in the bloody June days of the Roman Republic, three thousand would be buried in the shade of the cypress trees of the Cimitero di Santo Spirito.

"Rest not supine in your easier lives," Margaret exhorted her readers in a final *Tribune* letter from Rome. "I pray you *do something;* let it not end in a mere cry of sentiment." To Richard she wrote, "I shall go again into the mountains," giving yet another oblique explanation of her plans. "Private hopes of mine are fallen with the hopes of Italy. I have played for a new stake and lost it."

· VII ·

HOMEWARD

TASSO'S OAK. ROME.

From the Wreck of the Elizabeth

"Tasso's Oak, Rome," engraving by J. G. Strutt belonging to Margaret
Fuller, inscribed "From the Wreck of the Elizabeth"

20

"I have lived in a much more full and true way"

Nino was no longer "perfectly well" when Margaret arrived in Rieti. Had it not been enough to fear for Giovanni's life? On the night of the fiercest bombardment, when she had lain "pale and trembling" on the sofa in her "much-exposed" apartment, knowing that Giovanni was commanding a battery on the Pincian Hill, the most vulnerable position in the city, Margaret had vowed she would not spend another anxious night alone under fire. She arranged for Giovanni to come for her at the ringing of the Angelus the next evening and lead her to the Pincian gardens, now shorn of their towering oaks, preferring to die with him if they must. There she found many of the soldiers' wives already camped with their husbands. Spending the last night of the Roman Republic with Giovanni, making no secret of their connection among his comrades, may have helped Margaret begin to frame the revelations she would soon make to friends and family — "I have united my destiny with that of an obscure young man," she began one of them. The morning after that surprisingly peaceful night on the Pincian Hill came the assembly vote to surrender, and with it the imperative for republican soldiers to evacuate the city. Giovanni could no longer safely lead a separate life in Rome.

Through the weeks under siege, Margaret had often imagined she heard Nino crying for her "amid the roar of the cannon." And now here he was, the Young Italy that remained for Margaret and Giovanni, "worn to a skeleton" when they reached him in mid-July, "all his sweet childish graces fled." Nearly a year old, the boy was so weak he could barely lift the hand that Margaret reached out to kiss: "this last shipwreck of ho[pes] would be more than I could bear," she wrote to Lewis Cass of her fear that Nino would die in Rieti. The "little red-brown nest" of a village had seemed so healthful, the air so pure; even the garrisoning of Garibaldi's regiment in the town, once the stuff of nightmares for Margaret, turned out to have been the occasion for festivities, with the monks of the nearby monastery breaking their code of solitude to invite both Giuseppe and Anita Garibaldi in for "excellent coffee." But according to "the cruel law of my life," Margaret despaired, the safe haven threatened to become Nino's "tomb." And if so, she wished to die there with him, this "dearer self," her son. Margaret already knew what it meant to have a beloved infant—her little brother Edward—die in her arms.

Margaret had not fully understood the risk of leaving Nino with a wet nurse. She believed that by spending his infancy in the country town the boy would become "stronger," "better than with me." But the practice had never been common in New England and was increasingly out of favor in Europe, where mothers who were unable to nurse their newborns, or could afford not to, might still hire a nursing mother to live with the family; but they rarely sent infants away to the countryside. Experience warned of just what happened to Nino. Chiara's milk had slowed after nine months of nursing both Nino and her own child, and without Margaret on hand to supervise, Chiara had chosen in favor of her baby, weaning Nino onto bread and wine, pacifying him with the wine while withholding vital nourishment. The interruption of payments during the two-month siege probably forced the decision, which may have been ordered by Chiara's husband, Nicola, who by spousal right collected the income from his wife's breast milk. Margaret was appalled that Chiara had neglected Nino "for the sake of a few scudi," but money was the basis of a transaction that Margaret recognized too late transformed "the bosom of woman" from a "home of angelic pity" into "a shrine for offerings to moloch."

Wet-nursing in the Papal States followed rules dictated by the church. Some parents in villages like Rieti welcomed the extra income gained by raising another child alongside their own. But most wet nurses were unwed mothers, forbidden to rear their own children. Instead they were required by law to give up their babies at birth to foundling hospitals; permitting such women to nurture their own children was thought to lead the infants into sin. Knowing that local police would eventually confiscate their babies, many unmarried pregnant women took refuge in the foundling hospitals several months before giving birth and stayed there afterward, nursing other children, not their own, in exchange for lodging. Or, returning to their home villages immediately after the birth, they might hire themselves out, as did the young woman Margaret found next to revive Nino—a "fine healthy girl" with "two children already at the Foundling Hospital," yet who, to Margaret's frustration, was "always trying not to give him milk, for fear of spoiling the shape of her bosom!"

It took several weeks of feedings with the new nurse, who joined Margaret in the inn at Rieti where she now stayed with Giovanni, before the boy regained his "peaceful and gay" nature. He remained delicate into the fall, when Margaret and Giovanni moved to Florence, bringing the wet nurse with them, to join the "American Circle" of expatriates there. Nino had cried almost continuously those first weeks, "wander[ing] feebly on the surface between the two worlds"—life and death—perhaps suffering the effects of withdrawal from alcohol dependency. In her travels across Europe and Britain, Margaret had instinctively sympathized with women, like the factory workers in Manchester, who felt compelled to sedate their hungry babies with opium during long days away, and she'd applauded the visionary schemes of the French Fourierists to provide infant *crèches* to the children of laborers, where mothers might feed their babies at intervals through the workday. But as Margaret had declared to her *Tribune* readers, "woman's day has not come yet"—not for Margaret or Chiara, nor for the "fine healthy girl" who saved Nino but was marked as a sinner and deprived of her own two children.

How far was Margaret from that unwed girl? Was there ever a risk that Nino might be taken from her as a foundling? Margaret was an American citizen, and a prominent one. But Nino was born within the borders of the Papal States, and the country's strict laws on children of unwed mothers, surely known to Giovanni, may have been one reason Margaret and Giovanni almost certainly married in secret outside Rome sometime during Margaret's pregnancy. They knew, as well, that travel with Nino between the Italian states or abroad would require papers that showed all three to be a family. Perhaps the couple found an opportunity to marry in the early spring of 1848, as Margaret's depression and morning sickness abated and she visited the seaside town of Ostia, when revolutions were sweeping Europe and for a brief few days it had seemed as if all of Italy had become "free, independent, one." Possibly Giovanni arranged a private ceremony in Rieti, where Nino's baptismal record certified his birth "from the married Giovanni Angelo of Marquis Ossoli from Rome and Margarita Fuller heterodox from America." The term "heterodox" referred to her religion: not Catholic.

Margaret's love for Giovanni had intensified in the year of living at risk in Rome, the year they had been parents of "Angelo Eugenio Filippo," as Nino's name was entered in the baptismal records of the ancient cathedral at Rieti. But her views on marriage remained as "heterodox" as they had been when she debated the institution with Waldo Emerson in Concord years before—not just not-Catholic, but counter to any tradition. In the letters she sent from Rieti to her mother and a few close friends, letters that "half killed me to write" as she finally disclosed facts she had concealed for nearly two years, Margaret didn't use the word "marriage," and she never gave details of a ceremony, perhaps wishing to avoid drawing attention to Nino's premarital conception. To her mother she explained circuitously that "your eldest child might long ago have been addressed by another name than yours, and has a little son a year old." She apologized for the "pang" Margarett Crane would certainly suffer in learning this "piece of intelligence" so long after the fact. But she told her mother that if it had not become "necessary, on account of the child, for us to live publicly and permanently together," she would have preferred to keep the secret longer—perhaps, her words suggested, not to have married at all.

Writing to William Channing, Margaret simply launched in: "I am a mother now." As for the "tie" with her child's father, whom she did not name at first, their love existed independent of the "corrupt social contract" she had entered into for their son's sake, because "children involve too deeply." Margaret was frank. She and Giovanni—"my gentle friend, ignorant of great ideas, ignorant of books," but "never failing" in "pure sentiment"—were not ideally matched: "If earthly union be meant for the beginning of one permanent and full we ought not to be united." Margaret was older, nearly forty, and she no longer expected to find a lifelong soul mate; nor did she wish to bind the younger Giovanni to her if he should meet another woman he loved better. These principles did not diminish their love; they intensified it. But living by them "in the midst of a false world," one that prized legal and ecclesiastical bonds over relations freely chosen, like hers with Giovanni, came "easier to those" without children.

"Yet I shall never regret the step which has given me the experience of a mother," Margaret wrote to William; "my heart was too suffocated without a child of my own." She had discovered "I am not strong as we thought"—not strong enough to continue living as a solitary sibyl who prophesied a better day for women and waited stoically for its advent. Not strong enough to live openly with her lover and child in a foreign land without marriage license or birth certificate. Little wonder that when Margaret's startling news reached Sarah Clarke, she thought her old friend seemed "more afraid of being thought to have submitted to the ceremony of marriage than to have omitted it."

Margaret had long argued that marriage should be "only an experience," not a defining vocation for women. What mattered was *experience*. "I have lived in a much more full and true way than was possible in our country," she wrote to William Channing of her more than two years in Italy; "each day has been so rich in joys and pains, actions and sufferings, to say nothing of themes of observation"—material for her book. Despite the restrictive laws on women and children in the Papal States, Margaret had experienced more freedom of opportunity, both professionally and personally, in Rome than in New England or New York. And now she had a family, a child whose "little heart clings to mine" and a husband whose companionship, Margaret wrote to her sister, Ellen, is "an inestimable blessing." Giovanni had remained loyal when she was "more sick, desponding and unreasonable in many ways than I ever was before," and he had cheered and sustained her with "the sacred love, the love passing that of women." "In him," Margaret wrote to her mother, "I have found a home."

And yet they had no home. Giovanni and Margaret Ossoli, as they were now to be known, the marchese and marchesa d'Ossoli, as Margaret occasionally ventured to introduce her husband and herself, had "moored" themselves temporarily in Florence, in a small apartment at one corner of a broad piazza looking toward the ornate marble façade of the Church of Santa Maria Novella, and settled into a daily routine of walks in the *cascine* on the banks of the Arno, visits to museums, and quiet hours devoted to writing while the baby napped. Often they brought Nino out with them, but when they didn't, "What a difference it makes to come home to a child," Margaret exclaimed to Emelyn Story; "how it fills up the gaps of life." From his bed Nino could reach up to draw the heavy curtains and let in the sunlight when he woke in the morning or after his nap, and he bobbed and swayed by the window to the rhythms of the Austrian drum corps training in the piazza below. He played contentedly on the floor while Margaret and Giovanni dressed for the day and enjoyed "kicking, throwing the water about" in his bath. At fifteen months, Nino was beginning to speak in his parents' two languages. Kissing and then patting Margaret's cheeks, he would say "poor," perhaps mimicking his mother's solicitous gestures when he'd been ill; standing up and stretching to his full height, he called out "*bravo.*"

Nino was growing fat and was "not handsome," according to an American friend, George Curtis, an aspiring literary journalist who paid the family a visit that fall en route to Egypt and Syria. But could Margaret, once a plump and homely child, mind that about him? She had feared so recently that her son might waste away. But now "I feel so refreshed by his young life," Margaret wrote to Cary Sturgis Tappan of the boy she considered "very gay impetuous, ardent"—a word she had often used to describe herself—and a "sweet tempered child." Nino's cheerful nature, she believed, had been enhanced "by taking the milk of these robust women." And "Ossoli," as Margaret referred to her husband in letters, "diffuses such a peace and sweetness over every day." George Curtis observed this as well. To him, Giovanni seemed "a dark-haired, quiet, modest man" with "no appearance of smartness"; Curtis guessed that Margaret's husband would have trouble learning English. But he "clings to Margaret with quite a touching confidence & affection." As for Margaret, the "Marchesa Ossoli herself": she "seems as always." Curtis noted "a vein of intense enthusiasm threading with fire her talk about Rome, which was fine & wonderful at the same time." Like so many before him on both sides of the Atlantic, George Curtis had been stimulated by Margaret's conversational powers into a plethora of metaphor; her "heart is now too much rooted in Rome," Curtis supposed, "ever to bear a long, never a life-long separation."

To Margaret, Florence was "so cheerful and busy after ruined Rome" that she hoped she and Giovanni might manage to "forget the disasters of the day for awhile." But the vivid images of dead and dying Romans in the hospital and on the battlefield, of blasted city walls, ravaged villas, and gardens "watered in blood," would never leave their imagination, nor would the memory fade of those "glorious days that expand the heart, uplift the whole nature," that they had lived through before the siege. The Austrian presence in Florence was a continual reminder of the failed republic, posing an almost unbearable contradiction to Margaret's firm belief, as she wrote in a November dispatch to the *Tribune*, that "the world can no longer stand without" the "vast changes in modes of government, education and daily life" that *must* be brought about by "what is called Socialism." There was no other "comfort, no solution for the problems of the times." In Florence, Margaret took solace in viewing the figure of Dante painted on an interior wall of the Duomo, clad in red cloak and standing with book in hand just outside the gates of the city from which he had been banished, gesturing toward the lurid and divine landscapes of his epic poem. For him, both "Heaven and Hell are in the near view." It was the same for Margaret and Giovanni; the couple could not stay long in such painful proximity to terrifying memories, "blighted" hopes.

Giovanni had suffered even greater disappointments than Margaret — "it has ploughed great furrows into his life." He had lost home, employment, and now, it seemed, his small inheritance at the whim of an "angry" older brother who'd been forced to hide out in a cellar while republican soldiers occupied his house during the siege. Margaret accepted a job tutoring the daughter of the American businessman turned sculptor Joseph Mozier, with whom she had stayed on her solo tour of northern Italy three years before, and she expected, with Giovanni's savings and the remainder of her *Tribune* payments, to "eke out bread and salt and coffee till April." But perhaps that was long enough: "I should not be sorry to leave Italy till she has strength to rise again." Margaret and Giovanni, who frequently wore his dark brown, red-trimmed Civic Guard jacket at home as if to keep the cause alive, both looked forward to a successful second uprising — "a new revolution" — in perhaps two or three years' time: the vengeful despotism of "the restored authorities" had been so extreme, "it cannot be otherwise." Only then would they "find really a home in Italy." The plan of settling for several years in America, where

Margaret could publish her book more profitably if on hand to make the arrangements, began to solidify in both their minds.

Christmas in Florence was different from the last in Rieti, when Margaret and the infant Nino had huddled together in the cold mountain town, listening to church bells, missing Giovanni. This winter's cold was far worse: in Rome two feet of snow had fallen, and in Florence snow covered the piazzas, water froze overnight in the washbasins. On Christmas morning several packages arrived, perhaps gifts from the wealthy Mozier, all of them containing large toys—a bird, a horse, and a cat—that sent Nino into a "kind of fearful rapture," with "legs and arms, extended, fingers and toes quivering, mouth made up to a little round O, eyes dilated." Witnessing Nino's "pure delight" in the gifts made Margaret regret "any money I ever spent on myself or in little presents for grown people, hardened sinners." But Nino's favorite toy was one that Margaret had drawn in a lottery at a party in the home of another expatriate sculptor, Horatio Greenough, where a few American families with children had gathered to celebrate the holiday. This one was a tiger with a small child asleep on its neck. Nino whispered over the pair, "seeming to contrive stories," as the guardian tiger stood frozen in a watchful stance, "stretching up to look at the child."

Was Margaret "as always"? She tried hard to persuade her friends that this was so, that she had not been simply "running about" in "blind alleys" as she followed her "revolutionary spirit" into an actual revolution and an unlikely marriage. She was acting out her nature. "The heart of Margaret you know," she had written to Costanza Arconati Visconti, expressing hope that the surprising news of husband and child would not cause her friend to "feel estranged"—"it is always the same." Margaret wished her family and friends to understand "I have acted not inconsistently with myself," that "whatever I have done has been in a good spirit and not contrary to *my* ideas of right."

She needn't have worried about Costanza, who had heard the rumor of Margaret's romance with a soldier in the Civic Guard more than a year before; the marriage and perhaps Giovanni's tinge of nobility answered her concerns, and she wrote swiftly to assure Margaret of her continued affection. Costanza and her ten-year-old son had taken up residence in a villa outside Florence this year; proximity and shared motherhood drew the two women into an even closer friendship. But Margaret's report to Costanza that she had been received with "no questions" by the English-speaking residents of the city on her arrival "with the unexpected accessories of husband and child" gave only one side of the story.

Margaret had detected an "increased warmth of interest" from "the little American society of Florence," which she might have read as prurient. The poets Elizabeth Barrett and Robert Browning, whom Margaret had long hoped to meet, had settled in Florence three years before, mingling socially with the cluster of American expatriate artists settled there, and Elizabeth Browning's account of Margaret's sudden appearance in the city — "retiring from the Roman field with a husband & child above a year old!" — gave a more accurate version of the Americans' stunned reaction to the revelation of an "underplot." No one had "even suspected a word," Elizabeth Browning wrote to her friend Mary Russell Mitford in England, and Margaret's "American friends stood in mute astonishment before this apparition of them here."

The Brownings, whose elopement to Italy had provoked an international "warmth of interest," welcomed Margaret and her family to their spacious rooms at Casa Guidi near the Pitti Palace, happy to have their own year-old son acquire a playmate and eager to test Margaret's powers of conversation. But many of the Americans were inclined to judge more harshly, their response varying with the opinions they already held of Margaret. Frederick Gale, the older brother of one of Margaret's Greene Street School pupils, while passing through Florence on a European tour encountered Margaret and Giovanni at two different parties hosted by Joseph Mozier. Gale was no partisan of his sister's former instructor. He wrote home to relay the "strange story" of Margaret Fuller's transformation "by marriage, into no less a personage than the *Marchioness of Ossoli*": if "the scornful, manhating Margaret of 40 has got a husband, really no old maid need despair, while there is life in her body!" In his journal Gale noted after the first party, "There are wrinkles and lines in her face, old enough for 60!" while "her husband is handsome and hardly looks 30." Margaret appeared "sad and depressed," Gale observed, "an old woman before her time." She must have won him over at the second party, however. They danced two "cotillions," during which Margaret was "merry and agreeable" after the guests had dined on "cold turkey, duck, maryonaise [*sic*], champagne and whisky punch." The "transcendental ex-editress of the Dial devoted herself with unmistakeable ardor to them all." It was Giovanni, who "says nothing," whom Gale found fault with this time.

Joseph Mozier himself had long been a supporter of Margaret, welcoming her into his home in the summer of 1847 shortly after she had parted ways with the Springs and supervising her recovery from an attack of cholera. Since then, Mozier had established his reputation as a sculptor with a portrait bust in marble of Pocahontas; later he completed a similar one of Margaret. Whether she sat for the work during the earlier stay or during her 1849–50 winter residence in Florence with Giovanni and Nino, or whether the firm-jawed heroine he sculpted was, like Pocahontas, primarily a work of Mozier's imagination, his perception of Margaret as a mannish figure of steadfast resolve and scant femininity is evident in the piece. Bountiful in his generosity to Margaret, Mozier was privately contemptuous of Giovanni: "the handsomest man," yet he appeared to be "entirely ignorant," even "of his own language." In Mozier's estimation, Margaret's husband was "half an idiot." Giovanni's attraction for and to Margaret remained a puzzle he could not solve.

Giovanni's habitual silence in the company of Margaret's English-speaking friends, with whom he could not converse, was certainly the source of Mozier's uncharitable assessment. Most often Giovanni merely escorted Margaret to social events and returned for her later, not wishing "to impose any seeming restraint, by his presence, upon her friends," wrote William Hurlbert, a more sympathetic member of the American circle. But Giovanni's inability to speak English may not have been the only reason for his silences. Hurlbert, a recent graduate of Harvard Divinity School, visited the Ossoli apartment on several occasions and noted the "melancholy pleasure" Giovanni took in wearing his uniform at home, reading "from some patriotic book" while Margaret worked "surrounded by her books and papers." Giovanni's recollections of war "seemed to be overpoweringly painful," and his memories of Margaret's "terrible distress" over his safety caused her husband to break down in the telling; he could communicate well enough, it seemed, to a receptive listener. Perhaps the awkward muteness in formal gatherings that Mozier took for ignorance or near idiocy was a self-protective numbness, an aftereffect of wartime service and the forced flight from his devastated home city. Or perhaps Giovanni simply displayed a hushed reverence for his wife never before seen in a man of Mozier's acquaintance. His adoration may have seemed, to the rich American, a kind of mental defect.

Giovanni got along far better with Horace Sumner, the much younger brother of the Massachusetts anti-slavery lawyer Charles Sumner, although at first Giovanni took the "pale, erect, narrow little figure," a former denizen of Brook Farm, for "some insane person" when the young man accosted Margaret outside the Duomo one day at sunset. "Imagine Brook Farm walking the streets of Florence," Margaret wrote afterward to George Curtis; "every body turned to look." Margaret's nerves began to "tingle with old associations" as the twenty-five-year-old Sumner sputtered on about "walking into the country to see the green." But soon she was "listening with a sort of pleasure to the echo of the old pastoral masquerade." After that first chance encounter, Horace Sumner visited often to give Giovanni lessons in English. By spring he was considering sailing for home with the Ossolis.

It was harder still for Margaret to persuade her old friends in America that "I am just the same for them [as] I was before," a message she asked her sister, Ellen, to convey to Waldo Emerson in particular, hoping for a letter from him. For months Waldo did not write, although he passed along with no comment the news to his brother William that "Margaret F. has been near two years married" and "they will probably all come to America" as soon as he heard it in October of 1849. But then, Margaret had not written directly to Waldo, or to many others. Instead she had enclosed daguerreotype portraits of Giovanni, dressed in his Civic Guard uniform, in the few letters she did send, as if his handsome visage, when passed among the wider circle, might guard against the severe judgments she anticipated. "I expect that to many of my friends Mr Emerson for one, he will be nothing," she wrote to Ellen, "and they will not understand that I should have life in common with him," adding that she didn't think Giovanni would care: "he has not the slightest tinge of self-love."

But Margaret cared on Giovanni's behalf. Concerned that "he will feel very strange and lonely" in America, Margaret was "much more anxious about his happiness" than her own. And so she made an effort to prepare her friends and family in advance. "He is not in any respect such a person as people in general would expect to find with me," she had written to her mother. And to Ellen: surely "*some* of my friends and my family who will see him in the details of practical life, cannot fail to prize the purity and simple strength of his character." Margaret felt all the more relieved when Margarett Crane wrote a gracious letter of welcome that arrived in late November. Giovanni wept joyful tears—the only tears Margaret had seen him shed, except at the news of his father's death and the entry of the French into Rome—to think he would be greeted with affection by "*La Madre*."

Others, like Rebecca and Marcus Spring, wrote to express the kind of hurt that Waldo Emerson must also have felt, stunned that they should have been "left" to "hear these things from others." Margaret could only plead that she had been "worn out and sensitive from much suffering," and so could "make my communication" only to those few whose "hearts" had seemed "awake in love to mine at that time." Where the Springs were concerned, there was no hiding the fact that though Margaret had traveled with the Quaker couple for nearly a year, she had slowly drawn away from them as she made her visit to George Sand in Paris, then threw in her lot with Adam Mickiewicz, and finally took up with the young Italian she'd introduced to them simply as Giovanni. Their differences still jarred. In response to Rebecca Spring's well-intentioned blessing on Margaret's son—"it is still better to give the world this living soul than . . . a printed book"—Margaret bristled: "it is true; and yet of my book I could know whether it would be of some worth or not, of my child I must wait to see what his worth will be."

Margaret still planned to return to America "possessed of a great history," as she'd written to William Channing even before the climactic events of June 1849. Each day that it was not too cold in the apartment to take pen in hand, she gave her morning hours to assembling a complete manuscript from pages she had already written. In her letter to the Springs she argued hard in defense of the revolution she had joined, mourned, and hoped to see rise again. The Springs, as Quakers, would condone only "the peace way," which Margaret agreed was "the best," in principle. "If any one see clearly how to work in that way, let him," Margaret wrote. But "if he abstain from fighting against giant wrongs let him be sure he is really and ardently at work undermining them or better still sustaining the rights that are to supplant them. Meanwhile I am not sure that I can keep my hands free from blood."

Was this a changed Margaret? Nothing proved she was still herself more than such a declaration. Margaret had always been, as she'd once written in a poem, "the much that calls for more," constant in an ever-expanding ardency. Yet how would America receive a woman who refused to give the particulars of a mysterious marriage, who considered her book of greater present import than the baby she dearly loved, who condoned violent revolution? "These are not the things one regrets," she wrote to the Springs of an impulsive loan of money she'd made to the Danish radical socialist Harro Harring, whose roman à clef about Mazzini she had reviewed for the *Tribune;* "we must consent to make many mistakes or we would move too slow to help our brothers much."

Margaret's reputation in America was not helped by a very public strike against her the year before, from one of New England's most highly regarded poets of her generation, James Russell Lowell. Taking offense at Margaret's dismissal of his work as "absolutely wanting in the true spirit and tone of poesy" in *Papers on Literature and Art,* the collection she published as she left for Europe, Lowell had returned the blow with a mean-spirited caricature in his *Fable for Critics,* depicting Margaret as a self-aggrandizing virago who boasted of having "lived cheek by jowl, / Since the day I was born, with the Infinite Soul." Several of Margaret's friends, including William Story and Thomas Wentworth Higginson, wrote to Lowell in her defense, asking him to remove the lampoon from his next edition of the book, but he would not. Margaret, who learned of this "plot against me" while still in Rome, was stunned — the lines were "too cruel and too cunningly wrought," she wrote to Cary Tappan. She must have felt all the more irked to find that the caricature derived from the old days of the "pastoral masquerade" and to have this particular effigy of herself raised while she was tending grievously wounded Roman soldiers and reporting the latest news from an embattled Italy — coverage that, to his credit, Lowell openly admired.

Margaret never wrote to Lowell herself; "a useless resistance is degrading," she explained to Cary. Her stern critique of Lowell's poetry would always seem to her justified; his personal attack on her was not. But the experience helped inure her to slights she began to detect from American friends, several of whom now urged her not to return. "I pity those who are inclined to think ill, when they might as well have inclined the other way," Margaret wrote to Cary. "However let them go; there are many in the world who stand the test, enough to keep us from shivering to death." She was not without the capacity to see herself as her critics did, but "if my life be not wholly right," she wrote to William Channing, "it is not wholly wrong nor fruitless." When even William begged that for her own sake she reconsider her plans, Margaret advised her friend not to "feel anxious about people's talk concerning me. It is not directed against the real Margaret, but a phantom." To her mother she stated firmly, "I will believe I shall be welcome."

The Ossolis didn't have the funds for all three to travel by Cunard, the steamship line that had brought Margaret to Liverpool from Boston in a record twelve-day crossing four years earlier. Margaret learned of a barque, a three-masted merchant ship called the *Elizabeth*, leaving from Livorno for New York in May on a transatlantic voyage expected to last two months or longer. The captain was willing to take on a few passengers once he'd filled his hold with "marble and rags," Margaret's way of referring to the cargo: 150 tons of Carrara marble, silk and fine paintings, and a sculpture by the best known of America's expatriate artists, Hiram Powers. The *Elizabeth* would have to suffice, and the sturdy, slow-moving craft began to seem a wise choice as news reached Margaret of the wrecks of three swifter vessels making Atlantic crossings that spring, including the *Royal Adelaide*, a steamship whose 250 passengers all drowned off the British coast.

Through the last days of March, Margaret attended Easter week services in the Duomo and at the gleaming white Basilica of Santa Croce with Giovanni, then devoted herself to preparations for travel as the "Siberian winter" turned to a steady April rain—beginning, Margaret noted, on April 4, the day she and Giovanni observed as an anniversary. The time had come to wean Nino from "his great stout Roman mother in the flesh," as Margaret could not afford the wet nurse's passage nor continue to employ her in the United States. Margaret would need to acquire "an immense stock of baby-linen," since clean water for laundry would be in short supply on board ship, as well as "poultry, a goat for milk, oranges and lemons, soda hardbread, and a medicine chest." Her head was "full of boxes, bundles, pots of jelly, and phials of medicine," an array of necessities all the more bewildering as Margaret had never before given much thought to packing for "a journey for myself, except to try and return all the things, books, especially, I had been borrowing." But her energy was high. "I have never been so well as at present," she wrote to Sam Ward.

Margaret still found time for visits to the Uffizi, which during the winter months had been too cold for her to linger in front of Titian's Venuses or Fra Angelico's angels. "I feel works of art more than I have ever yet," she wrote to Sam. "I feel the development of my own nature as I look on them; so many hid meanings come out upon me." Two "new (old) Raphaels" had been discovered on canvases beneath other paintings in the collection — one of them a "lovely Madonna." A *Last Supper,* also attributed to Raphael, had turned up in a Florentine coach house, once the refectory of a nearby convent. Margaret thought the image, now being copied by a prominent engraver, would make a fit companion to the print of Leonardo da Vinci's famous *Cenacolo* in Milan that Sam had brought back so many years ago from his own European tour, the one Margaret had missed, during which he had fallen in love with Anna Barker.

The surge of aesthetic responsiveness inspired Margaret to write an essay describing her favorite works in the Vatican galleries, which she sent to the *United States Magazine and Democratic Review.* The published essay could serve as a reminder too for a "sufficient number of persons" in editorial posts of Margaret's wide-ranging journalistic capabilities, to "enable me to earn frugal bread" once back in America. In the essay's opening pages, Margaret could not help but recall the days of May and June 1849, when the gardens surrounding the Vatican had been "full of armed men" and cannons were concealed in the shrubbery. But Margaret's memory also carried her farther back to the "divine images" — sculpted figures of Perseus, Apollo, Ariadne — she'd studied on one particular torchlight tour of the galleries and knew would "remain to exhilarate and bless all my after life," the years ahead in America.

Returning home after errands or excursions to "find always the glad eyes of my little boy to welcome me" meant that Margaret had "never felt so near happy as now." Her "tie" with Nino, so "real, so deep-rooted," was an "unimpassioned love," which "does not idealize and cannot be daunted by the faults of its object" — so unlike the romantic passions she'd experienced, which had so often ended in disappointment. Nothing but a child "can take the worst bitterness out of life." Margaret realized the "great novelty, the immense gain" of motherhood: "nothing else can break the spell of loneliness."

Yet Nino's very existence raised the stakes of Margaret's new undertaking: "For his sake indeed, I am become a miserable coward. I fear heat and cold and moschetoes. I fear terribly the voyage home, fear biting poverty." To William Channing she admitted, "I never think of the voyage without fearing the baby will die in it." Headache and what felt like a "dangerous pressure on the brain" overcame her for more than a week, during which she felt "so sad and weary" about leaving Italy "that I seem paralyzed." A bleeding performed by one of Mozier's doctors brought relief. "One would think that so much fuss could not end in nothing," she wrote in another letter to William Channing, "so Patience Cousin and shuffle the cards, till Fate is ready to deal them out anew."

As the spring rains let up and the skies cleared for the *Elizabeth* to sail, Margaret continued to fret about Nino, his health on the voyage, his future in America: "I hope he will retain some trace in his mind of the perpetual exhilarating picture of Italy." Could Margaret retain the hopeful notes she had sounded in her final *Tribune* column, written for New Year's Day, 1850? As she had confided in William Channing, "It has long seemed that in the year 1850" — the year Margaret would turn forty — "I should stand on some important plateau in the ascent of life, should be allowed to pause for awhile, and take more clear and commanding views than ever before." But so far she had experienced "no marked and important change."

"Joy to those born in this day," Margaret had written for the *Tribune*. "In America is open to them the easy chance of a noble, peaceful growth, in Europe of a combat grand in its motives, and in its extent beyond what the world ever before so much as dreamed. Joy to them; and joy to those their heralds." Margaret had made herself one of those heralds of a better day. Could she, leaving Italy "with most sad and unsatisfied heart" along with so many "betrayed and exiled" comrades, rest content in the belief that "there come after them greater than themselves, who may at last string the heart of the world to full concord"?

21

"No favorable wind"

MARGARET HAD ONCE CONFIDED IN ANNA WARD THE STORY of her unfortunate uncle Peter Crane, her mother's only brother. In childhood, Peter and Peggy, as Margarett Crane had been called as a girl, were "the flower of the family, sweet-tempered, generous, gay and handsome," both "very dear to one another and to their parents." But as the two siblings grew older, Peter became restless, and one night he ran away from "the little farm-house home, without the consent of his parents," knowing they would not give it, certain that "in some distant Eldorado, he could do more and be happier than in the narrow path marked out for him at home." According to family legend, the "rashness of Peter" was offset by Peggy's "fortunate" marriage to Timothy Fuller soon after. For as long as he lived, Timothy Fuller helped support the Crane parents, supplying "the place of the wandering son."

What became of Peter? Although he had sent home to Peggy a sum of money "from the first fruits of his labors," out of which she purchased her "first white gown," Peter never prospered as he had dreamed, and he never returned home. In the end, he "could not bear to come back thus, old, sad, and poor to lift the latch again of the door from which he had stolen by night in presumptuous youth."

Uncle Peter was not really so old when he died, barely fifty. But his was one of those "long sad tales of ineffectual lives" that, Margaret told Anna, "move me deeply." Margaret was in her early thirties, an ambitious woman still uncertain of her capacity for achievement, when she learned the news of her uncle Peter's lonely death and wrote out the story for Anna. Margaret had not yet published her first book, and she had been turned aside painfully, both in love and in friendship. "It *is* sad when a man lays down the burden of life frustrated in every purpose," Margaret wrote to Anna. "Happy the prodigal son who *returns!*"

Three years later, Margaret left America as one of its most accomplished citizens, a cultural emissary to Europe. She was the author of a book on the woman question that had revived the cause and advanced it well beyond Mary Wollstonecraft's *Vindication of the Rights of Woman;* she was a widely read columnist for a national newspaper with a rare commission as foreign correspondent. But Margaret, "the much that calls for more," had still been searching. Now, after several "rich, if troubled years," although worried that "to go into the market, and hire myself out" would be "hard as it never was before," Margaret had fulfilled many of her longest-held desires. She had taken a lover who became her devoted husband; she had borne a child. Stored for travel inside her portable desk was the manuscript of a new book, her "great history" of the rise and fall of the Roman Republic. Margaret, who had played the role of eldest son to her father in girlhood and to her family since Timothy's death, whose heart was moved by Uncle Peter's story rather than Peggy's, could now play the prodigal who *returns.* Uncertain of her welcome in the United States, Margaret was sure of what she possessed, what she was bringing home — "my treasures, my husband and child," and her book, "what is most valuable to me . . . of any thing."

Another long-ago night in Boston with Anna Ward: Sam was away, and Margaret and Anna shared a bed, "together in confiding sleep," as they had done so often when Margaret visited Anna before her marriage to Sam. But this night, with her head on Sam's pillow, after listening to Anna's "graceful talk," Margaret fell into a restless sleep and dreamed "a frightful dream of being imprisoned in a ship at sea, the waves all dashing round." Dreaming, she suffered through "horrible suspense," knowing the crew had orders to throw their prisoner overboard. Into the nightmare scene entered "many persons I knew," who were "delighted to see me," yet when Margaret begged their help, "with cold courtliness" they "glided away." "Oh it was horrible these averted faces and well dressed figures turning from me . . . with the cold wave rushing up into which I was to be thrown."

The seventeenth of May, the day of sailing, came. Margaret and Giovanni spent their last night in Florence with the Brownings, Margaret almost giddy with anticipation. During the last days of packing her nerves jangled at the thought of America, of the "sense of fresh life unknown here," and of the "rush and bang" of Americans—more than twenty million of them now—"with their rail-roads, electric telegraphs, mass movements and ridiculous dilettant phobias." How many would "care for the thoughts of my head or the feelings of my heart"?

Margaret brought a Bible for the Brownings' little boy as a parting gift from Nino, inscribed "*In memory of* Angelo Eugene Ossoli." In the Brownings' handsomely furnished parlor, the couple joked nervously about a prophecy in the Ossoli family that the sea "would be fatal" to Giovanni, that he should "avoid traveling" by water. Then Margaret turned to Elizabeth Browning, "with that peculiar smile which lighted up her plain, thought-worn face," the poet would recall, and told her hostess, "I accept as a good omen that our ship should be called the ELIZABETH."

But despite—or because of—her fascination with the mystical and the magnetic, properties she regarded as certain to be proven empirically one day, Margaret had long ago put aside the notion of luck, whether good or ill. She preferred to practice perseverance in the face of adversity. When Timothy Fuller had announced the move from the Dana mansion in Cambridge to the farm in Groton and her brother Eugene had complained that "our family star has taken an unfavorable turn" and "we shall never be lucky any more," Margaret had made her own peace with the family's change of fortune. "We are never wholly sunk by storms," she chose to believe, even if "no favorable wind ever helps our voyages." Better to live by the words she had copied out from the *Aeneid* as a girl and explicated in an essay for her father, the determined oarsmen's credo: "*Possunt quia posse videntur.*" *They can conquer who believe they can.*

And yet, to those who reject the notions of luck and fate, the world still insists on offering up chance, accident. As Margaret, the prodigal who would return, boarded the *Elizabeth* at Livorno with her "treasures," having posted by separate vessel a last affectionate letter to her mother in the event she did not survive the voyage— "and I say it merely because there seems somewhat more of danger on sea than on land"—she accepted the laws of chance. Margaret knew, as she'd once taken the trouble to calculate and record in her journal, that "more than five hundred *British vessels alone* are wrecked and sink to the bottom *annually*."

A steady wind drove the ship westward across the Mediterranean toward Gibraltar and the broad Atlantic. Margaret's seasickness subsided by her fortieth birthday, May 23. Little Nino, almost two years old, made friends with the crew, with the goat that provided his milk, with Captain Hasty's young wife, Catherine, with twenty-two-year-old Celeste Paolini, a nurse Margaret had hired after all, enabling the young woman's return to a job she'd formerly held in New York. Horace Sumner was already a friend. All six passengers had comfortable rooms toward the stern of the ship, in a covered exterior cabin with its own parlor and exercise deck. The breeze tossed Giovanni's dark hair, which grew long as the days passed, curling into ringlets in the salty air.

But Captain Hasty was unwell. Fever and aches turned to smallpox, and after a seven-day sail and a night at anchor off Gibraltar, he was dead. There had been no chance for a doctor's attention. Margaret recorded the funeral at sea, when all the ships in the blue harbor raised their banners in the late-afternoon sun— "Yes! it was beautiful but how dear a price we pay for the poems of the world." She did her best to console Catherine Hasty. The *Elizabeth* was doused in sulfur and quarantined; no one could board or leave the ship during the required week in the harbor, spent waiting to see if anyone else on board contracted the illness.

Under the command of first mate Henry Bangs, the *Elizabeth* sailed onward, now over open ocean. Two days out, Nino, who had visited Captain Hasty in his sickroom before smallpox was confirmed, became ill, his body and face covered with pustules, his eyes swollen shut. The vaccine administered by the careless doctor in Rieti had been ineffective. Suffering high fevers, the child wandered once again "between the two worlds." But he was stronger now than he'd been the previous summer. When Margaret and Catherine Hasty sang to him, Nino waved his puffy hands in time to the music. On the ninth day, Nino *"could see"* again. The boy's swift recovery, the disappearance of the pockmarks from his face, brought comfort to the grieving Catherine Hasty. She had never known "two people happier or more devoted to each other & their child" than Margaret and Giovanni. Although she'd seen them quarrel once over Nino's care, she had also watched Giovanni draw Margaret into an embrace and calm his anxious wife, telling her "I wish we could always think the same thing—& I never could differ from you, if it were not that baby's life depends on it."

No one else on board succumbed to the illness, and the *Elizabeth* drifted lazily westward in a midsummer stillness at midocean. Casting her thoughts ahead to arrival in the old New World, Margaret might have recalled the last summer she'd stayed in Concord, inhabiting her sister's house all on her own, a welcome visitor to the Emersons and Haw- thornes: "I feel cradled,—with me the rarest happiest of feelings," she'd written to Cary Sturgis. "I am borne along on the stream of life."

Neither chance nor accident, but only time, the duration of a transatlantic crossing, prevented Margaret from receiving the letter Waldo Emerson had finally posted to her in April, just before she left Florence. But this was fortunate. Margaret did not have to read the advice of yet another dear friend who'd fallen under the influence of what she'd come to think of as "the social inquisition of the U.S." Waldo had joined the chorus rec- ommending that she "stay in Italy, for now." He offered to do the work of selling Margaret's book for her in America, as he had for Thomas Car- lyle's *Sartor Resartus,* and he marshaled his eloquence to press the "ad- vantages of your absenteeism" and a continued residence abroad: "not only as adding solidity to your testimony, but new rays of reputation & wonder to you as a star." No letter at all would be better than reading Waldo's oblique, subtly reproachful reference to her changed state: "but surprise is the woof you love to weave into all your web."

Margaret could remember instead Waldo's several letters written from London and Paris, urging her to return with him to America, express- ing at last the outright affection she had longed to hear from him: "Shall we not yet—you, you, also,—as we used to talk, build up a reasonable society . . . and effectually serve one another?" She could remember that Waldo's vision of a future life, an afterlife, had included her: "When we die, my dear friend, will they not make us up better, with some more proportion between our tendencies & our skills; that life shall not be such a sweet fever, but a sweet health, sweet and beneficent, and solid as Andes?"

Waldo's words, if she remembered them, might have brought some comfort as the wind picked up, blowing the *Elizabeth* rapidly past Bermuda on July 14, then close to port at New York on the evening of July 18—and then as night fell, the novice Captain Bangs all unwitting, beyond. Nino and Giovanni had to be Margaret's first thoughts when, at four in the morning on July 19, the *Elizabeth* ran aground off Fire Island, well north of their intended destination. Here, along the narrow southern rim of Long Island, there was no safe harbor, only shallow waters and treacherous shoals; no rescue party, only a lifeboat beached near a distant lighthouse and practiced scavengers on shore who would rather pillage under cover of darkness the flotsam of merchant vessels blown off course by storms and wrecked on Long Island's sandbars than aid in the dangerous rescue of passengers.

The six on board the *Elizabeth* had packed their trunks for arrival; Margaret had chosen Nino's outfit to wear ashore. But they huddled together now in their nightclothes, Margaret's white gown faintly visible in the darkness of the cabin, after the dreadful shock of impact woke them all and an ominous scraping sound from below confirmed their worst fears. Waves breached the sides of the ship and beat against the walls of the cabin, which rocked to and fro with each surging swell. The wind howled at near hurricane force. Nino cried until Margaret swaddled him in blankets in her arms as she sat bracing herself with her back to the leeward wall, her legs pointing up the slanting cabin floor toward the foremast. Celeste screamed and wailed until Giovanni persuaded her to kneel in prayer. "Cut away!" they heard, and sails, rigging, and two of the three masts crashed to the deck of the *Elizabeth*, whose hold, with its cargo of "marble and rags," now flooded with seawater. *She lay at the mercy of the maddened ocean.*

"We must die," Horace Sumner told Catherine Hasty. "Let us die calmly, then," the young widow replied. But shore was only three hundred yards off. At dawn, the first mate, Charles Davis, appeared to guide the passengers up to the forecastle where the crew had gathered, just as the flimsier walls of the passengers' cabin began to break apart. The ship's hull was stuck fast in the sands below, the vessel itself leaned to one side; waves poured over the main deck, littered with ropes and shards of the two downed masts. Nino made the trip in a canvas bag slung around a sailor's neck. Catherine Hasty was nearly swept overboard, but Davis grabbed her long hair and held fast until she was free of the wave. All six passengers reached the relative shelter of the forecastle, where they could see figures moving about on shore. Davis returned to the passengers' cabin to retrieve Margaret's purse — seventy dollars in gold coins — and her travel desk, which held "what is most valuable to me if I live," the manuscript. Margaret tied the doubloons into a kerchief and secured it at her waist. The tide was near its lowest point; surely someone would come to their rescue.

An hour passed, yet none of the figures on shore entered the water; their attention was fixed elsewhere, on trunks, hats, anything that washed up on land. The sailors — there were seventeen in all — began to leap overboard. Swimming to shore at low tide, for those who knew how, seemed the only possible means of salvation. As one man fought his way to safety on the beach, after nearly an hour wrestling with the waves, Horace Sumner plunged in to follow, but he never resurfaced, dragged under by currents or knocked unconscious by floating debris.

Here was death by drowning: silent, senseless. A life lost, not sacrificed, yielded up not in a battle for freedom, but in a desperate bid for survival. And Margaret could not swim. She had waded into the shallows of the East River at Turtle Bay to bathe on warm summer nights, imagining James Nathan's embrace; but she had never taken a stroke in the open ocean, and would not now in a storm that was smashing seaside cottages and boats at harbor as it battered the Atlantic coast all the way from North Carolina, where it made landfall, to Coney Island.

The tide turned. The waters began to rise again and the waves to swell ever higher, lifting the roof of the forecastle as they crested, drenching those who remained on board in spray. Soon the ship would be broken up entirely. Charles Davis proposed tying rope handles to wooden spars and towing passengers to shore. Catherine Hasty volunteered. Margaret watched as the younger woman held grimly to her plank, rolled over and over by the waves, her long hair streaming in the billows, her soaking nightdress dragging her downward, until she finally reached the shore, pulled out of the undertow by Davis at the last. She lived. *Now came Margaret's turn.*

But no single spar could support Margaret, Giovanni, Nino, and Celeste, the passengers still gathered about the foremast. With them were the *Elizabeth*'s cook, carpenter, steward, second mate, and Captain Bangs. Bangs insisted Margaret take hold of a plank; he would drag her next to shore. She refused. Bangs offered to take Nino first. She would not let him go. Margaret would not leave her family; they would not leave her. Surely first mate Davis would return with the lifeboat now visible on shore.

Another hour passed, after which the terrified, exasperated Bangs released his remaining crew members from duty; they could save themselves any way they wished. "I am a married man[.] I do not feel it right to throw away my life & can do nothing more on board," he yelled into the wind, and dove from the deck to fight his way to shore. No one followed. Later, on the beach, an enraged Davis dragged Bangs out of the surf, berating him for "breaking his pledge," leaving passengers behind on the sinking ship he'd dared to captain. Davis had had no greater success in persuading anyone on shore to help launch the lifeboat in the rough surf; the heavy craft could not be managed alone. But the passengers and crew still waiting aboard the wreck could not know this.

In midafternoon, more than ten hours since the *Elizabeth* ran aground, the storm raged more fiercely than ever. The cook, Joseph McGill, cried out as the ship's stern gave way. There could be no hope of rescue now. All must make "*one* desperate effort," dive in and swim if they could, grab whatever might float and jump if they couldn't, before the wreck itself dragged them under. The steward had just taken Nino in his arms, Margaret saw to it, when an enormous wave crashed over the forecastle, bringing down the ship's final mast, pulling up a stretch of deck, and sending Nino and the steward overboard. Celeste and Giovanni clung to the mast until the next wave swept them away. Margaret steadied herself for a moment, and then she too was gone. *When last seen, she had been seated at the foot of the foremast, still clad in her white night-dress, with her hair fallen loose upon her shoulders.*

• • •

It was over. Margaret would no longer suffer, or exult in, what Waldo had called life's "sweet fever." Did she share his belief in, his hope for, a compensating "sweet health" in death?

Margaret had believed that she and Giovanni "could have a good deal of happiness together in what remains of life," once they reached America. And Nino—would his small voice have spoken new words, deepened, and mingled with those of the other growing children of Concord? Through the years ahead there would be his cousins, Ellen and Ellery's Greta and Caroline; and Waldo and Lidian's Ellen, Edward, and Edith; Nathaniel and Sophia's Una, Julian, and Rose; Bronson and Abba's Anna, Louisa, Beth, and May. Theirs would be the voices of "children splashing and shouting in the river," once so pleasing to Margaret as she lay on a favorite boulder in the hot sun of a summer day years ago, a day such as this one should have been—"lustrous warm, delicious happy, tender." Farmers were "making hay in a near field" and the "fiddle of the village dancing master" could be heard "with its merry shriek and scrape in the distance, but all this noise"—all this *life*—was "harmonized by the golden fulness of light on the river on the trees, on the fields: it cared not where it lay: it loved and laughed on all."

Epilogue:
"After so dear a storm"

TWO NIGHTS BEFORE THE *ELIZABETH* STRUCK GROUND OFF Fire Island, the skies over the northeastern United States had been so clear that the daguerreotypist John Adams Whipple, experimenting with Harvard's powerful Great Refractor telescope, succeeded in capturing the first photographic image of a star, Vega. But the same winds that scoured the heavens on the night of July 16–17, enabling a technological marvel, had carried with them a lethal storm and a merchant ship, a remnant of the fading age of sail, that proved no match for nature's force.

When news of the wreck of the *Elizabeth* and Margaret's disappearance reached the *New-York Tribune* offices, Horace Greeley assigned the story to his finest young writer, the poet-journalist Bayard Taylor, who set out at nightfall, making a seven-hour journey over still-stormy waters to reach the scene just before daybreak on Saturday, July 20. Newly returned from California, where he'd been posting letters to the *Tribune* on the 1849 gold rush, the twenty-five-year-old Taylor traversed the shoreline, finding ruptured casks of almonds, sacks of juniper berries, and oil flasks, "their contents mixed with the sand." The ship's shattered timbers were strewn along the narrow beach for a stretch of three or four miles. Taylor marveled at the force of a storm that had "so chopped and broken" the once sturdy vessel that "scarcely a stick of ten feet in length can be found." A portion of the *Elizabeth*'s foremast, studded with broken spars and snagged in loose rigging, rose and fell on the swells about fifty yards off shore, held fast by the ship's sundered hull, a skeletal apparition beckoning in the dawn light.

Taylor had given up his post in mining country for the sake of a tubercular sweetheart back east; he was determined to marry, although his bride would survive only a few more months. At Fire Island, the waste of healthy lives, the "bruised and mangled" bodies of the dead that had washed to shore, seemed an abomination. Catherine Hasty had insisted on transporting Nino's small body, still warm when it reached the beach, to the nearest house, a mile off, where the surviving sailors paid tearful farewells and fashioned a makeshift coffin out of one of their own sea chests. They locked and nailed down the lid before burying the boy "in a little nook between two of the sand-hills some distance from the sea." The midsummer heat made a swift interment necessary. Nino's nurse, Celeste Paolini, was "enclosed in a rough box" and committed to the sand alongside two Swedish sailors and the ship steward who had held Nino in his arms at the last. In all, eight lives were lost. The bodies of Margaret, Giovanni, and Horace Sumner had not yet been found.

In his account of the wreck for the *Tribune*, Taylor placed blame squarely on the "inexperience" of Captain Bangs and made no secret of his disgust at the crowd of indifferent scavengers, whose number swelled to a thousand by Sunday morning as the greedy streamed in from as far off as Rockaway and Montauk to pilfer what they could of the *Elizabeth*'s cargo, valued at $200,000, roughly the equivalent of $4.5 million today. Taylor reported that a trunk filled with oil paintings destined for the Aspinwall family—kin to William Aspinwall Tappan, Cary Sturgis's husband—had floated to shore. The paintings might have been preserved had they not been immediately cut away and pocketed by looters, who left the frames in shambles on the beach. Only a few "shreds of canvas, evidently more than a century old, half buried in the sand" remained. Likewise, the "silk, Leghorn braid, hats, wool, oil, almonds, and other articles contained in the vessel, were carried off as soon as they came to land."

Taylor held out hope that the bodies of Margaret and Giovanni would be found "buried under the ruins of the vessel" or cast up on shore farther along the coast, dragged westward by the current that had set in since the storm. On Sunday afternoon, one of Margaret's trunks bobbed free of the wreck, claimed at once by Catherine Hasty "before the pirates had an opportunity of purloining it." She was said to be drying manuscripts by the fire in the same house where Nino had lain in state the day before. Taylor himself looked through "a pile of soaked papers," finding copies of French and Italian newspapers as well as "several of Mazzini's pamphlets," Margaret's reference materials. "I have therefore a strong hope that the work on Italy will be entirely recovered," he wrote in the *Tribune*.

Word of the tragedy took longer to reach New England, where Margaret's family had gathered at Arthur's house in Manchester, New Hampshire, anticipating a reunion with Margaret and first encounters with her husband and son. Instead, a telegram reprinted in the local paper brought the grim news, and Ellen, Arthur, Eugene, and Margarett Crane set out immediately for New York, where the Springs opened their Brooklyn home to the stricken family. As a child, Margaret had suffered from nightmare visions of her mother's death. Had Margarett Crane ever permitted herself to imagine her daughter's? Mrs. Fuller "sat like a stone in our house," Rebecca Spring remembered afterward, unable to eat or sleep or even cry. Ellen was as agitated as her mother was benumbed; she could not think of life without her older sister.

Arthur, Eugene, Marcus Spring, and Horace Greeley left together for Fire Island on the twenty-fourth, where they met Charles Sumner searching in vain for the body of his younger brother. William Channing was there too, along with his cousin, Ellen's husband Ellery Channing, and Henry Thoreau, who had traveled with Ellery from Concord. Waldo Emerson had handed Thoreau seventy dollars to cover expenses and charged him "to go, on all our parts, & obtain on the wrecking ground all the intelligence &, if possible, any fragments of manuscript or other property." Waldo had considered making the trip himself but changed his mind, instead staying home to begin filling the journal that would ultimately generate his portion of a memorial biography he already envisioned as marking out "an essential line of American history" devoted to this "brave, eloquent, subtle, accomplished, devoted, constant soul!"

At Fire Island, Thoreau made a full survey of the shoreline and interviewed as many survivors and witnesses as he could find, drawing up an inventory of the Ossolis' belongings: five trunks of varying sizes, a case of books, a tin box, and Margaret's jewelry, four rings, a brooch, and "one eye glass with heavy gold handles & chain." Aside from the large trunk recovered by Catherine Hasty, another had been found, but its contents had vanished, "whether emptied by the sea, or by thieves, is not known."

Late in the day he enlisted three fishermen to ferry him in an oyster boat to Patchogue on the mainland, where he'd heard many of the scavengers lived, but the trip proved fruitless and nearly cost Thoreau his life. The fishermen had delayed for several hours, drinking at a tavern as darkness fell, waiting for the tide to rise, they said. Two of the men spent the voyage stretched out in the bottom of the boat, sleeping off their bender in a swill of bilge and vomit; the third, taking the helm, narrowly missed running the boat aground when he mistook the light from a nearby cottage for the beam of a distant lighthouse. Thoreau got no answers in Patchogue other than what he gleaned from observing several youths at play with dominoes, dressed up in hats scavenged from the wreck; their mothers had stitched decorative tassels and buttons to the hats, filched, Thoreau guessed, from Margaret's wardrobe trunk.

Thoreau returned to Fire Island to learn that a few garments had been recovered: a shift embroidered with Margaret's initials, a child's underclothes, a man's shirt. But there were no more papers to be found anywhere, and Margaret's manuscript was not among those in the trunk, nor was it in the small portable desk that first mate Davis had retrieved from the passengers' cabin on Margaret's instructions. Ellery Channing had stayed behind to help Catherine Hasty dry the contents. Precious letters from Mazzini and Mickiewicz survived, along with Margaret's correspondence with Giovanni and a slim journal she'd kept in Rome during the early months of 1849, ending just as the siege began. Nothing more. Nothing, until Thoreau stumbled across Giovanni's guardsman's coat. He ripped off one button and pocketed it for his return to Concord, its solidity mocking his quest after vanished lives. "Held up," he would write of the button in his diary, "it intercepts the light and casts a shadow, — an *actual* button so called, — and yet all the life it is connected with is less substantial to me than my faintest dreams."

A week after the *Elizabeth* foundered off shore, "a portion of a human skeleton," mutilated beyond recognition by sharks, was reported on the beach, a mile or more from the lighthouse. Thoreau followed this lead as well, tracing once more on foot the now deserted shoreline until he spied the "relics of a human body," he later wrote, which had been draped with a cloth, their location marked with "a stick stuck up" in the air. "Close at hand," he wrote, "they were simply some bones with a little flesh adhering to them," with "nothing at all remarkable about them." He could not make out "enough of anatomy to decide *confidently*" whether the body was "that of a male or a female" — whether Margaret, Giovanni, Horace Sumner, or anyone else.

After so many days of futile searching, Thoreau felt acutely the insignificance of his place in the drama, and "as I stood there [the bones] grew more and more imposing. They were alone with the beach and the sea, whose hollow roar seemed addressed to them." It seemed to the thirty-three-year-old writer, whose early scribblings had passed beneath Margaret's stern editorial eye, "as if there was an understanding between them and the ocean which necessarily left me out, with my snivelling sympathies. That dead body had taken possession of the shore, and reigned over it as no living one could, in the name of a certain majesty which belonged to it."

Margaret's essay for the *United States Magazine and Democratic Review* recollecting her torchlight tour of the Vatican galleries had just appeared in print, in the July issue. Her concluding lines, describing her recent efforts in Florence to gain entrance to the Church of San Lorenzo for a nocturnal viewing of Michelangelo's interiors — "I doubt they cannot look grander by one light than another; but I hope to try" — stood in sharp contrast to the *Tribune*'s account of her last words, as reported by the *Elizabeth*'s cook: "I see nothing but death before me, — I shall never reach the shore." But there was no disputing it: Margaret was gone.

"To the last her country proves inhospitable to her," Waldo Emerson summed up in his journal, perhaps wishing to forget that he had been among the several friends who, unsettled by the surprising course Margaret's life had taken in Italy, discouraged her return to America. Now he could simply mourn: "I have lost in her my audience." Margaret had been his equal in intellect and, since leaving Concord, had bested him in experience. "We are taught by her plenty how lifeless & outward we were," he had once observed. "Her heart, which few knew," he wrote now, adapting an oft-quoted assessment of Margaret's idol Goethe, "was as great as her mind, which all knew." Fatherless since childhood, Waldo Emerson had grown up into a life of recurring loss, each death unleashing an inner fury that took the form of months-long depression. The loss of Margaret, his friend, collaborator, and intellectual sparring partner, affected him differently, if still personally, as a shock that warned of his own mortality: "I hurry now to my work admonished that I have few days left."

Privately, in his journal, Horace Greeley lamented the loss of Margaret's book—"pages so rich with experience and life," he conjectured. Greeley wrote her *Tribune* obituary himself, calling for new editions of her already published work and concluding, "America has produced no woman who in mental endowments and acquirements has surpassed Margaret Fuller." And he opened up the *Tribune*'s pages to memorial poetry. Christopher Cranch, who had known Margaret in Boston as a member of the Transcendentalist circle and later in Rome, contributed one of the first elegies on a subject that would beguile American poets far into the twentieth century, Robert Lowell and Amy Clampitt among them. Like the other lyrics written in direct response to her drowning and printed in the *Tribune*, Cranch's "On the Death of Margaret Fuller Ossoli" expressed unambiguous grief:

> *O still sweet summer days! O moonlit nights,*
> *After so dear a storm how can ye shine! . . .*
> *For she is gone from us—gone, lost for ever,*
> *In the wild billows, swallowed up and lost—*
> *Gone full of love, life, hope and high endeavor,*
> *Just when we would have welcomed her the most.*

But how warmly would Margaret have been welcomed? Her tragic death seemed only to invite further speculation on a topic that had preoccupied Margaret's friends ever since the news of her secret marriage and child had reached New England. Pondering the question became a form of mourning, a means of reconciling the loss. By August 1, Cary Sturgis Tappan had received a packet of papers sent from Concord containing the accounts that Ellery Channing and Henry Thoreau had written up for Waldo. It was like the old days of sharing letters and journals through the mail, but immeasurably sadder. "How characteristic," Cary decided, had been Margaret's actions in the crisis: offering her own life preserver to a sailor once she'd resolved not to make a bid for shore, "refusing to part with her child when she could not have saved him." And even Margaret's "securing the money about her" was a heart-rending sign of "how much she had felt the need of it." Someone "who had always been taken care of," Cary observed, someone like herself, "would not have done so when lives were in danger."

Then Cary's thoughts wandered to the now impossible future: "The waves do not seem so difficult to brave as the prejudices she would have encountered if she had arrived here safely." Margaret, as Cary remembered her, "was always so sensitive to coldness & unkindness, even from strangers." There was something fitting, even, about the way her life had ended: "Her return seemed like tearing a bird's nest from a sheltering tree and tossing it out on the waves." And Cary could not resist a last gibe at her former teacher, a woman she had resented as well as loved. Cary had suffered an early loss—her beloved older brother, knocked overboard by a wayward boom at sea, when she was a girl. Her mother had gone mad with grief. "Why should we all be afraid to lose everything?" Cary asked now, questioning Margaret's decision to remain on the sinking *Elizabeth* with her husband and son. "It is not sorrow but tedious days that we fear." Margaret had deserted Cary too.

Cary had never known Margaret as a married woman, as a mother. Did Cary believe her old friend could have saved herself from death at sea, like some Shakespearean heroine—Viola of *Twelfth Night* or Miranda of *The Tempest*, whose name Margaret had borrowed for her pseudonymous autobiographical sketch in *Woman in the Nineteenth Century*? Would this Margaret-Miranda have abandoned husband and child and fought her way to shore, crying out in the voice of the writer, "I must depend on myself as the only constant friend," proud that she had "taken a course of her own, and no man stood in her way"? Writing to Cary from London four years earlier, Margaret had reproached the younger woman similarly for giving up her "noble" independence to marry, for failing to "embark on the wide stream of the world" by continuing her work as an artist. And Margaret had been right: Cary was already unhappy in her marriage, already fearing tedious days ahead, a kind of death in life.

Cary had been the one to deliver the terrible news to Sophia and Nathaniel Hawthorne, who'd taken up residence with their two young children in a small farmhouse on the grounds of Highwood, the estate the Tappans leased from Sam Ward in Lenox, the property to which Nathaniel would one day give the name Tanglewood in his children's tales. Nathaniel's first novel, *The Scarlet Letter*, had been published in early spring, selling out its first edition within ten days and making its author an instant celebrity. But money was still in short supply, and Cary's offer of the "Red House," as Nathaniel dubbed the simple cottage—"as red as the Scarlet Letter," he'd noted with pleasure—for minimal rent, had been a welcome one, especially as Nathaniel's book, with its preface satirizing the denizens of Salem's Custom House, his colleagues until the political spoils system cost him his job the year before, had earned him enemies at home.

After reading the newspaper accounts of the shipwreck that Cary had brought her, Sophia could think of nothing "so unspeakably agonizing as the image of Margaret upon that wreck, alone, sitting with her hands upon her knees—& tempestuous waves breaking over her!" Sophia wished "at least Angelino could have been saved," she wrote to her mother in Boston, but of Margaret and Giovanni: "If they were truly bound together as they seemed to be, I am glad they died together." Years before, Sophia had dismissed Margaret's critique of marriage in *Woman in the Nineteenth Century*, arguing that unless "she were married truly"—like Sophia—Margaret had no right to pronounce on the institution. Now, however, Sophia felt that "with her new & deeper experience of life in all its relations—her rich harvest of observation . . . Margaret is such a loss."

But gossip about the Ossoli marriage traveled nearly as fast as reports of the drownings. George Ripley and Waldo Emerson puzzled over the precise meaning of Giovanni's title, figuring it "is about equivalent to *Selectman* here." Sophia Hawthorne's older sister Mary had heard from Maria Child that Giovanni "was wholly unfit to be [Margaret's] husband in this country . . . He would have been nothing here—he could do nothing, be nothing, come to nothing, and he would have dragged her down." Margaret was rumored to have been pregnant with a second child even as her young family's "only prospect of maintenance was by her pen." Maria Child guessed that Margaret would have "fully realized" the "unsuitableness of the match" once she'd arrived in America. "When we think of what a laborious and precarious living she would have had to earn," Mary had concluded, "I think that we may well be thankful that they all went to Heaven together, agonizing and melancholy as the departure was."

Maria Child's revelations had gone still further. She told Mary that "she never saw such a craving for affection as in Margaret" and recounted an incident from their days together as journalists in New York City when Margaret had "burst into tears," confiding that she "feared she should die" if she never had a child. Astonished that "Margaret, with her vaulting ambition was woman enough to say that," Mary Peabody, now married to the politician Horace Mann and herself the mother of three young boys, wrote to Sophia that "I do not wonder at her marrying the first man who showed devoted love to her even if he were not particularly intellectual."

"How infinitely sad about Margaret," Sophia wrote back. She too was convinced now that "if her husband was a person so wanting in force & availibility," Margaret would have found "no other peace or rest" back in America—"I am really glad she died." Sophia had harsh words for the loose-lipped Maria Child as well: "there is a vein of coarseness in her nature, not feminine. I hate reform-women, as a class do not you? I think it is designed by GOD that woman should always spiritually wear a veil, & not a coat & hat."

But Sophia and Mary's oldest sister, Elizabeth Peabody, still unmarried, reached a kinder appraisal of Margaret, the woman she once helped find her way in Boston's literary marketplace, and of her unconventional liaison in Rome. "It was not unpleasant to Margaret's romantic temperament," Elizabeth supposed, to have had "this little mystery for a season."

Sophia Hawthorne's distaste for "reform-women" signaled a conflict that might have distressed Margaret on her return to America more than any controversy resulting from bringing the diffident, undereducated Giovanni dei Marchesi Ossoli to live with her there. While Margaret was away in Europe, the women's rights cause she had helped to set in motion with *Woman in the Nineteenth Century* had surged ahead into activism with a first impromptu convention in Seneca Falls, New York, called by Lucretia Mott and Elizabeth Cady Stanton, once a participant in Margaret's Boston Conversations. The year was 1848, when revolutions swept the Continent. Had Margaret survived the Atlantic crossing in the summer of 1850, she would have been expected to attend the first National Woman's Rights Convention, scheduled for October in Worcester, Massachusetts. In later years, the president of the convention, Paulina Wright

Davis, an anti-slavery activist turned suffragist, recalled having written to Margaret in May of 1850—a letter Margaret never received—asking her to preside over the two-day assembly. "It can never be known if she would have accepted," Davis admitted, but "to her, I, at least, had hoped to confide the leadership of this movement."

Instead, when delegates from as far away as Ohio, Pennsylvania, Vermont, and upstate New York gathered in Worcester on October 23 and 24 to hear Sojourner Truth, Lucretia Mott, Frederick Douglass, Lucy Stone, and William Lloyd Garrison speak in favor of women's suffrage and a slate of other reforms, the assembled crowd observed a moment of silence. "We were left to mourn her guiding hand—her royal presence," remembered Davis. But aside from William Channing, who served as one of two vice presidents at the convention, these prominent radicals were not Margaret's comrades. Waldo Emerson had dodged the event, claiming he was hard at work on Margaret's memorial biography. Speaking at a convention like this one, with more than a thousand participants, had not so far been Margaret's way of doing business either.

Still, Paulina Wright Davis began her keynote address by citing a connection between the women's rights cause and "the European movement of 1848," the wave of revolutions that Margaret had so ardently championed and that had seemed, for a short while, certain to succeed. It would not be enough, Davis warned, to "rely upon a good cause and good intentions alone." A strong organization with clear aims would be necessary. Davis's language as she continued her speech might have been drawn from one of Margaret's *Tribune* columns or *Woman in the Nineteenth Century*. Davis advocated a "reformation," both "radical and universal" in nature, that "seeks to replace the worn out with the living and the beautiful." She envisioned "an epochal movement—the emancipation of a class, the redemption of half the world, and a conforming re-organization of all social, political, and industrial interests and institutions"—a movement for "human rights."

The question of Margaret's reception at her return, which led some of her closest friends to conclude that her death had been merciful, suggested a more troubling one—had she wished to die? Was there more than a tinge of the suicidal in a person who could "refuse" rescue, even for reasons of familial devotion? Anyone who had been close to Margaret knew her occasions of despair, her recurring wish in extremis for release. The question would not go away, thriving in the rich soil of Margaret's audacious life. To so many, Margaret's choices had always seemed unthinkable. In her final hours, might she have welcomed a way out?

As late as 1884, an elderly William Henry Channing was still "pained" by the thought that he might have abetted such speculation with his account of the wreck for the memorial volumes he'd joined Waldo Emerson and James Freeman Clarke in publishing soon after Margaret's death. There, "our blessed M. appears as almost *wilfully* . . . throwing away her own life," Channing wrote regretfully to Thomas Wentworth Higginson, at work on his own biography of Margaret, "out of a resolve not to be sundered from her husband & their boy." Indeed, after reading Channing's version of the tragedy in the 1852 *Memoirs of Margaret Fuller Ossoli*, Caroline Healey Dall, the young recorder of Margaret's Conversations, now unhappily married to a man she considered her intellectual inferior, thought it likely that "Margaret was happy to die," although for different reasons than Channing expected. Dall believed Margaret must have chosen death "before the mist dissolved": before she was forced to admit that her "romantic marriage" to Giovanni Ossoli was not a true "union of heart and flesh" — and — "mind."

But Margaret's own writings in the last year of her life show persistent resolve in the face of danger, not recklessness or fatalism, and an immunity to public censure. "I have never yet felt afraid when really in the presence of danger," she had written to her mother of the passage into Rome on flooded roads after Nino's birth. If Margaret was pregnant again, as rumored, or even if she wasn't, she was still in love with Giovanni. She believed in the future of their family. Margaret had known, as she'd written to William Channing from Florence on the eve of her return, that "there must be a cloud of false rumors and impressions at first, but you will see when we meet that there was a sufficient reason for all I have done."

All that Margaret had done in Italy, all that she had suffered and survived — a lonely birth, months of separation from Giovanni or Nino, the days under siege, Nino's brushes with death — had prepared her for the final crisis, caught in a "heavy storm" on a homeward journey. Unlike her father, to whom she'd written a first letter of concern for his safety in another violent storm — "i hope you will not have to come home in it" —

Margaret, the returning prodigal, was traveling with all that she most prized. In a brave decision worthy of the mythic heroines she took as her guides, Margaret would not leave them behind: "*having lived*, I shrink not now from death."

There could be no burial for Margaret and Giovanni, but within five years of the drownings, her family erected a stone monument at Mount Auburn Cemetery in Cambridge. Nino's remains, which had been transferred from Fire Island to Cambridgeport in the days following the wreck, as well as those of Timothy, Julia Adelaide, and Edward, were reinterred in a plot in the lush, gardenlike cemetery large enough to accommodate future generations, so that the Fullers might "mingle our dust together as we have our hearts," in Margarett Crane's plan. Margaret's sister, Ellen Channing, was the first to join them — dead of consumption in 1856.

In the years after, so many visitors — grieving, curious, inspired — made their way to Margaret's memorial stone that the route leading directly from the entrance up the hillside to the Fuller plot became a well-worn path and eventually the first paved road in the cemetery. Despite the reassuring solidity of the granite memorial — to "Margaret Fuller Ossoli" and "her Husband, Giovanni Angelo, Marquis Ossoli," as the monument read — Margaret could now only ever be "yours in the distance," as she had once signed a letter to a friend from abroad. Perhaps that is why so many wished to get as close as they could and say goodbye.

ACKNOWLEDGMENTS

My debts to previous scholars and biographers are legion. One will be immediately apparent to some readers: in homage to Margaret Fuller's first biographers, her three friends Ralph Waldo Emerson, William Henry Channing, and James Freeman Clarke, I have adapted the chiefly geographical section titles from their two-volume *Memoirs of Margaret Fuller Ossoli* for use in my account. These markers served as formal requirements do in a sonnet, permitting me to tell a new story without departing entirely from tradition. Several italicized sentences in Chapter 21 are quoted directly from *Memoirs*.

The Emerson-Channing-Clarke volumes kept Margaret Fuller's memory alive through the second half of the nineteenth century, along with later biographies by Julia Ward Howe and Thomas Wentworth Higginson. Although many now credit *Woman in the Nineteenth Century* with inspiring the American women's suffrage movement, Margaret Fuller was nearly forgotten by the time of the Nineteenth Amendment's ratification in 1920. She enjoyed a brief vogue as a feminist foremother in the 1970s, her face appearing on T-shirts, her famous injunction "Let them be sea-captains!" converted into a slogan. Her resurrection then was aided by the publication of important works by Bell Gale Chevigny and Paula Blanchard, just as Robert Hudspeth and Charles Capper embarked on decades-long efforts to document Fuller's life, in a six-volume edition of her letters and a two-volume definitive biography, respectively. During the same period, Joel Myerson, Judith Mattson Bean, Susan Belasco Smith, and Larry J. Reynolds issued complete editions of Fuller's nearly three hundred journalistic pieces written for the *New-York Tribune*. Joan Von Mehren and Meg McGavran Murray have produced thoroughly researched biographies; and two anthologies, Jeffrey Steele's *The Essential Margaret Fuller* and Mary Kelley's *The Portable Margaret Fuller*, have made a broad selection of writings accessible to general readers. Joel Myerson's contributions to Fuller scholarship extend well beyond his editions of her *Tribune* columns, beginning with his bibliographic work of the 1970s and surely not ending with his recent *Fuller in Her Own Time*. No new biography can be written without reliance on these crucial projects.

I am grateful to Phyllis Cole, Helen R. Deese, Kathleen Lawrence, and Robert D. Richardson Jr. for "conversations that make the soul," whether in person or by email, that have contributed greatly to my understanding of Margaret Fuller and her friends. The members of my biographers' group, Joyce Antler, Frances Malino, Susan Quinn, Lois Palken Rudnick, Judith Tick, and Roberta Wollons, as well as companions in biography Carol Bundy, Natalie Dykstra, Carla Kaplan, Louise W. Knight, Stacy Schiff, and Susan Ware, have prodded and praised in precisely the right measure. Deborah Friedell first suggested I write about Margaret Fuller, John Demos urged me to tackle a "big" subject, and Lindy Hess and Ann Hulbert believed I could. Deborah Pickman Clifford saw me begin, and I wish she were here to read the final pages.

Profound thanks to Charles Capper, Robert Hudspeth, Joel Myerson, and Joan Von Mehren, who always answered my questions, and to Lynn Hyde, Mary De Jong, Lucilla Fuller Marvel, Marie Cleary, Elton A. Hall, Alan Thomsen, and James Lawrence, dean of the Swedenborgian School of Studies, all of whom led me to new and fascinating material. Tom Rankin, Mario Bannoni, Wendy White, and Deb Theodore were my guides to Rome. Anne Gray Fischer assisted ably and often on short notice with a variety of research tasks, and Neil Giordano helped with illustrations. The comradeship of the Reverend Jenny Rankin and the Transcendentalist Council of First Parish Concord, as well as the Reverend Dorothy Emerson, Jessica Lipnack, Bonnie Hurd Smith, and others of the Margaret Fuller Bicentennial Committee, sustained me in moments when I felt, as Margaret once lamented, "I am little better than an aspiration."

The endurance of Margaret Fuller's legacy depends on the dedicated archivists who care for her private papers and make them available to the public. Leslie Morris, Heather Cole, and the staff of the Houghton Library at Harvard were generous with their time and guidance to the voluminous Margaret Fuller Family Papers. Peter Drummey, Brenda Lawson, Anne Bentley, Kathy Griffin, Conrad E. Wright, Ondine LeBlanc, Katheryn Viens, and Dennis Fiori continue to make the Massachusetts Historical Society my research home. Leslie Perrin Wilson of the Concord Free Public Library shared insights along with the treasures of the William Munroe Special Collections, and Kimberly Reynolds of the Boston Public Library Rare Books and Manuscripts Division made certain my research missions were successful. Sarah Hutcheon of the Schlesinger Library always had something new to show me, and Karen Kukil of the Sophia Smith Collection at Smith College introduced me to Caroline Sturgis Tappan's artwork. Nina Myatt and Scott Sanders, who against all odds maintain the Antiochiana Collection in Yellow Springs, assisted from afar. My research at the Berg Collection of the New York Public Library was conducted chiefly on Lola Szladitz's watch; Isaac Gewirtz offered aid in recent years.

My work on Margaret Fuller began as a result of a fellowship from the Radcliffe Institute of Advanced Study at Harvard University. I am grateful for the mix of minds in the RIAS class of 2007, particularly for conversations initiated by Jane Kamensky and William McFeely of the Biography Cluster and discussions on historical narrative writing with Katherine Vaz. Drew Gilpin Faust was dean, and her encouragement, as well as that of the Fellowship Program director Judith Vichniac and Nancy Cott, director of the Schlesinger Library, has been crucial. Current dean Lizabeth Cohen and the members of the 40 Concord Group make RIAS a continuing source of intellectual support. My colleagues in the Writing, Literature, and Publishing Department at Emerson College have abetted my interest in Margaret Fuller and Transcendentalism, especially Yu-jin Chang, who translated several German texts; I am grateful for a semester's leave during which I completed many chapters of the book, as well as for a Huret Faculty Development Award, which enabled research in Rome.

My agent, Katinka Matson, made certain this book found a safe home; my editor, Deanne Urmy, provided that home at Houghton Mifflin Harcourt as well as judicious advice at every stage of the project. Susanna Brougham, Larry Cooper, Nicole Angeloro, and Ashley Gilliam, also at HMH, offered invaluable assistance; Emily Bailen McKeage and Deborah Weisgall read the manuscript and supplied meaningful criticism and much-needed reassurance. Abundant thanks to Rebecca Newberger Goldstein, Christine Stansell, Diane McWhorter, Margo Howard, Gail Banks, and Joan Ensor, patient and inspiring friends; more gratitude still to my daughters, Josephine Sedgwick and Sara Sedgwick Brown, for all they teach me every day, and to Scott Harney, first reader and devoted partner.

NOTES

In quotations from primary sources I have retained the original spelling and punctuation, except in some instances where I have altered capitalization at the start of sentences for ease of reading.

ABBREVIATIONS

Names

CS: Caroline Sturgis
GAO: Giovanni Angelo Ossoli
JFC: James Freeman Clarke
MCF: Margarett Crane Fuller
MF: Margaret Fuller
RWE: Ralph Waldo Emerson
TF: Timothy Fuller
WHC: William Henry Channing

Books

CFI: Charles Capper, *Margaret Fuller: An American Romantic Life,* vol. 1, *The Private Years* (New York: Oxford University Press, 1992).

CFII: Charles Capper, *Margaret Fuller: An American Romantic Life,* vol. 2, *The Public Years* (New York: Oxford University Press, 2007).

Dispatches: Margaret Fuller, *"These Sad but Glorious Days": Dispatches from Europe, 1846–1850,* Larry J. Reynolds and Susan Belasco Smith, eds. (New Haven: Yale University Press, 1991).

EL: The Letters of Ralph Waldo Emerson, in ten volumes: vols. 1–6, Ralph L. Rusk, ed.; vols. 7–10, Eleanor M. Tilton, ed. (New York: Columbia University Press, 1939, 1990–95).

FL: The Letters of Margaret Fuller, in six volumes, Robert N. Hudspeth, ed. (Ithaca, N.Y.: Cornell University Press, 1983–94).

JMN: The Journals and Miscellaneous Notebooks of Ralph Waldo Emerson, in sixteen volumes, William H. Gilman et al., eds. (Cambridge: Harvard University Press, 1960–82).

MMM: Meg McGavran Murray, *Margaret Fuller: Wandering Pilgrim* (Athens, Ga.: University of Georgia Press, 2008).

OM: *Memoirs of Margaret Fuller Ossoli,* in two volumes. R. W. Emerson, J. F. Clarke, and
W. H. Channing, eds. (Boston: Phillips, Sampson, 1852).

SOL: Margaret Fuller, *Summer on the Lakes, in 1843,* Susan Belasco Smith, ed. (Urbana and
Chicago: University of Illinois Press, 1991).

VM: Joan Von Mehren, *Minerva and the Muse: A Life of Margaret Fuller* (Amherst: University of Massachusetts Press, 1994).

WNC: Margaret Fuller, *Woman in the Nineteenth Century* (New York: Greeley and McElrath, 1845).

Manuscript Collections

Antiochiana: Robert Lincoln Straker typescript collection of Peabody family papers, An-
tioch College

Berg: Henry W. and Albert A. Berg Collection of English and American Literature, New
York Public Library, Astor, Lenox, and Tilden Foundations

BPL: Rare Books and Manuscripts, Trustees of the Boston Public Library

FMW: Fuller Manuscripts and Works, Houghton Library, Harvard University

MHS: Massachusetts Historical Society

PSR: Swedenborgian House of Studies, Pacific School of Religion

Smith: Sophia Smith Collection, Smith College

PROLOGUE

xv "what is most": WHC, "Papers," BPL, quoted in *CFII,* p. 508.
"Nothing *personal*": MF, "1849 Journal" bMS Am 1086 [4] FMW.

xvi "first acquaintance": Ibid., p. 3.
"The people": Leona Rostenberg, ed., "Margaret Fuller's Roman Diary," *Journal of
Modern History,* vol. 12, no. 2, June 1940, p. 213.
"Monstrous are the treacheries": Ibid., p. 215.
"Rome is barricaded": Ibid., p. 220.
"will not take off": MF, "The Great Lawsuit. Man *versus* Men. Woman *versus*
Women," *Dial,* vol. 4, no. 1, July 1843, p. 30.

xvii a "fore-sayer": *FLIII,* p. 106.
"the great radical dualism": "The Great Lawsuit," p. 43.
"There is no wholly": Ibid.
"a woman whose": Ibid., p. 29.

xviii "fulness of being": Ibid., p. 35.
"history of feeling": *FLVI,* p. 76.
"represent the female": *WNC,* p. 161.

xix "takes rank in society": *FLIV,* p. 256.
"mind that insisted": *FLV,* p. 301.
"life rushes": MF, *Essays on American Life and Letters,* Joel Myerson, ed. (Albany,
N.Y.: NCUP, 1978), p. 379.
"expansive fellowship": *ELIII,* p. 394.
Nathaniel Hawthorne: For an in-depth treatment of the friendship of MF and Na-

thaniel Hawthorne, see Thomas R. Mitchell, *Hawthorne's Fuller Mystery* (Amherst: University of Massachusetts Press, 1998).

"When a writer": Nathaniel Hawthorne, *The House of the Seven Gables,* in *Collected Novels* (New York: Library of America, 1983), p. 351.

xx "we propose": "The Great Lawsuit," p. 10.

"young "lovers": *ELII*, p. 332.

"ardent and onward-looking": *FLIII*, p. 156.

"genius" would be: *FLII*, p. 172.

"From a very": *FLVI*, p. 134.

fifty thousand readers: "half a hundred thousand readers," *FLIV*, p. 56.

"Another century": *Dispatches*, p. 245.

xxi "The scrolls": *FLII*, p. 249.

"a little space": *FLII*, p. 249.

"empowering me": *FLII*, p. 187.

1. THREE LETTERS

5 "dear Father": *FLI*, p. 79, original document fMS Am 1086 [9:1] FMW.

"severe though kind": Quoted in *MMM*, p. 12.

"*original,*" worthy: Quoted in *CFI*, p. 38.

6 "I have learned": *FLI*, p. 81, original document fMS Am 1086 [9:3] FMW.

of her "*stile*": Quoted in *CFI*, p. 50.

"as near perfection": Quoted in *MMM*, p. 21.

"high scholar": *OMI*, p. 14.

"on the stretch": *OMI*, p. 15.

"absolutely no patience": *OMI*, p. 17.

"I do not": *FLI*, p. 81.

"To excel": Quoted in *MMM*, p. 17.

7 "speaks of": *FLI*, p. 81.

"soft, graceful": *OMI*, p. 14.

"severe sweetness": *OMI*, p. 13.

"My first experience": *OMI*, p. 14.

"She who would": *OMI*, p. 14.

"delicate" in health: *OMI*, p. 17.

8 "with loud cries": *OMI*, p. 13.

"I assure": *FLI*, p. 91.

difficult, "opinionative": Quoted in *CFI*, p. 67.

The Deserted Village: FLI, p. 91.

"*profoundly* into": Quoted in *MMM*, p. 21.

"my mother's hand": *OMI*, p. 23.

"flower-like nature": *OMI*, p. 12.

"Do not let": *FLI*, p. 91.

"power to disengage": Quoted in *MMM*, p. 36. Murray's discussion of MF's early reading has been formative to my work, and I refer readers to her chapter "The World of Books," *MMM*, pp. 33–44.

"a new tale": *FLI*, p. 94.
9 "P S I do not like": *FLI*, p. 95.

2. ELLEN KILSHAW

10 signed "Margaret": *FLI*, p. 89.
"first friend": *OMI*, p. 32.
"an English lady": *OMI*, p. 33.
"Elegant and captivating": *OMI*, p. 33.
"comfortable" yet "very ugly": *OMI*, p. 23.
11 "unsavory" soap factory: MF's brother Richard F. Fuller, *Recollections of Richard F. Fuller* (Boston: privately printed, 1936), p. 8.
"child of masculine energy": Martha L. Berg and Alice de V. Perry, eds., "'The Impulses of Human Nature': Margaret Fuller's Journal from June Through October 1844," *Proceedings of the Massachusetts Historical Society,* vol. 102, 1990, p. 115.
"violent bodily exercise": *OMI*, p. 41.
"a habit and a passion": *OMI*, p. 22.
"the girls supposed": *OMI*, p. 41.
"given up": *OMI*, p. 41.
12 presenting a "*mesquin*": *OMI*, p. 23.
"a new apparition": *OMI*, p. 33.
"the river": *FLIII*, p. 81.
"atmosphere of ": *OMI*, p. 41.
"I saw": *OMI*, p. 39.
"face most fair" ... "graceful pliancy": *OMI*, p. 33.
"my first real": *OMI*, p. 34.
"growing beneath": *OMI*, p. 33.
"heralds of ": *OMI*, p. 34.
13 "from a distance": *OMI*, p. 35.
"reserve" ... "self-possession" ... "timidity": *OMI*, p. 33.
"*All* accomplishments": Quoted in *VM*, p. 20.
"the heir of all": *OMI*, p. 14.
14 "no woman dares": Quoted in *MMM*, p. 9.
"so well pleased": Quoted in *VM*, p. 19.
"*delicious* hour[s]": Quoted in *CFI*, p. 14.
"the man looks": *WNC*, p. 59.
15 "piece of good fortune": Quoted in *CFI*, p. 16.
"throbs of ambition": Quoted in *CFI*, p. 17.
"hasty temper": Quoted in *MMM*, p. 11.
"a tyrant": *OMI*, p. 28.
"such an overflowing": Quoted in *CFI*, p. 18.
"*more romantically*": Quoted in *MMM*, p. 18.
"your absent *Lord*": Quoted in *MMM*, p. 24.
"disobedient spouse": Quoted in *MMM*, p. 24.
"wayward" behavior: Quoted in *MMM*, pp. 19–20.
"you in my eye": Quoted in *MMM*, p. 19.

16 "highly cultivated": *OMI*, p. 33.

"so surprising": Quoted in *CFI*, p. 41.

"better than my life": *FLI*, p. 94.

"the lonely child": *OMI*, p. 39.

"the voice": *OMI*, p. 38.

"a region": *OMI*, p. 39.

"shallow and delicate": *OMI*, p. 39.

17 "melancholy": *OMI*, p. 40.

"would not be pacified": *OMI*, p. 40.

"All joy": *OMI*, p. 40.

"In the more": *OMI*, p. 12.

"my *pair* of Ms": Quoted in *MMM*, p. 13.

"effeminate": Quoted in *CFI*, p. 29.

"I am rather": Quoted in *VM*, p. 22.

"she could never": Quoted in *CFI*, p. 54.

18 "Sarah Margarett": Quoted in *MMM*, p. 18.

"a very feasible": *FLI*, p. 115.

"impertinent": Quoted in *VM*, p. 21.

"I see in Sarah M.": Quoted in *VM*, p. 20.

"I have long thought" . . . "I intend": Quoted in *VM*, p. 22.

"to make": Quoted in *MMM*, p. 32.

19 "Whenever I find": Quoted in *CFI*, p. 38.

"how deep": *FLII*, p. 176.

"'Madeira' seemed": *OMI*, p. 36.

3. THEME: "POSSUNT QUIA POSSE VIDENTUR"

20 "They can conquer": I have used Dryden's 1697 translation of line 231 from book five of Virgil's *Aeneid*, the translation MF would have known.

"Theme corrected": bMS Am 1086A, FMW.

"man of business": *OMI*, p. 14.

"demanded accuracy": *OMI*, p. 17.

21 "had no conception": *OMI*, pp. 16–18.

"I thought": *OMI*, p. 22.

"Beauties of Nature": fMS Am 1086 [9] FMW.

22 "too much strength": *OMI*, p. 18.

"loved to conquer": *OMI*, p. 22.

"a victim": *OMI*, pp. 15–16.

23 "came with": Oliver Wendell Holmes, quoted in *CFI*, p. 46.

"a revelation" and further Holmes commentary: Quoted in *CFI*, p. 46; *VM*, p. 18.

"Miss Mary": *FLI*, p. 96.

her "deficiencies": Quoted in *MMM*, p. 48.

"very corpulent": Quoted in *MMM*, p. 48.

24 a "robust" girl: Frederic Henry Hedge, quoted in *CFI*, p. 65.

"polite forms": Quoted in *CFI*, p. 56.

"grown up gentlemen": *FLI*, p. 118.

"display" her "attainments": TF, quoted in *CFI*, p. 63.

"eye of Intelligence": *FLI*, p. 114.

"prodigy of talent": WHC, quoted in *CFI*, p. 60.

"wonderful child": Elizabeth Palmer Peabody, quoted in *MMM*, p. 47.

"had not religion": Elizabeth Palmer Peabody, quoted in *CFI*, p. 60.

25 "I get the card": *FLI*, p. 98.

"defies the god": Quoted in *MMM*, pp. 41–42.

"the dashing misses": Frederic Henry Hedge, quoted in *CFI*, p. 61.

"a sad feeling": WHC, quoted in *CFI*, p. 60.

26 "with indiscriminate": Frederic Henry Hedge, quoted in *CFI*, p. 61.

"rhapsodical intimations": Quoted in *CFI*, p. 58.

"this hopeful": MCF, quoted in *CFI*, p. 65.

"manners and disposition": Quoted in *CFI*, p. 69.

"address" . . . "that he never": *FLI*, p. 121.

"he had never": Quoted in *CFI*, p. 62.

27 "exceedingly agreeable": *FLI*, p. 127.

"*well over*": Quoted in *CFI*, p. 64.

"notoriously unpopular": Quoted in *CFI*, p. 65.

"nobility of blood": *FLI*, p. 89.

"my natural": *FLI*, p. 332.

4. MARIANA

28 red "flush": MF journal c. March 1834 FMW, quoted in *CFI*, p. 65.

"eruption" on Margaret's face: Quoted in *CFI*, p. 65.

"mortified to see": MF journal c. March 1834 FMW, quoted in *CFI*, p. 65.

need for "instruction": Quoted in *CFI*, p. 73.

"an odd and unpleasing": *FLVI*, p. 59.

"much taller": *FLIV*, p. 137.

"too independent": MCF, quoted in *CFI*, p. 66.

"wounded" vanity: MF journal c. March 1834 FMW, quoted in *CFI*, p. 65.

29 "for I should grieve": Quoted in *CFI*, p. 71.

having been "disappointed": Quoted in *CFI*, p. 64.

"cheapen her value": Quoted in *CFI*, p. 66.

"She certainly": Quoted in *CFI*, p. 65.

"I hope you will": *FLI*, p. 132.

"not see you": *FLI*, p. 135.

"judicious country": Quoted in *CFI*, p. 74.

30 "a fair opportunity": Quoted in *CFI*, p. 75.

"Orthography, Reading": Reprinted in Samuel Abbott Green, *Groton Historical Series*, vol. 3, no. 9 (Groton, Mass.: 1893), p. 405; quoted in *CFI*, p. 71.

"I feel myself ": *FLI*, p. 139.

"I did not intend": *FLI*, p. 139.

"those who had": *OMI*, p. 52.

"been unfortunately": The story of Mariana, *SOL*, pp. 51–58. Margaret may have borrowed the name and some personality traits from Goethe's headstrong and histrionic Mariana of *Wilhelm Meister*, a character who, as Margaret once wrote in her journal, liked to "range the orchards as a freebooter, & sit in the boughs of the withered apple tree like Charles 2d in the royal oak." Martha L. Berg and Alice de V. Perry, eds., "'The Impulses of Human Nature': Margaret Fuller's Journal from June Through October 1844," *Proceedings of the Massachusetts Historical Society*, vol. 102, 1990, p. 61.

32 "those sad experiences": *FLI*, p. 160.

33 "I feel the power": *FLI*, p. 151.
   "I am determined": *FLI*, p. 152.
   "a gladiatorial": *FLI*, p. 155.

5. THE YOUNG LADY'S FRIENDS

39 "I expect": *FLI*, p. 150.

40 "translate[d]" through her reading: *FLI*, p. 153.
   "so slow": *FLIII*, p. 105.

41 "one of the most": Thomas Wentworth Higginson, *Margaret Fuller Ossoli* (Boston: Houghton, Mifflin and Co., 1884), p. 27.

42 "a young girl": Ibid., p. 29.
   "feudal hall": *FLI*, p. 153.
   "There is a constant": Elizabeth Palmer Peabody to Maria Chase, May 1821, Peabody Family Papers, Smith.
   "born leader": Anna Parsons, quoted in *CFI*, p. 94.
   "How did she glorify": *OMI*, p. 78.

43 "sarcastic, supercilious": Kate Sanborn, quoted in Joel Myerson, *Fuller in Her Own Time* (Iowa City: University of Iowa Press, 2008), p. xxiii.
   disdain for "mediocrity": *OMI*, p. 64.
   "know as much": *Margaret Fuller Ossoli*, p. 25.
   "Each was": *OMI*, pp. 103–4.
   "never rested": *OMI*, p. 104.
   "be capable": *OMI*, p. 78.
   "should not": *OMI*, p. 64.

44 "marked the very dawn": Thomas Wentworth Higginson, quoted in Deborah Pickman Clifford, *Crusader for Freedom: A Life of Lydia Maria Child* (Boston: Beacon Press, 1992), p. 41.
   "restless insatiable": Ibid., p. 50.
   "harmless arrow": Ibid., p. 53.
   "possessed a large": Ibid., p. 57.
   "honest independence": Ibid., p. 50.

45 "a natural person": *FLI*, p. 154.
   "accidental advantages": Quoted in *CFI*, p. 95.
   "brilliant" de Staël: *FLI*, p. 154.
   "like a butterfly": *Crusader for Freedom*, p. 54.
   "a poor isolated": Ibid., p. 53.

46 "was the beginning": George Curtis, quoted in *Crusader for Freedom*, p. 70.

less "careful": Mrs. John [Eliza Rotch] Farrar, *Recollections of Seventy Years* (Boston: Ticknor and Fields, 1866), p. 171.

47 "an American freedom": Charles Eliot Norton, "Reminiscences of Old Cambridge," *Proceedings of the Cambridge Historical Society*, vol. 1, 1905, p. 17. See also Elizabeth Bancroft Schlesinger, "Two Early Harvard Wives: Eliza Farrar and Eliza Follen," *New England Quarterly*, vol. 38, no. 2, June 1965, pp. 147–67.

"elected" mother: Quoted in *CFI*, p. 97.

"mould her": *Margaret Fuller Ossoli*, p. 36.

48 "the most intolerable": Harriet Martineau, quoted in *Fuller in Her Own Time*, p. xxiii.

become a "gentlewoman": [Eliza Ware Rotch Farrar], *The Young Lady's Friend* (Boston: American Stationers' Company, John B. Russell, 1837), p. 318.

"In no country": Ibid., p. 319.

"dragged round": Ibid., pp. 112–14.

49 "who attend": Ibid., p. 318.

"run, jump": Ibid., p. 325.

"one of the highest": Ibid., pp. 385–86.

50 "the precious": Ibid., pp. 2–3.

6. ELECTIVE AFFINITIES

51 the "brutal" Constantine: *FLI*, p. 152.

"My whole being": *FLI*, p. 164.

"anxious suspense": *FLI*, p. 153.

"powerful eye" . . . "imposing maniere": *FLII*, p. 154.

"inclined to idealize": *FLIII*, p. 156.

52 "truly myself": *FLVI*, p. 234.

"like a plaything": John Wesley Thomas, ed., *The Letters of James Freeman Clarke to Margaret Fuller* (Hamburg: Cram, de Gruyter, 1957), p. 97.

"Her mind": *WNC*, p. 29.

"intellectual abandon": JFC, quoted in *CFI*, p. 102.

"pull people": Sarah Clarke, quoted in *CFI*, p. 103.

"gladiatorial disposition": *FLI*, p. 155.

"contempt for": *OMI*, p. 104.

"aching wish": *FLI*, p. 155.

"communicate more": *FLVI*, p. 272.

"so open" . . . "intimacy": *FLVI*, p. 234.

53 souls to be "conjugal": *FLVI*, p. 134.

"brilliant vivacity": *FLVI*, pp. 160, 159.

"I have determined": *FLI*, pp. 158–59.

"When disappointed": *FLI*, p. 159.

54 whose "pride": *FLI*, p. 158.

declared himself "satisfied": *FLVI*, pp. 161–62.

"Ah weakness": *SOL*, pp. 59, 58.

"insincerity and heartlessness": *FLVI*, p. 102.

"Thoughts he had": *SOL*, pp. 59–60.

55 If "separation" was possible: *FLI*, p. 347.
"given" to her: *FLIII*, p. 197.
"my child": *FLII*, p. 187.
"while night": *FLII*, p. 187.
"thirty-seven degrees": *FLI*, p. 161.
"answering store": *FLI*, pp. 162–63.

56 "pleasure . . . of finding": *FLVI*, p. 134.

57 "It seems": *FLI*, p. 177.
"extraordinary, generous": *OMI*, pp. 59, 64.
Elective Affinities: FLI, p. 174.

58 "E." should "suffice": *FLVI*, p. 166.
"loved and loving": *Letters of James Freeman Clarke to Margaret Fuller*, p. 17.
"the Elizabeth affair": *FLVI*, p. 166.
"What you have felt": *FLVI*, p. 172.
"fair Elschen": *Letters of James Freeman Clarke to Margaret Fuller*, p. 9.
"I looked upon": *FLVI*, p. 179.

59 "cross mouth": Quoted in *CFI*, p. 106.
"bitter months": *FLI*, p. 347.
"my nerves": MF journal, quoted in *CFI*, p. 112.

60 entering "prison": *OMI*, p. 135.
"a great burden": *FLI*, p. 347.
"the only person": *FLI*, p. 174.
"there is no": Quoted in *CFI*, p. 112.

61 "more sweet": *FLI*, p. 170.
"divinest love": *FLII*, p. 93.
"the same love": MF journal, quoted in *CFI*, p. 281.
"how she idolizes": *Letters of James Freeman Clarke to Margaret Fuller*, p. 112.
"I loved Anna": MF journal, quoted in *CFI*, p. 281.
"sympathies most wide": Quoted in *CFI*, p. 117.
"consciousness" of her abilities: Quoted in *VM*, p. 45.
"what is the effect": Quoted in *CFI*, p. 117.

62 "men never": *WNC*, p. 30. The quotation begins "But early I perceived that men never . . ."
"full of self": Quoted in *CFI*, p. 116.
"her kind": Quoted in *CFI*, p. 118.
"you are destined": *Letters of James Freeman Clarke to Margaret Fuller*, p. 35.
"should think me fit": *FLVI*, p. 195.

63 "I felt as I have so often": *FLVI*, p. 250.
"She has nothing": Quoted in *CFI*, p. 117.
"sphere of duty": Quoted in *CFI*, p. 118.

64 "from a very": *FLVI*, p. 134.
"more extended": *FLI*, p. 347.
that "self-dependence": *WNC*, p. 28.
"pilgrim and sojourner": *FLVI*, p. 134.
"not as a plaything": *WNC*, p. 27.
"conform to an object": *SOL*, p. 151.

"always suffered much": Thanksgiving Day narrative, *OMI*, pp. 139–42.
65 "communion with": *FLI*, p. 347.
"epoch of pride" . . . "haughty": *FLII*, p. 154.

7. "MY HEART HAS NO PROPER HOME"

71 "too tamely": *FLIII*, p. 85.
"neither beautiful": *FLVI*, p. 213.
"characters" . . . "amusing": *FLI*, p. 190.
"where there is never": *FLI*, p. 178.
"This is the first": *FLI*, p. 198.
72 "a sweet youth": *FLVI*, p. 212.
"collisions," Margaret called: *FLIII*, p. 85.
73 "in a dark room": *FLI*, p. 180.
"I greeted": *FLI*, p. 180.
"*only* grown-up daughter": *FLI*, p. 201.
"sitting-still occupations": *FLVI*, p. 212.
"My fingers": *FLVI*, pp. 215–16.
"domestic tyrant": MF, "Lives of the Great Composers," *Dial*, vol. 2, no. 2, October 1841, p. 178.
"hardening" labor: Richard Fuller, quoted in *CFI*, p. 122.
74 the spot "Hazel-grove": *OMI*, p. 154.
"I used to look": *OMI*, p. 170.
"ill-judged exchange": *FLIII*, p. 85.
"some might sneer": *FLVI*, p. 274.
75 "seems to have": *FLI*, p. 201.
"entirely absorbed": *FLVI*, p. 245.
"half so friendly": *FLI*, p. 88.
"oercloud" . . . "brought me": *FLVI*, p. 206.
"wild and free": *FLVI*, p. 210.
"I am not a nun": *FLVI*, p. 206.
"How free": John Wesley Thomas, ed., *The Letters of James Freeman Clarke to Margaret Fuller* (Hamburg: Cram, de Gruyter, 1957), p. 43.
"Whatsoever thy hand": Quoted in Paula Blanchard, *Margaret Fuller: From Transcendentalism to Revolution* (Reading, Mass.: Addison-Wesley, 1978), p. 81.
76 "The wor[ld] receives": *FLVI*, p. 210.
"engrossing object": *FLVI*, p. 216.
"compress all": *FLVI*, p. 210.
"thrilling at the heart": *Letters of James Freeman Clarke to Margaret Fuller*, p. 58.
"Why was she a woman?": Quoted in *CFI*, p. 117.
"Fair, pure" . . . "my sweet" . . . "best, truest": *Letters of James Freeman Clarke to Margaret Fuller*, pp. 52, 27, 58.
"Your manner": *FLVI*, p. 210.
"disappointed and tortured": *FLVI*, p. 208.
"prepared" to see: *FLVI*, p. 209.

"the breaking up": *FLVI*, p. 209.

77 "you are gone": *FLVI*, pp. 209–10.
"Margaret Good child": *FLVI*, p. 232.
"no sphere": Quoted in *CFI*, p. 117.
"I feel as if ": *FLVI*, p. 210.
"You envy": *Letters of James Freeman Clarke to Margaret Fuller*, p. 77.
"Now that I have": *FLVI*, pp. 210–11.
"there is no escaping": *FLVI*, p. 215.

78 "my heart has no": *FLVI*, p. 223.
"lay on the shelf ": *FLI*, p. 202.
"*icy* seclusion": *FLI*, p. 195.
"I rejoice": *FLVI*, p. 130.
"my Father has not": *FLVI*, p. 232.
"try my hand": *FLI*, p. 202.
"ten-thousand, thousand": *FLI*, p. 196.
"is peculiarly home-sickness": *FLI*, p. 182.

79 Writing from a biblical: *FLVI*, p. 234.
"could only write": *FLVI*, p. 243.
connection of Eliza Farrar's: *VM*, p. 57.
"walk into the Boston": *FLVI*, p. 260.
"onward spirit": *FLVI*, p. 252.
"to feed" . . . "Was I not": *FLVI*, p. 232.

80 "Earning *money*": *FLVI*, pp. 251–52.
"I am more": *FLI*, p. 209.
"coolness of judgement": Quoted in *FLI*, p. 228n.
"ROME! it stands": *OMI*, p. 19.
"mild in his temper": MF, "Brutus," *Boston Daily Advertiser and Patriot*, November 27, 1834.

81 "My father requested": *FLI*, p. 226.
"to lose this object": "Brutus."
"ability" as a writer: *FLI*, p. 226.

82 "topics of religion": *Letters of James Freeman Clarke to Margaret Fuller*, p. 88.
"Don't be afraid": Ibid., p. 91.
"most brilliant circle": Quoted in *VM*, p. 66.
"the ideal": Quoted in *CFI*, p. 149.
"no matter how severe": *FLVI*, p. 258.
"We feel like an explorer": *Letters of James Freeman Clarke to Margaret Fuller*, pp. 94–95.
"one [who] has": *FLVI*, p. 258.

83 "This going into": *FLI*, p. 223.
"the art of writing": *FLVI*, p. 257.
"My grand object": *FLVI*, p. 258.
"die and leave": *FLVI*, p. 254.
"common-place people": *FLVI*, p. 242.
"I am not yet *intimate*": *FLI*, p. 190.
"consent" to the time off: *FLI*, p. 230.

84 "romantic rocks": *FLI*, p. 232.
"gorgeous" . . . "immense" . . . "dropped": *FLI*, p. 233.
"dressed dolls": *FLI*, p. 217.
"see her": *FLVI*, p. 265.
"I was to him": *FLVI*, p. 267.
85 "has what I want": Quoted in *CFI*, p. 155.
"all the most": Elizabeth Palmer Peabody to Mary Tyler Peabody, [January 31, 1835], Berg.
"that only clergyman": *FLI*, p. 210.
"of any American": MF to Elizabeth Palmer Peabody, Groton, February 3, 1836, in "Biography of Elizabeth Palmer Peabody" [manuscript draft] by Mary Van Wyck Church, p. 298, MHS.
86 "the reverend": *FLVI*, p. 266.
"of character and manners": *FLI*, p. 225.
"restless desire": *FLI*, p. 223.
"write a novel": *FLVI*, p. 261.
"the most gentle": *FLVI*, p. 251.
87 "My dear": Quoted in *VM*, p. 71.

8. "RETURNED INTO LIFE"

89 "worn to a shadow" . . . "orphan" . . . "awful calm": *OMI*, pp. 155–56.
"the lifeless": Thomas Wentworth Higginson, *Margaret Fuller Ossoli* (Boston: Houghton, Mifflin and Co., 1884), p. 54.
"returned into life": *FLI*, p. 244.
"My father's image": *OMI*, p. 156.
90 "I have often": *FLI*, p. 237.
"a more heedful ear": *FLI*, p. 239.
"make things": *FLI*, p. 237.
91 "my boys": *FLI*, p. 231.
"become more tenderly": *FLVI*, p. 271.
"Art is Nature": Quoted in *CFI*, p. 150.
"write a *Life*": *FLVI*, p. 260.
92 "I should like": John Wesley Thomas, ed., *The Letters of James Freeman Clarke to Margaret Fuller* (Hamburg: Cram, de Gruyter, 1957), p. 94.
"She thinks the time": *FLVI*, p. 272.
"the first winter": *FLII*, p. 168.
"to tear my heart": *FLI*, p. 247.
"some isle": Jeffrey Steele, ed., *The Essential Margaret Fuller* (New Brunswick, N.J.: Rutgers University Press, 1992), p. 1.
"masculine traits": Ibid., p. 7.
"When with soft eyes": Ibid., p. 2.
93 "full of poverty": *FLII*, p. 168.
"the silent room": *FLII*, p. 168.
94 "an ascetic life": *FLII*, p. 168.
"bareness, her pure shroud": *FLII*, p. 169.

"to forget myself": *FLI*, p. 254.

"ask no more": *FLII*, p. 169.

"I *was* called": *FLI*, p. 244.

"a tower": Quoted in *CFI*, p. 166.

"happy sort": The story is recounted in "Death in Life," *OMI*, pp. 162–64.

96 "What I can do": *FLI*, p. 254.

"get money": *FLI*, p. 254.

"spiritual philosophy": MF, quoted in *CFI*, p. 198.

97 "cultivate the heart": Elizabeth Palmer Peabody to Love Rawlins Pickman, Thursday evening [July 1835], *Horace Mann Collection*, microfilm edition, 40 reels (Boston: MHS, 1989), reel 4.

"the advantage": Elizabeth Palmer Peabody, *Record of a School, Exemplifying the General Principles of Spiritual Culture* (Boston: James Munroe, 1835), pp. 62–63.

"I had seen the Universe": Elizabeth Palmer Peabody, "Miss Peabody's Reminiscences of Margaret's Married Life," *Boston Evening Transcript*, June 10, 1885. I am grateful to Mary De Jong for sharing her discovery of this important article.

"the pilot-minds": Quoted in *CFI*, pp. 178–79.

"mind-emotions": Quoted in *CFI*, p. 177.

"I would gladly": *FLVI*, p. 274.

98 "liberal communion": *FLIV*, p. 192.

"I believe we all": *ELII*, pp. 46–47.

"assuage grief's": MF, "LINES—On the Death of C.C.E.," *Daily Centinel and Gazette*, vol. 1, no. 32, May 17, 1836.

"little book": *FLII*, p. 128. In this letter to RWE of April 12, 1840, MF recalls that she never read *Nature* in book form because RWE had read it aloud to her. The book was in print by the time of her next long stay in the spring of 1837.

"We like her": Dolores Bird Carpenter, ed., *The Selected Letters of Lidian Jackson Emerson* (Columbia: University of Missouri Press, 1987), p. 49.

"like being set": *ELII*, p. 32.

99 even "question[ing]" them: Mary Tyler Peabody to Elizabeth Palmer Peabody, letter beginning "I did not get . . . ," n.d. [1836], *Horace Mann Collection*, microfilm edition, 40 reels (Boston: MHS, 1989), reel 4.

"more liberal": Quoted in *CFI*, p. 197.

the Unitarian "Pope": Theodore Parker, quoted in Wesley T. Mott, ed., *Biographical Dictionary of Transcendentalism* (Westport, Conn.: Greenwood Press, 1996), p. 186.

100 managed to "offend": *ELI*, p. 450.

"magnetic power" . . . "sympathy and time": *FLVI*, p. 261.

101 "Whoever would preach": Elizabeth Palmer Peabody, "Emerson as Preacher," in F. B. Sanborn, ed., *The Genius and Character of Emerson: Lectures at the Concord School of Philosophy* (Port Washington, N.Y.: Kennikat Press, 1971, reprint of 1885 edition), p. 161.

"greatly pained": *FLVI*, p. 287.

"forget what": Quoted in *CFI*, p. 195.

102 "Margaret alone": *FLI*, p. 95.

"born with knives": RWE, "Historic Notes of Life and Letters in New England," *Lectures and Biographical Sketches* (Boston: Houghton, Mifflin and Co., 1886), p. 311.

"vicious in": Quoted in Bruce Ronda, ed., *The Letters of Elizabeth Palmer Peabody* (Middletown, Conn.: Wesleyan University Press, 1984), p. 245.

"the only book": *ELVII*, p. 245.

103 "one third": Quoted in *CFI*, p. 198.

"an ignorant": Quoted in Madelon Bedell, *The Alcotts: Biography of a Family* (New York: Clarkson N. Potter, 1980), p. 131.

"more indecent": Joseph T. Buckingham, review in the *Boston Courier*, quoted in *CFI*, p. 198.

"one-sided": Quoted in *CFI*, p. 198.

"star of purest": *FLI*, p. 265.

"lost in abstractions": *OMI*, p. 172.

9. "BRINGING MY OPINIONS TO THE TEST"

105 "Here is the hostile": *FLI*, pp. 286–87.

"It is but a bad": *FLVI*, p. 293.

106 "too young": *FLIII*, p. 226.

"faded frocks" . . . "Now that": *FLI*, p. 258.

"vegetate" . . . "sunny kindness": *FLI*, p. 272.

"had a grand": *FLI*, p. 285.

"as soon as you can": *ELII*, p. 35.

"poppy & oatmeal": *ELII*, p. 37.

esteemed her "holiness": *FLI*, p. 328.

"We lead a life": *ELII*, p. 41.

"I am sure": *FLI*, p. 269.

privately "schooling" herself: *FLI*, p. 272.

107 "the excitement": *FLI*, p. 272.

Waldo's "Compensation": *FLI*, p. 285.

108 "learning geology": "Address on Education," in Stephen E. Whicher, Robert E. Spiller, and Wallace E. Williams, eds., *The Early Lectures of Ralph Waldo Emerson*, vol. 2, 1836–1838 (Cambridge: Belknap Press of Harvard University Press, 1964), pp. 195–96.

"Concord, dear Concord": *FLI*, p. 283.

"These black times": *ELII*, p. 77.

"peculiar aspects": "Address on Education," pp. 195–97.

"The disease": Ibid., p. 196.

"capital secret": Ibid., p. 202.

"teach self-trust": Ibid., p. 199.

"Amid the swarming": Ibid., p. 196.

"*Man Thinking*": Ralph Waldo Emerson, "The American Scholar," *Essays and Lectures* (New York: Library of America, 1983), p. 54.

109 "willing to communicate": Laraine R. Fergensen, "Margaret Fuller in the Classroom: The Providence Period," *Studies in the American Renaissance*, 1987 (Charlottesville: University Press of Virginia), p. 138.

"I believe I do": *FLI*, p. 292.

"There is room": *FLI*, p. 288.

"hearts are right": *FLI*, p. 292.

"absolutely torpid": To Bronson Alcott, *FLI*, p. 287.

"this experience": *FLI*, p. 292.

110 "antipathy" to worms: Laraine R. Fergensen, "Margaret Fuller as a Teacher in Providence: The School Journal of Ann Brown," *Studies in the American Renaissance*, 1991 (Charlottesville: University Press of Virginia), p. 70.

"spoke upon": Mary Ware Allen, quoted in *VM*, p. 102.

"wished to live": "Margaret Fuller as a Teacher," p. 102.

Daphne, Aspasia, Sappho: Judith Strong Albert, "Margaret Fuller's Row at the Greene Street School: Early Female Education in Providence, 1837–1839," *Rhode Island History*, vol. 42, May 1983, p. 46.

"Lament of Mary": "Margaret Fuller as a Teacher," p. 70.

Princess Victoria's ascension: Ibid., pp. 67–68.

"How and when": Mark Shuffleton, "Margaret Fuller at the Greene Street School: The Journal of Evelina Metcalf," *Studies in the American Renaissance*, 1985 (Charlottesville: University Press of Virginia), p. 39.

"I wish": Anna Gale, quoted in *CFI*, p. 230.

111 "serve two masters": *FLI*, p. 327.

"barbarous ignorance": Quoted in Bell Gale Chevigny, *The Woman and the Myth: Margaret Fuller's Life and Writings* (Old Westbury, N.Y.: The Feminist Press, 1976), p. 174.

"miserably prepared": *FLI*, p. 292.

"satirical" . . . "I often" . . . "too rough" . . . "I dare": "Margaret Fuller in the Classroom," pp. 134–35.

"we must *think*": Quoted in *CFI*, p. 231.

message of "self-trust": "The American Scholar," pp. 53–71 *passim*.

112 Emerson's "sermons": *OMI*, p. 195.

"Who would be": *JMNV*, p. 407.

"what is any": *ELII*, p. 82.

"*O my friends*": *FLI*, pp. 294–95.

"Mr. Hedge's Club": *ELII*, p. 95.

club of the "Like-Minded": JFC, quoted in *CFI*, p. 182.

113 "all-day party": Dolores Bird Carpenter, ed., *The Selected Letters of Lidian Jackson Emerson* (Columbia: University of Missouri Press, 1987), p. 59.

"the progress": Tess Hoffman, "Miss Fuller Among the Literary Lions: Two Essays Read at 'The Coliseum' in 1838," *Studies in the American Renaissance*, 1988 (Charlottesville: University Press of Virginia), p. 45.

"who knows": *ELII*, p. 95.

plying the "Spiritualists": *Selected Letters of Lidian Jackson Emerson*, p. 59.

114 "incompleteness" in the reasoning: "Miss Fuller Among the Literary Lions," p. 51.

"immense wants": Ibid., p. 46.

"a woman may": Ibid., p. 50.

"marriage, mantua-making": *FLVI*, p. 279.

"Too bright": "Miss Fuller Among the Literary Lions," p. 50.

"the idea": Ibid.

115 "I feel": *FLI*, p. 302.

"I grow": *FLI*, p. 325.

"school for": *FLI*, p. 322.

"those who would reform": *FLI*, p. 287.

"This was just": *FLI*, pp. 322–23.

"there were no": *FLI*, p. 304.

116 "It is no longer": *FLI*, p. 316.

"I *must* leave": *FLI*, p. 295.

"Holiness" and "Heroism": *FLI*, pp. 327–28.

"all the scandal" . . . "a poor": *FLI*, p. 293.

117 "You must not": *FLI*, p. 318.

she'd been expelled: *FLII*, p. 149.

"As to transcendentalism": *FLI*, pp. 314–15.

118 "nothing striped": *FLI*, p. 311.

"the heroic element": *FLII*, p. 41.

"I keep on": *FLI*, p. 327.

"three precious": *FLI*, p. 320.

"two years": *FLI*, p. 349.

"that I may": *FLI*, p. 320.

"There is a beauty": *FLI*, p. 331.

"devote to writing": *FLI*, p. 349.

"Its superior tone": *ELII*, p. 135.

119 "it is regal": *FLI*, p. 332.

"We are the children": "Margaret Fuller as a Teacher," p. 91.

"those means": *FLI*, p. 327.

"gabbled and simpered": *FLI*, p. 351.

any "May-gales": "Margaret Fuller as a Teacher," p. 90.

"eat up": *ELII*, p. 143.

"as handsome": *ELII*, p. 135.

"I am better": *FLI*, p. 328.

"It seems": *ELII*, p. 168. This passage may have been the germ of Emerson's well-known statement "Men descend to meet," in his essay "The Over-Soul." *Essays and Lectures*, p. 391.

120 "persons except": *ELII*, p. 129.

"Devoutly" . . . "Always": *FLI*, pp. 328, 337.

"For a hermit": *ELII*, p. 143.

"Will you commission": *ELII*, p. 169.

121 "I heard": *FLI*, p. 352.

"a new young man": *FLI*, pp. 341–42.

"full of affection": *FLI*, p. 342.

"elegantly bound": "Margaret Fuller at the Greene Street School," p. 45.

"vestal solitudes": *FLI*, p. 351.

"I do not wish": *FLI*, pp. 353–55 *passim*.

10. "WHAT WERE WE BORN TO DO?"

127 "all the value": *FLVI*, p. 312.

"pitiful" and "clumsy": *FLI*, p. 300.

"Lines" ... "F": "LINES–On the Death of C.C.E.," *Daily Centinel and Gazette*, vol. 1, no. 32, May 17, 1836.

128 "huntsman's dart": From "Eagles and Doves," in John Sullivan Dwight, ed., *Select Minor Poems, Translated from the German of Goethe and Schiller* (Boston: Hilliard, Gray, and Co., 1839), pp. 104–5.

"To a Golden Heart": Ibid., p. 31.

129 "there is reason": Ibid., p. xv.

"in course": Ibid.

"lying in heaps": *FLVI*, p. 309.

"monologue" by Goethe: MF translation, *Conversations with Goethe in the Last Years of His Life, Translated from the German of Eckermann* (Boston: J. Munroe, 1839), p. viii.

"He knew both": Ibid., p. xx.

"it was all tea": *FLVI*, p. 309.

"hackneyed moral": *FLII*, p. 56.

130 "the disorders": *FLIII*, p. 85.

"is the natural": MF, "The Great Lawsuit. Man *versus* Men. Woman *versus* Women," *Dial*, vol. 4, no. 1, July 1843, p. 35.

"as if an intellectual": *FLII*, p. 32.

"a brilliant": *ELII*, pp. 202–3.

"daunts & chills": *ELII*, p. 197.

131 "ransom more time": *FLIII*, p. 198.

"speed the pen": *ELII*, p. 203.

threw herself "unremittingly": Robert N. Hudspeth, "Margaret Fuller's 1839 Journal: Trip to Bristol," *Harvard Library Bulletin*, vol. 27, 1979, p. 454.

begun negotiations: *FLII*, pp. 113–14.

practice of billing: *FLI*, p. 350.

"the richest": "Margaret Fuller's 1839 Journal," p. 456.

"ill stocked" library: Ibid., p. 457.

"destitute of all": Ibid., p. 464.

132 "live wire": Quoted in *CFI*, p. 271.

"unsustained" and "uncertain": "Margaret Fuller's 1839 Journal," p. 464.

"fine houses": *FLIII*, p. 69.

"A man's ambition": Quoted in *VM*, p. 114.

"Ministry of Talking": *VM*, p. 114.

"circle" of women: *FLII*, p. 87.

133 "great instincts": Nancy Craig Simmons, "Margaret Fuller's Boston Conversations: The 1839–1840 Series," *Studies in the American Renaissance*, 1994 (Charlottesville: University Press of Virginia), p. 204.

"These Greeks": *FLII*, p. 40.

134 German Romantic "mythomania": Marie Cleary, "Margaret Fuller and Her Timeless Friends," in Gregory A. Staley, ed., *American Women and Classical Myths* (Waco, Tex.: Baylor University Press, 2009), p. 46.

"state their doubts": *FLII*, p. 86.

"willing to communicate": Laraine R. Fergensen, "Margaret Fuller in the Classroom: The Providence Period," *Studies in the American Renaissance*, 1987 (Charlottesville: University Press of Virginia), p. 138.

"an age of consciousness": *OMI*, p. 186.

"era of experiment": *FLIII*, p. 120.

of "illumination": *FLIII*, p. 55.

"undefended by rouge": *FLII*, p. 88.

"digressing into personalities": *FLII*, p. 86.

"simple & clear": "Margaret Fuller's Boston Conversations," p. 203.

"learn by blundering": *FLII*, p. 88.

"to question" . . . "a precision": *FLII*, pp. 88, 87.

most women felt "*inferior*": "Margaret Fuller's Boston Conversations," p. 203.

"few inducements": *FLII*, p. 87. For a discussion of young ladies' academies, many of which provided a more thorough education than MF realized, see Mary Kelley, *Learning to Stand and Speak: Women, Education, and Public Life in America's Republic* (Chapel Hill: University of North Carolina Press, 2006).

"that practical" . . . "application": "Margaret Fuller's Boston Conversations," p. 203.

"magic about me": *FLII*, p. 175.

135 rate of pay: *CFI*, p. 293.

"the most entertaining": *OMI*, p. 308.

"finished and true": *OMI*, p. 95.

136 "a kind of infidel": Sarah Clarke, quoted in *CFI*, p. 293.

"dreaded" the feeling: *FLII*, p. 97.

"nucleus of conversation": "Margaret Fuller's Boston Conversations," p. 203.

"the real trial": *FLII*, p. 98.

"playful as well as deep": "Margaret Fuller's Boston Conversations," p. 204.

137 "the embodiment": Undated manuscript [ca. fall 1839], "Comments on Margaret Fuller's Conversations, in hand of Miss Mary Peabody," Robert Lincoln Straker typescripts, pp. 1313–14, Antiochiana.

"not as the Goddess": Ibid.

"set forth": Ibid.

"Why was it" . . . "What do": "Margaret Fuller's Boston Conversations," p. 207.

138 "was inevitable": "Comments on Margaret Fuller's Conversations."

"credulous simplicity" . . . "Many questions": "Margaret Fuller's Boston Conversations," pp. 207, 208.

"wisdom" . . . "the conversation": Ibid., pp. 208, 209.

"rather little": Ibid., p. 210.

"kept clinging": *FLII*, p. 97.

"seeking out": "Comments on Margaret Fuller's Conversations."

139 "what was the distinction": "Margaret Fuller's Boston Conversations," p. 214.

"women were instinctive": Ibid., pp. 214–15.

"*feminine* or receptive": Joel Myerson, *The New England Transcendentalists and The Dial* (Cranbury, N.J.: Associated University Presses, 1980), p. 21.

"repressing or subduing": "Margaret Fuller's Boston Conversations," p. 215, italics added for readability.

"something higher": Ibid., p. 214.

140 "want of isolation": Ibid., pp. 215–16.

"Let men": Ibid., p. 216.

141 "passionate wish": *OMI*, p. 215.

"There I have": *FLII*, p. 118.

11. "THE GOSPEL OF TRANSCENDENTALISM"

142 "It is true": *FLVI*, p. 314.

"any other record": *FLVI*, p. 310.

"wise mind": MF, *Life Without and Life Within; or, Reviews, Narratives, Essays, and Poems*, Arthur B. Fuller, ed. (New York: The Tribune Association, 1869), p. 31.

143 "I shall love": *FLVI*, p. 315.

"all sorts of": John Wesley Thomas, ed., *The Letters of James Freeman Clarke to Margaret Fuller* (Hamburg: Cram, de Gruyter, 1957), p. 91.

144 "enlist all": Henry Hedge, quoted in *VM*, p. 64.

"speak truth": RWE, quoted in Joel Myerson, *The New England Transcendentalists and* The Dial (Cranbury, N.J.: Associated University Presses, 1980), p. 31.

"dreamy, mystical": Ibid., p. 26.

"obey thyself": RWE, "An Address Delivered Before the Senior Class in Divinity College, Cambridge, Sunday Evening, July 15, 1838," *Essays and Lectures* (New York: Library of America, 1983), pp. 81, 79, 76, 92.

"nature itself": "Abner Kneeland," *Dictionary of UUA Biography*, www25.uua.org/uuhs/duub/.

"the famine": "An Address Delivered Before the Senior Class in Divinity College," p. 84.

145 "incoherent rhapsody": Robert D. Richardson Jr., *Emerson: The Mind on Fire* (Berkeley: University of California Press, 1995), p. 299.

"As long as all": Ibid., p. 300.

"They call it": Ibid., p. 292.

"I begin": *ELII*, pp. 168–69.

"If utterance": "An Address Delivered Before the Senior Class in Divinity College," p. 83.

"Never forget": *Family School*, vol. 1, no. 2, p. 20.

146 "the snore": *New England Transcendentalists and* The Dial, p. 34.

"There will be": Ibid., p. 30.

"entire freedom": Ibid., p. 38.

"we of the sublunary": Ibid., p. 44.

"A perfectly free": *FLII*, p. 126.

"afternoon and evening": *New England Transcendentalists and* The Dial, p. 38.

147 "unemployed force": *FLII*, p. 126.

"you prophecied": *FLII*, p. 111.

"wish it to be": *ELII*, p. 243.

"looking for the gospel": *FLII*, p. 131.

"My position": *FLII*, p. 109.

148 "small minority": *FLII*, pp. 108–10.

"the public": *FLII*, p. 131.

"everlasting yes": MF, "Lives of the Great Composers," in *Art, Literature, and the Drama* (New York: The Tribune Association, 1869), p. 283.

149 "intolerable that there": *New England Transcendentalists and* The Dial, p. 31.

"literary lions": Thomas L. Woodson, Neal Smith, and Norman Holmes Pearson, eds., *The Letters, 1813–1843: Centenary Edition of the Works of Nathaniel Hawthorne*, vol. 15 (Columbus: Ohio State University Press, 1984), p. 382.

the couple had "feasted": Sophia Peabody to her brother George Peabody, May 21, 1839, Berg.

"measuring no hours": "The Editors to the Reader," *Dial*, vol. 1, no. 1, July 1840, p. 4.

"*a little beyond*": *New England Transcendentalists and* The Dial, p. 26.

"gladly contribute": *ELII*, p. 229.

"your labors": *ELII*, p. 243.

"this flowing": *ELII*, p. 234.

150 "We have nothing": *ELII*, pp. 285–87 *passim*.

"those parts": *FLII*, p. 132.

"Every body": Entry of April 17, "Notebook for 1840," FMW.

"these gentlemen": *JMNXI*, p. 471.

second American "revolution": "The Editors to the Reader," pp. 2–4 *passim*.

151 "A Short Essay on Critics": *Dial*, vol. 1, no. 1, July 1840, pp. 5–11.

"power & skill": *ELII*, p. 281.

"the laws": "A Short Essay on Critics," p. 5. Margaret also worked to establish standards of criticism for musical performance in her *Dial* writings and later reviews for the *New-York Tribune*. See Megan Marshall, "Music's 'Everlasting Yes': A Romantic Critic in the Romantic Era," in *Margaret Fuller and Her Circles*, Brigitte Bailey, Katheryn Viens, and Conrad E. Wright, eds. (Lebanon, N.H.: University Press of New England, 2013), pp. 148–60, 277–79.

"critics are poets": Ibid., p. 7.

"He will teach": Ibid., p. 11.

152 "In books": Ibid., p. 10.

"I know": *FLII*, pp. 124–25.

"Nature is ever": "A Short Essay on Critics," p. 10.

153 "in an unpoetical": "A Record of Impressions Produced by the Exhibition of Mr. Allston's Pictures in the Summer of 1839," *Dial*, vol. 1, no. 1, July 1840, p. 74.

"When I look": *FLII*, p. 127.

"adapt myself": *FLII*, p. 125.

"We shall write": *FLII*, p. 126.

"urge on": *FLII*, p. 131.

"a large": *FLIII*, p. 39.

"my protestor": Quoted in *Emerson: The Mind on Fire*, p. 309.

154 "The Problem": *Dial*, vol. 1, no. 1, July 1840, p. 122.

a sonnet she'd written: "To W. Allston, on Seeing His 'Bride,'" *Dial*, vol. 1, no. 1, July 1840, pp. 83–84.

"a type" . . . "Woman's heaven": *FLII*, p. 166. MF explains her intended meaning of the sonnet to WHC in this letter of October 19, 1840. "Where Thought": "To W. Allston," p. 84.

"Orphic Sayings": *Dial*, vol. 1, no. 1, July 1840, pp. 85–98.

155 "you will not": *ELII*, p. 294.

"quite grand": *FLII*, p. 135.

"in a new spirit": *ELII*, p. 313.

"O queen": *ELII*, p. 316.

"pleading . . . affinity": "Orphic Sayings," p. 85.

"infidelity in its higher": Critical responses quoted in *New England Transcendentalists and* The Dial, p. 51.

prized "imagination": Ibid., pp. 51–52.

156 "one of the most": Ibid., p. 51.

managed to "explode": *ELII*, p. 305.

"Our community": Quoted in *New England Transcendentalists and* The Dial, p. 53.

"the word *Dial*": *ELII*, p. 311.

"honest, great": *Dial*, vol. 1, no. 2, October 1840, p. 227.

"I think when": *FLII*, p. 152.

157 "deserve greater": *Dial*, vol. 1, no. 2, October 1840, pp. 260–61. One of the two paintings by Sarah Clarke, *Kentucky Beech Forest*, remains in the Boston Athenaeum's collections.

"the task": *FLII*, p. 175.

"peace": *FLII*, p. 181.

"better and perhaps": Quoted in *New England Transcendentalists and* The Dial, p. 59.

"truly interested": *FLII*, p. 182.

158 "all that is lovely": *Günderode* (Boston: E. P. Peabody, 1842), p. x.

suicide of the older: The events leading up to Karoline's death, including Bettine's attempt to distract her from heartbreak with the attentions of a "young French Officer of Hussars," are recounted in *Goethe's Correspondence with a Child* (London: Longman, Orme, Brown, Green, and Longmans, 1839), vol. 1, pp. 98–122.

"a prophet": "Menzel's View of Goethe," *Dial*, vol. 1, no. 3, January 1841, pp. 340–47.

159 "rich in thoughts": *FLII*, p. 185.

"A man's idea": *Dial*, vol. 1, no. 3, January 1841, p. 357.

"exponent of Literary Liberty": Critical response quoted in *New England Transcendentalists and* The Dial, p. 62.

"most original": Theodore Parker, "German Literature," *Dial*, vol. 1, no. 3, January 1841, p. 320.

"No one of all": *Dial*, vol. 1, no. 3, January 1841, p. 405.

essay titled "Woman": *Dial*, vol. 1, no. 3, January 1841, pp. 362–66.

160 "not like a botanist": *FLII*, pp. 165–66.

"singing to herself": MF, "The Magnolia of Lake Pontchartrain," *Dial*, vol. 1, no. 3, January 1841, pp. 299–305.

161 "I cannot": *FLII*, p. 167.

"prize the monitions": "The Magnolia of Lake Pontchartrain," p. 299.

162 ticket fees: *New England Transcendentalists and* The Dial, p. 63.

"the good Public": *ELII*, p. 376.

"fervid Southern": *ELII*, p. 378.

12. COMMUNITIES AND COVENANTS

163 "to hear you": *ELII*, p. 364.

"I thought": *ELVII*, p. 445.

missed the opening session: *ELII*, p. 383.

"a more simple": Quoted in Sterling F. Delano, *Brook Farm: The Dark Side of Utopia* (Cambridge: Harvard University Press, 2004), p. 34.

164 "simple earnestness": *FLII*, p. 101.

"I was no longer": Ednah Dow Cheney, *Reminiscences* (Boston: Lee & Shepard, 1902), p. 205.

"the club": *ELII*, p. 293.

"when once": *JMNXI*, p. 476–77, and *FLII*, pp. 101–2.

165 "denationalize" and subsequent quotations from 1841 opening Conversations: Caroline W. Healey Dall, *Margaret and Her Friends* (Boston: Roberts Brothers, 1895), pp. 26–29, 31–38. See also Joel Myerson, "Mrs. Dall Edits Miss Fuller: The Story of Margaret and Her Friends," *Papers of the Bibliographical Society of America*, vol. 72, no. 2, 1978, pp. 187–200.

166 "seemed melted" . . . "relation" . . . "perfectly true": MF to WHC in *JMNXI*, p. 477.

"We have time": MF to Sarah Helen Whitman, *FLII*, p. 118.

"all kindled": MF to WHC in *JMNXI*, p. 477.

167 "distinct in expression": MF, "The Great Lawsuit. Man *versus* Men. Woman *versus* Women," *Dial*, vol. 4, no. 1, July 1843, p. 21.

"met as": *Margaret and Her Friends*, p. 13.

"perpetual wall": *FLVI*, p. 322.

"*bounteous giver*" and passages from this Conversation: *Margaret and Her Friends*, pp. 41–46.

"there were too many": Ibid., p. 117.

"few present": Ibid., p. 156.

"they will get free": *FLII*, p. 205.

"never enjoyed" . . . "in no way": *Margaret and Her Friends*, p. 13.

168 "I love her": Ibid., p. 156.

"blunder" and subsequent Conversation on Psyche: Ibid., pp. 113–15.

"pilgrimage of [the] soul": Ibid., p. 97.

"the Productive Energy": Ibid., p. 38.

"what is dear": Ibid., p. 41.

"bound in the belt": *JMNXI*, p. 256.

169 "more alone": *FLIII*, p. 47.

their "constellation": *FLIII*, p. 154.

"the young people": *ELII*, p. 384.

"game of wits": *ELII*, p. 385.

"We have a great": RWE, "Friendship," *Essays and Lectures* (New York: Library of America, 1983), p. 341.

"our friendship": *ELII*, p. 385.

"my need": *FLII*, p. 159.

"most unfriendly": *FLII*, p. 171.

"masculine obligations": *FLIII*, p. 213.

"this light": *FLII*, p. 159.

170 budding "Genii": *FLII*, p. 124.

Concord "sage": *FLII*, p. 170.

"the much that calls": MF, poem dated January 1, 1841, in Jeffrey Steele, ed., *The Essential Margaret Fuller* (New Brunswick, N.J.: Rutgers University Press, 1992), p. 18.

"gipsy" freedom: *JMNVIII*, p. 289.

"belong[ed] to the": *FLII*, p. 205.

"good letters": *FLII*, p. 53.

"guests so queenly": *ELII*, p. 129.

"surprised me into": *ELII*, p. 143.

"the fair girl" . . . "inspires the wish": Quoted in Kathleen Lawrence, "The 'Dry-Lighted Soul' Ignites: Emerson and His Soul-Mate Caroline Sturgis as Seen in Her Houghton Manuscripts," *Harvard Library Bulletin*, vol. 16, no. 3, fall 2005, p. 44. I am grateful to Kathleen Lawrence for conversations about the Fuller-Sturgis-Emerson triangle, which have advanced my understanding of this crucial period in the lives of all three, and for the evidence of a lifelong "connexion" between RWE and CS that she introduces in this important essay.

"engaged my cold": *JMNVII*, p. 15.

171 "her blasphemies": Quoted in "The 'Dry-Lighted Soul,'" p. 47.

"lofty" willfulness: Quoted in "The 'Dry-Lighted Soul,'" p. 48.

"Greatly to Be": CS, "Life," *Dial*, vol. 1, no. 2, October 1840, p. 195.

"the right poetry": *JMNVII*, p. 372.

"Be not afraid": *FLII*, p. 103.

"good vagabond": *JMNVIII*, p. 289.

"full of indirections": *JMNVIII*, p. 289.

"a great genius": *JMNVIII*, p. 352.

"I think": *FLII*, p. 150.

172 taken to calling "Raphael": *FLII*, p. 49.

"gone so much" . . . "a joyful song": *FLII*, p. 171.

"How did you": *FLII*, p. 90.

"You would not": *FLII*, pp. 80–81.

"bitterness of checked": *FLII*, p. 81.

"incapable of feeling": *FLII*, p. 90.

"We knew": *FLII*, p. 81.

would "spoil" him: *FLII*, p. 91.

173 "You have given": *FLII*, p. 91.

"star of stars": *FLII*, p. 47.

"I understand": *FLII*, p. 95.

"though I might": *FLII*, pp. 95–96.

"strip of paper": *JMNVII*, p. 259.

"A new person": RWE, "Friendship," p. 343.

174 "Cold as I am": *JMNVII*, pp. 273–75.

"young man": *FLII*, p. 81.

"The wind": *JMNVII*, p. 260.

"chill wind": *FLII*, p. 95.

"vexation" of business: Quoted in Eleanor Tilton, "The True Romance of Anna Hazard Barker and Samuel Gray Ward," *Studies in the American Renaissance*, 1987 (Charlottesville: University of Virginia Press), p. 59. See also Carl Strauch, "Hatred's Swift Repulsions: Emerson, Margaret Fuller, and Others," *Studies in Romanticism*, vol. 7, no. 2, winter 1968, pp. 65–103.

175 "bird has flown" . . . "ague": Samuel Gray Ward, quoted in "The True Romance," p. 67.

"emaciated," by Margaret's: *FLII*, p. 150.

"implied another": *ELVII*, p. 404.

"eldest and divinest": *FLII*, p. 93.

"soaring like": *FLII*, p. 150.

"willing" to be: MF, quoted by RWE in *ELII*, p. 325.

176 "I count & weigh": *ELII*, p. 325.

"a good horse": *ELII*, p. 323.

"the debt": *ELVII*, p. 402.

"More fleet": RWE, "The Visit," *Dial*, vol. 4, no. 4, April 1844, p. 528.

"I thought she": *ELVII*, p. 404.

177 "angel has appeared": *ELII*, p. 339.

"The duration": RWE, "The Visit," p. 528.

"with a certain": *ELVII*, p. 404.

"If you will": *FLII*, p. 69.

"Persons were": *JMNXI*, p. 494. See also Jeffrey Steele, "Transcendental Friendship: Emerson, Fuller, and Thoreau," in Joel Porte and Saundra Morris, eds., *The Cambridge Companion to Ralph Waldo Emerson* (Cambridge: Cambridge University Press, 1999), pp. 121–39; and Susan Belasco, "'The Animating Influences of Discord': Margaret Fuller in 1844," *Legacy*, vol. 20, no. 1/2, 2003, pp. 76–93.

178 "The higher": RWE, "Friendship," p. 352.

"What a spendthrift": *JMNX*, p. 94.

"absolute all-confiding": *JMNXI*, p. 495.

"Life is" . . . "On comes": *JMNVII*, p. 48.

"We are armed": *JMNVII*, p. 106.

"stricken soul": *JMNVII*, p. 48.

"a man wakes": Quoted in Robert D. Richardson Jr., *Emerson: The Mind on Fire* (Berkeley: University of California Press, 1995), p. 280.

179 "taxed" Waldo: *ELII*, p. 325.

"It is even so": *JMNVII*, p. 301.

"friendship of": *JMNVII*, p. 315.

"see the ludicrousness" . . . "privation": *JMNVII*, p. 301.

"in my heart": *JMNVII*, p. 315.

"might destroy": *FLII*, p. 104.

"Wise man": *Dial*, untitled lines of prose, vol. 1, no. 1, p. 136.

"admire the winding up": *FLII*, p. 146.

"of being often": *ELII*, p. 327.

"dared" to entertain: *ELII*, p. 351.

180 "I have lived": *ELII*, p. 327.

"tell you how": *FLII*, p. 157.

her promise: *FLII*, p. 154.

"for the joy": *ELII*, pp. 327–28.

"I need to": *FLII*, p. 160.

"I ought never": *ELII*, p. 352.

"live as": *ELII*, pp. 352–53.

181 "I write" . . . "I have dreamed" . . . "these extraordinary": *ELII*, p. 332.

"new covenant": *ELII*, p. 339.

Waldo wrote "gladly": *JMNVII*, p. 512.

"I am yours": *ELII*, p. 336.

"reconcile our": *ELII*, p. 349.

"Sometimes you appeal": *ELII*, p. 352.

"If Love": RWE, "The Visit," p. 528.

182 "a life more intense": *FLII*, p. 66.

"O these tedious": *FLII*, p. 170.

"You are intellect": *FLIII*, p. 209.

"I have felt": *FLII*, p. 159.

"deep living force": *FLIII*, p. 120.

"Could I lead": *FLII*, p. 159.

"highest office": *FLII*, p. 159.

"faithful through": *FLII*, p. 214.

"I know not": *FLII*, p. 160.

"Did not you": *FLII*, p. 160.

"I value you": *FLII*, p. 213.

"no mortal": *FLII*, p. 111.

"my own priest": *OMI*, p. 99.

183 "new alliance": *FLII*, p. 183.

she was her "Priestess": *FLII*, p. 187.

"the deepest privacy": *FLII*, p. 173.

"I grow": *The Essential Margaret Fuller*, p. 12.

an ideal "community": *FLII*, pp. 179–80.

"tangled wood-walks": *FLII*, p. 64.

"Waldo is": *FLII*, p. 170.

"I wish": *FLVI*, p. 330.

184 "to sail downward": *FLII*, p. 163.

"a sort of ": *OMI*, p. 308.

"all things": *FLII*, p. 160.

"To you": *ELVII*, p. 402.

"Friendship," Waldo would: RWE, "Friendship," p. 343.

"fine war": Elizabeth Palmer Peabody, "Miss Peabody's Reminiscences of Margaret's Married Life," *Boston Evening Transcript*, June 10, 1885. I am grateful to Mary De Jong for bringing this article to my attention.

"purest ideal": *FLII*, pp. 191–92.

"fledglings of Community": *FLII*, p. 209.

"transcendental heifer": Thomas L. Woodson, Neal Smith, and Norman Holmes Pearson, eds., *The Letters, 1813–1843: Centenary Edition of the Works of Nathaniel Hawthorne*, vol. 15 (Columbus: Ohio State University Press, 1984), p. 527.

185 "with common": *OMI*, p. 99.

"I serve you not": "Étienne de la Boéce," *The Collected Works of Ralph Waldo Emerson*, vol. 9, *Poems* (Cambridge: Harvard University Press, 2011), p. 158.

"Now all seems": *FLII*, p. 106.

"Is it not better": *JMNVII*, p. 63.

186 "dissonance, of transition": *FLVI*, p. 332.

"a total failure" ... "I will not": *FLII*, p. 194.

"one thing": *FLII*, p. 180.

difference between "Living": *FLII*, p. 184.

"a firmer hold": *FLII*, p. 180.

"The Phalanx": *FLII*, p. 163.

"who have dared": Elizabeth Palmer Peabody, "A Glimpse of Christ's Idea of Society," *Dial*, vol. 2, no. 2, October 1841, p. 222.

187 "limitations of human nature": *FLII*, p. 109.

"At the name": *ELII*, p. 364.

"University": *ELII*, pp. 323–24.

188 "indifference" might "seem incredible": *FLII*, p. 197.

"The Abolition cause": *FLII*, pp. 197–98.

"women are Slaves": *JMNVII*, p. 48.

"constellation, not a phalanx": *FLIII*, p. 154.

"Once I was": *FLII*, p. 202.

"living so long": *FLII*, p. 69.

nine-thousand-word essay: MF, "Goethe," *Dial*, vol. 2, no. 1, July 1841, pp. 1–41. For the epigraph, Fuller quotes Goethe in the original German. I am grateful to Yu-jin Chang for the English translation I have provided.

189 "do something frivolous": *FLII*, p. 107.

"Love and Insight": CS, *Dial*, vol. 1, no. 3, January 1841, p. 305.

"field[s] of outsight": Quoted in "The 'Dry-Lighted Soul,'" pp. 56–57.

190 "I have walked": *FLII*, pp. 422–23. Kathleen Lawrence expands on RWE's positive association of sea imagery with Cary Sturgis in "The 'Dry-Lighted Soul'"; he had also described Margaret Fuller's heart, sympathetically, as "a sea that hates an ebb."

"modern men": *Margaret and Her Friends*, p. 101.

Transcendentalist "Coterie": *FLVI*, p. 332.

191 "If ever": *FLIII*, p. 66.

"a good neighborhood": *JMNVIII*, pp. 172–73.

"living in": *JMNVIII*, p. 93.

"an earnest" . . . "a great deal": *FLII*, p. 210.

"*that* seems feasible": *FLII*, p. 208.

"fled out of": *ELIII*, p. 7.

"Nature . . . has crushed": *ELIII*, p. 9.

"how bad": *ELIII*, p. 9.

"our fair boy": *ELIII*, p. 9.

"every cherished": *ELIII*, p. 10.

"Margaret Fuller": *JMNVIII*, p. 165.

192 "Shall I": *ELIII*, p. 8.

"Must every": *ELIII*, p. 9.

Lidian was "saintly": *FLII*, p. 160; "holiness": *FLI*, p. 328.

"a bible": *FLII*, p. 160.

"so anti-Christian": Joel Myerson, "Margaret Fuller's 1842 Journal: At Concord with the Emersons," *Harvard Library Bulletin*, vol. 21, no. 3, July 1973, p. 338.

"Marriage should": *JMNVIII*, p. 95.

"all the marriages": Conversation reported by RWE to Elizabeth Palmer Peabody and recorded in her journal, entry of November 25, 1836. In "Biography of Elizabeth Palmer Peabody" [manuscript draft] by Mary Van Wyck Church, p. 280, MHS.

193 "every one": Nancy Craig Simmons, "Margaret Fuller's Boston Conversations: The 1839–1840 Series," *Studies in the American Renaissance*, 1994 (Charlottesville: University Press of Virginia), p. 215.

"ruined health": *FLII*, p. 81.

"lack of ": *FLIII*, p. 164.

"mourned that I": *OMI*, p. 99.

"perfect" friends: "Margaret Fuller's Boston Conversations," p. 218.

"We cannot": *JMNVIII*, p. 95.

"Never confess": Lidian Jackson Emerson, "Transcendental Bible," in Joel Myerson, ed., *Transcendentalism: A Reader* (Oxford: Oxford University Press, 2000), pp. 381–82.

194 "Let there": *ELIII*, p. 53.

"we shall": *ELIII*, p. 81.

"our poor Dial": *ELIII*, pp. 36–37.

"rotation in martyrdom": *ELIII*, p. 35.

"desk & inkhorn": *ELIII*, p. 75.

"red room" . . . "long word": "Margaret Fuller's 1842 Journal," p. 338.

"questioning season": MF to WHC, *FLIII*, p. 91.

"we go but" . . . "more at home" . . . "we do not": "Margaret Fuller's 1842 Journal," p. 323; "are moderate now": p. 326.

195 "burst into tears" . . . "a painful": Ibid., p. 331.

"looked at": Ibid.

"lurking hope": Ibid., p. 332.

196 "more his companion": Ibid., p. 331.

Lidian's "magnanimity": Ibid., p. 332.

"wonderful sleepless": *ELIII*, p. 62.

"when my soul": *FLII*, p. 160.

197 "You would have": *JMNVII*, p. 400.

"the holy man": *FLII*, p. 147.

"I see": *JMNVII*, p. 400.

"my long": *ELIII*, p. 62.

"interrogating, interrogating": *JMNVIII*, p. 196.

"talking, as we almost": "Margaret Fuller's 1842 Journal," p. 330.

"Man," he told her: Ibid.

"claim a devotion": Ibid., pp. 330–31.

198 "Great Sage": Martha L. Berg and Alice de V. Perry, eds., "'The Impulses of Human Nature': Margaret Fuller's Journal from June Through October 1844," *Proceedings of the Massachusetts Historical Society*, vol. 102, 1990, p. 105.

"it has not": "Margaret Fuller's 1842 Journal," pp. 329, 327.

"capital" letter: Ibid., p. 333.

"some ill": Ibid., p. 334.

199 "nowise convinced": Ibid., p. 335.

"my poor": Ibid.

"left Ellen": Ibid.

"He reads": Ibid., p. 336.

"took it": Ibid., pp. 335–36.

"no tragedy": Ibid., p. 336.

200 "be impossible": Robert D. Habich, "Margaret Fuller's Journal for October 1842," *Harvard Library Bulletin*, vol. 33, no. 3, 1985, p. 285.

"sublimo-slipshod" . . . "to the very end": Quoted in Joel Myerson, *The New Eng-*

land Transcendentalists and The Dial (Cranbury, N.J.: Associated University Presses, 1980), pp. 111, 109.

"a succession": "Margaret Fuller's Journal for October 1842," p. 286.

"the true": "Margaret Fuller's 1842 Journal," p. 336.

201 "because he dont": Ibid., p. 332.

"radiant genius": *JMNXVI*, p. 22.

"woman, self-centred": MF, "The Great Lawsuit," p. 47.

"lumber waggon": *FLIII*, p. 137.

"To Rhea": RWE, *Dial*, vol. 4, no. 1, July 1843, p. 104.

13. "THE NEWEST NEW WORLD"

202 "fire winged": *FLIII*, p. 131.

203 "lost its interest" . . . "the newest": *FLIII*, p. 147.

"the birth": MF, journal passage dated July 1844, quoted in *JMNXI*, p. 461.

"dripping" rain: *FLIII*, p. 126.

"known it all": Quoted in *CFII*, p. 125.

"with eyes full": *JMNIX*, p. 19.

"woo the mighty" . . . "the Americanisms": *SOL*, pp. 18, 6.

"continual stress" . . . "so much": *SOL*, p. 3; *FLIII*, p. 131.

"no escape": *SOL*, p. 3.

"hordes" of immigrants: MF journal, quoted in *CFII*, p. 125.

"life-blood rushes": *SOL*, p. 19.

204 "for a plaything": *SOL*, pp. 6–7.

"the conspiring": *SOL*, p. 9.

"aboriginal population": RWE to Martin Van Buren, April 23, 1838, published in the *Daily National Intelligencer*, Washington, May 14, 1838, and the *Yeoman's Gazette*, Concord, May 19, 1838.

205 "real old": *FLIII*, p. 131.

"glut the steamboat": MF journal, quoted in *VM*, p. 173.

"rudeness of conquest": *SOL*, p. 18.

"make amends": MF journal, quoted in *CFII*, p. 125.

"for business": MF journal, quoted in *VM*, p. 173.

"*material* realities" . . . "do not ape": *FLIII*, p. 129.

"talking not": *SOL*, p. 12.

"I say": *FLIII*, p. 132.

206 "oak shaded" . . . "room enough": MF journal, quoted in *VM*, p. 174.

"country [where]": *SOL*, p. 25.

"one of the band": MF letter, quoted in *JMNXI*, p. 485.

"pleasant or natural": *JMNXI*, p. 464.

"born to rove": *SOL*, p. 26.

"every anecdote": MF journal, quoted in *VM*, p. 174.

"blissful seclusion": *SOL*, p. 28.

"we do not": MF journal, quoted in *VM*, p. 174.

"so all life": *FLIII*, p. 143.

"overpaid for coming": *FLIII*, p. 133.

207 "free careless": *FLIII*, p. 169.

"drinking visiters": *SOL*, p. 26.

"I had never": *SOL*, p. 33.

"puffs of Ameriky": *SOL*, p. 37.

"decked with" . . . "My companions": *SOL*, p. 33.

"from the blood": *SOL*, p. 41.

"seated in the Indian": *SOL*, p. 41.

"the body": *FLIII*, p. 133.

"standing at gaze": *SOL*, pp. 71–72.

208 "most engaging": *FLVI*, p. 348.

"Roman figure" . . . "sullenly observing": *FLIII*, p. 135.

"he felt": *SOL*, p. 75.

"beautiful looking": *FLIII*, p. 135.

"medicinal virtues": *SOL*, p. 41.

"sweet melancholy": *SOL*, p. 74.

"delicacy of manners": *SOL*, p. 112.

"the educated": *SOL*, p. 109.

209 *"fair rich"*: MF journal, quoted in *JMNXI*, p. 461.

"vast flowery": *FLIII*, p. 169.

"mode of cultivation": *SOL*, p. 29.

"the harmony": *FLIII*, p. 169.

"rightful lords": *SOL*, p. 29.

"new, boundless" . . . "neither wall" . . . "gain from": *SOL*, p. 40.

"omnivorous traveler": *SOL*, p. 29.

"for affection's": *SOL*, pp. 38–39.

"students of the soil": *SOL*, p. 41.

"canoe-men in pink": *SOL*, p. 150.

210 "sportsman stories": *SOL*, p. 152.

"such childish": *SOL*, p. 152.

"I have given": *FLVI*, p. 151.

"writ[ing] constantly": *FLII*, p. 126.

"every arbitrary": MF, "The Great Lawsuit. Man *versus* Men. Woman *versus* Women," *Dial*, vol. 4, no. 1, July 1843, pp. 14, 44, 47.

most enduring: Even at the time, Theodore Parker recognized the essay to be "the best piece that has seen the light in the Dial," letter to RWE, August 2, 1843, MHS, quoted in *CFII*, p. 121.

"look abroad": *FLVI*, p. 143.

"noble career" . . . "take share": *FLVI*, p. 151.

211 "the man to be with": *FLIII*, p. 148.

"those dim": *FLIII*, p. 52.

"the student": *FLIII*, p. 151.

"poor shady": *FLIII*, p. 151.

"have sweets": *FLII*, p. 65.

"had never": Thomas Wentworth Higginson, *Margaret Fuller Ossoli* (Boston: Houghton, Mifflin and Co., 1884), p. 194.

212 "no lives" . . . "little book": *FLIII*, pp. 160, 159.

"in addressing": *OMI*, p. 130.

"my mind": *Margaret Fuller Ossoli*, p. 195.

"you would": *FLIII*, pp. 160–61.

"friend at once": *FLVI*, p. 260.

213 "the Public": *FLIII*, p. 196.

her initials: See Joel Myerson, *Margaret Fuller: A Descriptive Bibliography* (Pittsburgh: University of Pittsburgh Press, 1978), for title pages of first editions of MF's published work.

"an important era": MF journal, quoted in *CFII*, p. 142.

seven hundred copies: *Margaret Fuller: A Descriptive Bibliography*, p. 11.

"literary sect" . . . "excellencies" . . . "graphicality": Quoted in *CFII*, p. 155.

"one of the most": Quoted in *CFII*, p. 165.

"the only" . . . "your house" . . . "has a fine": Quoted in *CFII*, p. 155.

214 "reflective tendency" . . . "a heathen": Quoted in *CFII*, p. 156.

"seems to be": *FLIII*, p. 204.

"world of infants": *FLIII*, p. 211.

215 "men do not feel": *FLIII*, p. 175.

"Girls are": *FLIII*, p. 197.

"I love best": *FLVI*, pp. 143–44.

"live truly": *FLVI*, p. 144.

"I have no child": MF journal, quoted in *CFII*, p. 171.

"feel withdrawn": MF journal, quoted in *JMNXI*, p. 464.

inducing "palsy": *FLVI*, p. 144.

sixty dollars: *FLIII*, p. 181.

216 "companion" or "to be loved": *FLVI*, p. 348.

"not to be": MF journal, quoted in *CFII*, p. 137.

"keen pangs": *FLIV*, p. 66.

"wide digressions": *OMI*, pp. 350–51.

"there is no": *FLIII*, p. 161.

"Life *is* worth": *FLIII*, p. 187.

"Our intercourse": MF, "Dialogue," *Dial*, vol. 4, no. 4, July 1844, pp. 458–59.

217 "doubt whether": MF journal, quoted in *JMNXI*, p. 499.

"the stream": MF to CS, May 3, 1844, quoted in *JMNXI*, p. 464.

"I am not": MF journal, quoted in *JMNXI*, p. 468.

"independent life": *FLIII*, p. 199.

"get beyond": *FLIII*, p. 229.

"transcendental fatalism": Martha L. Berg and Alice de V. Perry, eds., "'The Impulses of Human Nature': Margaret Fuller's Journal from June Through October 1844," *Proceedings of the Massachusetts Historical Society*, vol. 102, 1990, p. 93.

"disappointments" in Waldo: *FLIII*, p. 209.

"Life here": *FLIII*, p. 213.

218 "deep yearnings": MF journal, quoted in *JMNXI*, pp. 463–64.

"adventurous course": *FLIII*, p. 210.

"remarkable justness": Quoted in *CFII*, p. 122.

"degradation" had less: *FLIII*, p. 223.

219 "so pleasantly": *FLIII*, p. 242.

thirty thousand subscribers: *CFII*, p. 195.

"already eminent": *CFII*, p. 197.

"the wiser mind": *FLVI*, p. 343.

"at least try": MF journal, quoted in *CFII*, p. 166.

"the busy": *FLIII*, p. 245.

"spinning out": *FLIII*, p. 241.

220 "When it comes to": *FLIII*, p. 143.

"a delightful": *FLIII*, pp. 241–42.

14. "I STAND IN THE SUNNY NOON OF LIFE"

223 "holy and equal": Martha L. Berg and Alice de V. Perry, "'The Impulses of Human Nature': Margaret Fuller's Journal from June Through October 1844," *Proceedings of the Massachusetts Historical Society*, vol. 102, 1990, p. 89.

"What do you think": Quoted in Julian Hawthorne, *Nathaniel Hawthorne and His Wife*, vol. 1 (Hamden, Conn.: Archon Books, 1968, reprint of 1884 edition), p. 257.

"A wife only": Quoted in *Nathaniel Hawthorne and His Wife*, vol. 1, p. 258. Sophia and Nathaniel Hawthorne together wrote a letter to MF that was far less critical of the book, judging from MF's response (*FLIV*, p. 103), but the letter does not survive.

"No unmarried": Orestes Brownson, quoted in *CFII*, p. 188.

224 first printing: *FLIV*, p. 56.

"the liberal": *Charleston Mercury*, quoted in *CFII*, p. 188.

"a *bold* book": Quoted in *CFII*, pp. 186–88.

"There exists": *WNC*, p. 22.

"While any one": *WNC*, p. 10.

"interests were": *WNC*, p. 156.

225 "no home": *WNC*, p. 25.

"as a nature": *WNC*, p. 27.

"live without": *WNC*, p. 25.

"a noble piece" . . . "quite an important": Quoted in Larry J. Reynolds, "From *Dial* Essay to New York Book: The Making of *Woman in the Nineteenth Century*," in Kenneth M. Price and Susan Belasco Smith, eds., *Periodical Literature in Nineteenth-Century America* (Charlottesville: University Press of Virginia, 1995), p. 25.

"The world": *WNC*, p. 95.

"rouse their" . . . "assume [their]": *WNC*, pp. 159, 162.

226 "'Girls can't'": *WNC*, p. 33.

"Let it not": *WNC*, p. 31.

"If she knows": *WNC*, p. 107.

"better companions": *WNC*, p. 84.

"must marry": *WNC*, p. 58.

"an adopted child": *WNC*, p. 59.

"seal of degradation": *WNC*, p. 66.

"belong[s] to": *WNC*, p. 162.

"there is no": *WNC*, p. 51.

"household partnership": *WNC*, p. 60.

227 "intellectual companionship": *WNC*, p. 60.

"work together": *WNC*, p. 67.

"in public life": *WNC*, p. 60.

"two minds" . . . "express an onward": *WNC*, p. 66.

"seeking clearness": *WNC*, p. 62.

"highest grade": *WNC*, p. 69.

"the thirst": *WNC*, p. 157.

"reverent love": *WNC*, pp. 70–71.

"need to be": *FLII*, pp. 159–60.

228 "ordinary attachment" . . . "age, position": *FLII*, pp. 90, 81.

"mutual visionary": "'The Impulses of Human Nature,'" p. 105.

"his only true": *WNC*, pp. 71–72.

"chastity and equality": *WNC*, p. 120.

"Woman, self-centred": *WNC*, p. 162.

"excessive devotion": *WNC*, p. 161.

"so entirely": *WNC*, p. 146.

"her whole existence": *WNC*, pp. 161–62.

229 "men never": *WNC*, p. 30.

"the ennui": *WNC*, p. 160.

"absorbed" in marriage: *WNC*, p. 162.

"self-reliance and self-impulse": *WNC*, p. 161.

"compromise" and "helplessness": *WNC*, p. 107.

"obedient goodness": "'The Impulses of Human Nature,'" p. 89.

"sign of the times": *WNC*, p. 82.

"despised auxiliaries": *WNC*, pp. 84–85.

"celibacy is the great": *WNC*, p. 106.

"cherished no sentimental": *WNC*, pp. 27–29.

230 "Saints and geniuses": *WNC*, p. 86.

"much greater": *WNC*, p. 159.

"remove arbitrary": *WNC*, p. 158.

"We would": *WNC*, p. 26.

"men do *not*": *WNC*, pp. 158–59.

"a ship at sea": "'The Impulses of Human Nature,'" p. 94.

"man . . . is man": Joel Myerson, "Margaret Fuller's 1842 Journal: At Concord with the Emersons," *Harvard Library Bulletin*, vol. 21, no. 3, July 1973, p. 330.

"male and female": *WNC*, p. 103.

231 "every faculty": Nancy Craig Simmons, "Margaret Fuller's Boston Conversations: The 1839–1840 Series," *Studies in the American Renaissance*, 1994 (Charlottesville: University Press of Virginia), p. 214.

"There is no": *WNC*, p. 103.

"no discordant": *WNC*, p. 26.

"Patient serpent": "'The Impulses of Human Nature,'" p. 74.

"I stand": *WNC*, p. 163.

232 "their wounds": *FLIV*, p. 59.

"Great Book": *FLIV*, p. 59.

"The thousands": Quoted in *CFII*, p. 187.

"the opposition": *FLIV*, p. 59.

"loose" . . . "chaste ideal": Quoted in *CFII*, p. 189.

she had been "heard": *FLIV*, p. 56.

"demure Boston": Francis B. Dedmond, "The Letters of Caroline Sturgis to Margaret

Fuller," *Studies in the American Renaissance,* 1988 (Charlottesville: University Press of Virginia), p. 232.

"The style": Ibid., p. 239.

233 one of her "trances": Ibid., p. 231.

"It makes me": Ibid., p. 239.

"I have found": *FLIV,* p. 64.

"first time": "'The Impulses of Human Nature,'" p. 101.

"prison" of Captain Sturgis's: "The Letters of Caroline Sturgis to Margaret Fuller," p. 235.

234 "has the physical": Quoted in *Nathaniel Hawthorne and His Wife,* vol. 1, p. 258.

15. "FLYING ON THE PAPER WINGS OF EVERY DAY"

235 "dull and dubious": Judith Matson Bean and Joel Myerson, eds., *Margaret Fuller, Critic: Writings from the* New-York Tribune, *1844–1846* (New York: Columbia University Press, 2000), p. 98.

"should be looked at": Ibid.

236 building plan: Alison R. Brown, "Reform and Curability in American Insane Asylums of the 1840's: The Conflict of Motivation Between Humanitarian Efforts and the Efforts of the Superintendent 'Brethren,'" *Constructing the Past,* vol. 2, no. 1, 2010, p. 12.

"parsimony" was "the worst": *Margaret Fuller, Critic,* p. 104.

"intelligent sympathy": Ibid., p. 99.

"vagrant, degraded": Ibid., p. 98.

"openings to a better": Ibid., p. 99.

"careless scrutiny": Ibid., pp. 99–100.

237 "a school": Ibid., p. 100.

"show[ed] by their": Ibid., p. 101.

"no eye": Ibid., p. 101.

"one of the gloomiest": Ibid., p. 102.

"I have always": *FLIV,* p. 46.

"women like myself": Quoted in *CFII,* p. 205.

238 "receive the punishment": *Margaret Fuller, Critic,* p. 102.

"to aid": *FLVI,* p. 359.

"for those": Francis B. Dedmond, "The Letters of Caroline Sturgis to Margaret Fuller," *Studies in the American Renaissance,* 1988 (Charlottesville: University Press of Virginia), p. 329.

"made acceptable": Quoted in Susan Belasco Smith, "Margaret Fuller in New York: Private Letters, Public Texts," *Documentary Editing,* vol. 18, no. 3, September 1996, p. 66; ten dollars: *CFII,* p. 198. See also Paula Kopacz, "Feminist at the 'Tribune': Margaret Fuller as Professional Writer," *Studies in the American Renaissance,* 1991 (Charlottesville: University Press of Virginia), pp. 119–39.

"an excellent": John Wesley Thomas, ed., *The Letters of James Freeman Clarke to Margaret Fuller* (Hamburg: Cram, de Gruyter, 1957), p. 145.

"mutual education": *FLVI,* p. 359.

239 "scenes" . . . "materials": Martha L. Berg and Alice de V. Perry, eds., "'The Impulses

of Human Nature': Margaret Fuller's Journal from June Through October 1844," *Proceedings of the Massachusetts Historical Society*, vol. 102, 1990, pp. 77, 101.

"would have suggested": *Margaret Fuller, Critic*, pp. 99–100.

"Do you want": MF, "Asylum for Discharged Female Convicts," *New-York Daily Tribune*, June 19, 1845, C143 in CD-ROM accompanying *Margaret Fuller, Critic*.

"chief mental focus": *Margaret Fuller, Critic*, p. 2.

"more fine": "'The Impulses of Human Nature,'" p. 86.

"the old spirit": *Margaret Fuller, Critic*, p. 8.

240 "the contributions": Ibid., p. 29.

"nature" . . . "excommunicated" . . . "regret": Ibid., pp. 94, 96, 97.

"performed with a degree": MF, "Music in New-York," *New-York Daily Tribune*, January 18, 1845, C088 in CD-ROM accompanying *Margaret Fuller, Critic*.

"There is no reason": *Margaret Fuller, Critic*, pp. 102–3.

"worthy the admiration": "Music in New-York." Background sources for New York City in the 1840s: Lydia Maria Child, *Letters from New-York*, Bruce Mills, ed. (Athens: University of Georgia Press, 1998); Gloria Deak, *Picturing New York: The City from Its Beginnings to the Present* (New York: Columbia University Press, 2000); John Doggett Jr., *The Great Metropolis; or, New York in 1845* (New York: John Doggett Jr., 1845); Eric Homberger, *The Historical Atlas of New York City* (New York: Henry Holt, 1994); Eric Homberger, *Scenes from the Life of a City: Corruption and Conscience in Old New York* (New Haven: Yale University Press, 1994); George K. Lankevich, *American Metropolis: A History of New York City* (New York: New York University Press, 1998); Howard B. Rock and Deborah Dash Moore, *Cityscapes: A History of New York in Images* (New York: Columbia University Press, 2001); Nathan Silver, *Lost New York* (Boston: Houghton Mifflin, 1967); Edward K. Spann, *The New Metropolis: New York City, 1840–1857* (New York: Columbia University Press, 1981); François Weil, *A History of New York* (New York: Columbia University Press, 2004); Norval White, *New York: A Physical History* (New York: Atheneum, 1987).

241 "go-ahead, fearless adroitness": *Margaret Fuller, Critic*, p. 127.

"mother of men": *ELIII*, p. 19.

unkempt newspaperman: See Robert C. Williams, *Horace Greeley: Champion of American Freedom* (New York: New York University Press, 2006), p. xii.

242 "thickly settled": *FLIII*, p. 250.

"Grahamites and Hydropaths": *FLIV*, p. 45.

"strong potations" . . . "Skin": Quoted in *CFII*, pp. 218, 219.

"a winding": Quoted in *Scenes from the Life of a City*, pp. 214–15.

"I like living": *FLIV*, p. 51.

243 "in his habits": *FLIV*, p. 56.

"what turmoil": Horace Greeley, quoted in *CFII*, p. 199.

"flying on the paper": *Margaret Fuller, Critic*, pp. 14–15.

16. "A HUMAN SECRET, LIKE MY OWN"

244 "like an inspired": Rebecca Spring and MF, quoted in *CFII*, pp. 206–7.

245 "dismal inky": Richard Henry Dana Jr., quoted in *CFII*, p. 197.

"to make": *ELIII*, p. 268.

"fine head" . . . "her large gray": Quoted in *CFII*, p. 216.

246 "not pleasant": *FLIV*, pp. 59–60.

"merry season": MF, *Essays on American Life and Letters*, Joel Myerson, ed. (Albany, N.Y.: NCUP, 1978), p. 277.

"even those": Ibid., p. 279.

"how very little": Ibid., p. 280.

"partial inferiority": *FLIV*, p. 158.

247 "supersensual" science: *Essays on American Life*, pp. 271–72.

"this ugly": MF journal, quoted in *CFII*, p. 137.

"a prospect": *FLVI*, p. 356.

"rule of life" . . . "means by which": *Essays on American Life*, pp. 273, 272.

Woman's "intuitions": *WNC*, p. 91.

248 "we do not": MF, "Review of Theodore Leger, *Animal Magnetism; or, Psychodunamy*," *New-York Daily Tribune*, May 30, 1846, C294 in CD-ROM accompanying Judith Matson Bean and Joel Myerson, eds., *Margaret Fuller, Critic: Writings from the New-York Tribune, 1844–1846* (New York: Columbia University Press, 2000).

"patience" . . . "more rapid": *Essays on American Life*, pp. 273, 276.

"free from prejudice": "Review of Theodore Leger."

"no sleep": *FLIV*, p. 59.

reports from friends: *FLIV*, p. 61n.

"held his right hand": *FLIV*, p. 61n.

"a power": "Review of Theodore Leger."

249 "what I meet": *FLIV*, p. 59.

"stronger passions": *WNC*, p. 136.

"a truly happy": *FLIV*, p. 65.

"the new knowledge": *Margaret Fuller, Critic*, p. 14.

meeting had taken place: James Nathan, letter dated 1873, in Julia Ward Howe, ed., *Love-Letters of Margaret Fuller, 1845–1846* (New York: D. Appleton, 1903), p. 4.

of her "beloved": *FLIV*, p. 82; James Nathan's travel letters in the *Tribune: FLIV*, pp. 146, 159.

"nameless relation": *FLIV*, p. 75.

250 "some day": *FLIV*, p. 47.

"the utmost": *WNC*, p. 55.

"prized . . . both as a warning": *Margaret Fuller, Critic*, pp. 57–58.

251 "there are": *FLIV*, p. 95.

"boldness, simplicity": *FLIV*, p. 74.

252 "never know" . . . "wholly": *FLIV*, p. 65.

"wish to hear": *FLIV*, p. 62.

"show me how": *FLIV*, p. 47.

"restless sad": *FLIV*, p. 100.

"my mind": *FLIV*, p. 52.

"twenty four": *FLIV*, p. 68.

"*my dear*": *FLIV*, p. 64.

"these little": *FLIV*, p. 65.

"last Winter's": *FLIV*, pp. 66–67.

"one feels": *FLIV*, p. 62.

"suffer an untimely": *FLIV*, p. 66.

"there is to be": *FLIV*, p. 65.

"a cold faintness": *FLIV*, p. 69.

253 "I love sadness": Martha L. Berg and Alice de V. Perry, eds., "'The Impulses of Human Nature': Margaret Fuller's Journal from June Through October 1844," *Proceedings of the Massachusetts Historical Society*, vol. 102, 1990, p. 70.

"an injured woman": *FLIV*, p. 68.

"broken through": *FLIV*, p. 67.

"English maiden": *FLIV*, p. 191.

"deserted" a woman: Rebecca Spring, quoted in *CFII*, p. 223.

"I have elected": *FLIV*, p. 70.

"Could the heart": *FLIV*, pp. 68–70.

"*That* I know": *FLIV*, p. 67.

"the path": *FLIV*, pp. 69–70.

254 "The golden time": *FLIV*, p. 70.

she draped: *FLIV*, p. 114.

"I am with you": *FLIV*, pp. 72–73.

"approached" Margaret "so nearly": *FLIV*, p. 75.

"Yesterday was": *FLIV*, p. 77.

"the sweet": *FLIV*, p. 73.

255 "earth-stain" ever be: *FLIV*, p. 77.

"It seemed the work": *FLIV*, pp. 75–76.

the man of "force": *FLIV*, p. 100.

"'*the dame*'": *FLIV*, p. 78.

"so much": *FLIV*, p. 75.

"that if Margaret": *FLIV*, p. 76.

"crave" all the more: *FLIV*, p. 87.

"noble enough": *FLIV*, pp. 82–83.

"come tomorrow": *FLIV*, p. 102. Although the source of Margaret's quotation from Novalis is not known, she may have been offering a loose translation of the closing lines of his poem "Astralis," which include "Das Herz als Asche niederfaellt" — "The heart, as ashes, falls down." I am grateful to Yu-jin Chang for suggesting this possible attribution.

"Platonic affection": "'The Impulses of Human Nature,'" p. 77.

256 "Your views": Ibid.

"the class": MF, "The Great Lawsuit. Man *versus* Men. Woman *versus* Women," *Dial*, vol. 4, no. 1, July 1843, p. 35.

"read not": "'The Impulses of Human Nature,'" p. 77.

"childish rest": *FLIV*, p. 87.

"was not enough": *FLIV*, p. 98.

"called on for wisdom": *FLIV*, p. 137.

"and now am": *FLIV*, p. 98.

257 "the crimson ones": *FLIV*, p. 98.

"works which": *Margaret Fuller, Critic*, p. 57.

"get out": *FLIV*, p. 87.

"but a mortal": *FLIV*, p. 95.

"able to stand": *WNC*, p. 161.

"life seems": *FLIV*, p. 97.

"so much for me": *FLIV*, p. 99.

258 *"mein liebste"*: *FLIV*, p. 96.

"since you have": *FLIV*, p. 104.

"carried . . . many": *FLIV*, p. 91.

"must know": *FLIV*, p. 99.

"you must always": *FLIV*, p. 109.

"take it gently": *FLIV*, p. 97.

"You have touched": *FLIV*, p. 75.

was no "mistake": *FLIV*, p. 107.

"your moon": *FLIV*, p. 100.

"To the Face Seen in the Moon": Quoted in *CFII*, p. 172.

"The Woman in me": Quoted in *CFII*, p. 172.

259 a "queenly" moon: *FLIV*, p. 102.

"A human secret": *FLIV*, p. 105.

"have no confidant": *FLIV*, p. 159.

"we improve": *FLIV*, p. 136.

"men have the privilege": *FLIV*, p. 117.

"last letter": *FLIV*, p. 111.

"magnetic power": MF, *Art, Literature, and the Drama* (New York: The Tribune Association, 1869), p. 83.

"it is well": *FLIV*, pp. 110–11.

260 "I cannot do": *FLIV*, p. 77.

"fair girl": *FLIV*, p. 147.

"She must suffer": *FLIV*, p. 139.

"who combined": *FLIV*, p. 100.

"beautiful summer": *FLIV*, p. 153.

"prettiest dresses": *FLIV*, p. 148.

"the waters": *FLIV*, p. 137.

"concentrated on": *FLIV*, p. 141.

"indeed there *are*": *FLIV*, p. 121.

"I have never": *FLIV*, p. 141.

261 "no poem": *FLIV*, p. 92.

"is it not by living": *FLIV*, p. 141.

titled "Clairvoyance": *New-York Daily Tribune*, July 23, 1845, C163 in CD-ROM accompanying *Margaret Fuller, Critic*.

"the affair": *FLIV*, p. 146.

"poor maiden": *FLIV*, p. 139.

"*Now* is the crisis": *FLIV*, p. 147.

"tender and elevated": *FLIV*, p. 134.

"the precious": *FLIV*, pp. 134–35.

"a good miniature": *FLIV*, p. 149.

262 "I like them better": *FLIV*, p. 121.

"has rent from me": Quoted in *JMNXI*, pp. 507–8.

"our moods": *FLIV*, p. 167.

"seldom" . . . "because he": Quoted in Joel Myerson, *The New England Transcendentalists and* The Dial (Cranbury, N.J.: Associated University Presses, 1980), pp. 208, 209.

"very lonely": *FLIV*, p. 167.

263 "just about": *FLIV*, p. 163.

17. LOST ON BEN LOMOND

270 "would have given": *FLIV*, pp. 192–93.

"great mutual": MF, "Thom's Poems," *New-York Tribune*, August 22, 1845, C175 in CD-ROM accompanying Judith Matson Bean and Joel Myerson, eds., *Margaret Fuller, Critic: Writings from the* New-York Tribune, *1844–1846* (New York: Columbia University Press, 2000).

"If I persevere": *FLIV*, p. 193.

"a desire for you": *FLIV*, pp. 204–5.

"retouching" several: *FLIV*, p. 146.

"never be": *FLIV*, p. 205.

271 "I am going": *FLIV*, p. 195.

"full of distaste": *FLIV*, p. 216n.

"and then thanks": Quoted in *VM*, p. 227.

"brief and vivid": *FLIV*, pp. 218–19.

272 "very glad to find": *FLIV*, p. 166.

"close calculator": *CFII*, p. 271.

"The attractive force": *FLIV*, p. 213.

"slower, solider": *Dispatches*, p. 41.

"packages of seed": MF, *Essays on American Life and Letters*, Joel Myerson, ed. (Albany, N.Y.: NCUP, 1978), p. 380.

273 "nine days of wonder": *Dispatches*, p. 39.

"florid, fair": *Dispatches*, p. 53.

"the real wants": *Dispatches*, p. 57.

"merely the retirement": *Dispatches*, p. 53.

"I care not": Julia Ward Howe, ed., *Love-Letters of Margaret Fuller, 1845–1846* (New York: D. Appleton, 1903), p. 187.

274 "drenching" equinoctial: *Dispatches*, p. 69.

"Life seems": *FLIV*, p. 97.

"alone, as usual" . . . "I have no real": *OMII*, pp. 166, 167.

275 nickname "Sibyl": Bettine von Arnim, *Goethe's Correspondence with a Child*, vol. 1 (London: Longman, Orme, Brown, Green, and Longmans, 1839), p. 91. Margaret had also written a breathlessly admiring letter to the sixty-five-year-old von Arnim in 1840, before she had given up her project of writing a biography of Goethe. It appears that she received no answering letter. *FLVI*, pp. 328–29.

"Officer of Hussars": *Goethe's Correspondence with a Child*, vol. 1, p. 102.

"drink in": *Dispatches*, p. 74.

276 "all fevered" and remainder of account: *Dispatches*, pp. 75–77.

"*if* I had not tried": *FLIV*, p. 228.

277 "cessation of intercourse": Quoted in *CFII*, p. 291.

"my Yankee method": *Dispatches*, p. 77.

"life rushes": MF, "Farewell," *New-York Daily Tribune*, August 1, 1846; *Essays on American Life*, p. 379.

"the *feeble*": MF, review of Thomas L. McKenney, in *Memoirs, Official and Personal, New-York Daily Tribune*, July 8, 1846, C308 in CD-ROM accompanying *Margaret Fuller, Critic*.

"heightening and deepening": *Essays on American Life*, p. 380.

"she had seen": *JMNXI*, p. 498.

278 "making some good": *FLIV*, p. 188.

"glad Margaret Fuller": Quoted in *CFII*, p. 278.

had just "*eloped*": *FLIV*, p. 235.

"especially women": *Dispatches*, p. 79.

"I found" . . . "persons of celebrity": *FLIV*, pp. 239–40, 235.

"preconceived strong": *FLIV*, p. 228.

"others of a radical": *FLIV*, p. 235.

279 "habits of conversation": *FLIV*, p. 228.

"a woman of tact": Quoted in *JMNXI*, p. 471.

"European society": *FLIV*, p. 245.

"chosen the profession": *FLIV*, pp. 240–41.

"the miserable": *FLIV*, p. 194.

280 "waited long enough": Martha L. Berg and Alice de V. Perry, eds., "'The Impulses of Human Nature'": Margaret Fuller's Journal from June Through October 1844," *Proceedings of the Massachusetts Historical Society*, vol. 102, 1990, p. 109.

"full of grace": *FLIV*, pp. 248–49.

"full of all nobleness": Quoted in *VM*, p. 235.

281 "Beyond any": Quoted in *VM*, p. 240.

"beauteous and pure": *FLIV*, pp. 248–49.

18. "ROME HAS GROWN UP IN MY SOUL"

282 "the city of pleasures": *FLIV*, p. 252.

"*getting dressed*": *FLIV*, p. 241.

"thick, flowered": *FLIV*, p. 253.

"in a little": *FLIV*, p. 229.

"the devotion": *FLIV*, p. 241.

"openings were made": *FLIV*, p. 244.

283 "only way": *FLIV*, p. 234.

"besetting danger": MF, *Essays on American Life and Letters*, Joel Myerson, ed. (Albany, N.Y.: NCUP, 1978), pp. 369–70.

"habit of feeding": *Dispatches*, p. 128.

verbal "sharp-shooters": *Dispatches*, p. 122.

"true kings": *Dispatches*, p. 111.

284 Fourier's estimate: *WNC*, p. 160.

285 "lives on the footing": *FLIV*, p. 262n.

"Madame Sand": *FLIV*, p. 256.

"*La dame Americaine*" and account of meeting with George Sand: *OMII*, pp. 194–98.

287 "the man I had": *FLIV*, p. 261.

"the present": Alexander Chodzko, quoted in *CFII*, p. 318.

"deep-founded mental connection": *FLIV*, pp. 261–62.

288 "the very few": *FLV*, p. 175.

"the only one": *FLV*, p. 176.

"vow never": Alexander Chodzko, quoted in *CFII*, p. 318.

"He affected": *FLIV*, p. 263.

"an embodied": Quoted in *Dispatches*, p. 6.

"How much time": *FLIV*, p. 261.

"the attraction": *FLIV*, p. 263; "frightful": MF, "1849 Journal," p. 2, bMS Am 1986 [4] FMW.

"I speak and act": *FLIV*, p. 259.

289 "I do not know": *FLIV*, p. 263.

"prostrate multitude": William Ellery Channing, *Conversations in Rome: Between an Artist, a Catholic, and a Critic* (Boston: William Crosby and H. P. Nichols, 1847), p. 6.

"natal day": *Dispatches*, pp. 136–37.

290 "not great enough": Rebecca Spring, quoted in *VM*, p. 254.

"perpetual hurra": *Dispatches*, p. 136.

no sermon: *Dispatches*, p. 185.

"elaborate, expressive": George Stillman Hillard, *Six Months in Italy* (Boston: Ticknor and Fields, 1868), p. 145. See also John Paul Russo, "The Unbroken Charm: Margaret Fuller, G. S. Hillard, and the American Tradition of Travel Writing on Italy," in Charles Capper and Cristina Giorcelli, eds., *Margaret Fuller: Transatlantic Crossings in a Revolutionary Age* (Madison: University of Wisconsin Press, 2007), pp. 124–55.

"Rome is an all hacknied": *FLIV*, p. 156.

291 "an earnest": *FLVI*, p. 216.

"singular, fateful": *FLV*, p. 292.

"little book": *FLV*, p. 208.

"certainly did not": Quoted in *VM*, p. 256.

292 "say nothing": *FLV*, p. 291.

"simplicity" . . . "unspoiled nature": *FLV*, p. 271.

"ignorant of great": *FLV*, p. 248.

consider "nothing": *FLV*, p. 291.

"excellent practical": *FLV*, p. 261.

"I wish to be": *FLIV*, p. 262.

293 "all of me": Leopold Wellisz, "The Friendship of Margaret Fuller d'Ossoli and Adam Mickiewicz," *Bulletin of the Polish Institute of Arts and Sciences in America*, vol. 4, 1945–46, p. 99.

"offered me": *FLV*, p. 292.

"the splendidest": *FLV*, p. 305.

"I have not": *FLIV*, p. 266.

"a person": *FLV*, p. 250.

"Nature has been": *FLV*, p. 271.

"an obscure": *FLV*, p. 250.

"Giovanni," as Margaret introduced: Rebecca Spring, quoted in *VM*, p. 261.

"gentle friend": *FLV*, p. 248.

294 "never dream[ing]": *FLV*, p. 292.

"Do not": "The Friendship of Margaret Fuller d'Ossoli and Adam Mickiewicz," p. 102.

"try to bring away": "The Friendship of Margaret Fuller d'Ossoli and Adam Mickie-wicz," p. 103.

"A single": *FLIV*, p. 273.

295 "I take interest": *FLIV*, p. 271.

"a kind of springtime": *FLIV*, p. 273.

"busy and intellectual": *FLIV*, p. 291.

"a circle": *FLIV*, p. 295.

"very profitable": *FLIV*, p. 285.

"nearly killed": *FLIV*, p. 286.

"quiet room": *FLIV*, p. 283.

296 "advantage I derive": *FLIV*, p. 284.

"Who can": *Dispatches*, p. 140.

"I passed": *FLIV*, p. 284.

"alone with glorious Italy": *FLIV*, p. 290.

"a yearning": *FLIV*, p. 277.

"a wicked irritation": *FLIV*, p. 291.

"I begin": *FLIV*, p. 293.

"In this Europe": *FLIV*, p. 288.

"most fortunate": *FLIV*, pp. 295–96.

"specimen of the really": *FLIV*, p. 294.

297 "into contact": *FLIV*, pp. 291–92.

"women in Europe": *FLVI*, p. 48.

"fair and brilliant": *FLIV*, p. 291.

"one of the emancipated": *FLIV*, p. 311.

"pretty girls": *FLV*, p. 42.

298 "account of his": *ELIII*, pp. 377–78 and 378n.

"everlasting struggles": Quoted in *CFII*, p. 324.

"one to whom": *ELIII*, p. 377.

"these millennial": *ELIII*, p. 400.

"run out": *ELIII*, p. 394.

"O Sappho": *ELIII*, p. 401.

299 "rugged" translation: *ELIII*, p. 183. For the translation, see J. Chesley Matthews, ed., "Emerson's Translation of Dante's *Vita Nuova*," *Harvard Library Bulletin*, vol. 11, nos. 2, 3, 1957.

"almost unique": *JMNVIII*, p. 369.

"the Polander": *ELIII*, p. 400.

"Give All to Love": *The Collected Works of Ralph Waldo Emerson*, vol. 9, *Poems* (Cambridge: Harvard University Press, 2011), pp. 179–81.

300 *"give all for love"*: "The Friendship of Margaret Fuller d'Ossoli and Adam Mickie-wicz," pp. 105–6.

words were "*harsh*": Ibid., p. 107.

"Do not forget": Ibid., p. 106.

"Literature is not": Ibid., pp. 107–8.

"The relationships": Ibid., p. 106.

earned far less: *FLIV*, p. 256.

301 "Tumbledown-Hall": *ELIII*, p. 411.

"peristyle gables": *ELIII*, p. 413.

"we all succeed": *ELIII*, p. 394.

"legal fraction": *FLV*, p. 71.

"ten or even five": *FLIV*, p. 300.

"My uncle": *FLV*, pp. 70–71.

302 "the inward man": Quoted in *CFII*, p. 324.

"poor text": *FLIV*, p. 297.

"Amid the prayers": *FLIV*, p. 298n.

"American friend": Quoted in *VM*, p. 252.

"You do not": Quoted in *CFII*, p. 324.

303 "I feel": *FLIV*, p. 283.

"It must": *FLIV*, p. 290.

"every stone": *Dispatches*, p. 140.

"more attractive": *FLIV*, p. 275.

"worth an age": *FLIV*, p. 290.

"all the motions": *FLIV*, p. 308.

304 "elegantly furnished": *FLIV*, p. 301.

"my books": *FLIV*, p. 301.

second copy: *FLV*, p. 42.

"I find myself ": *FLIV*, p. 310.

"I live alone": *FLIV*, p. 309.

almost no "Amerns": *FLIV*, p. 275.

"I have seen": MF, "Recollections of the Vatican," *United States Magazine and Democratic Review*, vol. 27, July 1850, p. 65.

305 "Since I have": *FLIV*, pp. 310–11.

"in a sort of beatitude": *ELIII*, p. 444.

"quite by myself ": *FLIV*, pp. 308–9.

"a full communion": *FLV*, p. 192.

saltarello that "heated": *Dispatches*, p. 176.

"has developed": *Dispatches*, p. 135.

306 "I acted": *FLV*, p. 292.

"corrupt social contract": *FLV*, p. 248.

"lonely position": *WNC*, p. 86.

"viewed the whole": *FLIII*, p. 236.

"The union": *FLV*, p. 41.

"the existence": Martha L. Berg and Alice de V. Perry, eds., "'The Impulses of Human Nature': Margaret Fuller's Journal from June Through October 1844," *Proceedings of the Massachusetts Historical Society*, vol. 102, 1990, p. 77.

307 "Had I never": *FLV*, p. 292.

"thoughts of consecration": *OMII*, pp. 293–94.

"energetic and beneficent": *FLV*, p. 51.

"earthly union": *FLV*, p. 248.

"I wanted to forget": *FLV*, p. 42.

"mixture of fancy": *FLV*, p. 300.

"acts, not words": *FLVI*, p. 53.

"simple affinity": *FLV*, p. 300.

"inestimable blessing": *FLV*, p. 291.

"great faults": *FLV*, p. 270.

308 "wholly without vanity": *FLVI*, p. 53.

"the slightest": *FLV*, p. 291.

"very unlike" . . . "affections": *FLVI*, p. 53.

"lost" when he was: *FLV*, p. 299.

"spontaneously bound": *FLV*, p. 291.

"something of the violet": *FLV*, p. 283.

"mutual tenderness" . . . "except": *FLV*, pp. 301, 300.

more "precious" even: *FLVI*, p. 65.

their "tie" was not: *FLV*, p. 248.

309 "all human": *FLV*, p. 291.

"the time": *FLV*, p. 248.

"need of manifold": *FLII*, p. 159.

"a part of ": *FLV*, p. 300.

"when I am occupied": *FLV*, p. 291.

"no refreshment": *FLIV*, p. 312.

"highly prize": *FLIV*, p. 299.

"is happy": *FLV*, p. 291.

"I have not": *FLIV*, p. 312.

"first acquaintance": "1849 Journal," p. 3, FMW.

"pious" Catholic youth: *FLV*, p. 278.

"habitual attachment": *FLV*, p. 291.

"loves . . . to serve": *FLV*, p. 300.

"*I* am": *FLV*, p. 182.

310 "indolently joyous": *FLIV*, p. 273.

"this fantastic": *FLV*, p. 251.

"I liked": *FLVI*, p. 65.

"blessed, quiet": *FLIV*, p. 315.

"intoxicated" months: *FLV*, p. 43.

"like retiring": *FLV*, p. 283.

"I should have wished": *FLVI*, p. 65.

"I now really live": *Dispatches*, p. 168.

"nightly fever": *FLIV*, p. 310.

311 "professional beggars" and account of visit to Santo Spirito Cemetery: *Dispatches*, pp. 169–71. See also Katherine A. Geffcken, "Burials on the Janiculum: The Cemetery of Santo Spirito," in Katherine A. Geffcken and Norma W. Goldman, eds., *The Janus View from the American Academy in Rome: Essays on the Janiculum* (Rome: The American Academy in Rome, 2007), pp. 195–201.

"noble exiles": *FLIV*, p. 288.

312 "The Sunset": *The Complete Poetical Works of Shelley* (Boston: Houghton Mifflin, 1901), pp. 345–46.

"truly the gentleman": *FLVI*, p. 53.

"none to help" . . . "incubus": *FLIV*, p. 315.

"accident or angel": *FLV*, p. 43.

"I am tired" . . . "nothing less": *FLIV*, p. 314.

313 "I rejoice": *ELIII*, pp. 446–48.
    "God knows": *FLV*, p. 40.
    "There are circumstances": *FLV*, p. 57.
314 "this year, I enter": *FLV*, pp. 43, 41.
    "Rome is Rome": *FLV*, p. 46.

19. "A BEING BORN WHOLLY OF MY BEING"

315 "my view of the present": *FLIV*, p. 315.
    "made a law": *FLV*, p. 286.
    "God 'twas delicious": Quoted in *Dispatches*, pp. 1–2.
    "*my* America": *Dispatches*, p. 230.
316 "Still Europe toils": *Dispatches*, p. 164.
    "Our age is one": *Dispatches*, p. 155.
    "the fortieth": *Dispatches*, p. 203.
    "As to eating": *Dispatches*, p. 206.
    "authentic news": *Dispatches*, p. 207.
    "full insurrection": *Dispatches*, p. 202.
    "revolution has now": *Dispatches*, p. 208.
    "war is everywhere": *FLV*, pp. 58–59.
317 "I cannot": *FLV*, p. 58.
    King Louis Philippe's "dethronement": *Dispatches*, p. 211.
    "I am nailed": *FLV*, p. 61.
    "It is a time": *FLV*, p. 58.
    "a great past": *FLV*, p. 174.
    "squadron" of Polish: *Dispatches*, p. 223.
    "Mickiewicz is with me": *FLV*, p. 55.
    "if bullets have ceased": *ELIV*, p. 27.
    "I have him much better": *FLV*, p. 55.
    "unswerving and most tender": *FLV*, p. 261.
    "At present": *FLV*, p. 55.
318 "a bestower" ... "a being": *OMII*, pp. 294, 293.
    "Children, with all": *FLV*, p. 64.
    "The Gods themselves": *FLV*, pp. 59–60.
    "A million birds": *Dispatches*, p. 216.
    "Now this long dark": *Dispatches*, p. 209.
319 "official" news: *Dispatches*, p. 216.
    "*Miracolo, Providenza!*": *Dispatches*, p. 212.
    "O, Dante": *Dispatches*, p. 223.
    "most beauteous": Leona Rostenberg, "Mazzini to Margaret Fuller, 1847–1849," *American Historical Review*, vol. 47, no. 1, October 1941, p. 73.
    "gorgeous shows": *FLV*, p. 62.
    "abide in close": *FLV*, p. 65n.
    "Italy was so happy": *FLV*, p. 65.
    "bird's-nest village": *Dispatches*, p. 237.
320 "I am going" ... "into the mountains": *FLV*, pp. 64, 67, and 69.

"mountain solitude": *FLV*, p. 86. Thomas Hicks's portrait of MF can be seen in the National Portrait Gallery, Washington, D.C.

"a piece of the porphyry": *FLV*, pp. 63–64.

"only artist": *FLV*, p. 307.

"The artists'": *FLV*, p. 168.

321   "You must always": *FLV*, p. 71.

"What mystery": Quoted in *VM*, p. 284.

"sit in my obscure": *FLV*, p. 69.

"debility and pain": *ELIV*, p. 61.

"come live": *ELIV*, p. 28.

"a poverty": *ELIV*, p. 33.

"You are imprudent": *ELIV*, p. 61.

"there was a revolution": *ELIV*, p. 72.

"come to London": *ELIV*, p. 79.

322   "I have much to do": *FLV*, p. 66.

"say to those": *FLV*, p. 66.

"Fortune favors": *FLV*, pp. 64–65.

323   "lonely mountain home": *FLV*, p. 73.

"frightened at a very": Leopold Wellisz, "The Friendship of Margaret Fuller d'Ossoli and Adam Mickiewicz," *Bulletin of the Polish Institute of Arts and Sciences in America*, vol. 4, 1945–46, p. 116.

"All life": *FLV*, p. 210.

324   "lonely, imprisoned": *FLV*, pp. 79, 78. Margaret wrote to Giovanni in Italian; in some instances, as here, I have given both the English translation and the Italian to remind readers that the correspondence was conducted in Giovanni's native tongue and to give a sense of Margaret's fluency in the language.

"According to these women": *FLV*, p. 85.

"hid[ing] thus in Italy": *FLV*, p. 251.

"fits of deep longing": *FLV*, pp. 76–77.

"a lively Italian": *FLV*, p. 77.

325   "The country": *FLV*, p. 77. "Mrs. M.": quoted in *CCII*, p. 390.

"I don't like": *FLV*, pp. 81, 80.

"I never see": *FLV*, pp. 85–86.

"hive of very ancient": *FLV*, p. 208.

326   "we are of mutual": *FLVI*, p. 65.

"figs, grapes, peaches": *FLV*, p. 104.

"if it is necessary": *FLV*, p. 99.

"All goes wrong": *FLV*, pp. 105, 103.

"ordeal" of the birth: *FLV*, p. 109.

"seem worth": *FLV*, pp. 74–75.

"was I not cruel": *FLV*, p. 292.

327   "Carissimo Consorte": *FLV*, p. 111. "Carissimo" is abbreviated as "Cmo."

"mio caro": *FLV*, pp. 114, 115.

"he refuses": *FLV*, p. 116.

"I am delighted": *FLV*, p. 113.

"very beautiful": *FLV*, p. 112.

"has your mouth": *FLV*, p. 117.

"he is still": *FLV*, p. 124.

"odious brothers": GAO, quoted in *CFII*, pp. 348–49.

"He knows": *FLV*, p. 125.

328 "seemed to look": *FLV*, pp. 125–26.

"exstatic smiles": *FLV*, p. 302.

"entire" nights: *FLV*, p. 199.

"becomes more interesting": *FLV*, p. 139.

"has grown much fatter": *FLV*, p. 141.

329 "seclusion" in summer and December 1848 column: *Dispatches*, pp. 238–39.

"Were you here": *FLV*, p. 145.

"this kind of pain": *FLV*, p. 303.

330 "empty of foreigners": *Dispatches*, p. 239.

"remained at their posts": *FLV*, pp. 146–47.

stormed the Quirinal: *Dispatches*, p. 242.

331 "Thank Heaven": *FLV*, p. 147.

"Utopia is impossible": *FLII*, p. 109.

"at one time": *FLV*, pp. 145, 147, 149.

"These events": *FLV*, pp. 147, 149.

332 "Another century": *Dispatches*, pp. 245–46.

"Rome has at last": Leona Rostenberg, "Margaret Fuller's Roman Diary," *Journal of Modern History*, vol. 12, no. 2, June 1940, p. 211.

"seems to be well": *FLV*, pp. 163–64.

"seemed to recognize": *FLV*, p. 165.

333 "He seemed very excited" . . . "leave": *FLV*, p. 167.

"Rome is always": *FLV*, p. 169.

"men of princely": *Dispatches*, p. 244.

"the Murray": *FLV*, p. 159.

"veiled" . . . "struck up": *Dispatches*, p. 255.

"walked without": *Dispatches*, p. 256.

334 "ring all the bells": *Dispatches*, p. 256.

"The revolution": *Dispatches*, p. 250.

"people in U.S.": *FLV*, p. 159.

"large and brilliant": *FLIII*, p. 39.

"O Jamie": *FLV*, p. 174.

"I am leading": *FLV*, p. 187.

335 "screwed my expenses": *FLV*, p. 158.

"nothing can be more": *Dispatches*, p. 260.

"France is not to": *FLV*, p. 171.

"accomplish at least one": *FLV*, p. 213.

"I am not": *FLV*, pp. 205–6.

336 "true consolation": *FLV*, p. 207.

"little swaddled child": *FLV*, p. 209.

"a strangely precocious": *FLV*, pp. 209–10.

"I only live": *FLV*, pp. 209–10.

337 "The Roman Republic": *Dispatches*, pp. 260–61.

"King Wobble": "Margaret Fuller's Roman Diary," p. 220.

"Let us not": *Dispatches*, p. 264.

"I heard a ring": *FLV*, p. 201. See also Denis Mack Smith, *Mazzini* (New Haven: Yale University Press, 1994), pp. 68–69.

338 "the celestial fire": *FLV*, p. 201.

"as tranquil": *Dispatches*, p. 274.

"struggling unaided": *Dispatches*, pp. 265–66.

"the setting sun": *Dispatches*, p. 274.

339 "la cittadina": *VM*, p. 299.

"in excellent": *FLV*, p. 218.

"tell our secret": *FLV*, p. 220.

"We must pray": *FLV*, p. 223.

340 "I rose and went": *Dispatches*, p. 256.

"refreshment, keen and sweet": MF, "Recollections of the Vatican," *United States Magazine and Democratic Review*, vol. 27, July 1850, p. 65.

"reaction" in Florence: "Margaret Fuller's Roman Diary," p. 220. I have amended the punctuation in the final sentence of this entry to conform to that of the original, MF "1849 Journal" bMs Am 1086 [4] FMW.

"I wish I were": Jeffrey Steele, ed., *The Essential Margaret Fuller* (New Brunswick, N.J.: Rutgers University Press, 1992), p. 19.

341 "called to act": *FLV*, p. 58.

"fought like a man": *FLV*, p. 241.

Princess Belgioioso: *Dispatches*, p. 281.

"Margherita Fuller": Donato Tamblé, "Documents in the State Archive of Rome: Margaret Fuller's Hospital Service During the Roman Republic," in Charles Capper and Cristina Giorcelli, eds., *Margaret Fuller: Transatlantic Crossings in a Revolutionary Age* (Madison: University of Wisconsin Press, 2007), pp. 243, 242.

"female invasion": Ibid., p. 246.

"the soldiers": *Dispatches*, p. 275.

342 "quick and shameful": *Dispatches*, p. 275.

"Roman blood": *Dispatches*, p. 276.

"the terrible": *Dispatches*, p. 280.

"grand and impassioned": *FLVI*, p. 83.

"we climbed": "Recollections of the Vatican," p. 65.

343 "mock confessions": *Dispatches*, p. 279.

six priests: Larry Reynolds, "Righteous Violence: The Roman Republic and Margaret Fuller's Revolutionary Example," in *Margaret Fuller: Transatlantic Crossings in a Revolutionary Age*, p. 188 n. 10.

"brotherly scope": *Dispatches*, p. 279.

"the female": Quoted in "Righteous Violence," pp. 175–76.

Casa Diez: Although several recent biographies of MF use the spelling "Dies," I have chosen to use "Diez," the spelling employed by Robert Hudspeth in *FL* and in the popular Murray guides of the period.

344 "The French seem": *FLV*, p. 229.

"I am alone": *Dispatches*, p. 284.

"became a coward": *FLV*, p. 292.

"my heart": *FLV*, p. 257.

"could not see": *FLV*, p. 293.

"What shall I write": *Dispatches*, p. 285.

"terrible" battle: *FLV*, p. 238.

345 "The Italians fought": *FLV*, p. 239.

"cannonade" continued: *FLV*, p. 238.

"fails this time": *FLV*, p. 240.

"Rome is being destroyed": *FLV*, p. 240.

"how terrible"; university student: *FLV*, p. 239; *Dispatches*, p. 300.

346 "forget the great ideas": *FLV*, p. 258.

"the way of observation": *FLV*, p. 240.

"is perfectly well": *FLV*, pp. 236, 235.

"I am caught": *FLV*, p. 240.

347 "underrated" his friend: *JMNVIII*, pp. 368–69.

"who pretend": *Dispatches*, pp. 298–99.

"the fatal": *Dispatches*, p. 303.

348 "watered with the blood": "Recollections of the Vatican," p. 64.

"the balls": *Dispatches*, p. 303.

"for you only" . . . "My soul": "Mazzini to Margaret Fuller," p. 78.

"whizzed and burst": *Dispatches*, p. 303.

"I don't know": "Mazzini to Margaret Fuller," p. 78.

"Government, Army and all": Ibid., p. 79.

"Wherever we go": Arnold Whitridge, *Men in Crisis: The Revolutions of 1848* (New York: Scribner's, 1949), p. 190.

349 "ready to dare": *Dispatches*, p. 304.

"Never have I seen": *Dispatches*, pp. 304–5.

"to and fro": *Dispatches*, p. 306.

"the holocaust": *Dispatches*, p. 264.

350 "But for my child": *FLV*, p. 243.

"left helpless": *FLV*, p. 247.

"A marble": *Dispatches*, p. 310.

three thousand: Katherine A. Geffcken, "Burials on the Janiculum: The Cemetery of Santo Spirito," in Katherine A. Geffcken and Norma W. Goldman, eds., *The Janus View from the American Academy in Rome: Essays on the Janiculum* (Rome: The American Academy in Rome, 2007), p. 195.

"Rest not supine": *Dispatches*, p. 311.

"I shall go": *FLV*, pp. 243–44.

20. "I HAVE LIVED IN A MUCH MORE FULL AND TRUE WAY"

353 "pale and trembling": Lewis Cass Jr., quoted in *CFII*, p. 457.

"much-exposed" apartment: *Dispatches*, p. 303.

"I have united": *FLV*, p. 250.

"amid the roar": *FLV*, p. 258.

354 "worn to a skeleton": *FLV*, pp. 245–46.

"the cruel law": *FLV*, pp. 258–59.

"dearer self ": *FLV*, p. 257.

the practice [of wet-nursing]: Michelle M. Dowd, *Women's Work in Early Modern English Literature and Culture* (New York: Palgrave Macmillan, 2009); Valerie Fildes, *Wet Nursing: A History from Antiquity to the Present* (Oxford and New York: Basil Blackwell, 1988); Janet Golden, *A Social History of Wet Nursing in America: From Breast to Bottle* (Cambridge and New York: Cambridge University Press, 1996); Susan C. Greenfield and Carol Barash, eds., *Inventing Maternity: Politics, Science, and Literature, 1650–1865* (Lexington, Ky.: University Press of Kentucky, 1999); David I. Kertzer, *Amalia's Tale: A Poor Peasant, an Ambitious Attorney, and a Fight for Justice* (Boston: Houghton Mifflin, 2007); George D. Sussman, *Selling Mothers' Milk: The Wet-Nursing Business in France, 1715–1914* (Urbana, Chicago, London: University of Illinois Press, 1982).

"for the sake": *FLV,* p. 249.

355 "fine healthy girl": *FLV,* p. 249. For laws on foundling children in the Papal States, see *Amalia's Tale,* pp. 11–12.

"peaceful and gay": *FLV,* p. 254.

"American Circle": *FLV,* p. 280.

"wander[ing] feebly": *FLV,* p. 249.

"woman's day": *Dispatches,* p. 245.

356 "free, independent, one": *Dispatches,* p. 216.

"from the married": Joan Von Mehren, "Establishing the Facts on the Ossoli Family: An Experiment in E-Mail Research," *Margaret Fuller Society Newsletter,* vol. 9, winter 2001, p. 2. I have altered Von Mehren's translation slightly to correspond more closely to the original Latin, which is reprinted in "Margaret Fuller, the Marchese Giovanni Ossoli, and the Marriage Question: Considering the Research of Dr. Roberto Colzi," *Resources for American Literary Study,* vol. 30, 2005, p. 122. For a thorough discussion of theories as to the timing of the Ossolis' wedding, including the possibility that it may have taken place long after Nino's birth when the family lived in Florence, or not at all, see "Margaret Fuller, the Marchese Giovanni Ossoli, and the Marriage Question," pp. 104–43. Von Mehren concludes definitively that the wording of Nino's baptismal record confirms that the couple had married in advance of the baptism.

"half killed me": *FLV,* p. 304.

"your eldest child": *FLV,* p. 260.

"I am a mother": *FLV,* p. 248.

357 "Yet I shall never": *FLV,* p. 248.

"more afraid of being": Quoted in *FLVI,* p. 9.

"I have lived": *FLV,* p. 283. Although this letter survives without identification of the recipient, a reference to "something of the violet" suggests that it was written to WHC, who initiated this shared metaphor.

"little heart": *FLV,* p. 270.

"an inestimable": *FLV,* pp. 291–92.

"In him" . . . "I have found": *FLV,* p. 261.

"moored" themselves: *FLV,* p. 273.

358 "What a difference": *FLV,* p. 280.

"kicking, throwing": *FLV,* p. 302.

"not handsome": *FLV,* p. 288n.

"I feel so refreshed": *FLV,* p. 302.

"a dark-haired, quiet, modest": *FLV,* p. 288n.

"so cheerful and busy": *FLV,* p. 265.

359 "glorious days that expand": *FLVI,* p. 66.

"the world can no longer": *Dispatches*, p. 320.

"comfort, no solution": *FLV*, p. 295.

"Heaven and Hell": *FLV*, p. 273.

"blighted" hopes: *FLV*, p. 257.

"it has ploughed": *FLV*, p. 301.

"angry" older brother: *FLV*, p. 262.

"eke out bread": *FLV*, p. 285.

"I should not be sorry": *FLV*, p. 284.

frequently wore: William Henry Hurlbert, quoted in Joel Myerson, ed., *Fuller in Her Own Time* (Iowa City: University of Iowa Press, 2008), p. 97.

"a new revolution": *FLV*, p. 299.

"the restored authorities": *FLV*, p. 287.

"find really a home": *FLV*, p. 299.

360 two feet of snow: *Dispatches*, p. 320; *FLV*, p. 306.

"kind of fearful": *FLV*, pp. 305–6.

"running about" . . . "blind": *FLV*, p. 269.

"revolutionary" . . . "The heart": *FLV*, p. 250.

"I have acted": *FLVI*, p. 88.

"whatever I have done": *FLV*, p. 285.

361 "no questions": *FLV*, p. 269.

"increased warmth of interest": *FLV*, p. 269.

"retiring from the Roman": *FLV*, p. 280n.

"strange story": *Fuller in Her Own Time*, pp. 92–93.

362 figure of steadfast resolve: Joseph Mozier's portrait bust of MF is in the collection of the National Portrait Gallery. A photo can be seen in Robert N. Hudspeth, "A New Image of Margaret Fuller," *Thoreau Society Bulletin*, no. 273, winter 2011, p. 4.

"the handsomest": Nathaniel Hawthorne's account of Joseph Mozier's views, in *Fuller in Her Own Time*, p. 176.

"to impose": Ibid., pp. 97, 94, 98.

363 "pale, erect, narrow": *FLV*, pp. 275, 277.

"I am just the same": *FLV*, p. 293.

"Margaret F. has been": *ELIV*, p. 168.

"I expect that to many": *FLV*, p. 291.

"he will feel very strange": *FLV*, p. 286.

"He is not in any": *FLV*, p. 261.

"*some* of my friends": *FLV*, p. 291.

364 "*La Madre*": *FLV*, p. 299.

"left" to "hear": *FLV*, pp. 294–95.

"possessed of a great": *FLV*, p. 58.

"the peace way": *FLV*, p. 295.

365 "the much that calls": Jeffrey Steele, ed., *The Essential Margaret Fuller* (New Brunswick, N.J.: Rutgers University Press, 1992), p. 18.

"These are not the things": *FLV*, p. 296.

"absolutely wanting": MF, *Essays on American Life and Letters*, Joel Myerson, ed. (Albany, N.Y.: NCUP, 1978), p. 390.

"lived cheek by jowl": Quoted in *VM*, p. 294.

"too cruel": *FLV*, p. 199.

"a useless resistance": *FLV*, p. 199.

"I pity those": *FLVI*, p. 77.

366 "if my life be not": *FLVI*, p. 57.

"feel anxious": *FLVI*, pp. 87–88.

"I will believe": *FLVI*, p. 86.

"marble and rags": *FLVI*, p. 83.

the wrecks of three: *FLVI*, p. 81.

"Siberian winter": *FLVI*, p. 85.

"his great stout Roman": *FLVI*, p. 68.

"an immense stock": *FLVI*, p. 75.

"full of boxes": *FLVI*, p. 85.

"I have never": *FLVI*, p. 67.

367 "I feel works of art"; A *Last Supper*: *FLVI*, p. 68; John Ruskin, *The Complete Works of John Ruskin*, vol. 4, E. T. Cook and Alexander Wedderburn, eds. (London and New York: Longmans, Green, and Co., 1903), p. 40.

"sufficient number": *FLVI*, p. 70.

"full of armed men": MF, "Recollections of the Vatican," *United States Magazine and Democratic Review*, vol. 27, July 1850, pp. 65, 64.

"find always" . . . "can take": *FLVI*, p. 69.

"great novelty": *FLV*, p. 293.

"nothing else can break": *FLVI*, p. 69.

"For his sake": *FLVI*, p. 70.

368 "I never think": *FLV*, p. 284. See note following "I have lived" on page 445.

"dangerous pressure": *FLVI*, p. 74.

"so sad and weary": *FLVI*, p. 86.

"One would think": *FLVI*, p. 70.

"I hope he will": *FLV*, p. 305.

"It has long seemed": *FLV*, p. 300.

"Joy to those born": *Dispatches*, pp. 322–23.

"with most sad": *FLVI*, p. 85.

"betrayed and exiled": *Dispatches*, pp. 322–23.

21. "NO FAVORABLE WIND"

369 "the flower": *FLIII*, pp. 165–66.

"from the first": *FLIII*, pp. 166–67.

370 "rich, if troubled": *FLVI*, p. 85.

"to go into the market": *FLV*, p. 284.

"my treasures": *FLVI*, p. 86.

"what is most": WHC, "Papers," BPL, quoted in *CFII*, p. 508.

"together in confiding": Robert D. Habich, "Margaret Fuller's Journal for October 1842," *Harvard Library Bulletin*, vol. 35, 1985, p. 290.

371 *The seventeenth*: *OMII*, p. 338. The italicized sentences in this chapter are quoted directly from William Henry Channing's account of the wreck of the *Elizabeth*, in *OMII*, pp. 341–49.

"sense of fresh life": *FLVI*, p. 64.

"*In memory*": Quoted in *CFII*, p. 503.

"We are never": *FLV*, p. 57.

372 "and I say it merely": *FLVI*, p. 87.

"more than five hundred": Quoted in *CFII*, p. 500.

Celeste Paolini: Although the nurse's name is given variously as Celesta Pardena, Celeste Panolini, and Celeste Paolini in other accounts, I have adopted the third spelling, used by William Henry Channing, *OMII*, p. 338.

"Yes! it was": *FLVI*, p. 90.

Nino "*could see*": Catherine Hasty, quoted in *CFII*, p. 505.

373 "I feel cradled": *FLVI*, p. 354.

"the social inquisition": *FLV*, p. 285.

"advantages of your absenteeism": *ELIV*, p. 199.

"Shall we not yet": *ELIII*, pp. 447–48.

374 "Cut away!" . . . *She lay*: *OMII*, p. 342.

"We must die": Catherine Hasty, quoted in *CFII*, p. 507.

375 "what is most valuable": WHC, "Papers," BPL, quoted in *CFII*, p. 508.

376 *Now came Margaret's*: *OMII*, p. 346.

"I am a married": Quoted in *CFII*, p. 510.

"*one* desperate effort": Quoted in *CFII*, p. 511.

When last seen: *OMII*, p. 349.

377 "could have a good deal": *FLV*, p. 273.

"children splashing and shouting": Martha L. Berg and Alice de V. Perry, eds., "'The Impulses of Human Nature': Margaret Fuller's Journal from June Through October 1844," *Proceedings of the Massachusetts Historical Society*, vol. 102, 1990, p. 89.

EPILOGUE: "AFTER SO DEAR A STORM"

379 "their contents": "Letter of Bayard Taylor," Fire Island, July 23 [1850], first published in *New-York Tribune*, reprinted in MF, *At Home and Abroad; or, Things and Thoughts in America and Europe*, Arthur B. Fuller, ed. (New York: The Tribune Association, 1869), p. 425.

fifty yards: Citing "H. Thoreau's Notes," BPL, Charles Capper gives the distance of "less than three hundred yards," *CFII*, p. 506, in contrast to Bayard Taylor's location of the wreck at "not more than fifty yards from the shore," in "Letter of Bayard Taylor," p. 425. Perhaps the changing tide accounts for this discrepancy.

"bruised and mangled": "Letter of Bayard Taylor," pp. 427–28.

380 "inexperience" . . . "shreds": Ibid., pp. 426, 428.

"buried under the ruins": Ibid., pp. 427–28.

381 "sat like a stone": Quoted in *CFII*, p. 512.

"to go, on all our": *ELIV*, p. 219. See also Robert D. Richardson Jr., *Henry Thoreau: A Life of the Mind* (Berkeley and Los Angeles: University of California Press, 1986), pp. 212–13. The precise timing of the travel and arrivals of Fuller's friends and family at the site of the wreck is difficult to determine. I have relied on the somewhat contradictory accounts in *CFII*, p. 513, and Walter Harding and Carl Bode, eds., *The Correspondence of Henry David Thoreau* (New York: New York University Press, 1958), p. 261.

"an essential" . . . "brave": *JMNXI*, pp. 258, 256.

"one eye glass": RWE to Hugh Maxwell, August 3, 1850, PSR.

382 "whether emptied": RWE to Hugh Maxwell, August 3, 1850.

"Held up": Bradford Torrey and Francis H. Allen, eds., *The Journal of Henry D. Thoreau*, vol. 2, 1850–September 15, 1851 (Boston: Houghton Mifflin, 1949), p. 43. Thoreau wrote similar lines in a letter to H.G.O. Blake, dated August 9, 1850, in *Correspondence of Henry David Thoreau*, p. 265. See also Walter Harding, *The Days of Henry Thoreau: A Biography* (New York: Dover Publications, 1982), pp. 278–79.

"a portion": *Correspondence of Henry David Thoreau*, p. 263.

"relics" . . . "Close": Henry D. Thoreau, *Cape Cod* (New York: Thomas Y. Crowell, 1961), pp. 123–24.

383 "enough of anatomy": *Correspondence of Henry David Thoreau*, p. 263. Charles Capper traces an intriguing report of two bodies discovered "some time after the wreck" by a Fire Island boatman. After attempting delivery of the bodies to Horace Greeley, who refused them in the belief that too much time had passed for identification to be possible, the boatman buried the pair without ceremony or marker at Coney Island. The source of the tale was the owner of a Fire Island public house, Felix Dominy, one of the men Thoreau consulted during his search. Dominy brought his story to the attention of Margaret's family by letter four years after the drownings; with no clues as to the whereabouts of the graves, and perhaps unsure of the reliability of the source, the family chose not to undertake a search; *CFII*, pp. 513–14 and 622 n. 26. By this time too, claims and counterclaims on the part of both the Fuller and Ossoli families about the estates of the deceased had been resolved, partly due to an affidavit sworn by Captain Bangs "verifying that the remains of Count Ossoli and his wife had never been found" and that Margaret had "no property" and was "in debt." Perhaps a late discovery of the couple's remains would have revived the dispute between the families; Joan Von Mehren, "Margaret Fuller, the Marchese Giovanni Ossoli, and the Marriage Question: Considering the Research of Dr. Roberto Colzi," *Resources for American Literary Study*, vol. 30, 2005, p. 130.

"as I stood": *Cape Cod*, p. 124.

"I doubt they cannot": MF, "Recollections of the Vatican," *United States Magazine and Democratic Review*, vol. 27, July 1850, p. 71.

"I see nothing": "Letter of Bayard Taylor," p. 427.

"To the last" . . . "I have lost": *JMNXI*, pp. 256, 258.

"We are taught": *JMNVIII*, p. 368.

"Her heart" . . . "I hurry": *JMNXI*, pp. 257, 258.

384 "pages so rich": Quoted in *CFII*, p. 514.

"O still sweet summer": C. P. Cranch, "On the Death of Margaret Fuller Ossoli," "From the Tribune," undated newspaper clipping c. August 1850, bMS Am 1086 (misc.) B, FMW. In later versions of the poem "dear" was amended to "drear," and the title was changed to "Margaret Fuller Ossoli," as in *At Home and Abroad*, p. 436.

"How characteristic": Quoted in *VM*, p. 339.

385 "The waves": Quoted in *VM*, p. 339.

"I must" . . . "taken": *WNC*, pp. 29, 28.

386 "as red as the Scarlet Letter": Quoted in James R. Mellow, *Nathaniel Hawthorne in His Times* (Boston: Houghton Mifflin, 1980), p. 317.

"so unspeakably": Sophia Peabody Hawthorne to Mrs. Elizabeth Palmer Peabody, August 1, 1850, Berg.

it "is about": *JMNXVI*, p. 210.

"was wholly": Mary Peabody Mann to Sophia Peabody Hawthorne, [1850], Berg.

387 "she never": Ibid.

"How infinitely": Sophia Peabody Hawthorne to Mary Peabody Mann, September 9, 1850, Berg.

"there is a vein": Sophia Peabody Hawthorne to Elizabeth Palmer Peabody, December 29, 1850, Berg.

"It was not unpleasant": Elizabeth Palmer Peabody, "Miss Peabody's Reminiscences of Margaret's Married Life," *Boston Evening Transcript*, June 10, 1885. I am grateful to Mary De Jong for alerting me to this letter, written in 1870 and published to mark the occasion of Margaret Fuller's seventy-fifth birthday.

388 "It can never": Paulina Wright Davis, *A History of the National Woman's Rights Movement, for Twenty Years* (New York: Journeymen Printers' Co-operative Association, 1871), p. 14.

"We were left": Ibid., p. 14; moment of silence: *VM*, p. 339.

"the European": *The Proceedings of the Woman's Rights Convention, Held at Worcester, October 23 and 24, 1850* (Boston: Prentiss & Sawyer, 1851).

389 "pained" by the thought: WHC to Thomas Wentworth Higginson, January 5, 1884, MF Papers, Folder 194, BPL.

"Margaret was happy": Joel Myerson, ed., *Fuller in Her Own Time* (Iowa City: University of Iowa Press, 2008), p. 117.

"I have never": *FLV*, p. 149.

"there must be": *FLVI*, p. 57.

390 "*having lived*": MF poetry fragment, Fuller Papers, Folder 141, BPL.

"mingle our dust": Quoted in *VM*, p. 339.

"yours in the distance": *FLIV*, p. 274.

INDEX